A Lady Of England

The Life And Letters Of Charlotte Maria Tucker

by
Agnes Giberne

A Lady Of England
The Life And Letters Of Charlotte Maria Tucker
by Agnes Giberne

Copyright © 2024

All Rights reserved.

No part of this publication may be reproduced, stored in a retrieval system, or transmitted in any form or by any means, electronic, mechanical, photocopying or Otherwise, without the written permission of the publisher.
The author/editor asserts the moral right to be identified as the author/editor of this work.

ISBN: 978-93-62769-85-5

Published by

DOUBLE 9 BOOKS

2/13-B, Ansari Road
Daryaganj, New Delhi – 110002
info@double9books.com
www.double9books.com
Tel. 011-40042856

This book is under public domain

ABOUT THE AUTHOR

The British author Agnes Giberne lived from November 19, 1845, to August 20, 1939. She wrote a lot of novels and science papers. Her stories were typical of Victorian Christian stories for kids that had religious or moral themes. For kids, she wrote science books, and she also wrote a few historical stories and a well-known biography. Giberne was born in Belgaum, Karnataka, India. Her parents were Captain Charles Giberne (16 June 1808 – 21 December 1902) of the Bengal Native Infantry and Lydia Mary Wilson (c. 1816 – 20 May 1890). The Huguenots in her family tree came from Languedoc in France. The "de Gibernes" lived in Chateau de Gibertain. Charles Giberne came from a big family. Besides his brother, he had eight sisters. It was also where three of his brothers served. The wedding took place at St. Mary the Virgin, Walthamstow, on December 11, 1838, and Giberne was born. There is some doubt about how many brothers Giberne had. The India Family History and Families in British India Society records at the British Library show. By the 1851 census, Lydia Mary was living with the Rector of Eyam in Derbyshire and his family at Beach in Weston-super-Mare with her four children who were still alive.

CONTENTS

AUTHOR'S PREFACE 9
PREFACE 12

PART I
LIFE IN ENGLAND

CHAPTER I
A.D. 1771-1835 THE STORY OF HER FATHER 13

CHAPTER II
A.D. 1821-1835 CHILDHOOD AND GIRLHOOD 20

CHAPTER III
A.D. 1835-1848 EARLY WRITINGS 31

CHAPTER IV
A FARCE OF GIRLISH DAYS 41

CHAPTER V
A.D. 1847-1849 HOME LIFE 66

CHAPTER VI
A.D. 1847-1850 GRAVITY AND FUN 73

CHAPTER VII
A.D. 1849-1853 THE FIRST GREAT SORROW,
AND THE FIRST BOOK 86

CHAPTER VIII
A.D. 1854-1857 CRIMEA, AND THE INDIAN MUTINY 100

CHAPTER IX
A.D. 1857-1865 LIFE'S EARLY AFTERNOON 111

CHAPTER X
A.D. 1864-1866 A HEAVY SHADOW 123

CHAPTER XI
A.D. 1867-1868 GIVING COMFORT TO OTHERS 134

CHAPTER XII
A.D. 1868-1872 THE OLD HOME BROKEN UP 142

CHAPTER XIII
VARIOUS CHARACTERISTICS 154

CHAPTER XIV
1875 AN UNEXPECTED RESOLVE 166

CHAPTER XV
1875 BESIDE NIAGARA 177

PART II
LIFE IN INDIA

CHAPTER I
A.D. 1875 FIRST ARRIVAL IN INDIA 185

CHAPTER II
A.D. 1875-1876 A HOME IN AMRITSAR 197

CHAPTER III
A.D. 1876 CURIOUS WAYS 211

CHAPTER IV
A.D. 1876 A PALACE FOR A HOME 224

CHAPTER V
A.D. 1877 DISAPPOINTMENTS AND DELAYS 235

CHAPTER VI
A.D. 1877-1878 A BROWN AND WHITE 'HAPPY FAMILY' 249

CHAPTER VII
A.D. 1878 PERSECUTIONS 265

CHAPTER VIII
A.D. 1878-1879 EARLY CHRISTIAN DAYS IN
THE 19TH CENTURY 281

CHAPTER IX
A.D. 1879 THE CHURCH AT BATALA 297

CHAPTER X
A.D. 1880-1881 LOYAL AND TRUE 310

CHAPTER XI
  A.D. 1881-1882 CLOUDS AFTER SUNSHINE 321

CHAPTER XII
  A.D. 1882-1883 THE FIRST STONE OF BATALA CHURCH 336

CHAPTER XIII
  A.D. 1884-1885 SOME OF A. L. O. E.'S POSSESSIONS 353

CHAPTER XIV
  A.D. 1885-1886 ON THE RIVER'S BRINK 372

CHAPTER XV
  A.D. 1886-1887 IN HARNESS ONCE MORE 384

CHAPTER XVI
  A.D. 1887-1888 A VISIT FROM BISHOP FRENCH 399

CHAPTER XVII
  A.D. 1888-1890 THE DAILY ROUND 415

CHAPTER XVIII
  A.D. 1890-1891 IN OLD AGE 431

CHAPTER XIX
  A.D. 1892 LIGHT AT EVENTIDE 445

CHAPTER XX
  A.D. 1892-1893 THE LAST GREAT SORROW 462

CHAPTER XXI
  A.D. 1893 THE HOME-GOING 472

FOOTNOTES 483

AUTHOR'S PREFACE

The principal mass of materials for this Biography was placed in my hands last summer by the Rev. W. F. Tucker Hamilton, nephew of Charlotte Maria Tucker (A. L. O. E.), and since then many other relatives or friends, both in England and in India, have contributed their share of help, either in the way of written recollections or of correspondence. A paucity of materials exists as to the early part of the life; but in later years the difficulty is of a precisely opposite description, arising from a superabundance of details. Hundreds of letters, more or less interesting in themselves, have had to be put ruthlessly aside, to make room for others of greater interest. From first to last the long series between Charlotte Tucker and her own especial sister-friend, Mrs. Hamilton, takes precedence of all other letters in point of freedom, naturalness, and simplicity. The perfect trust and unshadowed devotion which subsisted between these two form a rare and beautiful picture.

It has seemed to me, and it may seem to others, that the main question in the Life of Miss Tucker is, not so much what she *did* here or there, in England or in India, as what she *was*. Many a discussion has taken place, and doubtless will again take place, as to the wisdom of her modes of Missionary work, and as to the degree of success or non-success which attended her labours. I have endeavoured to give fairly certain opposite views upon this question, even while strongly impressed with the conviction that no human being is capable of judging with respect to the worth of work done in his own age and generation. Subtle consequences, working below the surface, are often far more weighty, far more lasting, than the most approved 'results' following immediately upon certain efforts,—results which are, not seldom, found after a while to be of the nature of mere froth. Nothing can be more unprofitable, usually, than the task of endeavouring to 'count conversions.' It is of infinitely greater importance to note with what absolute self-devotion Miss Tucker entered into the toil, with what resolution she persevered in the face of obstacles, with what eagerness she did the very utmost within her power.

In writing the story of Miss Tucker's life at Batala, it has been impossible not to write also, in some degree, the story of the Infant Church at Batala. My main object has of course been simply to show what Charlotte Maria Tucker herself was; and Mission work, Mission incidents, Missionaries themselves, come in merely incidentally, as part of the background to her figure. Mention of them is accidental and fragmentary; not systematic. At the same time there is no doubt that nothing would have gratified Miss Tucker more than that any use should have been made of her letters likely to help forward the great work of Missions among the Heathen. Some years before the end, when in severe illness she thought herself to be passing away, she spoke of the possibility that her long correspondence about Batala might be so employed, and earnestly hoped that, if it were so, no one-sided account should be given, but that shadow as well as sunshine, the dark as well as the bright aspect, should be frankly presented. I have endeavoured to carry out her wishes in this particular.

It is to be regretted that at least a few letters from Mrs. Hamilton to Miss Tucker cannot be interspersed among the many from Miss Tucker to Mrs. Hamilton. None, however, have come to hand. Before Miss Tucker went to India she destroyed the bulk of her papers, after a ruthless fashion; and it does not appear that while in India she kept any of the letters that she received.

After some hesitation I have decided to give generally the names in full of those Missionaries, with whom she was most closely associated. I have also decided *not* to give the names of Indian Christians, with very few exceptions,—as of the Head Master of the Native Boys' School at Batala, whom she counted a personal friend; also of one or two Ordained Native Clergymen, and one or two contributors of slight material towards this *Life*. In many instances it would be very difficult to decide wisely at so great a distance, and without a knowledge of the individuals themselves. It is therefore best to be on the safe side. Many of the initials are the true initials; but many are not even that,—especially in the case of those who are still Heathen or Muhammadan.

In the spelling of Indian words and names I have endeavoured to follow mainly the more modern plan, adopted of late years, except in the case of a very few words which are practically Anglicised. Miss Tucker's own spelling of Indian words and names varies extremely; the word being often given differently when occurring twice in a single page. The spelling has therefore been altered throughout her correspondence. To avoid confusion in the minds of English readers, I have also taken the same liberty with letters from some others who have not adopted the modern mode.

In conclusion, I have only to express my sincere thanks for the most kind trouble taken by many friends of A. L. O. E. in contributing materials for my guidance.

AGNES GIBERNE.

Worton House, Eastbourne.

PREFACE

It would scarcely be fitting that this Volume should go forth to the Public without a few words of Preface from one of A. L. O. E.'s own family.

Only my beloved Mother—the 'Laura' of these pages—could have penned the words which should adequately tell all that my dear Aunt was to those who knew her best and loved her most fondly. And *she*, little as she had expected it, was the first of the two to be called Home.

It has, however, been a great satisfaction to me to intrust the preparation of the *Life* to Miss Giberne; and I am glad to have this opportunity of expressing my hearty appreciation of the literary skill, the sympathy, and the fidelity to truth with which she has accomplished her task.

Averse as my Aunt ever was to any fuss being made about her, nothing would have reconciled her to the publication of a Biography, save the hope that its story might be used of God to stimulate others to consecrate their lives to the Service of Christ, whether in the Foreign or Home Mission Field. It is in such hope that it is now sent forth, with the earnest prayer that His blessing may rest upon it.

W. F. TUCKER HAMILTON.

Christ Church, Woking.

Note.—Any profits derived by A. L. O. E.'s relatives from the publication of this volume will be apportioned among those Missionary Societies in which she was especially interested.

PART I
LIFE IN ENGLAND

'Constant discipline in unnoticed ways, and the hidden spirit's silent unselfishness, becoming the hidden habit of the life, give to it its true saintly beauty, and this is the result of care and lowly love in little things. Perfection is attained most readily by this constancy of religious faithfulness in all minor details of life, in the lines of duty which fill up what remains to complete the likeness to our Lord, consecrating the daily efforts of self-forgetting love.'—T. T. Carter.

CHAPTER I
A.D. 1771-1835 THE STORY OF HER FATHER

Charlotte Maria Tucker, known widely by her *nom de plume* of A. L. O. E.,—signifying A Lady Of England,—as the successful author of numberless children's books, deserves to be yet more extensively known as the heroic Pioneer of elderly and Honorary volunteers in the broad Mission-fields of our Church.

Her books, which were much read and appreciated in the youth of the present middle-aged generation, may to some extent have sunk into the background, as the works of successive story-tellers do in the majority of cases retire, each in turn, before newer names and newer styles; but the splendid example set by Charlotte Tucker, at a time of life when most people are intent upon retiring from work, and taking if they may their ease,—an example of *then* buckling on her armour afresh, and of entering upon the toughest toil of all her busy life, will surely never be forgotten.

She was the sixth child and third daughter of Henry St. George Tucker, a prominent Bengal Civilian, and, later on, Chairman of the East India Company. All her five brothers went to India, and all five were there in the dark days of the Mutiny. Thus by birth she had a close connection with that great eastern branch of the British Empire, to which her last eighteen years were entirely devoted. People in general go out early, and retire to England for rest in old age. Miss Tucker spent fifty-four active years in England, and then yielded her remaining powers to the cause of our fellow-subjects in Hindustan.

It seems desirable that a slight sketch of her father's earlier life should precede the story of hers.

Henry St. George Tucker came into this world on the 15th of February 1771. He was born in the Bermudas, on the Isle St. George, whence his name, and was the eldest of ten children. An interesting reference to this event is found in a letter of Charlotte Tucker's, written February 15, 1890: 'As I went in my duli to villages this morning, I thought, "One hundred and nineteen years ago a precious Baby was born in a distant island"; and I thanked God for our beloved and honoured Father.'

Henry St. George's father was a man of good descent, of high reputation, and of a leading position in the islands. His mother, a Miss Bruere before marriage,—probably the name was a corruption of *Bruyere*,—was daughter of the then governor of the Bermudas, a gallant old soldier, possessing fourteen children and also a particularly irascible temper.

The elder Mr. Tucker appears to have been a man of gentle temperament and liberal views; I do not mean 'Liberal' in the mere party sense, but liberal as opposed to 'illiberal.' Whatever his own opinions may have been, he did not endeavour to force them upon his children; he did not, in fact, petrify the children's little fancies by opposition into a lasting existence. It is amusing to read of the opposite tendencies among his boys, one taking the loyal side and another the republican side in the dawning struggle between England and her American Colonies. Long after, Henry St. George spoke of himself as having then been 'a bit of a rebel'; adding, 'But my republican zeal was very much cooled by the French Revolution; and if a spark of it had remained, our own most contemptible revolution of 1830 would have extinguished it, and have fixed me for life a determined Conservative.'

He had on the whole a strong constitution, though counted delicate as a child; and his early life in the Bermudas was one of abundant fresh air and exercise. Much more time was given to riding and boating than to books; indeed, his education seems hardly to have been begun before the age of ten years, when he was sent to school in England. Whether such a plan would answer with the ordinary run of boys may well be doubted. Henry St. George Tucker was not an ordinary boy; and he showed no signs of loss in after-life through ten years of play at the beginning of it.

One piece of advice given to him by his mother, when he was about to start for England, cannot but cause a smile. She was at pains to assure him that it would be unnecessary to take off his hat to every person whom he might meet in the streets of London. Henry St. George, speaking of this in later years, continues: 'But habit is strong; and even now, when I repair to the stables for my horse, I interchange bows with the coachman and the ostlers and all the little idle urchins whom I encounter in the mews.' One would have been sorry indeed to see so graceful a habit altered. It might far better be imitated. Exceeding courtesy was through life characteristic of the man, and it descended in a marked degree upon many of his descendants, notably so upon Charlotte Maria, the A. L. O. E. of literature.

School education, begun at ten, ended at fourteen. The boy worked hard, and rose in his classes quickly; though at an after period he spoke of his own learning in those days as 'superficial.' He had been intended by his father for the legal profession, and many years of hard work were supposed to lie before him. These plans were unexpectedly broken through. One of his aunts, who lived in England, acting impulsively and without authority, altered the whole course of his career. She asked him, 'Would he like to visit India?' A more unnecessary question could hardly have been put. What schoolboy of fourteen would *not* 'like to visit India'? Young Henry seized upon the idea; and the said aunt, under the impression that she was kindly relieving his father of needless school expenses, actually shipped the lad off as middy in a merchant vessel bound for India, not waiting to write and ask his father's permission. She merely wrote to say that the deed was done.

Officious aunts do exist in the world; but surely few so officious as this. The deepest displeasure was felt and shown when Henry's father learned what had happened. But by the time that his grieved remonstrances reached the boy, Henry was fifteen thousand miles away, 'hunting wild animals on the plains of Behar.' In the present day a boy so despatched might be sent back again; but in those days India was separated from England by a vast gulf of distance and of time. Any one writing from India to England could not look for a reply in less than a year; and his father was at Bermuda, not even at home, which made a further complication.

The boy's condition must at first have been forlorn enough. After a petted and luxurious boyhood, he had to live for months together upon salt junk; and his bed was only a hencoop. But there was 'stuff' in him, and hardships of all kinds were most pluckily endured. On landing at Calcutta he found himself in a strange country, among strange faces, without money and without work, though happily not quite without friends. His mother's brother, Mr. Bruere, was one of the Government Secretaries in Calcutta; and in the house of Mr. Bruere and of Mr. Bruere's pretty little sylph-like wife the young adventurer found shelter for some months, until an opening could be secured for him.

Fifteen years followed of a hard and continuous struggle. As long after he said of himself, he 'looked the world in the face' in those days; and while a mere boy of fifteen or sixteen he set himself resolutely to get on. From the first he grappled with the Native languages, showing a vigour and persistency in the study which, many many years later, were visible again in his daughter Charlotte, when grappling with the very same task. Only he was young; and she, when she followed his example, was well on in middle life.

Towards the end of those fifteen years resolution and untiring energy triumphed; and from the age of about thirty Mr. Tucker's rise to a good position was steady.

In 1792 he became a member of the Bengal Civil Service. In 1809 he was made Secretary in the Public Department. But he had had heavy work and many troubles, and his health began to fail; so the following year, after a quarter of a century of unbroken exile, he set off for England, carrying with him Government testimonials, couched in the warmest terms. These testimonials spoke of his 'long and meritorious services,' of his 'peculiar abilities,' of his 'talents and acquirements of the highest order,' of his 'unwearied diligence,' of his 'unimpeached integrity.' All this, of one who, twenty-five years before, had landed on Indian shores an almost penniless adventurer, without so much as a definite plan of what to do with himself and his energies!

That very year he was engaged, and the year after he was married, to Jane Boswell, daughter of a Mr. Robert Boswell of Edinburgh, who was related to the well-known biographer of Dr. Johnson. The Boswell family was known to have first settled in Berwickshire as far back as in the days of William Rufus, and afterwards in Fifeshire and Ayrshire at Balmute and Auchinleck. Mr. Robert Boswell's grandmother, Lady Elisabeth Bruce, was a daughter of the first Earl of Kincardine. Mr. Boswell was a devotedly good and also an able man; a minister, not in the Scottish Presbyterian Church, but in some smaller religious body; and his death took place in a somewhat tragic manner, before the date of his daughter's marriage to Mr. Tucker. While preaching, he quoted the text which begins, 'All flesh is as grass— —,' and as he uttered the words he fell back, dead!

A characteristic anecdote is told of his wife,—A. L. O. E.'s grandmother. She had a large family, and was badly off. One day a poor woman applied to her for help; and Mrs. Boswell called out to her daughter Jane, to know what money they happened to have in hand. 'Only one seven-shilling piece,' was the answer. Mrs. Boswell's voice sounded distinctly,—'Give it, then; give it to the woman.' 'But, dear mamma, there is no more money in the house,' remonstrated Jane. More decisively still came the response, 'Give it, then; give it to the woman.' And given it was. The story almost inevitably recalls that of the Widow's Mite; even though from certain points of view one is dubious as to the wisdom of the act.

Despite the poverty of the family Mrs. Boswell's daughters settled well in life. One married Mr. Egerton of the High Court in Calcutta; one married Dr. Roxburgh; one married General Carnegie; one married Mr. Anderson; one only, Veronica by name, remained unmarried; and Jane became the wife of Henry St. George Tucker. She was at that time a gentle and beautiful girl of about twenty-one, while Mr. Tucker was already over forty.

Early in the following year, 1812, they went out to India together; and his delight was great in returning to the country where he had toiled so long, and had made many friends. This time, however, his stay in the east was to be brief.

His first child, Henry Carre, was born that same year; and two years later came his eldest daughter, Sibella Jane. Also in 1814 fell the blow of his Mother's death, over which, strong man that he was, he wept passionately. Then his wife's health seemed to be seriously failing; and this decided him to leave the land of his adoption, throwing up all prospects in that direction. In 1815, the first year of European peace, at the age of forty-five, he 'retired from the active service of the Company,' travelling by long sea with his invalid wife and his two little ones, and spending some time at the Cape by the way. Before they arrived in England another little one, Frances Anne, had been added to their number.

A home was found in Charlotte Square, Edinburgh; and for some years, till 1819 or 1820, he was well content to remain there, living a quiet home-life, with a little family growing around him. Two more boys came, George William and Robert Tudor,—the former dying in babyhood, the latter growing up to be slain in the Indian Mutiny. Losing the infant George was a dire trouble to his parents; and Mrs. Tucker, believing that he had succumbed to the keen cold of Edinburgh, was never at rest in her mind until the northern home had been exchanged for one in the south. Such a change was not to be accomplished in a day, but in the course of time it came about; and meanwhile the remaining children were a constant source of interest and delight. The 'baby' at this date was Robert; afterwards a very favourite elder brother of A. L. O. E. His children, known in the family by the name of 'The Robins,' became in later years as her own.

Mr. Tucker could not long remain contented without definite work. He was still in the prime of life, still under fifty; and an eager desire took hold of him to enter public life once more, to serve again his own country, as well as the eastern land of his adoption. These purposes he thought might best be carried out by his becoming, if possible, one of the Directors of the East India Company. For the fulfilment of his desire—a desire, not for gain or wealth or position, but for the means of doing good—he had to wait a considerable time. He had indeed to wait until his next little daughter, Charlotte Maria, was five years old. Then, at length, he was appointed Director; one of the Twenty-four who, in those days, practically ruled India. Thereafter his influence was steadfastly exerted in the direction of a wise and righteous government of the dark millions of Hindustan; the land in which he had spent a quarter of a century of his life, and to which afterward not only all his five sons went, but one of his five daughters also, in the advanced years of her life.

While he waited for this long-desired appointment, other changes took place. They left their home in Edinburgh and moved south, first spending some months at Friern Hatch, in Barnet, near Finchley; and there it was that little Charlotte first saw the light of day. In 1822 they went to live in London, settling into No. 3 Upper Portland Place, whence no further move was made until after the death of Mrs. Tucker, more than forty-five years later.

In Portland Place the family was completed. Two years after the birth of Charlotte came her next brother, St. George; two years later still her next sister, Dorothea Laura, her peculiar companion and friend. The three youngest, William, Charlton, and Clara, finished the tale of ten living children.

Mr. Tucker was, as may have been already gathered, a man of unusual force of character and of indomitable will; robust in body and mind; unwearying in work; self-reliant, yet never presumptuous; an absolute gentleman, remarkable for the polished courtesy of his bearing, alike to superiors, equals, and inferiors in social position; open and straightforward as daylight; firm in his own convictions, but well able to look on both sides of a question, and liberal towards those who differed from him; entirely fearless in doing what he held to be right, and entirely free from all thought of self-seeking. He was, as his Biographer Mr. Kaye observes,—'pre-eminently a man amongst men,'—'a statesman at eighteen, and a statesman at eighty.' He was also a man of deep and true religion; a religion not much expressed in words, but apparent in every inch of his career. In a letter written long after his death by his daughter Charlotte, she remarked, when speaking of the biography of some well-known man: 'There is nothing to indicate that he ever said, as our beloved Father said, "The publican's prayer is the prayer of us all!"' Probably religious speech never came easily to him. His life, however, spoke more eloquently than mere words could have done.

One of his main characteristics was an abounding generosity. He was always ready to help those who needed help, up to his power, and beyond his power. In his own home he was charming; full of wit, full of fun, full of gay spirits and laughter; full also of the tenderest affection for his wife and children, an affection which was abundantly returned. He was an intensely loving and lovable man; his wonderful sweetness and evenness of temper, never disturbed by heavy work or pressing cares, endearing him to all with whom he came in contact. While he talked little of his own feelings, he did much for the good of others; and his life was one long stretch of usefulness. The union in him of strength with gentleness, of a masterful intellect with a spirit of yielding courtesy, of nobility with playfulness, of generosity with self-restraint, of real religious conviction and experience with frolicsome gaiety, made a combination not more rare than beautiful.

Many of his characteristics were distinctly inherited from him by his daughter Charlotte; among others, his literary bent. He was fond of writing, and in his well-occupied life he found some time to indulge the play of his fancy. In the year 1835 he published a volume of plays and enigmas, called *The Tragedies of Harold and Camoens*, dedicated to the Duke of Wellington, for whom he and his family had the deepest esteem and admiration.

CHAPTER II
A.D. 1821-1835 CHILDHOOD AND GIRLHOOD

Charlotte Maria Tucker was born on the 8th of May 1821, not within the sound of Bow bells, but, as already stated, at Friern Hatch, in Barnet, no long time before the family settled down in Portland Place.

Details of her very early life are greatly wanting. We should like to know how the childish intellect began to develop; what first turned her thoughts into the 'writing line'; whether authorship came to her spontaneously or no. But few records have been kept.

It is not indeed difficult to imagine the general character of her childhood. She was clever, quick-witted, full of fun, overflowing with energy, abounding in life and vigour. One of a large and high-spirited family, living in a home of comparative comfort and ease, and surrounded by a wide circle of friends and acquaintances, Charlotte must have had a happy childhood.

Long years after, when old and wellnigh worn out with her Indian campaign, she wrote—

> 'It seems curious to look back to the birthday sixty-one years ago, when sweet Mother called me "her ten-years old." Do you remember my funny little cards of invitation to a feast of liquorice-wine,—with possibly something else,—
>
> '"This is the eighth of May,
>
> Charlotte's Happy Birthday."
>
> 'I would not change this time for that. What a proud ambitious little creature I was! I have a pretty vivid recollection of my own character in youth. I should have liked to climb high and be famous.'

In another letter she alludes to the fact that as a child she had been accused of 'liking to ride her high horse.'

No doubt in those early days her ambition pointed to higher game than children's tales written 'with a purpose.'

In the gay young family party, two daughters and two sons were older than herself. Of the latter the nearest in age was Robert, four years her senior, the future dying hero of the Indian Mutiny. 'Our noble Robert' she calls him long after; and there appears to have been an early and close tie between Robert and his ambitious, eager little sister. Of Fanny, too, the next sister above her in age, two years older than Robert, she was particularly fond. But *the* tie in her life which was most of all to her, perhaps taking precedence of even her passionate love for her Father, was the bond between herself and Laura, the next youngest sister, about four years her junior. From infancy to old age these two were one, loving each other with an absolutely unbroken and unclouded devotion.

The two were counted to some extent alike, though with differences. Laura was the gentler, the more self-distrustful, the more disposed to lean. Charlotte was the more impulsive, the more eager, the more energetic, the more independent, the more self-reliant. In fact, Charlotte never did 'lean' upon anybody. Both were equally full of spirits and of frolicsome fun.

In another letter from India to this sister, dated January 18, 1886, when referring to a recent illness, she wrote—

> 'My memory is very acute. I thought lately that it was a great shame that I never should go back to dear old No. 3, which really was the happy home of our childhood before our griefs. So what do you think, Laura dear, I did lately? I acted over in my mind Christmas Day, as in the old times, when you and I were girls. I do not think that I left out anything; our jumping on dearest Mother's bed; the new Silver;[1] the Holly and the Mistletoe; the Christmas Box; the choosing the gowns; the Cake, etc. Then I went to Trinity Church; I heard the glorious old hymn, "High let us swell triumphant notes." It was such a nice meditation. Then Aunt Anderson and her dear daughters came for dinner. Of course Aunt had her little yellow sugar-plum box!'

It is a pretty and vivid description of the olden days in that dear old home, always spoken of among themselves as 'Number Three,' which she loved ardently to the last. Charlotte's affections for everything connected with her youth were of a very enduring nature.

Another short extract from her later letters may be given here, describing something of what the loved sister Laura was to her in those early days. It is dated December 10, 1892.

'My Laura loved me so fondly; we were so close to each other. How we used to share each other's thoughts from youth, as we shared the same room! Our honoured Father loved to hear his Laura's merry ringing laugh; when we chatted together he would say to her favourite sister,'—meaning herself—'"*She combines so much.*" I doubt that he saw any imperfection in a being so bright, so sweet.'

And in yet one more letter to this same Laura, dated November 1, 1884—

'You underrate your own qualifications as a companion, darling. Don't I know you of old, how playful and genial you are, as well as loving?... You are choice company for a tête-à-tête.'

The earliest writing of Charlotte's which comes to hand is indorsed, 'Charlotte, 1832,' and is addressed to 'Miss D. L. Tucker, 3 Upper Portland Place.' It is a valentine written to her sister; and it shows that at the early age of eleven she had at least begun a little versifying; usually the line first adopted by incipient authors.

'The snow-drops sweet that grace the plain
Are emblems, love, of you,
With innocence and beauty blest
Pure as the morning dew.

'Sweet rosebud, free from every storm
Of life, may peace incline
To hover ever round thy bed,
My dearest Valentine.'

Another early effort, undated, but possibly a year or two later, is addressed, 'To Dolly, the sweet little bud of the morn,'—no doubt to the same favourite sister, Dorothea Laura.

'Sweet bud of the morning, what poet can speak
The glories that beam in thy eye?
The rosebuds that bloom on thy fat little cheek,—
And thy round head so stuffed full of Latin and Greek,
Arithmetic and Geology.

'I send you a character-teller, my love,
'Tis little and poor, but it may
My kindness, affection, *etcetera*, prove,

And show you, my dear little Dolly, I strove
To make mine a happy birthday.'

What the 'character-teller' may have been it is difficult even to conjecture. Since Laura was four years her junior, the Latin, Greek and Geology were of course meant in the symbolical sense, standing for learning in general.

One more apparently early effort remains; not this time versification, but a birthday letter to Laura, inscribed, 'To my dear Lady Emma, from her affectionate Tosti.' Why Lady Emma?—and why Tosti? In these three effusions the handwritings are curiously unlike one another, though all are childish. One is large and unformed; another is small and cramped; the third is neat and of a copperplate description. It may be that her writing was long before it crystallized into any definite shape; often the case with many-sided people. But for the juvenile handwriting, it would be almost impossible to believe that the following middle-aged production was not written in later years. Children were, however, in those days taught to express themselves like grown people; and no doubt she counted that she had accomplished her task well.

> 'Many joyful returns of this day to you, dearest Laura, and may each find you better and happier than the last. I send you a little piece of velvet, which you may find useful, for I do not think you will value a present only for the money it costs; and I dare say you will agree with me that a *trifle* from an affectionate friend is often more valuable than great gifts from those who love you not.
>
> 'I hope, dearest Lautie, you may enjoy *a very particularly* happy birthday, and that you may have as few sorrows in the year you are just entering as in that you have just passed.—Accept my kindest love, and believe me to be
>
> 'Your affectionate friend and sister,
>
> 'C. M. T.'

This letter may have been some years later than the two copies of verses; but that hardly does away with the difficulty. The style is almost as pedantic for the age of sixteen or seventeen as for the age of ten or twelve.

Side by side with the intense devotion for her sister Laura, there was a considerable degree of reticence in Charlotte's nature. It may have developed more fully as time went on; yet it must surely have been a part of herself even in childhood. It was not with her a superficial reserve, an acted reticence, such as may sometimes be seen in essentially shallow women. On the surface she was free, frank, chatty, quick in response, ready to converse, full of liveliness, fun, and repartee. But underlying the freedom and brightness there was a habit of silence about her own affairs—that is to say, about affairs which concerned only and exclusively herself—which to some extent was a life-long characteristic.

Neither Charlotte nor any of her sisters ever went to school. Their father had a very pronounced objection to schools for girls; indeed, he had himself made an early resolution never to marry any girl who had been educated at school, and he kept that resolution. The same idea was followed out with his own daughters. A daily governess came in to superintend their studies; and occasional masters were provided. In reference to the latter Charlotte wrote, many years afterward, to a niece: 'No one can do as much for us in the way of education as we can do for ourselves. A willing mind is like a steam-engine, and carries one on famously. When I was young my beloved parents did not feel able to give us many masters. We knew that, and it made us more anxious to profit by what we had.'

Twenty-five years of hard toil in India had not made a rich man of Mr. Tucker; nor did his position as a Director bring him wealth. It was his daughter's pride in after-life to know that he had died comparatively poor, because of his inviolable sense of honour. Not that more money would not have been acceptable! Ten children, including five sons, to be launched in life, are a serious pull upon any purse of ordinary capacity; and Mr. Tucker was of an essentially generous nature. He had many relatives, many friends, and the demands upon his purse were numerous. On a certain occasion he gave away about *one-quarter of his whole capital*, a sum amounting to several thousands of pounds, to help a relative in a great emergency. One who met him immediately afterwards spoke of his appearing to have suddenly grown into an old man.

In Charlotte's earlier years anxiety as to money matters was often experienced; and recurring Christmastides saw a repeated difficulty in making both ends meet. This state of things continued up till about the year 1837, when an unlooked-for legacy was left to Mr. Tucker, as a token of great esteem, by a friend, Mr. Brough. Besides the main legacy to Mr. and Mrs. Tucker, the sum of two hundred pounds came to each of the children, and was treated as a 'nest-egg' for each. From this date serious pressure ceased, and Mr. Tucker became able to meet the various calls upon him; not indeed without care and economy, but without a perpetual weight of uneasiness. Some few years later another friend, Mr. Maclew, left another legacy in the same kind and unexpected manner.

These facts serve to explain the paucity of masters when Charlotte was young. But the sisters bravely accepted the condition of things, and worked hard to make up for any disadvantages. One distinct gain in such a home education was that at least they were free to develop each in her own natural lines, instead of being all trimmed as far as possible into one shape.

Charlotte's 'lines' were many in number.

She had a marked talent for drawing, and could take likenesses of her friends; good as regarded the salient features, though apt to grow into more of caricatures than the young artist intended. Musical gifts also were hers, including an almost painfully sensitive ear. Though her voice was never really very good, she sang much; and while well able to take a second at sight, she was in after years equally ready to undertake any other part in a glee, inclusive of the bass, which often fell to her share when a man's voice happened to be lacking.

A gift for teaching showed itself early; and as a child she would try to impress geographical facts upon her younger brothers and sisters by an original system of her own. In the Park Crescent Gardens, near Portland Place,—their playground; described by one friend in those days as a "jungle," because of its unkempt condition,—she would name one bed England, another France, another Germany, and so on, and would thus fix in the children's minds their various positions, though the shapes and sizes of the beds were by no means always what they ought to have been. That the mode of instruction was effective is evident from the fact that her brother, Mr. St. George Tucker, can recall the lessons still, after the lapse of fifty years, and can say, 'By that means I learnt that England was in the north-west corner of Europe.'

Another direction in which she excelled was that of dancing. Even in walking she possessed a peculiarly springy step, remarked by all who knew her; and this in dancing was a great advantage. She was at home alike in the dignified minuet and in the active *gavotte*, and she would perform the *pas de basque* with much spirit. Indeed dancing was an exercise in which she found immense enjoyment through half a century of life.

At home Charlotte was a leader in the games, herself flowing over with fun and frolic. Her fertile imagination left her never at a loss for schemes of amusement. Naturally eager, impulsive, vehement, she had from beginning to end an extraordinary amount of energy, and in childhood her vigour must have been almost untirable.

One can imagine how the house echoed with the gay voices and laughter of the young people, as they pursued their various games, led by the indefatigable Charlotte. Mr. Tucker loved the sound of those merry voices; and when he could join them he was probably the merriest of the whole party. At one period, heavy and long-continued work in 'clearing up the finances' of the East India Company kept him much apart from the family circle; and the delight was great when he could leave his big dry books, and be as a boy among the children again.

Bella, the elder girl, was pretty and of gracious manners, with dark eyes, and with a capacity for dressing herself well upon the very moderate allowance which her father was able to bestow. Fanny, the next sister, though not at all handsome, had also soft dark eyes, and a peculiarly sweet disposition; and she too dressed nicely. It was commonly said amongst themselves that Fanny was 'the gentle sister,' and that Charlotte was 'the clever heroic sister.' But Charlotte was not gifted with the art of dressing well.

In those early days, and for many a year afterwards, it would not appear that gentleness or sweetness were characteristics belonging to Charlotte. They were of far later growth, developing only under long pressure of loss and trial. In her childhood and girlhood, though doubtless she *could* be both winning and tender to the few whom she intensely loved, yet it was impossible to describe her generally by any such adjectives. She was chiefly remarkable for her spring and energy, her originality and cleverness, her wild spirits, and her lofty determination. With all her liveliness, however, she was in no sense a madcap, being thoroughly a lady.

In appearance Charlotte was never good-looking; and in girlhood she could not have been pretty; though there was always an indescribable charm in the vivid life and the ever-varying expression of her face.

One friend remembers hearing her tell a story of her young days, bearing upon this question of personal appearance. With a mirror and a hand-glass she examined her own face, the profile as well as the full face, and evidently she was not satisfied with the result. A wise resolution followed. Since she 'could never be pretty,' she determined that she 'would try to be good, and to do all the good in the world that she could.' It was a resolve well carried out.

This sounds like a curious echo of an early experience of her father. When a boy of about ten, he caught smallpox, and 'came forth,' as he related of himself long after, 'most wofully disfigured.... "Well," observed one of my aunts, "you have now, Henry, lost all your good looks, and you have nothing for it but to make yourself agreeable by your manners and accomplishments." Here was cold comfort; but the words made an impression upon my mind, and may possibly have had some influence on my future life.'

And much the same thought is reproduced in Charlotte Tucker's own clever and amusing little book, *My Neighbour's Shoes,*—when, as Archie gazes into the mirror, he says of himself, 'One thing is evident; as I can't be admired for my beauty, I must make myself liked in some other way. I'll be a jolly good-natured little soul.'

In girlish days it may have been a prominent idea with Charlotte. By nature she not only was impulsive, but she no doubt inherited some measure of her great-grandfather Bruere's irascible temper; and the amount of self-control speedily developed by one of so impetuous a temperament is remarkable. High principle had sway at a very early age; but this thought, that her lack of good looks might be compensated for by good humour and kindness to others, may also have been a motive of considerable power in the formation of her character.

It must be added that not all thought so ill of her looks as Charlotte herself did. An artist of repute, who saw her in the later days of her Indian career, has said unhesitatingly, in reply to a query on this subject,—'Plain! No! A face with such a look of intellect as Miss Tucker's could never be plain.' If matters were thus in old age, the same might surely have been said when she was young. But beauty of feature she did not possess.

In addition to her other gifts, Charlotte had something at least of dramatic power, and in her own home-circle she was a spirited actress.

Mr. Tucker's published volume of plays and enigmas has been already named. Both *Harold* and *Camoens* were acted by the young folk of the family, with the rest of their number for audience. It is uncertain whether any outside friends were admitted on these occasions.

In the second play Charlotte took the part of the heroine, Theodora; and her brother, St. George, took the part of Ferdinand. Camoens, the hero, is betrayed to the Inquisition by Theodora; the betrayal being caused by a fit of fierce jealousy on the part of Theodora, who loves, and is apparently loved by, Camoens. The jealousy has some foundation, since Camoens decides to marry, not Theodora but Clara. Theodora in her wrath is helped by another lover, Ferdinand, to carry out her plot, and together they bring a false charge against Ferdinand, who is speedily landed in the dungeons of the Inquisition. Theodora then, finding that Clara does not love Camoens, and repenting too late her deed, goes mad with remorse. Camoens is after all set at liberty, none the worse for his imprisonment; but the distracted Theodora, meeting her other lover and her companion in evil-doing, Ferdinand, attacks him vehemently, with these words—

'Theod. Ha! Ferdinand!
Thou hast recalled a name!

It brings some dreadful recollections.

'Twas he who basely did betray my husband.

Go, wretched man! bring back the murdered Camoens!

Go, make thy peace. (*She stabs him.*)

Bian. Oh! help!

Ferd. I bless the hand that gave the wound.
Thou hast redeemed me from a deadly sin,
Or mortal suffering.
Farewell, beloved unhappy Theodora.
Guard her, ye pitying angels!

Theod. Where am I?
What have I done?
I have some strange impression of a dream—
A fearful dream of death.
Young Ferdinand, who loved me!
Dead—dead—and by this desperate hand!'

After which Clara enters, and Theodora dies, completing the tragedy. One can picture the force and energy with which Charlotte would have poured forth her reproaches upon the head of Ferdinand, before giving him the fatal stab.

It may have been somewhere about this time—it was at all events before the year 1842—that Charlotte had once a scientific fit, and for several weeks threw herself with ardour into the study of Chemistry. At intervals in her life a marked interest is shown in certain scientific facts or subjects; sufficient, perhaps, to indicate that, had the bent been cultivated, she might possibly have shown some measure of power in that direction also. Books on Natural History always proved an attraction to her; and many little Natural History facts come incidentally into her correspondence, sometimes given from her own observation. In later years she even wrote two or three little books for children on semi-scientific subjects,—not without making mistakes, from the common error of trusting to old instead of to new authorities. But the early influences with which she was surrounded were not of a kind to call forth this tendency, if indeed it existed in any but a very slight degree. Her Father's bent was strongly poetical and classical; and probably his influence over her mind in girlhood was stronger than any other. The poetic and the scientific may, and sometimes do, exist side by side; but the combination is not very usual.

A great event of Charlotte's young days was the fancy-dress ball given by her parents in the spring of 1835. The Duke of Wellington himself was present; prominent still in the minds of men as the Deliverer of Europe, only twenty years earlier, from a tyrant's thraldom. All the young Tuckers, not to speak of their parents, were ardent admirers of the Duke. Laura, still a mere child, in her enthusiasm slipped close up behind, when the Duke was ascending the stairs, and gently abstracted a fallen hair from the shoulder of the hero, which hair she preserved ever after among her choicest treasures; and Charlotte was no whit behind Laura in this devotion.

At the ball Frances made her appearance dressed as Queen Elizabeth,—'very neat and very stately,'—while Charlotte represented 'the star of the morning,' in a dress of pure muslin, full and well starched, so nicely made and so beautifully white that the impression of it lasts still in the mind of a brother, after the lapse of more than half a century. The prettiness of her dress on that particular occasion was no doubt accentuated by the fact that in general Charlotte did *not* attire herself becomingly; and also by the fact of another young lady being present as a second 'star of the morning.' For the other 'star' had hired a dress for the evening; a muslin dress, which was by no means white, but dingy and tumbled. In contrast, Charlotte's pure whiteness, relieved by a star upon her forehead, drew much attention. Since she was then only a girl of about fourteen, it appears that a close distinction was not drawn in those days, as in these, between girls 'out' and girls 'not out.' Her brother, St. George, a boy of twelve or thirteen, was also present, wearing a Highland costume.

The hero of the day appeared in evening dress, according to the then fashion, with a star on his breast. Frances, in her queenly apparel, presented him with a bag which contained a Commission to defend England,—a business which, one is disposed to think, he had already pretty well accomplished! The Duke received this offering graciously; and a day or two later the following playful letter arrived from him to Mr. Tucker:—

'Strathfieldsaye.
Ap. 26, 1835.

'My dear Sir,—When Queen Elizabeth gave me that beautiful bag on Friday night, I was not aware that it contained a Letter Patent which I prize highly; and for which I ought to have returned my grateful acknowledgment at the time it was delivered.

'I beg you to present my thanks; and to express my hopes that her Majesty continued to enjoy the pleasures of the evening; and that she has not been fatigued by them.

'Ever, my dear Sir,

      'Your most faithful humble servant,

            (Signed) 'Wellington.

'H. St. George Tucker, Esq., etc.'

The delight and enthusiasm amongst the young people, aroused by this letter, may be imagined. It seems to have come later into the possession of Charlotte; and when she went to India it was presented by her to her sister Laura,—the envelope which contained it having in Charlotte's handwriting the following inscription:—

'*What I consider one of my most valuable possessions, and therefore send to my beloved Laura, to whom it will recall past days.*'

CHAPTER III
A.D. 1835-1848 EARLY WRITINGS

One after another the brothers of Charlotte went out to India. Henry Carre, the eldest, well known in Indian story, had left in 1831, when she was only ten years old; and in 1835 her particular companion, Robert, went also. He was a tall, handsome young fellow; and though only eighteen years old, he had already done well in his studies. At Haileybury his remarkable abilities won him the admiration of the Professors; and at his last examination for the Civil Service he signalised himself by actually carrying off *four* gold medals.

Among other gifts he had a keen touch of satire, and a power of easy versification. Some of the early verses preserved show considerable power, and are very spirited as well as amusing. A main feature of his character was, however, his intense earnestness. He was of the same stern and heroic cast of mind as Charlotte herself; with perhaps less fun and sparkle to lighten the sternness. Like her, he was markedly self-reliant, and was never known to lean upon the opinion of others.

With all Charlotte's gaiety and merriment, her delight in dancing and acting, and her love of games, there was a stern side, even in those early days, to her girlish nature; and in this respect she and Robert were well suited the one to the other. She was, as one says who knew her well, 'a born heroine'; indeed, both she and Robert were of the stuff of which in former centuries martyrs have been made.

At what date Charlotte first began to think seriously upon religious questions it is not possible to say. Probably at a very early age. Underlying her high spirits was a stratum of deep thought; and strong principle seems almost from the beginning to have held control over her life. One of her brothers speaks of her as 'always religious.' She may have thought and may have felt to any extent, without expression in words of what she thought or felt. The innate reticence, which veiled so much of herself from others, would naturally in early years extend itself to matters of religion. Later in life reserve broke down in that direction; but silence in girlhood was no proof whatever of indifference.

An undated letter to her niece, Miss Laura Veronica Tucker, written in middle life, gives us something of a clue here.

> 'I am much interested in hearing from your dear Mother that you are so soon to take upon you the vows made for you in Baptism, and I wish specially to remember you, my love, in prayer on the 18th.
>
> 'To-morrow, too, you attain the age of fifteen.... I was about your age, dear Laura, when the feeling of being His—of indeed having the Saviour as *my own* Saviour, came upon me like a flood of daylight. I was so happy! This was a little time before my Confirmation. Though I have often often done wrong since, and shed many many tears, I have never *quite* lost the light shed on me then, and now it brightens all the future, so that I can scarcely say that I have any care as regards myself—the Lord will take care of me in advancing age—in the last sickness—in what is called death, (it is only its shadow).'

To the majority of people religious conviction and experience come as daylight comes; not in one sudden burst, but gradually, heralded by grey dawn, slowly unfolding into brightness. Brought up as Charlotte was in an atmosphere of kindness, of gentleness, of unselfish thought for others, of generosity, of high principle, and of most real religion, albeit not much talked about, she would naturally imbibe the latter almost unconsciously, and as naturally would say little. The spiritual life, begun early in her, would expand and develop year by year, as fresh influences came, each in turn helping to shape the young ardent nature.

She was essentially independent; one who would of necessity think questions out for herself, and form her own opinions; and when an opinion was once formed, she would act in accordance with that opinion, fearlessly and conscientiously. All this came as a logical result of what she was in herself. But the very independence was of gradual growth; and side by side with it existed always a spirit of beautiful and reverent submission to her Father and Mother.

Although she never published anything during her Father's lifetime— whether because she was slow to recognise her own capabilities, or because he failed to encourage the idea, does not distinctly appear,—her pen was often busy. A small magazine or serial in manuscript, for family use, was early started among the brothers and sisters, and to this, as might be expected, Charlotte was a frequent contributor.

She also wrote several plays, following in her Father's footsteps; and some of these are extant, not *written* but exquisitely printed by her own hand. She was indeed an adept at such printing, as at many other things; and one amusing story is told anent this particular gift. About 1840, when her brother St. George was at Haileybury College, the latter wrote an essay, which was copied for him by Charlotte in small printed characters. Whereupon a rumour went through the College that one of the competitors had actually had his essay printed for the occasion. Inquiries were made; and the 'printed copy' was discovered to be the essay of Mr. St. George Tucker.

The earliest in date of these unpublished plays, composed for the entertainment of the home-circle, appears to have been *The Iron Mask*; achieved in 1839, when Charlotte was about eighteen years old. It was 'Dedicated, with the fondest esteem and affection, to her beloved Father, Henry St. George Tucker, to whom she is indebted for the outline of the characters and plot, by the Author, Charlotte Maria Tucker.' By which Dedication may be plainly seen that Mr. Tucker encouraged his daughter's literary bent, so far as actual writing went, though he does not seem to have helped her into print. The Preface to this early work is quaint enough to be worth quoting. The young Author had evidently studied Miss Edgeworth's style.

> 'I cannot pretend to offer that most common excuse of Authors that their works have been written in great haste and consequently under great disadvantages. I have been a considerable time about my little performance, and its defects are not owing to want of care or attention on my part.
>
> 'I once had thoughts of myself writing a Critique on *The Iron Mask*, to show that I am sensible of its faults, though I do not think I have *the power* to remove at least all of them. But I have dropped the idea, and am determined to leave them to be found out, or perhaps overlooked, by the eye of partiality and affection.'

The play is, of course, historical, and is of considerable length. One short quotation may be given as a specimen of her girlish powers, taken from Scene ii.

> '*Apartment in the Castle of Chateaurouge: a grated window seen in the background.*
>
> The Iron Mask.

> 'The glorious Sun hath reached the farthest west,
> And clouds transparent tipt with living fire
> Hang o'er his glory, bright'ning to the close.
> Now gently-falling dews refresh the earth,
> And pensive Silence, hand in hand with Night,
> Already claims her reign.
>
> Another day
> Has past! another weary weary day,
> And I am so much nearer to my grave!
> Oh that I could, like yon broad setting Sun,
> For one day tread the path of Liberty,
> For one day shine a blessing to my Country,
> Then, like him, set in glory!
> Still come they not?—then Chateaurouge deceived me!
> He said e'er sunset that they must be here,
> And I have watched from the first blush of morn,
> Before the lark his cheerful matins sung,
> Before the glorious traveller of the skies
> Had with one ray of gold illumed the east,
> And still they come not!—'Tis in vain to watch,
> They will not come to-night!—my sinking heart
> For one day more must sicken in suspense.'

The writing of the play as a whole is unequal,—what girl of eighteen is not unequal?—but in these lines, as well as elsewhere, there are tokens of genuine power, alike poetical and dramatic.

Next came, in the year 1840, *The Fatal Vow; a Tragedy in Three Acts*; on the title-page of which is found a dedication—'To Jane Tucker; the Mother who in the bloom of youth and beauty devoted herself to her children, and whose tender care can never by them be repaid.' The play was written in less than two months; its scene being laid in Arabia, while the characters are of Arabian nationality. It is an ambitious and spirited effort for a girl under twenty.

Two years later she wrote another, *The Pretender; a Farce in Two Acts*; respectfully dedicated to 'Fair Isabella, the Flower of the East.' This witty and amusing little farce shall be given entire in the next chapter, as a fair example of what she was able to accomplish at the age of twenty-one. It also shows conclusively her love of fun, and the manner in which she delighted in any play upon words.

In 1842, the same year which saw her produce *The Pretender*, her brother St. George went out to India; and two years later a paper of extracts from different letters, in her handwriting, records the sister's loving pride in the warm opinions sent home about that brother. Also the same paper contains an account of an affair in which he was engaged; but the said account not being correct in all details, I give it in different words.

In 1844, one year and a quarter after the arrival of Mr. St. George Tucker in India, he volunteered to assist his joint magistrate, Mr. Robert Thornhill, to capture the celebrated dacoit,[2] Khansah. Upon the receipt of further orders from his chief magistrate, Mr. Thornhill decided not to make the attempt. Mr. Tucker, however, having volunteered, thought it was his duty to go; and go he did, accompanied by a Thannadar,[3] four horsemen, and some Burkandahs. On a January morning, in early dawn, they reached the village in which the dacoit leader, Khansah, was supposed to be concealed; and after many inquiries they induced an alarmed little native boy to point out silently which hut sheltered Khansah.

Leaving the horsemen and the Burkandahs outside, Mr. Tucker and the Thannadar went into the courtyard of the house. In the darkness of the entry to one of the huts stood Khansah, holding a loaded blunderbuss. At first he was unperceived; but suddenly the Thannadar exclaimed, 'There he is!' and as Mr. Tucker turned to the right, Khansah fired off the blunderbuss. The Thannadar dropped dead; and Mr. Tucker's right arm fell helpless, from a wound in the shoulder. He climbed quickly over the low walls of a roofless hut, then turned about, and with his left hand steadying the right hand on the top of the outer wall, he fired his pistol at the dacoit,—and missed him. Mr. Tucker then went round the back of the hut to a tree which stood near the entrance; and shortly afterward Khansah came out, calling—'Kill the Sahib!' A struggle followed between Khansah and one of the native police, which lasted some three or four minutes. Then Khansah, having apparently had enough, made away on the Thannadar's pony; and Mr. Tucker, regaining his own horse, rode back to the station, accompanied by the Burkandahs and horsemen, who had carefully kept in the background when most needed, but whose courage returned so soon as the peril was over.

Eighteen months later an offer was made by Government of ten thousand rupees to any one who should give up Khansah,—the dacoit being a very notorious robber and murderer. His own relatives responded promptly to this appeal, and Khansah speedily found himself in durance vile. Mr. Tucker failed to identify the man in Court; but other evidence was forthcoming, and Khansah, being convicted, was hung. Charlotte, when noting down particulars of the above stirring episode, observes: 'We cannot feel too thankful to a merciful God for my precious George's preservation.' The brief account which she copied out from the letter of a friend in India ends with these words: 'My husband tells me he (Mr. Tucker) acted with great spirit, and showed much cool, determined courage, and deserved great credit; but from being almost a stranger to the habits of this country, he failed in his attempt to capture the dacoit.'

Another paper of copied extracts has a particular interest, because it seems to show, even then, a dawning sense in the mind of Charlotte Tucker of the needs of heathen and semi-heathen lands. The sheet is dated 1844; and the passages are selected from a book of the day, called *Savage Life and Scenes*. But probably at that period nothing was further from her dreams than that she herself would ever go out as a missionary to the East.

The following undated letters belong to the years 1846-7. A little sentence in the first, as to the solution of Mr. Tucker's enigma, is very characteristic of one who through life was always peculiarly ready to give praise to others.

TO MISS D. LAURA TUCKER.

'How sweet, good, and kind you are! I hardly know how to thank you and dearest Mother for *such* notes as I have received from both, but I truly feel your kindness at my heart....

'My eye is exceedingly improved. Such a fuss has been made about it here by my affectionate Fannies, that one might suppose that, like your friend Polyphemus, I had but one eye, and that as rudely treated as was his by Ulysses.

'We think that the solution of my noble Father's enigma is "Glass" or "Mirror." Fanny was the first to imagine this. As for going to Gresford the 3rd of next month, I do not wish to be one of the party at all, at all! I calculate that Robin will then have been on the waves 76 days; and though I do not expect him till October, the S— — *may* be a fast sailer, and fast sailers *have* accomplished the whole voyage in about that time, I believe. I drink the port wine which Papa brought down, which I hope may serve instead of bark.'

TO MISS SIBELLA J. TUCKER.

'Having concluded my reading of old Russell, how can I do better than employ the interval before the arrival of the

Indian letters in sitting down and writing to my fair absent sister? Colonel Sykes let me know last night that Robin would not come by *this* mail, which was, he says, only from Bombay, so that letters being all we must expect before Saturday fortnight, you need not hurry home on account of Robin's return.

'Now doubtless you would like to hear a little how the world in Portland Place has been going on since your fair countenance disappeared from our horizon. In the first place *all* the three Misses —— are coming. A comical party we shall have! There has been no letter from Lord Metcalfe yet, that I know of. We had a very nice evening yesterday. I wish that yours may have been equally agreeable. The beginning was by no means the worst part of it. I dressed early, and while Mamma and Fanny were upstairs, Charlie and I enjoyed quite a stream of melody from my dear Father, who sang us more than twenty songs, most of which I had never heard before. I wonder that he did not sing his throat quite dry, particularly after a Wednesday's work. I must now write Lautie an account of the Ball.'

TO MISS D. L. TUCKER.

'Well, dearest Lautie, we had a nice Ball last night. There were the Vukeels of S——, with their dark intelligent countenances, Colonel Sykes, your friend, who is really becoming quite a friend of mine, and honest, handsome Sir Henry Pottinger, the very look of whom does one good. I chatted with both the latter amusing gentlemen, and heard from Sir Henry a circumstantial account of his attack of gout, when, he said: "I felt as though I could have roared like a bull." Sir Henry thinks that ladies should have a glass of champagne after *every* dance, quadrille, waltz, or polka! "You would see," said he, "if my plan were followed, how many ladies would come." ... Papa has had applications for cadetships from Lord Jocelyn and H—— T——. I suppose that in both cases it will be, "I wish you may get it!"'

TO THE SAME.

'We have had such an amusing breakfast. Lord Glenelg was here. And he and Mamma have been making us laugh so,— he with his quiet jokes, and dear Mamma with her *naïveté*. Mamma very freely criticised Sir R. Peel's and Lord John

Russell's manner of speaking, to the great amusement of our guest, who threw out a hint that he might inform, and that Mamma had compromised herself. "It would be rather awkward," he observed, "if I were to sit beside Sir Robert this evening,[4] after what has passed"; and when he heard that Sir Robert was not to be present, he hinted that Mamma was in the same danger in regard to Lord John Russell. "But if I tell him that he opens his mouth too wide," said Lord Glenelg, "he may think I mean that he eats too much!"

'I am sure that our guest enjoyed his morning's gossip, and it gave us all a merry commencement to what I hope may be a very enjoyable though rather anxious day. Tudor is to take luncheon with us, so we have amusement provided for that meal also; and what a business it will be in the evening! Such a phalanx of ladies as dear Mother is to head. The Misses Cotton, two Misses Galloway, two Misses Shepherd, Miss Kensington, and our three selves, all to set off from No. 3! It will look like a nocturnal wedding.

'I have just come in from paying a round of visits, with a card of admission in my hand.... My hand trembles with the heat, for it is warm walking at this hour, and I always walk fast when I walk in the streets alone. I look forward with much pleasure to the evening's entertainment. I only wish that you and dear Bella could enjoy it too; but I hope that *your* dinner in September may afford you as much gratification as this would have done....

'We ... went to Mrs. Bellasis' Ball last night. Mamma and I thought it a nice one, but — — considered it very dull. The Eastwicks were not there, but your friend, Colonel Sykes, appeared, with his stern bandit-like countenance. He so reminds me of you! His fair lady and sons were also there.... Sir de Lacy and Lady Evans, the Hinxmans and Galloways were also at the Ball.

'How are the dear little Robins? I hope that we may soon have them with us again. Pray give them plenty of kisses from Auntie Charlotte.... I hope dear Robin got home comfortably.'

Some of the above-mentioned names were of men well and widely known. Lord Metcalfe, at one time Acting Governor-General of India, was a wise and most courteous Indian statesman, whose life has been written by Sir John Kaye. Colonel Sykes was one year Chairman of the Court of

Directors. Sir Henry Pottinger was a famous diplomatist. Lord Glenelg, living near, was often in and out, and loved to have a cup of tea at hospitable No. 3.

The habit of the family at this time, while spending the main part of the year at Portland Place, was to go to some country place in the summer, for several weeks, sometimes renting a house where they could stay all together, sometimes breaking into smaller parties. In 1846 they were at Herne Bay; in 1847 at Gresford; in 1848 at Dover and Walmer. While at Walmer they were a good deal thrown with the Duke of Wellington, and the former acquaintanceship ripened into more of intimacy. Before deciding on Walmer, two or three of the party went to Dover, and they had a somewhat perilous voyage thither, to which the following letter makes allusion:—

TO MISS D. LAURA TUCKER.

'I hope that you will all write us very affectionate letters of congratulation on our escape from the waves. How talented it was in Mamma to manage to send us letters so soon! We had no idea of hearing from home by 6 o'clock on Monday morning. We are all quite well. I was not well yesterday morning,—I imagine from the effects of our adventure; but I am, like the rest of our dear party, quite well to-day.

'We are to set out in a pony-chaise for Walmer, to see about a house. Papa is to drive, and I have no doubt but that we shall have a delightful little excursion.

'The immense cliff is a great objection to Dover. Unless we undergo the great fatigue of getting up it, we should be quite prisoners. Walmer is *much* flatter. We are anxious to hear what has become of the poor *Emerald*. She landed us here on Saturday morning, and proceeded on her perilous journey at about five in the afternoon. Papa saw the carpenter's wife, who told him that the leak could not be got at because of the coals, that they would not get to Boulogne, but must return in two hours. The poor woman's husband was in the vessel. She said that her eyes were tired with looking at the steamer, but philosophically observed that those who are doomed to sup salt water must sup it. The *Emerald* has *not* returned, however. It is probable that she has put in to some other port. I should like to hear about her fate. I should feel for our kind sailor.

'My darling Papa has rather taken fright at Mamma's letter. He fears that she is not well, that she has been hysterical at the thought of our danger, and seems anxious to go up to London himself, in order to assist her and see about her. Fanny and I expostulate. He is the best of husbands and fathers. I hope, however, that dearest Mamma is *not* unwell, and that the sea-air may do her good and strengthen her. Another objection to Dover is that the voyage is likely to be rougher to it than to Walmer. Walmer is not situated so near that terrible South Foreland.... This is Papa's opinion, but we cannot decide till we see Walmer.'

Further particulars of the adventure alluded to are unfortunately not forthcoming.

CHAPTER IV
A FARCE OF GIRLISH DAYS

THE PRETENDER;
A FARCE IN TWO ACTS; by Charlotte Maria Tucker

Characters:—

COLONEL STUMPLEY.

CHARLES.

DARESBY.

CORPORAL CATCHUP.

WEASEL—A Butler.

O'SHANNON—A Soldier.

MRS. JUDITH RATTLETON.

MISS SOPHIA RATTLETON.

MISS BARBARA RATTLETON.

MISS HORATIA RATTLETON.

Scene laid in Northumberland, in and near the house of Mrs. Judith.

ACT I
SCENE I
THE HIGHROAD BEFORE MRS. JUDITH'S HOUSE

Enter Charles.

Charles. A cold, wet, and misty evening, and above all to one whose pockets are not lined! My foolish fancy for the Stage has brought me to a declining stage, if not a stage of decline. Heigh ho! how dark it is getting! Just the sort of place to meet with a ghost of Hamlet, not the sort of hamlet that I'm looking after, for I have done with theatrical effects,—I wish that I had done with the effects of cold. How dark and gloomy that church steeple looks over the trees! I'm close to a churchyard, I suppose. And—ey! ey!

what on earth are those white things upon the grass? Clothes put out to dry; what an ass I was not to see that before! but fasting makes one nervous. There's a house. How cheerful the lights look in it! I hear the sound of a piano going. There must be ladies there, and ladies are ever good and kind. What if I were to try my fortune at the door? My poor namesake Prince Charlie must have put wanderers into fashion. Northumberland is near enough to Scotland to have imbibed a little of its spirit of romance. Poor Prince! we are fellows in misfortune as we were partners in ambition. We both sought to play the King, I on the boards, he in Britain; but his frea-king and my moc-king are both changed to aching on the moors, and a skul-king too, which makes us as thin as skeletons. I'll try and muster up courage for a knock. [*Knocks.*]

I should not look the worse for a new coat, I think. My knee-ribbons are bleached quite pale with the wind and the rain. *Mais n'importe!* the man, the man remains the same! These locks have proved the keys to a Lady's heart e'er now; and then wit and eloquence! When I was flogged at school for affirming that a furbelow must be an article, as I knew it to be an article of dress, my Master observed that all my brains lay at the root of my tongue; and the best position for them too, say I! Who would keep a prompter to bellow to one from the top of the Monument, and where's the use of carrying one's brains so high, that one must send a carrier pigeon express for one's thoughts before one can express them at all? Better have wit to cover ignorance, than silence to conceal sense. One can't squint into a man's head to see what it contains. Here comes a light to the door: now for the encounter.

Weasel *opens the door.*

Is Mrs. [*coughs*] at home? Pray present my compliments to her, and say that a gentleman who has lost his way entreats the favour of shelter for a night under her hospitable roof.

Weasel. Shall I take up your name, Sir?

Charles. No, Sir, you may take up my words. [*Exit* Weasel.] Had the fellow been a Constable he might have taken me up also, for in this apparel I look more like a highwayman than a gentleman in a highway. How very cold it is! I wish that the triangular-nosed fellow would make haste; and yet my heart misgives me. I must 'screw my courage to the sticking point!' Impudence, impudence is my passport! I hear him shuffling downstairs. Be hardy, bold, and resolute, my heart.

Weasel *opens the door.*

Weasel. Sir, my Mistress begs you to walk up.

Charles. Go on, go on, I'll follow thee! [*Exeunt.*]

SCENE II
THE PARLOUR OF MRS. JUDITH'S HOUSE

Charles. Mrs. Judith. The Misses Sophia, Barbara, *and* Horatia Rattleton.

Charles. For all this unmerited kindness, most kind and fair ladies, a lonely wanderer can only return you thanks.

[*The young Ladies whisper together.*]

Sophia. Handsome, isn't he?

Horatia. Such a flow of eloquence, such a command of language.

Barbara. I wonder, Ratty, who he is.

Mrs. Jud. Do you come from the North, Sir?

Charles. I have spent the last few months there, Madam, though I was not born in Scotland. They were unfortunate months to me. I came to England on my Company's being broken up.

Horatia. Your Company! did you serve King George?

Charles. No, Miss, I tried to serve myself.

Horatia. [*Aside to Barbara.*] Strange, is it not?

Sophia. Why was your company broken up?

Charles. Because we were not able to raise a Sovereign amongst us. We were sadly cut up.

Horatia. [*Eagerly.*] By the Dragoons?

Charles. [*Laughing.*] Do not inquire too closely, fair Lady.

Mrs. Jud. May I ask your name, Sir?

Charles. Charles Stu— [*Aside.*] Ass that I am!

Mrs. Jud. I beg your pardon, Sir, I did not hear you.

Charles. [*Aside.*] The first word that comes! [*Aloud.*] Dapple, Madam, Dapple. [*Aside.*] I might have hit on a more romantic name, but my brain seems in a whirl.

Horatia. It is a very curious study to trace the derivations....

Mrs. Jud. Any way related to the Dapples of....

Sophia. Down, Adonis, down! your dirty little paws....

Horatia. One would suppose them sometimes prophetical of future events. Who can deny that Hanover....

Barbara. Our family name of....

Horatia. [*Raising her voice.*] Who can deny that Hanover has a great resemblance to Hand-over, or that Cumberland is as just a denomination for the bloody Duke as if....

Sophia. Pretty little pet he is, is he not?

Barbara. Our family name of Rattleton is said to be derived from a famous Ancestor of ours, a chief of the ancient Britons....

Mrs. Jud. My Cousin by the Mother's side....

Barbara. Whose head being cleft from his shoulders as he was driving his chariot into the thickest of....

Mrs. Jud. The family of the Goslings....

Horatia. Also passionately fond of Heraldry....

Barbara. His spirit seemed unconquered even by the blow which decapitated him, and he drove on....

Horatia. A Lion rampant over 6 grasshoppers....

Barbara. Whence our name of Rattle-ton or Rattle-on is said to be derived.

Charles. [*Aside.*] This is beyond endurance. They stun me. What a nest of parrots I am in! I cannot get in a word.

Horatia. Thus, Sir, your name of ... I beg your pardon, Sir, it has slipped my memory.

Charles. [*Aside.*] Hang me, if it has not fairly bolted from mine!

Mrs. Jud. Mr. Charles Dapple.

Charles. [*Aside.*] I'll change the conversation. [*To Horatia.*] You seem much devoted, Miss, to scientific pursuits.

Horatia. O, they are my delight, my recreation! Ornithology, Mythology, Geology, Conchology, fascinate me. I was first given my taste for the higher branches of these intellectual sciences by....

Sophia. Mr. Dapple, have you remarked my pretty little....

Horatia. My Uncle in the Scilly Isles, whose mind....

Sophia. Have you remarked....

Horatia. A profound genius....

Sophia. My little poodle, Adonis?

Horatia. By-the-by, Mr. Dapple, may I ask your opinion on a much disputed point, where I venture to differ even from my Uncle? What do you think of the Aerolites?

Charles. [*Turning to Sophia.*] A sweet little dog, indeed: what fine eyes!

Horatia. Do you think them....

Charles. The little pink ribbon round its neck is so becoming.

Horatia. [*Raising her voice.*] Mr. Dapple, Mr. Dapple, do you think the Aerolites....

Charles. [*Aside.*] Help me, my mother-wits!

Horatia. Do you agree in the generally received opinion....

Charles. [*Aside.*] Some political party perhaps!

Horatia. Or do you think them....

Charles. Why, ma'am, I think—I—I am decidedly of opinion—that—that—the....

Horatia. The Aerolites....

Charles. Are nothing more or less than Jacobites.

All the Ladies. Jacobites!

Horatia. Why, Sir, I always thought them a sort of stone....

Charles. Stone-fruit, true, true; I spoke without thinking. Stone-fruit, a species of—of—apricots.

Barbara. Hark, there is a knock at the door. Peep through the shutters, Ratty, and see who it is.

Charles. [*Aside.*] A little diversion for me. I am growing so hot. Silence to cover sense would in this case....

Horatia. 'Tis old Colonel Stumply.

Charles. [*Starting up.*] Colonel Stumply! I'm dished.

The Ladies. Why—what—who——

Charles. Perhaps you will permit me, ladies, to retire. I feel indisposed—faint! [*Exit.*]

Mrs. Jud. I must go and welcome my old friend. [*Exit.*]

Horatia. Bab!

Barbara. Ratty!

Horatia. What a flash of electricity has burst on my intellect!

Sophia. His noble air; his wan features....

Horatia. A fugitive....

Sophia. A wanderer....

Horatia. His sudden alarm....

Sophia. [*Rushing into her arms.*] O Ratty, Ratty, what a day! what an honour! what a surprise!

Barbara. How now, what's the matter?

Horatia. Brain of adamant! could not instinct direct you to the feet of your adored Prince?

Barbara. The Prince! Is it possible?

Sophia. Charlie! Charlie! O! what a moment!

Horatia. Did you not hear him describe the ruin of his army....

Sophia. Did you not hear 'Charles Stew—' upon his noble tongue....

Horatia. How he started when he recollected himself....

Sophia. And O, how exquisitely pathetic, how touchingly appropriate, the name he gave instead! Dapple; to signify how his fortunes are chequered—Dapple....

Barbara. How the Jacobites were running in his head when he even....

Sophia. Little reason had he to fear us. If Daresby had been here....

Barbara. And this vile Colonel: no wonder he started off!

Sophia. What shall we do to get rid of him?

Horatia. All that woman ever attempted I am ready to perform.

Sophia. I would die for him.

Barbara. And I too.

Sophia. The handsome, brave, dear, darling young Prince! And to think that Daresby's a Whig!

Enter Mrs. Judith *and* Col. Stumply.

Col. Good evening, young Ladies, good evening. I have just returned from the North, where we are everywhere triumphant, and our laurels should ensure us a welcome from beauty. 'None but the brave, none but the brave deserve the fair,' you know. Hey, Miss Sophy?

Sophia. [*Aside.*] Monster!

Horatia. [*Aside.*] Traitor!

Barbara. [*Aside.*] Butcher!

Col. What, all silent and aghast? I shall begin to fear myself unwelcome. Hey, Mrs. Judith? But my Regiment is quartered for the night in the village, and I was sure that I might throw myself on the hospitality of an old friend.

Mrs. Jud. We are delighted to see you.

Col. Is your little room unoccupied to-night?

Mrs. Jud. To tell the truth there is a young....

Horatia. [*Aside.*] I could beat her! [*Aloud.*] It is quite unoccupied, Sir, except—except in this cold weather we keep the pigs there.

Col. The pigs!

Mrs. Jud. Why, Ratty....

Horatia. Oh, it is not fit to receive you, Sir. The chimney tumbled in during the last gale....

Mrs. Jud. Why, Ratty....

Horatia. And every pane of glass is broken.

Sophia. [*Aside to Barbara.*] O Bab, such lying can never thrive.

Mrs. Jud. What strange non....

Horatia. [*Aside.*] How on earth can I stop her tongue? [*Aloud.*] Aunt, Aunt, is there any supper prepared for the Colonel?

Col. Anything; anything; the cold ride has sharpened my appetite; but a good blaze like this cheers the heart, and gives me courage to face even the pigs, Miss Ratty!

Mrs. Jud. The pigs! why....

Horatia. Would you like to see that everything is comfortable yourself, Aunt? [*Aside.*] I am in a fever!

Col. Turn out the pigs, hey, Mrs. Judith?

Mrs. Jud. If I ever....

Horatia. Go, dear Aunt, precious Aunt, do go.

Sophia. A nice little dish of your own making would be so acceptable.

Barbara. We'll take care of the Colonel.

Mrs. Jud. I cannot com—pre—hend—I—— [*The girls half lead, half push her out.*]

Col. You will excuse me, young ladies; I always make a point of looking after my horse myself. [*Exit.*]

Horatia. [*Sinking on a chair.*] I am exhausted. Stupid sticks, why did you not assist me?

Sophia. I tried, but....

Barbara. What shall we do now?

Sophia. My heart beats so, I shall expire.

Barbara. The Colonel will stay in spite of the pigs.

Sophia. Where can we hide the Prince?

Horatia. [*Starting up.*] A thought has struck me.

Sophia. What, what?

Horatia. You shall hear—it has been done before. You will aid me in the execution of it.

Sophia. [*Throwing herself into her arms.*] O my Ratty!

Horatia. We will save him.

Barbara. We will, we will!

Horatia. Or perish with him.

Sophia. We will.

Horatia. Come, come, no time is to be lost; let us fly to his succour.

> 'Come weal, come woe,
> We'll gather and go,
> And live or die wi' Charlie!'

SCENE III
A CHURCHYARD BY MOONLIGHT

Enter Charles, Sophia, Barbara, *and* Horatia.

Charles. Where on earth are you taking me?

Sophia. To safety, to safety.

Barbara. We know all.

Charles. You know all?

Horatia. Your name, your situation....

Charles. Then you must know that the coming of the Colonel is hangably inconvenient to me.

Sophia. We tremble at your danger.

Horatia. We will defend you with our lives.

Charles. Excessively kind, but it is not quite come to that yet. A kick or a caning....

Sophia. You make us shudder.

Charles. But I do not like promenading at this hour in winter! Is it a country fashion? I am very cold, and tired, and sleepy, and I would rather retire to rest.

Horatia. Here then we have arrived at the spot. Descend, and you will find a bed prepared for you.

Charles. Descend! why, hang me if it isn't a vault!

Sophia. If it would please you to descend....

Charles. Please me, you barbarous witches! would it please any one to be buried alive? What on earth do you mean?

Barbara. The only way to preserve your rights....

Charles. Rites, do you call these rites? They are very inhuman rites. Anything but the rites of hospitality. To offer a stranger the shelter of your roof, and then make his bed in a vault! This is your spare-room, is it? If I had guessed what you meant to do with your guest, I would not have troubled you with my company.

Horatia. O, for your Country's sake....

Charles. My Country's sake! what good can it do my Country? I know your motives, you scientific Monster! you want to make a petrifaction of me.

Horatia. Is it possible that a treatment so....

Charles. A treat meant is it? If you mean it for a treat, I assure you that I do not consider it as one. You may go in yourself and enjoy it.

Barbara. So short a space ...

Charles. A very short space I can see, and a very narrow space too. I'll be hanged if I get into it!

Horatia. Who could have expected opposition from such a quarter?

Sophia. Can the Hero shrink from so small a trial of his constancy? Oh, descend, descend, and we will admire....

Charles. Add mire, you cruel wretches! is there not enough at the bottom already?

Horatia. We would preserve you.

Charles. Didn't I say so? Some inhuman experiment! But I'll not be preserved to please you, not I.

Sophia. [*Throwing herself at his feet.*] O noblest of men! doubt not our fidelity! yield to our agonized entreaties!

[*The others kneel.*]

Charles. Yield, indeed! I beg you will rise, fair Ladies. I know not if you are jesting; 'tis but a cold jest to me. As for entering that vault, you may kill me before you bury me, for while I'm alive I'll not go, Ladies; I say I will not go.

Horatia. Then we must leave him to his fate.

Charles. Leave me, leave me, all alone in a churchyard. Ladies, ladies, for pity's sake....

Horatia. I am beside myself.

Charles. Remain then beside me. Or rather, why cannot we return to the house? I am half frozen with cold and ... and excitement!

Barbara. You forget the Colonel.

Charles. The Colonel. O, is that all? Can't you hide me in some quiet corner?

Horatia. I have it! the storeroom.

Barbara. But if a search should be made?

Charles. Search! who'll search? The storeroom is the very place. Come, come, the air is piercing; come.

Barbara. This way; by the kitchen door.

Charles. Once more into the house, dear friends, once more. [*Exit.*]

Horatia. Is this the Prince? the Hero?

Sophia. O Ratty! our duty remains the same! [*Exeunt.*]

ACT II

SCENE I
THE PARLOUR

Colonel Stumply. Weasel.

Col. Good-morrow, Weasel. An old campaigner, you see, learns to be an early riser.

Weasel. I wish your honour a good morning. I hope you found your room comfortable.

Col. Most comfortable. No traces of the pigs, ha, ha! none the worse for the chimney-top; ha, ha, ha! That Comet has a tail, I guess. Well, Weasel, how has all gone on these two years, since I last found myself at Rattleton Hermitage? Hey?

Weasel. Much the same as usual, your honour. Our only varieties are Dr. Daresby and the rheumatics; till last night when....

Col. The girls—the young Ladies seem much grown, much improved.

Weasel. O, for the matter of that, yes, though Miss Ratty's sadly taken up with the books, d'ye see. She's poring all day long over a lot of different sorts of learnings; I don't remember their names, but they all ends in *oddity*. Then she's an out and out Jacobite, and thumps the piano when she sings 'Charlie is my darling,' as though she took it for a Whig. Indeed, your honour, last night....

Col. And Miss Barbara?

Weasel. She's quiet like, Sir. She's never off her chair stitching away. They says, your honour, that she makes holes on purpose to sew them up again, d'ye see?

Col. Sophy—Miss Rattleton is a charming girl.

Weasel. Ah, so thinks some one else. Did your honour ever see young Dr. Daresby?

Col. No, what of him?

Weasel. O, nothing, Sir. But they walks alone together, and sings duets together, and he gave her the little poodle, and they says, your honour, d'ye see....

Col. Yes, yes, I understand.

Weasel. She always feeds that fat little dog herself, your honour. She gives it slices of bread and strawberry jam. But she's a good young Lady, Sir. Often I sees her going to the cottages with her little pink bag filled with the good things which Mrs. Judith makes. (I knows that from Mrs. Marjory who has to wash out the grease-spots every day for Miss Sophy.) And there she goes mincing along with her long veil hanging behind, and her little poodle running on before her. But may I make bold to ask how Master Stumply is? He was a very little boy when....

Col. Not a word of him, Weasel, not a word of him! He's a wayward ... don't speak of him! folly and indiscretion have been his bane.

Weasel. [*Shaking his head.*] There's some others I know seem running the same road.

Col. How? Who?

Weasel. O, it is not for me to say, your honour.

Col. Speak; explain yourself.

Weasel. I dare say 'twas all a frolic, your honour, but there were odd doings here yesterday.

Col. Tell me, tell me.

Weasel. [*Mysteriously.*] Perhaps as an old friend of the Family your honour ought to know all, and such a rum affair....

Col. Go on, go on.

Weasel. Well then, your honour, yesterday was a cold evening, d'ye see, and as I was stirring the kitchen fire there comes a knock, and I goes to the door, your honour.

Col. Well.

Weasel. There stands a tall, genteel-like lad with a ragged coat. And he would give me no name, but he said he was a Wanderer, and asked for a night's lodging. So Mrs. Judith, who never can refuse any one, ordered the spare bed to be got ready for him.

Col. So I turned him out, hey, Weasel? There's the secret of the pigs; but why this mystery?

Weasel. Mystery, Sir, ay, that's the word; but if your honour was to hear what followed!

Col. What? where did they put him?

Weasel. [*Lowering his voice.*] When it was night, your honour, what sees I through the chink of the kitchen door in the passage but the three young Ladies lugging along a great bundle, and stopping and panting and puffing? So says I, I'll see to the bottom of this, so I pops out suddenly and says, 'Can I help you, Misses?' quite civil like. But O Sir, how Miss Sophy trembled and turned as white as a lily, and Miss Ratty stamped and sent me to the village—at that hour, your honour, company in the house—the ground covered with frost—I subject to the rheumatics—and what for, d'ye think? to get her twopenceworth of shoe-ribbon, your honour; and when I brought it, would you believe it?—she roared out that it was too narrow and sent me back again.

Col. Most strange! most unaccountable! Have you any guess what was in the bundle?

Weasel. I winked at it, your honour. There was a mattress and blankets, I'm sure.

Col. For the Stranger, I suppose. But this mystery! I cannot understand it. Where could they be going?

Weasel. To the churchyard, I thinks.

Col. The churchyard!

Weasel. Why, your honour, they certainly did not go into the kitchen, and the back-door leads straight across the yard to the Church, and the vault would be no bad hiding-place, your honour. Miss Ratty has hid there herself, I knows, when the dentist was here.

Col. Have you no other clue? What an extraordinary affair!

Weasel. Why, Sir—your honour, last night Mrs. Marjory overheard Miss Ratty whispering Miss Sophy, and she said, Sir....

Col. What? speak out!

Weasel. 'As long as the Colonel remains here the Prince must keep concealed.'

Col. [*Springing up.*] The Prince! ha, ha! I smell a rat! the Pretender! the Pretender! if there was ever such luck, such fortune! Hang me if I could not—but there's not an instant to be lost. Fly, Weasel, to the village. Bid Corporal Catchup and a dozen stout fellows be with me directly. Fly, I say, and if it be all as I hope, I'll cram you with gold till you choke. Begone! Fly! [*Exit* Weasel.] Thirty thousand pounds and a baronetship! Sir Stephen Stumply! Ah, if that wayward boy—the Pretender! the Pretender! he's in a net, in a net, and I'll be hanged if I let him out of it. [*Exit.*]

SCENE II
THE DRAWING-ROOM

Enter Horatia.

Horatia. What a sleepless night I have passed, what anxiety, what excitement! and yet how unlike is he to what I had imagined! so timid, so petulant! and that perpetual punning! It matters not, however,—his title to our services remains the same! A strange misgiving is on my soul; is it the shadow of approaching danger, or only the fear of it? The Colonel gave me a strange meaning look as he passed me this morning, and said, 'You are early up, Miss Ratty; I fear that your rest was broken last night.' Can he suspect anything? That sneaking wretch, Weasel! Hark, I hear the Colonel's step and a strange voice. I'll conceal myself behind this screen. Perhaps....

Enter Colonel Stumply *and* Corporal Catchup.

Col. Plant two stout fellows at the front door, and half a dozen in the garden. Place them so that there shall be no possibility of escape either from the house or the churchyard adjoining.

Cor. I will, Sir.

Horatia. [*Aside.*] Horror and despair!

Col. Yourself and four of your best men go and search the open vault at the right-hand corner of the churchyard, and on your lives let not your prisoner escape. Go, plant your Sentinels, and then to your business. [*Exit* Corporal Catchup.] I will go and superintend myself. [*Exit.*]

Horatia. Day of horror and misery! All is lost. All is discovered. If I but knew of one who could divert the attention of these wretches till the Prince escaped! If I ...

Enter Daresby.

Daresby! He's a Whig! but I'll make him my tool.

Daresby. Good morning, I came thus early....

Horatia. [*Speaking very fast.*] You are so welcome—you came just a moment ...

Daresby. My Sophy! nothing is the matter with her?

Horatia. O no. It's a poor soldier—got the cholera—lying in the vault ...

Daresby. In a vault!

Horatia. Run, run, dearest Daresby, or you will be too late.

Daresby. What do you mean? Explain yourself.

Horatia. The cholera, I say—in the vault—O! you put me in a fever. For my sake, for Sophy's—O run, fly!

Daresby. Whatever can you ...

Horatia. Go, or I shall run wild! You know the way, go!

Daresby. If I can be of any use to the poor sufferer. [*Exit.*]

Horatia. O, what a relief! he's gone! I should never survive another day of such excitement. If they once suppose that their object is gained and the Prince caught, the sentinels will be removed from the garden, and he can escape through the window. If the deception can be carried on for one half-hour he may be saved. I must go and put my sisters on their guard, and prepare the Prince for flight. If Aunt Judith or Weasel see and recognise

Daresby all is lost. I wish I could lock them both up. What a labyrinth I am in! The greatest comfort is that the Colonel is a blockhead, and would not know a prince from a pancake! [*Exit.*]

SCENE III
THE STORE-ROOM

Charles. Something better than a vault this, methinks. I could not have found a hiding-place more to my mind. Excellent cherry-brandy she makes, this Mrs. Judith. I have entered half a dozen professions since I entered this room; it will be hard if I do not make my fortune out of one of them. I am an Historian, for I have been discussing old dates; a Merchant, for I add plum to plum; a Lawyer, for I have opened many a case; a Lord Mayor, for the mace is before me; and a Navigator, for I am led to seize and gulf! What if I were to stay here altogether, or set up a new company with my fair hostesses? Miss Ratty is cut out for a tragedy Queen. Such passion! such emphasis! [*Mimicking.*] 'That my keen knife see not the wound it makes' — but the puzzle is that they are all ladies; not one to take a gentleman's part. It is a shame in me to say so, for I am sure that they have taken mine. My only hope would be in Weasel. That fellow has such a desperate squint, that I am sure he would make a capital Lear!

Enter Horatia.

Horatia. Fly! fly! while yet there is a moment's respite.

Charles. Fly! and wherefore?

Horatia. Rouse all the ancient courage of your race ...

Charles. There can be no courage in a race, for a race is running away.

Horatia. Let the spirit of your Ancestors glow in your bosom, for the hour of danger is come.

Charles. 'I dare do all that may become a man' ...

Horatia. Does this trifling become a man and a hero?

Charles. I know of but one thing, fair Ratty, that can become a man and a hero.

Horatia. What is that?

Charles. A boy, to be sure!

Horatia. Enough, enough of this perpetual play of words. We must think, we must act. Another is now taking your place at the vault ...

Charles. My place! how excessively obliging!

Horatia. Every moment is invaluable. Put on this dress of my Aunt's which I have brought for you, and fly, fly, while the deception lasts!

Charles. The brandy must have got into my head.

Horatia. Put it on, I entreat you, if not for your own or your Country's sake, yet for your noble Father's.

Charles. My Father's! Either you or I ... Why, what's the matter with him? Is he in the farce too?

Horatia. [*Aside.*] He is the worse for liquor! O horrible! and at such a moment! [*Aloud.*] The soldiers are here—sent to seize you—to drag you to a dungeon, perhaps an ignominious death.

Charles. [*Alarmed.*] And why? what have I done?

Horatia. I heard the orders given. One hour's delay will lead you to the scaffold.

Charles. The scaffold!

Horatia. The block.

Charles. The block! why, what is my crime? Why does not my Father come to my assistance?

Horatia. Your Father cannot—he is exiled from his native land. Were he to appear, he must perish too.

Charles. Have you hid him? have you hid him?

Horatia. [*Aside.*] Horridly drunk! [*Aloud.*] Put on this dress and fly. It is your only chance of life.

Charles. You have put me into a shiver. I cannot half believe, nor a quarter comprehend you.

Horatia. Believe then these tears, this agony of apprehension in which you see me. This moment the soldiers may be mounting the staircase—cutting off all hope ...

Charles. Give me the slip then, and I will give them the slip! quick, quick, and the cloak and hood.

Horatia. Here, here! O despatch! while you remain here I tread on hot iron.

Charles. I am to personate your Aunt.

Horatia. Yes, yes, any one, but make haste.

Charles. So, I'm equipped. Farewell, Lady!

Horatia. Pull the hood over your face. O farewell! [*Exit* Charles.]

Horatia. One hour more of excitement, and then ... [*Exit*.]

SCENE IV
THE CHURCHYARD

Enter Corporal Catchup *and Soldiers.*

Corp. Silence! Silence! halt! advance bending down and with your bayonets presented. Comrades, this is a glorious day, and if we catch the Pretender we shall have little cause to grieve that we arrived a day too late for the Battle of Culloden. What were the deeds of the Duke of Cumberland to ours? He but wounded the fox, we catch him by the nose. We shall be made Aldermen, every man of us. Take ground behind those bushes; keep silence. I hear a voice in the vault. On your lives be silent—be steady!

Daresby. [*In the vault.*] I can find no one, yet here is a bed prepared. What a strange place to make an hospital of! [*Emerging from the vault.*] Perhaps the poor fellow has got frightened and delirious ...

Corp. Stand!

Daresby. Ah, here is my Patient. So you have got the cholera, my Friend!

Corp. No, unless that's one of your titles. Surrender or die!

Daresby. He must be in a high fever! Be calm, my good man, I will render you all the assistance in my power.

Corp. You will, will you?

Daresby. Come with me to the house, come. This is no place for a person in your state.

Corp. Well, if this arn't droll! he's trying to humbug me.

Daresby. You may catch your death of cold.

Corp. I'll catch nothing but you. Come along, Sir, offer no resistance, for it's of no use. I'm sorry for you, but I've a duty to perform, and a reward to get.

Daresby. What do you mean, fellow? Stand off!

Corp. Ho! guards there! [Daresby *is surrounded.*]

Daresby. This is some error. By whose warrant do you dare to apprehend one of his Majesty's subjects?

Corp. No use in all that deception, Sir: all's discovered now.

Daresby. What's discovered, fellow, what deception? Who dares use such terms to me! You shall answer for your conduct, Sir; this shall not be passed over, I'll warrant you.

Corp. I hope not, Sir.

Daresby. This is not to be endured. By whose orders do you presume to place me under arrest?

Corp. We are under the orders of Colonel Stumply.

Daresby. I must see the Colonel instantly. He shall give me an explanation of this extraordinary affair. Take me to him directly.

Corp. All in good time, Sir. Stickum, have you handcuffs with you?

Daresby. Handcuffs, villain!

Stickum. No.

Corp. Keep your hand on his collar, then. Soldiers, present bayonets. Let him attempt to escape, and he dies.

Daresby. With what effrontery ...

Corp. Move on, Sir, if you please. [*To the Soldiers.*] Keep your eye on him. If he but raise his hand or turn his head — fire! [*Exeunt.*]

SCENE V
THE GARDEN GATE

O'Shannon.

O'Shan. A could, misty, morning, and I am left here to keep watch without a drop of the cratur to cheer my heart or keep my spirits from sinking. There's all the rest of them gone to catch the Pretender and get the prize-money, and it's nothing that I'm likely to catch here but a cold. I wish that I had never left the tallow business, that I do, for all this murthering work. It was a lucky chance that we were a day too late for the fair at Culloden; it's no fancy I have for the Highlanders' dirks. Awful slashing work they made, 'tis said. Well-a-day! I must shoulder my gun; if the Corporal found me standing at ease, he would order me a round dozen: there's no fear of it's going off for its own accord, the cratur, for I forgot to load it this morning.

Enter Charles *in disguise.*

Charles. [*Aside.*] And there is a Sentry! Horatia was right! But what they should want to arrest either me or my Father for is more than I can comprehend! This is really nervous work. I fear that I shall find it as difficult to pass this fellow as I found it at school to parse a sentence from my grammar-book. Notwithstanding the dress with which Ratty provided me, I shall need all the address of which I am master to get through this scrape should he address me. I must put on an air of confidence. Perhaps he may let me pass without question.

O'Shan. A black morning, Ma'am.

Charles. [*Attempting to slip past.*] Did you ever see mourning any other colour?

O'Shan. Can't pass here, Ma'am.

Charles. No! and why?

O'Shan. 'Cause I am posted here to keep a good watch.

Charles. [*Attempting to pass again.*] Easier to keep a good watch than to get one!

O'Shan. I have orders to let no one pass.

Charles. O but, my good fellow, I have very important business. You must let me go.

O'Shan. Keep back, Ma'am. Now I thinks on't, your hood looks rather suspicious.

Charles. [*Retreating a step.*] Does it? A sort of robbin' hood, I suppose. [*Aside.*] I wish the fellow were at Jericho.

O'Shan. And that dress was never made for you? Let me see a little closer. [*Advancing.*]

Charles. [*Retreating. Aside.*] Shall I run for my life?

O'Shan. Stop, stop, my good Lady! Methinks your dress is uncommon short, too, it hardly reaches to the clocks of your stockings.

Charles. Mind your watch, and leave my clocks alone. [*Aside.*] O dear! O dear! If I were but once fairly off! [*Attempts to run.*]

O'Shan. Stop, or I'll shoot ye! I'll send a bullet through your head if ye stir an inch farther.

Charles. [*Aside.*] I'm done for!

O'Shan. [*Aside.*] I'll make sure. [*Suddenly darts towards Charles and pulls back his hood.*] Hillo! hillo! I've caught him! I've caught him, 'tis the man himself.

Charles. [*Aside.*] One struggle for life. [*Aloud.*] Beware, fellow, I have arms. [*Aside.*] None but what nature gave me.

O'Shan. [*Retreating a step. Aside.*] Murther! and the gun is not loaded!

Charles. [*Aside.*] I've staggered him! [*Aloud.*] Lay but a finger on me and I'll lay you with the dust.

O'Shan. Keep off, or I'll shoot ye.

Charles. [*Retreating.*] A fig for your gun!

O'Shan. [*Aside. Retreating.*] I wish some one would come. I've heard he's a raal hero. I'll call for help. Holloa! there.

Charles. Hold your peace, or I'll cut you piece-meal.

O'Shan. I'll blow your brains out, I will! [*Aside.*] He can't guess that it's not loaded.

Charles. [*Aside.*] If he should fire!

O'Shan. [*Aside.*] If he should fight! My poor Mother; och, if she could see me now, 'twould pit her into high-strikes. Is no one coming to help me?

Charles. [*Aside.*] If I could but touch his kinder feelings! I have been accustomed to steal hearts, but I fear that I should find his steeled already. I must make one more effort to steal past him. But the sight of his matchlock makes my blood run cold.

O'Shan. Och! he's coming nearer. O for pity's sake ...

Charles. If mercy ever touched your bosom ...

Enter Corporal Catchup.

O'Shan. Catch him! catch him! 'tis he, the Pretender! catch him, Corporal! collar him! never fear!

Corp. Who? the old woman?

O'Shan. Catch him, I say, and never be frightened for him, man. I found him out.

Charles. So—all is lost.

Corp. A man in disguise! it must be he. Bind him, O'Shannon. This is a prize indeed.

O'Shan. Ah, poor gintleman, your troubles will soon be pit an end to. Ah! ye may well sigh, for no man laughs on his way to the gallows.

Charles. The gallows! is it possible that so inhuman a murder can be contemplated?

O'Shan. O ye may be satisfied of it! There's only one thing that's doubtful, I'm thinking.

Charles. What's that?

O'Shan. Whether they'll stick your head on the Lord Mayor's mace before or after they've hung you!

Charles. O horrible, horrible, most horrible! It cannot, O it cannot be! What a dreadful, what a fearful fate! O that the first step I took from my Father's home had been into a horse-pond! that I had died e'er I left it!

O'Shan. Ay, there's the pity! Had ye stayed peaceably at home, this would never have happened to ye.

Charles. The gallows! can it be?

O'Shan. Ah, how all the Ladies will pity ye! such a likely lad, and so young, and ...

Charles. Silence! you distract me.

O'Shan. Poor gintleman! when it comes to the pinch, when the rope ...

Corp. No more, O'Shannon! You have secured his arms. Bring him speedily along with you. No delay!

Charles. My limbs can scarcely support me! O day of agony, of misery, and despair! [*Exeunt.*]

SCENE VI.
THE PARLOUR.

Colonel Stumply.

Col. [*Rubbing his hands.*] Caught! caught! This is indeed a good day's work.

Enter Sophia, Barbara, *and* Horatia.

Col. Ah! ha! my pretty Jacobites, this comes of your plotting. The Pretender is in safe hands now. Who would have thought you up to such a conspiracy?

Horatia. Alas, our unhappy Prince!

Sophia. [*Aside to* Horatia.] Poor Daresby! It makes my heart faint to think of him. I cannot stay to look on.

Horatia. You must stay to keep him silent. 'Tis but for an hour. I am ashamed of you. Remember that you have a part to perform.

Sophy. I cannot say what is not true.

Horatia. Say nothing, then.

Enter Daresby *guarded.*

Daresby. [*To the* Col.] Sir, I demand an explanation of this most extraordinary and unjustifiable treatment. Sir, I am a gentleman and ... [Horatia *makes earnest signs to him to be silent.*]

Col. You shall be treated, Sir, with all the respect due to your station, consistent with your safe custody.

Daresby. Of what am I charged? Who is my accuser? what wretch dares? [Horatia *repeats the signs.*] What is the meaning of all this nonsense? Do you wish to make a fool of me? I'll not endure this ...

Col. Be calm, Sir, and submit to destiny.

Daresby. I'll not submit to such treatment. My name is ...

[Horatia *in an agony throws herself at his feet, exclaiming*] O noble man! for the sake of all you love....

Daresby. Horatia, I am in a dream. Sophy, of you I ask, I entreat, an explanation. Why am I thus confined? Why do you stand calmly looking on my disgrace?

Sophy. Calmly! O Da ... [*Aside.*] I cannot restrain my tears.

Daresby. Are you too my enemy?

Sophy. Your enemy! O!

Daresby. [*To the* Colonel.] Are my political opinions suspected? Am I supposed to be a Ja....

Horatia. You are known—you are known—to be—to be—to be ... [*Enter* Weasel.]

Horatia. [*Springing to* Sophia's *side.*] O Sophy, for pity's sake take that creature off, or....

Sophy. Weasel, Weasel! [*Aside.*] What can I say?

Weasel. What! Dr. Da....

Sophia. Weasel, Weasel, will you go directly to the garden and fetch....

Weasel. What, Miss?

Sophia. Fetch, fetch—some spinach.

Weasel. Spinach don't grow in November, Miss, as Dr....

Horatia. Go to the village directly for....

Weasel. Can't go to the village no more, Miss, till I've laid the cloth for breakfast. The Doc....

Horatia. We must have wine. Go to the cellar.

Weasel. Haven't got the keys, Miss. If I might make bold to ask why....

Horatia. Begone this instant ... we shall want poultry. Wring every chicken's neck in the yard, or I'll wring yours as sure as I stand here! [*Exit* Weasel.]

Col. What an extraordinary temper!

Daresby. Sophy, Sophy, if you are still the ingenuous being I ever believed you to be, tell me in what farce I am thus forced to act a part against my will. Tell me the secret of the conspiracy which seems formed against me. Are you an accessory?

Col. Why, the Ladies have been turning every stone in your defence! They never let out the secret! As far as they were concerned you might have remained in your vault until you were old enough to stay there altogether!

Daresby. Every sentence that I hear bewilders me yet more. Ratty Rattleton, Ratty Rattleton, you are at the bottom of the plot.

Enter Mrs. Judith.

Horatia. [*Aside.*] Aunt Judy! this is distraction!

Mrs. Jud. Young Daresby, my....

Horatia. Aunt, Aunt....

Mrs. Jud. What's the matter?

Horatia. The ... [*aside*] at last I seem come to my wits end! [*Aloud.*] The....

Daresby. Mrs. Judith Rattleton, you are my friend, you will bear witness....

Horatia. The most important....

Sophia. O dear Aunt....

Barbara. If you would only hold your tongue!

Mrs. Jud. What a racket! what ... why....

Daresby. Mrs. Judith, I am here charged with....

Mrs. Jud. You, Daresby! Why, Colonel, this is....

Col. Not the Prince! Then he is concealed in the house! I see all; follow me, Guards ... [Sophy *throws herself at his feet;* Horatia *and* Barbara *rush to the door.*]

Horatia. You shall pass over my corpse! I am desperate! [*The door suddenly opens. Enter* Charles *guarded by* O'Shannon *and the* Corporal.]

All the Young Ladies. The Prince! horrors! the Prince!

Daresby. My chum, Charles Stumply!

Charles. My Father!

Col. Ah, Scapegrace! dare you present yourself before me? Under what false and shameful pretences have you entered this house?

O'Shan. Charles Stumply! hang the fellow, he's only a man after all.

Daresby. I cannot contain my surprise.

Mrs. Jud. The ungrateful vagabond! he has stolen my best gown and hood.

Horatia. I shall sink to the cellar.

Sophia. O Daresby, how comical!

Col. Speak, you scamp! What has induced you to dress yourself like—a—speak! nor add a falsehood to your other faults and follies.

Charles. My dear Father, I have used no deception except that of changing my name. I am the deceived, not the deceiver. No one present is as much surprised at seeing me, as I myself am at finding myself thus. These fair Ladies kindly and willingly took me in, and I see that, quite unwittingly, I have taken them in also! I own that I merit your displeasure, but I will do so no longer. I have received a lesson which I will not soon forget. I will no longer run counter to your wishes, but return to the counter for which you destined me. I have long devoted myself to a-muse, but now I will learn to obey. I own that I too fondly sought the giddy cheer of an applauding audience. Romance and her knights had taken possession of my fancy, but I have found the nights too cold, and the cheer too indifferent. I return with humble regret to my loving Sire, and if he will receive me a-gain, he may perhaps be able to make a-gain of me yet!

Col. Ah, you Rogue, you little merit that I should look at you again. The Pretender, indeed! so farewell to my dreams of fortune! I always thought it too good to be true. Ladies, I have to beg a thousand pardons for my rudeness in breaking in....

Charles. I must bear that blame, my Father. Had I not broken out, you would not have broken in.

Horatia. Deceiving Wretch! could I for a moment....

Charles. No anger, fair Miss Ratty, we had enough of this indignation at the brink of the vault, when you were near falling out with me because I would not fall in with your ideas, and fall into the vault.

Daresby. Ah, Sophy, how you treated me!

Sophia. I thought it my duty, dearest.

Daresby. I can pardon you anything; but that deceiving Ratty, whose word I can never again believe....

Charles. No more of that, Daresby. The farce is ended, the mists of mistake are clearing up, the reign of Folly must fall, let not Anger survive its cause!

> Now that we have ended all this War of Words,
> And fall to drawing corks instead of swords,
> Now the Pretender may his Captors mock,
> And view with glee a match without the lock,
> Let each resentful thought and feeling cease,
> And General Harmony conclude the Piece!

CHAPTER V
A.D. 1847-1849 HOME LIFE

In 1847 a new interest entered the life of Charlotte Tucker. The three little ones of her brother Robert and his wife,—Louis, Charley, and Letitia,—came to live at No. 3, and were made her especial charge. All of them, but particularly the pretty little dark-eyed Letitia, then only two years old, were thenceforward as her own; first in her thoughts, and among the first in her love. She taught them, trained them, devoted herself to them; and their names will often be found in her letters. The death of Letitia, nearly twenty years later, was one of the heaviest sorrows she ever had to endure. One is disposed to think that the care and responsibility of three little ones, undertaken in the midst of a full and busy family life, and in addition to all the duties of that life, could have been no sinecure, and must have been fraught with many a difficulty.

The Tuckers were much in society, as may indeed have been already gathered. Mr. Tucker was a man greatly sought after, alike on account of his position and influence, and because of his personal attractiveness. Open house was kept; and the large circle of friends and acquaintances never failed to find a welcome. So many indeed would drop in and out, that three lunches in succession were occasionally known to take place at No. 3; and so frequent were the 'parties' to which the family was invited, that sometimes they would appear at three different houses in the course of one evening. 'Party' in those days was a wide term, embracing divers kinds of entertainment, from a simple musical gathering to a large ball.

Dinner-parties also were numerous. In reference to these, Charlotte Tucker wrote rather drolly to her sister late in life, speaking of—'those formal affairs, which you and I remember in our earlier days. We *must* ask So-and-so; and how shall we find gentlemen to counterbalance Mrs. and Miss out of one house? Slow concerns those great dinner-parties were; a kind of social duty, which cost much trouble and expense, and gave not much pleasure. A kind of very stiff jelly, with not many strawberries in it.'

An amusing story is told about these large dinners. In those days the custom of 'drinking healths' had gained sway to an absurd and objectionable extent; gentlemen being expected to respond to every toast, and not only to sip their wine, but very often to empty their glasses, under pain of giving serious offence. Mr. Tucker always had by his side a decanter of toast and water, from which his glass was filled for the various toasts; and probably those not in the secret counted him a marvellously hard-headed man. One day a guest requested leave to taste this especial wine, which was kept for the host alone, supposing it to be of some very rare and choice vintage. His request was immediately complied with; and the face of the *bon-vivant* may be imagined when he discovered himself to be drinking toast-and-water.

No doubt these dinners *were* a 'social duty'; and no doubt some of them may have been extremely dull. Yet it must not be supposed that Charlotte did not thoroughly enjoy London society, and did not fully appreciate intercourse with polished and intellectual minds. That which in her old age would have been a mere weariness to her, was no weariness in youth and early middle age. One of her brothers remarks: 'She was very sociable, lively, and threw her whole heart into the kindly entertaining of guests of all ages.' Such powers of entertaining as she possessed could not but have gone with enjoyment in the use of those powers.

Moreover, the study of different characters, the drawing out of other people's thoughts, the gaining of new ideas for herself, must have had some fascination. And, despite all her kindness, all her readiness to see the best in everybody, she could not, with her keen sense of humour, have failed to be a good deal amused with the various foibles and absurdities which certain people are wont to display, even in the best society, and when upon their most circumspect behaviour.

Ever merry, and ever making others merry, she could, as one friend says, 'keep a whole tableful laughing and talking,' without difficulty. In fact, whatever the dinner-parties may have seemed to herself, her own presence, her bright smile and sparkling conversation, effectually prevented sensations of dulness on the part of others who were there.

Whether Charlotte ever had what, in the language of fifty or sixty years ago, was delicately termed a 'preference' for anybody, cannot be known. Her hand was at least once sought in marriage, while she was still a girl; and some signs seem to have been visible that she was disposed to 'like' the gentleman in question. Her parents, however, disapproved of the match, and it came to nothing. If at any time she really were in love, it is pretty certain that she never would have revealed the fact to any mortal being until sure that her 'preference' was returned. The reticence which was so marked a feature in her otherwise frank and open nature would undoubtedly have had sway in this direction.

Speaking to a friend, long after in old age, she said that in her young days 'at home,' when a certain nameless gentleman was supposed to be paying his addresses to Fanny, the other sisters were 'very indignant' at the idea of any man wishing to break into their sisterly circle. This probably preceded her own little affair, since Fanny was four years her senior. The pretty notion of home-life and of the unbroken sisterly circle had in time to yield before stern facts, as first one sister and then a second proved faithless to nursery traditions.

Wide as was the circle of family acquaintances, the girls possessed few intimate outside friends. Mr. Tucker rather discouraged such intimacies, considering that his five daughters ought to be content with the close companionship of one another. Charlotte had above all her Laura, whom she devotedly loved; and so satisfying was this friendship that she probably cared little for others by comparison.

Mrs. Tucker, in her quiet way, was no less a power in the house than was her husband. Though less brilliantly gifted, she was very observant, very quaint, very wise, a most affectionate Mother, intensely loved and revered by all her children. She had her own peculiar mode of looking upon things. For instance,—having noticed that girls in an evening party, glancing at a mirror, were apt to be disquieted to find their dresses disorganised, she resolved to have no mirrors at all in her rooms, hoping thereby to secure greater peace of mind among her guests. It does not seem to have occurred to her, that a vague uneasiness about the state of their attire might possibly trouble them quite as much as even an uncomfortable certainty.

Another short story of Mrs. Tucker, showing her quiet, incisive force of character, may well come in here. She had a very strong objection to unkind discussion of people behind their backs. On one occasion, when in the drawing-room of a certain lady, other callers beside herself were present, and one of the latter rose to leave. No sooner was the unfortunate lady gone, than the hostess began to speak of her in disparaging terms. Mrs. Tucker made no immediate observation; but presently, turning to the hostess, she said mildly, 'I ought to be going,—but I really am afraid to do so.' Much surprised, the other asked why. 'Because,' Mrs. Tucker replied, 'I am afraid that when I have left the room you will begin to speak of me as you did just now of Mrs. — —.' The courteously uttered reproof—a pretty sharp one, however gently bestowed—was accepted in an equally courteous spirit; and the hostess earnestly assured her that nothing of the kind should take place.

There is no need to imagine, because Charlotte was gay and bright in society, that she never knew the meaning of depression. Shadows of loss and sorrow had not yet begun to fall across her pathway; yet even in those happy days she must have grasped the meaning of 'down' as well as 'up.' Rather curiously, she spoke of herself in old age as having been when young 'subject to very low spirits'; or more strictly, she said that she would have been so subject, but for the counteracting influences of 'religion' and 'work,' the latter arising from the former. High spirits seldom exist without some tendency to occasional re-action. But certainly the sense of depression, whenever it may have assailed her, was not allowed to be a weight upon others in her everyday life.

It was most likely somewhere between 1847 and 1849 that she began to feel uneasy about going to certain kinds of amusement. Fanny was the first to dwell upon this subject, and to be unhappy as to exactly what she ought or ought not to do. Long years after Charlotte Tucker wrote: Sweet Fanny suffered *much* from her sensitiveness of conscience'; and the words may perhaps in part have borne reference to such debatings as these.

Fanny's gentle, yielding nature went no farther than being troubled. She did not speak out. But when the same questionings spread to the younger sister, matters were different. Charlotte was not one who would hesitate as to action, in the face of her own conscience. To some extent here lies the gist of the matter. While she could go with a clear and perfectly easy conscience, able to enjoy herself, and untroubled by doubts, she probably did so without harm to herself, so long as her life was not 'given to pleasures,' that is to say, so long as she did not unduly *love* these things, or allow them to occupy a wrong place in her life. The moment conscience became uneasy, however, there was nothing for her but to stand still and carefully to consider her next step. For 'he that doubteth is condemned if he eat,' even though the eating may not be actually and intrinsically evil. Whether or no the things were in their essence wrong,—and to decide this, each thing would have to be regarded apart, entirely on its own merits,—they became wrong for Charlotte, so soon as she could no longer accept them with a free and happy mind. They became wrong, at least, *unless* she felt her doubts to be overridden by the duty of obedience.

Fanny had doubted and hesitated; Charlotte doubted, and did not hesitate. She went straight to her parents, told them frankly what she felt, and asked whether she might give up going to such places of entertainment as caused her uneasiness.

Wisely and generously Mr. and Mrs. Tucker yielded. If it had become a matter of conscience with her, she might remain at home. Although they did not view the question in precisely the same light, they would not make their conscience the rule for her actions, but would leave her free to be guided by the dictates of her own.

Had they not so responded, had they insisted on having her with them still wherever they went, Charlotte would have given way. Hers was a high ideal of filial submission; and though she had reached an age when she had a right to an independent opinion, yet obedience to them ranked in her mind before the necessity to decide for herself, in a question where opinions might so greatly differ. If they desired her to go, she would go. If the matter were left to herself, she would be on the safe side in all cases which seemed to her dubious, and would remain at home.

There is little or nothing in her letters of that date bearing on this subject; but the above seems to have been her manner of regarding it. While feeling the need to draw for herself some line of demarcation between things expedient and things inexpedient, she does not appear to have fallen into the error, so common amongst really earnest and excellent people, of counting that the line which she rightly drew for herself must of necessity be the only right line for everybody else. Such a view leads to many a harsh and un-Christian judgment. What is dangerous for one may not be perilous for another, who is differently constituted. What is needless for one may be an absolute duty for another, who is in quite a different position. Probably Charlotte saw this. It is worth remarking that, while she kept aloof from many entertainments out of the house, she never, either then or in later years, refused to join in home-parties, or failed to do her utmost to entertain the guests. There was nothing morbid or repellent about the development of her sense of duty.

TO MISS D. LAURA TUCKER.

'*July 12, 1848.*

'You are my lovely, loving, and lovable Laura; a Diamond among gems, and a Rosebud among flowers. Why do you mention so often the mere handwriting of your letters? Do you think that I see anything in them but the kindness of her who has, in the midst of all her engagements, found so much time to devote to me? My own Mother too—how very good to me she has been! I am grateful to her for all her most kind endeavours to set my mind quite at ease on the subject of the poor little Robins....

'We have taken it into our heads that, what between music and teaching and writing and visiting, *you* may have more work on your hands than may suit your taste. Under this idea, Fanny, like a dear Quixote as she is, formed a grand plan of rushing up to town on Thursday by coach with uncle Charlton, who happened to be coming, and turning you off the music-stool, or snatching the spelling frame from your delicate hand instanter.

'But I opposed this double-quick march for several reasons, which I hope you may think cogent. In the first place, I hope that you are not *so* hard-worked that it would be too much for you for a few days more to go on with only the assistance of the fair Sibella and Clara. 2ndly, The country seems really doing sweet Fan good. She told me yesterday that she did not know when she had felt so well. I too am perfectly well. 3rdly, I think at your full table on Friday our room would be better than our company. 4thly, We are engaged to take tea with Mrs. Edgecombe on that day. 5thly, For Fanny to start off by coach and me to follow by fly, would appear to me both an extravagant and extraordinary procedure. So, after all these reasons, I thought that we had better fix on Saturday for the day of our departure, until I heard that Aunt *must* come up to Town on Monday. She offered to take us up with her, but as it would of course be more agreeable to her to come with *us*, I think that we shall find ourselves in dear old Portland Place on Monday morning.

'I am so much obliged to dearest Mamma for her kind intention of taking me to Thalberg's splendid Concert on Monday. It would really give me more pleasure if I might present my ticket to dear Fanny Lanzun, who has been all kindness and attention to us. You know how we wished that *one* of our family might hear Jenny Lind. Now I can hear through your ears; and none of the Lanzuns have had that treat, you know.'

TO MISS D. L. TUCKER.

'Oct. 13, 1848.

'Many thanks for your last sweet note to me, and kind consent to fill my place.... I do hope that you may not find teaching the wearisome task which I sometimes do. Perhaps Aunt Laura may succeed better in fixing the attention of her little pupils. At all events, *I* am grateful to you for undertaking the trouble. You are dear to a sister's heart, sweet Laura, and I hope that you are one of the blessings for which I am *not* unthankful....

'I had two delightful games of chess yesterday with my dear Father.... What an awful state Vienna is in! Is not the murder of Count Latour dreadful?'

TO THE SAME.

'Oct. 10, 1849.

'Another sweet note from my darling Laura. I am rich in letters to-day, for I have received three such nice ones.

'Yesterday evening I spent about an hour at the piano. I did not, however, sing any of your especial songs. I began one day—'The world is so bright'—but my heart and voice failed, because you were away. However, I daresay that I shall try again this evening. How it would cut up my music, were you to go to any great distance, for most of my favourite songs are yours. How I have enjoyed hearing you sing them.... Farewell, sweet Laura. I must go and hear my children their lessons. I hear their little feet and voices above me.'

CHAPTER VI
A.D. 1847-1850 GRAVITY AND FUN

Though verging now on her thirtieth year, Charlotte Tucker was still unknown to the public as an Author. If the initials A. L. O. E. existed in her mind as a future possibility, they had at least not yet appeared upon any printed page.

From time to time, however, her pen was busy; still in the old line of comic or tragic plays, for home amusement. In 1847 she wrote *The Castle of Sternalt; a Tragedy in Two Acts*; belonging to the Cavalier and Roundhead period of England's history. In that same year she also accomplished *Grimhaggard Hall; a Farce in Two Acts*—not historical, but highly comic. After which came apparently a gap of two or three years; and in 1850 she wrote, *Who Was The Witch? a Drama in Three Acts*—historical again, belonging to the days of the Saxons and of King Harold, half comic, half tragic.

It does not appear from these three plays that her gift in the dramatic line had made any marked advance during the ten years or more which had elapsed since first she launched out in this direction. Probably an entirely different mode of life from hers, a less sheltered existence, a more extensive knowledge of human nature in its countless phases, is an absolute necessity to such development. There is in them much latent power, however unequal and undeveloped, whether it be of the grave or of the sparkling and humorous description. The following quotation from the *Castle of Sternalt* will give an idea of her tragic style at that period. Ravensby, the hero, is a Cavalier, imprisoned and condemned to death on a false charge of murder.

ACT IV.—SCENE I.
A DUNGEON.

Ravensby.
'Th' intensity of grief destroys itself.
The torturer beholds his Victim stretched
Unconscious, pain itself o'ercome by pain.
Fate dooms me now to death; last punishment
Which mortal can inflict,—and yet I feel

There's mercy in the doom. Thus to live on
Were lingering martyrdom; it were to die
By inches, drain my heart's blood drop by drop.
One flash ends all! O Clara, when my soul
Hath ceased to suffer, can it cease to love?
Methinks, when quitting Earth, 'twill still retain
Her image, who was more than Earth to me!
It is a portion of my being, twined
With every thought and feeling; thou wilt weep,
My Clara; thou canst not believe him false
To faith and friends, who is so true to thee.
Gazing into the uncorrupted depths
Of thy pure feelings, thou wilt judge of mine.
When all denounced me, thou wert still my friend
When all forget, thou wilt remember still!

     Enter Agnes.

Agnes, *aside.*
I ne'er have feared the eye of mortal man,
Why should I shrink from his?

Rav. Who comes to break
The prisoner's solitude?

Agn. One who would be
The prisoner's friend.

Rav. I have no friend—save one.

Agn. Can he speak thus who hath so long espoused
The Royal cause, and served that cause so well?
Who, girt with honours, well deserved, hath stood
One in a noble Brotherhood of Fame!
Where are the Cavaliers who fought with thee
In battle, side by side, who with thee shared
The feast, and drained the wine-cup to your King?
Where are they now? what, gone? not one remains,

T'assert thy innocence, or shield thee from
An ignominious death. Friends! out upon them!
They mock the name; it were not thus, if thou
Hadst drawn thy gallant sword with those who wear
No chains but those of Virtue, those who own
No earthly Monarch, and uphold no power
But that of Liberty; whose friendship lasts
Not only when the red wine sparkles high,
And revelry and song profane the night;
If such had been thy comrades and thy friends,
Thou hadst not been forsaken thus.

Rav. No more!

Agn. The gate thou hast defended with thy blood,
To-morrow casts thee forth, led out to die;
And the proud towers coldly will look down
Upon the closing scene; for hearts more hard
And more impregnable decree thy doom.
Thou diest a traitor's death;—but wert thou *ours*,
Then ev'ry bush around the fatal spot
Should hold an armed defender, ev'ry knoll
Conceal an ambushed friend, and at a word
A wall of steel should bristle round thy breast;
hen swords should clash with swords, and they who came
To shed thy blood lie weltering in their own.
If thou wert ours—and yet thou mayst be ours,——

Rav. Cease, for I know thee, Temptress; words like these
Betray the fair false lips from which they flow.
Thou'rt Agnes, own it,—Gasper Tarlton's love.
Agn. Agnes I am, not Gasper Tarlton's love.

The thistledown that floats upon the breeze,
The thorny weed which from my path I spurn,
The insect which I crush beneath my tread,

Are not to me more insignificant,
More worthless—than the Slave whom thou hast named.

Rav. Thank Heaven! then my last doubt melts away;
He yet is true, yet faithful to his King;
My sacrifice will not be made for nought.
Maid, he is honoured in thy hate!

Agn. And thou——
Rav. Leave me.

Agn. To perish!

Rav. Thou canst not defend.
Agn. I could,—yes, I could arm in thy behalf
A thousand gallant hands, might I but say,
'The injured will on the oppressor turn,
Unite the love of freedom with revenge,
A thousand-fold repay the debt he owes
To your brave confidence; in Ravensby
Ye will destroy a foe and win a friend!'
Could I speak thus——

Rav. Thy sex protects thee, Maid,
Or thou shouldst learn the meed of treason. Hence!

Agn. From other lips such words I had not borne.
Why should I thus urge life upon thee,—why
Seek to preserve thee in thine own despite?
O thou art worthy of a nobler cause;
I see in thee one who can nobly dare,
Firmly resolve, and boldly execute;—
And what a bright career before thee lies——

Rav. A brief one,—from the dungeon to the tomb.

Agn. To die a Traitor in the eyes of men.

Rav. Better than live a villain in my own.
Depart, and leave me to my fate. Away!

Agn. O brave and glorious! I will tempt no more.
My pride is humbled. I have found a soul
That soars beyond mine own. I would not rob
Thy pinion of one plume. I watch thy flight
With kindling emulation. O for power
To follow it, that I above this sphere
Might rise; companion, not unworthy thee!

Rav. A step approaches.

Agn. None must see me here. [*Retires into shade.*]

Agnes in the end confesses herself guilty of the crime for which he is condemned to death;—in time to save his name from lasting disgrace, though not in time to save his life.

Who Was The Witch? though in parts amusing enough, is hardly so good as the others. Modern English puns sit oddly upon a background of pre-mediæval Saxon history. *Grimhaggard Hall* is perhaps one of A. L. O. E.'s most comic and laughable *jeux-d'esprit*, over which one can picture the family as enjoying many a hearty laugh. The perpetual play upon words, and the almost rollicking fun and nonsense of the whole, remind one of her earlier effort, *The Pretender*, already given at length; though the later-written farce is in some respects scarcely equal to the girlish achievement. Both these plays illustrate well the frisky and frolicsome side of a character which was in some respects not only intensely serious, but absolutely stern. Charlotte Tucker's was truly a many-sided nature.

Whether at this time she had already begun to write anything in the shape of children's story-books does not appear. It is by no means unlikely, since the date of her first appearance in print was now fast drawing near.

The chief characters in *Grimhaggard Hall* are—Mr. Cramp; Mr. Scull, an artist; Mr. Wriggle, a tutor; Miss Cob; and Nellie, daughter of Mr. Cramp.

ACT I.
Library in Grimhaggard Hall. Nellie and Mr. Wriggle.

Nellie. O my dear old Tutor, I shall be so sorry to lose you! I wish that my good Father had kept to his old plan, and instead of sending Bob to College had kept both you and him here. This house is so intolerably dull. When you are gone I shall sit looking at the old stones in the old wall, till I petrify into one myself. Why, the very spiders' webs look as though there were no business doing in them, and not a *fly* nor even a *broom* would call at the door! Heigh-ho!

Wrig. You forget, honoured Madam, the governess, Miss Cob, who is expected here to-morrow.

Nell. A governess; the horror! then I hear that she is an oddity; so absent; very learned though, and extremely well-informed. I am rather old for a governess; I was seventeen last March. It would have been quite a different thing to have gone on with my studies here with you and Bob. Do you know that, without vanity, I consider that I have made amazing progress during the month that you have been here?

Wrig. In Geography, Madam, for instance. Let me have the honour of recalling to your oblivious memory that only yesterday you forgot the situation of Guinea.

Nell. Nonsense! I said that it was on the *Gold* Coast, and wished I had it in my own pocket.

Wrig. I have remarked with regret, if you will permit me to say it, an aversion to consulting the Atlas, which— —

Nell. Keep me from you and your atlas! Atlas carried the world, and you would burden me with the Atlas. I hardly consider myself competent yet to carry the whole globe on my poor little shoulders. I should like to know what is the use of knowing the situation of this place and that place, to one who never has the satisfaction of seeing any place at all beyond the walls of our stupid garden. I wish that the cross old gentleman who bequeathed my father Grimhaggard Hall, had lived to repent it, that I do! I would rather live in the narrowest lane in the City than be cooped up here like a toad in a block. I've no fancy to be a Penelope,—stitch, stitch, stitch!

Wrig. Penelope was a distinguished ornament to her sex.

Nell. O dear Tutor, I know that she was a duck of a queen, but distinguished for nothing but her *web-feat*.

Wrig. The resource of literature remains to you, Madam, which was never open to her. I would again venture to draw your attention to the subject of Geography.

Nell. O no more of that, I beg, my dear Mr. Wriggle. I know that *Ham* and *Sandwich* are in the kitchen, *China* in the cupboard, and *Madeira* in the cellar. That is enough for me. I regard Geography simply in reference to utility. I'm quite a utilitarian by principle. You know that the greatest navigator was a *Cook*; I dare say that he discovered *Chili, Cayenne,* and *Curaçoa*. Now do you know, my wise old Tutor, in spite of your white hair and all your learning, I think that I could puzzle you.

Wrig. It would be difficult, Madam, to place a limit to your powers.

Nell. Tell me, why is Botany Bay called Botany Bay?

Wrig. I am not, I must own, aware from what the name is derived. Probably the Botanist has there discovered some new and curious specimens of plants.

Nell. O you must have come from *Dunse* or the *Scilly* Isles. Botany Bay is called Botany Bay, because blossoms of the *birch* and sprigs of the *gallows-tree* are transplanted there *without their leaves.*

Wrig. I see! I see! Ha, ha!

Nell. I wonder if Miss Cob will understand a joke,—if she will ever perpetrate a pun. Do you know I fancy her such a prim old quiz? I should like to know whether she will play at chess with Papa, or teach me the guitar, as you do. Do you think that she will endure this house?

Wrig. The total want of all society, except that which the walls of Grimhaggard Hall have the honour constantly to enclose, may perhaps have an effect upon the lady's spirits not altogether exhilarating; but when your brother returns from College, perhaps he may be accompanied by some of his fellow-students.

Nell. Students; what an idea! When my Father would sooner see a Goblin than a young man under any circumstances!

Wrig. Is not this rather a peculiar—rather a singular—I would say prejudice? Could such a word be applicable to the excellent Mr. Cramp?

Nell. I should say very singular indeed, did I not know its cause.

Wrig. Is it presumptuous to inquire what that cause may be?

Nell. O I'll tell you in a moment. It all arises out of the freaks and folly of Mr. Grim of Grimhaggard Hall, who had, I am sorry to say, the kindness to leave us this property, and thereby consigned me to the dolefuls for the rest of my life.

Wrig. Was the estate bequeathed under any unpleasant conditions? I never heard your respected father complain of such.

Nell. O it is all *right* to my father because it was all *left* to him. But you shall hear. This Mr. Grim had a promising nephew, ... and this nephew, Mr. Atherton by name, was very naturally considered as Mr. Grim's heir, the old gentleman never having persuaded any lady to marry him, and reign like another Proserpine over the gloomy shades of Grimhaggard Hall.

Wrig. How then came the estate to your Father?

Nell. Have a little patience, my dear Mr. Wriggle, and you shall be as learned as myself upon the subject. Well, this old uncle quarrelled with this young nephew. I think that it was about politics or some such absurdity; the elder was a Tory and the junior a Radical; no, the young one was the Tory, and the old one the Radical; and this *radical* question was the *root* of the quarrel. Now what do you think the spiteful old gentleman did?

Wrig. Disinherited his nephew, and left the property to Mr. Cramp.

Nell. That would have been a pretty severe lesson to the young man; but what do you say to the affectionate uncle leaving such a clause as this in his will? That my father must only have and hold this said Grimhaggard Hall, on condition of poor Mr. Atherton's never even crossing the threshold of what he once considered his home! The place must be perfectly *heir*-tight. If he ever passes twelve hours under this roof, the whole estate is to revert to him.

Wrig. Such a clause argues little charity; but perhaps it may ultimately prove for the benefit of him whom it was designed to injure.

Nell. Ah, you think that Mr. Atherton may still manage to get his property out of his old uncle's *clause*! I am sure I wish that Mr. Grim had left the dull place to him, or any one but us; but then my Father is not of my mind. Yet even he has not an atom of enjoyment of his prize, from the perpetual fear of losing it. He has heard that young Atherton is very sharp and clever; of course he will try to regain his rights by any means that may present themselves; so I really believe that Papa expects him to appear some day or other through the key-hole. The gate is kept constantly locked,—luckily, one can see the high-road from the house,—nothing in the shape of a Man is permitted to pass it; we have even parted with all men-servants, lest Mr. Atherton should manage to get in disguised as a lackey. Grimhaggard Hall is a regular Convent. A travelling pedlar is regarded with suspicion; the butcher-boy must hand the leg of mutton over the gate; the young apothecary is an object of terror,—I could not have a tooth pulled out, were I to die for it. Dear me, how it is raining! The weather seems endeavouring to find out whether it be possible to make Grimhaggard Hall look a little duller than usual.

Wrig. I hope Miss Cob may be fortunate in having finer weather for her journey to-morrow.

Nell. She is on the road to-day, like John Gilpin's hat and wig. She was to leave Puddingham this morning, and rest to-night at the Jolly Bridecake at Mouseton. I hope the coach is provided with oar and rudders, for she will certainly have to swim for it!...

In the midst of this talk an artist's gig is smashed outside the front gate; and the artist, Mr. Scull, being much shaken, is actually admitted within the walls of the old Hall, to the great disquiet of Mr. Cramp, who is determined that, come what may, the young man shall not remain through the night. It is a pelting day, and no other conveyance seems likely to pass; while the artist is plainly unable to walk the distance which separates Grimhaggard Hall from the next town. While this matter is still under discussion, a ring at the front-door bell is heard, and 'a woman of very singular appearance' is seen 'standing in the rain, without an umbrella, as if water were her native element.'

Nell. Who can it be? [*Runs to the window.*] Why, how tall she is! she looks as though she had grown a foot since that dress was made for her. What an extraordinary figure! Why, Sarah is actually letting her in. Papa, we have not had so many visitors since we came here. Grimhaggard Hall is growing quite gay.

Cramp. I will go and meet this strange guest. [*Exit.*]

Nell. It cannot be—it cannot be Miss Cob! Such a governess would kill me either with terror or with laughter.

Wrig. You were in expectation, Madam, of some one remarkable for eccentricity. We must not always judge of the qualities of the mind by the singularity of the exterior.

Enter Mr. Cramp *and* Miss Cob.

Cramp. Miss Cob,—my daughter. [Nelly *makes a curtsey,* Miss Cob *a bow.*]

Nell. [*Aside to* Wriggle.] I shall never keep my countenance.

Wrig. [*Aside.*] That is to be regretted, for it is a very fair one.

Cramp. We did not expect you to-night, Ma'am. Did you not purpose sleeping at Mouseton?

Miss C. The inn was chock-full.

Cramp. But how came you to be on foot? You never have walked all the way! Where is your conveyance? It would be of the utmost service to me.

Miss C. Smashed on the road.

Cramp. Well, if all the gigs and cabs in England are not in coalition against me this day! And where is your luggage?

Miss C. Coming. You did not expect me to carry it on my back, like a snail, did ye?

Wrig. Miss Cob, like an experienced general, leaves her baggage in the rear.

Nell. I should rather have expected to find it in the *van.* You are very wet, Ma'am; shall I help you off with your cloak?

Miss C. O never mind. I'm neither sugar nor salt; only it's a plaguy thing to have one's dress so long, walking through such a bog.

Nell. [*Aside.*] How *long* she may have had her dress, I know not; but in one sense I am sure it is short enough.

Miss C. This seems a good big house, but rather too much like a prison. Have you those bars on all the windows?

Cramp. On all.

Miss C. And how many men-servants do you keep?

Cramp. None at all. [*Aside.*] What impertinent curiosity!

Nell. [*Aside.*] Shall I venture to address her again? I can scarcely command myself. [*Aloud.*] Pray, Ma'am, are you fond of music?

Miss C. I'm a regular dab at it.

Nell. What instrument do you play?

Miss C. All sorts of instruments, from the drum to the Jew's harp.

Nell. You don't play the cornopion?

Miss C. Like bricks,—and sing all the time. You shall hear me to-morrow. [*All stare in mute amazement.*]

Cramp. May I trouble you, Ma'am, to let me see your letter of introduction from Lady Myres again?

Miss C. Heartily welcome. You will read all about me there. Full details of manners and accomplishments. She says I'm a little absent sometimes; so if ever I make a few trifling blunders, I hope you'll set them down to that score.

Nell. [*Aside to* Wriggles.] I wish she were absent now, for I think I shall die in convulsions.

Miss C. I'll teach you all sorts of things suitable for a lady. Knitting, netting,—crow—crowfoot ...

Wrig. I see that nothing is beyond your apprehension.

Miss C. What do you say about *apprehension*? Are you a police officer?

Wrig. No, Madam, I am a humble Professor of Geography, Geology, Algebra, and ...

Miss C. O I'm a match for you in all that, and I know Latin, Greek, and American besides.

Wrig. And what tongue, Madam, do you prefer?

Miss C. O I'm not particular about those sort of things; but if you want my opinion, why I think pickled tongues are excellent.

Wrig. [*Turning away laughing.*] This is either too bad or too good! [*Aloud.*] And your other studies, Ma'am?

Miss C. As for Arithmetics, they're at my fingers'-ends.

Nell. I have not yet got beyond the Rule of Three.

Miss C. You shall know the Rule of Four-and-twenty, before I have done with you. We'll skip the 4, 5, and 6.

Nell. And the Rule of Three inverse?

Miss C. In verse? Yes, you shall have it in all sorts of verse, merry, tragical, and comical.

Nell. [*Aside.*] I shall expire with laughter. [*Retires to the window.*]

Wrig. [*Aside.*] I really cannot stand this any longer. [*Follows her.*]

Scull (the artist). Pray, Madam, may I venture to ask if you paint?

Miss C. You are a very impudent fellow, to ask a gentle—woman if she paints. Do I look as if I painted?

Scull. I beg a million pardons, Ma'am, but as I paint myself ...

Miss C. You paint precious badly then, for you're as yellow as a cowslip!

Cramp. [*Aside.*] Is the woman intoxicated or insane?

Scull. I think—I imagine that there is a little misapprehension, Ma'am, on your part. My vocation is that of an artist.

Nell. O Miss Cob, you must see his sketches.

Scull. You see, Ma'am, there is a new work to come out at Christmas, which is to be entitled,—*The Mouse on the Mantelpiece*. The letterpress is in very able hands,—a very pretty little fairy-tale for grown-up children,—that's all the rage now, you know, in this enlightened age. But the illustrations will be the great thing. A steel-plate frontispiece, of course, in which will be introduced a number of winged mice in a variety of positions,—a very clever thing, I can assure you; and then wood-cuts,—I have the honour of being intrusted with the designs for them. We are to have a different illustration for the top of every column.

Nell. That will no doubt be *capital*.

Scull. It will form a very elegant little volume altogether,—the most remarkable publication of the day.

Miss C. Well, after my wet walk, I think I'd be the better for something to warm me.

Nell. You shall have some tea directly, Ma'am.

Miss C. Tea! Wishy-washy stuff!

Nell. Would you prefer gruel?

Miss C. Gruel! I wish you joy of your fare!

Nell. [*Aside.*] The fair Arithmetician looks as though she would not have 3 *Scruples to a Dram*!

Cramp. I dare say Miss Cob is fatigued after her long walk. Nelly, show her the apartment. I hope everything is comfortable there.

Nell. Certainly, Papa. [*Aside to* Wriggle.] At any rate, I will venture to say that her room is better than her company. [*Exeunt* Nelly *and* Miss Cob.]

And so on,—the wind-up of the story being that Miss Cob is found to be a burglar in woman's disguise; while the artist is a harmless nobody. But elderly Wriggles, the tutor, who has lived quietly in the house for a month past, and of whom even Mr. Cramp has had no suspicions, turns out to be the much dreaded nephew, and to him by right Grimhaggard Hall now appertains. As, however, he has managed to fall deeply in love with the punning heroine, all difficulties are solved by their marriage,—Nellie being equally in love with him. Thus the nephew gains the old home, and the uncle does not lose it.

CHAPTER VII
A.D. 1849-1853 THE FIRST GREAT SORROW, AND THE FIRST BOOK

It must have been at about this time that Charlotte became increasingly anxious for more of definite outdoor work among the poor. Her wish was to be allowed to visit in the Marylebone Workhouse; but difficulties for a while barred her way. Mr. Tucker objected strongly, fearing the risk of infectious diseases for his daughters; and no doubt the risk in those days was far greater than in these, considering the then condition of Workhouses generally.

So long as permission was refused, Charlotte seems to have contented herself with the simple duties of home-life. She was not one who would restlessly fight for and insist upon her own way at all costs, under the plea of doing what was right. Rather, one may be sure, she counted the prohibition as in itself sufficient indication of the Divine Will. However, while submitting, she probably used from time to time some little pressure to bring about another state of things; and somewhere about the beginning of 1851 her parents' 'reluctant consent' was, we are told, at length given. From that time she and Fanny visited regularly in the Workhouse.

In 1849 Charlotte's eldest sister, Sibella, was married to the Rev. Frederick Hamilton, for some time Curate to Mr. Garnier, the Vicar of Holy Trinity Church, which they all regularly attended. Mr. Garnier and his wife, Lady Caroline, were especial friends of Charlotte, through many a long year. Thus the first break in the charmed circle of sisters was made; and Fanny was now 'Miss Tucker,' Charlotte being the second home-daughter.

Until the spring of 1850 Mr. Tucker kept his health and vigour to a marvellous extent for a man eighty years old, — for one too who had worked more or less hard through life from the age of fourteen or fifteen. He still attended to his India House business, not seeming to find it too much for his strength; and in the April of that year, after making a speech in Court, he was congratulated by a brother-Director upon the force and energy with which he had spoken. 'Ah,' he replied, 'it is only the last flicker of the taper before it goes out.'

No one had noticed aught to be wrong with him, but perhaps he had himself been conscious of failing power. Soon afterwards a sharp attack of fever and inflammation laid him low, and most serious fears for his life were felt. It was a time of terrible suspense to his own family; not least so to Charlotte, who had always loved him with an intense devotion. Probably few fathers are quite so devotedly beloved as was old Mr. Tucker; but not many men, and especially not many men of his years, can throw themselves into the interests and amusements of their children, as he was able to do.

They had till then hardly realised how suddenly the call might come. As his biographer says, he had been always 'so full of life, there had been so much activity of body, so much energy of mind, so much elasticity of spirit, that they had never associated with all this vitality a thought of the stillness of death.' Now, without warning, the foe was at their very door; and the shadow of his great danger weighed heavily upon them all.

In answer to many prayers he was given back to them again, just for a little while. But they could never quite forget how nearly he had been taken from them, how unexpectedly the great separation might come.

Another event of 1850 was the marriage of Charlotte's brother, William Tucker, at Brussels. It came almost immediately upon Mr. Tucker's rally from his severe illness; and Charlotte had the pleasure of being taken to Brussels for the wedding by her brother, St. George Tucker, then home for a short time from India. It would be interesting to know her first impressions of the Continent, but not many letters of this date are available. The two which follow are among the last belonging to her unshadowed younger life, before the true meaning of loss and sorrow had dawned upon her. One black cloud had gathered and dispersed; but it was soon to roll up again; and then the storm would break.

'Oct. 3, 1850.

>'Dearest Laura,—We have finished the volume of stories which we were reading—which by the way resembled the pottles of strawberries sold in the streets, capital at the beginning, but as one gets further on, miserably inferior—and now Fanny has gone to her dear Will-making, so I keep her pen in company by writing to you. I soon knocked off my Will, and we have just the same sum to dispose of, but her large sheets of paper are not covered yet.
>
>'Now what shall I write to you about, dear—for we write so often that it is impossible that we should often have much to write about? The sun shines one day, and does not shine

another; the sea is rough one morning and calm the next. I may have to follow the style of Letitia in her well-known note, "sometimes we pass Fummity, and sometimes we do not." Things go on quietly, nothing changed but my half-sovereign. I had to buy new ribbons for Letitia to-day, and fear that I shall have to supply the children with fresh gloves.

'I have been reading about our poor friend, the first of the Blacks, to-day; and it appears that his character was very fairly drawn by Miss Martineau. I was glad to know a little about the after doings in Hayti, and find that Dessalines—that fierce fellow, husband of Theresa—was made first Emperor, and killed in about two years. He was a great savage, but his wife an amiable lady. Then came King Henri I.—our friend Christopher the Cook—who was king at the time that my informant wrote, that is to say, in 1819. A famous king he seems to be, or have been, with a good palace, standing army of 25,000 men kept in strict discipline, a hereditary aristocracy—all of the colour of coal—and ecclesiastical establishment. He was considered in person very much like King George III.—barring complexion, I suppose—and, in short, that part of Hayti which owned him for king seemed in a very flourishing condition in 1819.

'Do you remember the name of Thaurepas (?), the blacky General who weakly surrendered his post to the French? What do you think the grateful Monsieurs did to him? Nailed epaulettes on his shoulders and a cocked hat on his head, and then threw him with his wife and children into the sea! Would one believe such things of men in the 19th century? I should like to know something of the present state of Hayti, and whether the throne is filled by a son of Henri I., for I suppose that Christopher is hardly living still. If he were, would you not like to have his autograph?

'I have told you all this about Hayti, because I thought that, like myself, you would be pleased to know what really became of the characters in Miss Martineau's Romance, and one seldom meets with a book which throws any light upon such an out-of-the-way subject.'

'Oct. 18, 1850.

'Dearest Laura,—We have been luxuriating in the letters from Paris.... All things look so bright and joyous! I have twice sung "The World is so Bright" to-day *con amore*, and my heart is so lightsome that I could dance. I do not think that I have *once* seen precious Father dull since my return. He desires me to say that he cannot quite countenance a visit to Lebanon. It is rather too far, and Lord Ellesmere was very ill on his way thither; so dear —— must give up her Blackbeard, and content herself with Sir Peter. Now Mamma is reading St. George's note. Papa is smiling away,—his dear lips apart. He looks so nice in Clara's beautiful cap!

'Henry thinks so much of you, dear. He says that you are a sweet girl, and that he loves you extremely. I cannot tell you all the kind things he says of you....

'We are such a comfortable party, and our loved absent ones help to make us more so.... This is a very disconnected sort of note, a sort of patchwork, for my ears are as much employed as my hand, and I have every now and then a message to darn in,—then, O my chilblains! But I am determined to complain of nothing, for I am so overloaded with blessings. Dearest Parents are just going out. The weather is delicious. The world is so bright, the world is so fair! Yes, even now, when she has only a wreath of dahlias, and decks herself in yellow like the sweet little Blossom!...

'I should like to think that our dear trio are enjoying themselves as much at Paris as I am at home. I hope and trust that we may all have such a happy winter together, when "Love's shining circlet" has all its gems complete except the dear Indian absentees.'

This was written in the autumn following Mr. Tucker's dangerous illness. After a long and tedious convalescence, his health had steadily improved through the summer months, and during the autumn he seemed to be almost himself again,—able to walk out regularly, able to read much and thoroughly to enjoy being read to by his wife and daughters. In the evenings he would delight in their music, varied by merry talk and by an occasional rubber of whist.

With the coming of winter acute neuralgic pains took possession of him; and though some little improvement was seen with the advent of spring, it was not permanent. In the end of May 1851 he was taken to Brighton for a few days' change; after which he became worse and then again better. Amid these fluctuations, which included at times very severe suffering, his manly courage and patience were never known to fail.

On the tenth of June he seemed so far improved as to talk of going next day to the India House, for the Wednesday's Council. The Doctor strongly opposed this; and Mr. Tucker went instead to a Flower-Show, with his daughters. For two days afterward he seemed particularly well. On Friday night there was no apparent change for the worse; and his usual tender good-night to them all had in it no shadow of approaching calamity.

But the end was at hand. Before morning sharp illness had seized upon him; and before twelve o'clock he had passed away.

It was a heavy blow to all who knew him; above all to his wife and children. He had been the very life of the house, the very spring of home-brightness. Charlotte's little niece, Bella Frances, daughter of the elder brother, Henry Carre Tucker, came to spend her first English holidays in the house, not long after Mr. Tucker's death, and she found the whole family 'plunged in gloom,'—Charlotte Tucker being exceedingly sad and grave. The only one, indeed, of the whole party who was able to speak cheerfully was Laura. It is probable that Laura had at that date a dawning outside interest in her life, not possessed by any of the others, which may have enabled her to bear up somewhat better than they could.

Many months earlier, after the sharp illness of the preceding year, Mr. Tucker had written a letter to all his children, thanking them for their 'late unwearied and devoted attentions' to him. After desiring them 'not to give way to strong emotions,' he had gone on to say,—'I have reached a very advanced age, and must be prepared for a change. Old age has its infirmities and suffering, and a prolonged existence is not to be desired. Your care should now be to comfort and console your beloved mother, who has been everything to me and everything to you all. I trust that she will not leave this house, in which we have all enjoyed so much happiness; and I feel assured that you will all tenderly watch over her, and contribute by every means in your power to her future comfort.'

This wish was fulfilled. Mrs. Tucker never did leave No. 3 Upper Portland Place, except of course for necessary change. It remained her home, and the home of her daughters, from the year 1851, when her husband died, until her own death in the year 1869.

How much of life's sunshine had been swept out of Charlotte's life by the loss of her Father, it is perhaps impossible for any one to estimate who did not personally know Mr. Tucker. Not that *all* her sunshine had departed!

Apart from her own inherent elasticity of spirit, she was devotedly attached to her Mother; and she had still the tender and satisfying companionship of Laura.

That while deeply saddened, she was not crushed, is shown by the following letter to her little niece, Bella F. Tucker, dated August 9, 1851:—

> 'The sun has been shining so beautifully lately, and the reapers have been busy in the fields. It is a sight to warm the heart, to see the yellow sheaves covering the land, and we should bless God for an abundant harvest. There is a clover-field near us, and it looks like a beautiful carpet of lilac and green. I was calculating that there must be more than two million blossoms in that one field; and each blossom may be perhaps the home of many insects.... Then what is that field compared to all England, or England to Europe, or Europe to the whole world? Neither your little head, nor the wisest man's, can imagine how many blossoms and how many insects there are on this great globe,—it makes one almost giddy to think of it,—and then to consider that all the world itself is only like a speck in God's Creation, that there are said to be *eighty millions* of fixed stars, each of which has very likely worlds moving round it. And God made all. How very great and wonderful He must be! It seems surprising that He should care for every one on this little ball,—how much more astonishing that He should have condescended to come and live upon it, to have appeared as a feeble Child in one of the worlds that He had made, and then actually to *die*, like one of the creatures that He had formed! Is not God's power wonderful, and His love more wonderful still?
>
> 'When you look at the bright blue sky, do you never long to fly up like the birds,—no, much higher than the birds can fly, to your Home, to your Father which is in Heaven? I hope that time may come, sweet Bella, but now is the time to prepare. I sometimes think that this life is our school-time. We are now to learn lessons of faith and patience and love. When our education is finished we shall be allowed to go Home; and Death will be the gentle Messenger to say,—"Your Heavenly Father sends for you; come and join your loved ones who have gone before. O that will be joyful, when we meet to part no more!"'

There is a tone of quiet sadness running through the letter, in marked contrast with those joyous epistles to her sister Laura quoted earlier in this chapter. The world could never again be to her 'so bright, so fair!' as in the days when her Father was still upon earth. No doubt as time went on the buoyancy of her temperament reasserted itself; but life was no longer unshadowed; and other troubles soon followed.

One of these must certainly have been the marriage of her sister Laura, though no letters are at hand to show what she felt. Mr. Otho Hamilton, elder brother to the Rev. Frederick Hamilton, who had married Charlotte's eldest sister, sought Laura's hand; and he was accepted.

Not entirely without hesitation. Perhaps few girls can say, or ought to say, 'Yes' at once, without time for consideration. When the offer came, Laura's first impulse was, naturally, to go to her Mother for advice; her second impulse was to go to her friend-sister. It is not hard to realise what the thought must have been to Charlotte of losing this dearly-loved companion,—her room-mate and the constant sharer of her thoughts and interests from very infancy; nor is it difficult to believe how bravely she would put aside the recollection of herself, viewing the question from Laura's standpoint alone. It must, however, be remembered that Charlotte was romantically enthusiastic on the subject of others' engagements, and was through life ardently interested in the marriages of her friends. In the present case her knowledge of how highly her Father had thought of Mr. Hamilton would be an additional incentive to put no obstacle in the way. It seems that Laura's hesitation had arisen, not from any doubt as to her own feelings, but simply from a desire to be sure of her duty. The engagement took place; and on the 19th of October 1852, Laura Tucker became Mrs. Hamilton. So another leaf was turned in the story of Charlotte's life.

And now, in the very midst of these changes and losses arose a new interest. Hitherto, Charlotte had written a good deal, but she had never published, perhaps had never even thought of publishing. What first led her to adopt the style of fiction, by which she was soon to become known, it is possible at least to conjecture. In 1850, as we have seen, she wrote another of her merry plays, full of fun and humour. Now, suddenly, she seems to have plunged into the line of children's stories, having each a very prominent 'purpose,'—her earliest being *The Claremont Tales*. It may be that the shock of her first great sorrow, the death of Mr. Tucker, making her to realise intensely the shortness of life on earth, and the supreme weight of things unseen, had the effect of turning her mind with a new energy to the thought of doing good by means of her pen. It may be also that, now *he* was gone for whom and with whom she had written her plays, all zest in that direction was gone with him, and the gift of writing, like a river dammed up in one direction and forced to turn elsewhere, sought naturally a fresh outlet,— an outlet with which there should be no overpoweringly sad associations.

Moreover, the home-circle was no longer what it had been. Two of the sisters, to whom she had read her plays, were gone; and with the changed order of life came a new order of writing.

Exactly when she began or finished *The Claremont Tales* is not known. With her usual reserve she at first said nothing about the completed ms.—beyond, at all events, reading the stories to the children. Probably she felt doubtful about her own venture; and some little time seems to have passed before she showed it to her Mother. Mrs. Tucker was much delighted with the attempt, said at once that it ought to be published, and insisted on action being taken.

So, on November 19, 1851, the ms. was sent to Messrs. W. and R. Chambers, with the accompanying letter:—

> 'Sir,—It has for some time been my anxious desire to add my mite to the Treasury of useful literature, which you have opened to the young as well as the old.
>
> 'The Tales which I now venture to offer to you for publication were originally composed for young children under my own charge, and were listened to with an appearance of interest, which gives me hopes that they may meet with no unfavourable reception from others of the same tender years.
>
> 'I ask for no earthly remuneration; my position in life renders me independent of any exertions of my own; I pray but for God's blessing upon my attempts to instruct His lambs in the things which concern their everlasting welfare; and deeply gratified should I feel, were my little work to be classed among the numerous valuable publications which you have already given to the world.
>
> 'The Tales might be printed separately, as each forms a complete story, though all are united by connecting links.'

The date is given, but no name and no address; and a letter more quaintly stiff and unbusiness-like can surely never have won a Publisher's smile. To return the ms. to herself, if disapproved of, was not possible; and, as it happened, *The Claremont Tales* did not belong to the class of publications undertaken by Messrs. Chambers. Very kindly, however, they passed it on to the house of Messrs. Gall and Inglis; and by them the little book was brought out. One can imagine how eagerly Charlotte, while preserving her strict incognita, must have watched for the possible appearance of her Tales, and how delighted she would be to see the name advertised. When this occurred, she wrote again—

'May 24, 1853.

'A. L. O. E. presents her compliments to Messrs. Gall and Inglis, and, admiring the elegant form in which they have presented The Claremont Tales to the public, is happy to offer to them for publication the accompanying volume of poems,—asking no further remuneration than 20 copies of the work, when printed, for *gratuitous* distribution. A. L. O. E. proposes sending a few copies of her poems to the principal Reviews, as a means of extending their circulation.

'A. L. O. E. would be glad to know whether Messrs. Gall and Inglis propose adopting her suggestion of printing some or all of *The Claremont Tales* in a *very cheap* form, for distribution amongst poor children, Ragged Schools, etc.

'Any communication will be received by the Authoress, if addressed to—"Miss Aloe; care of Miss Lanzun; S——; Middlesex."

'P.S.—Miss —— would much like to know whether *The Claremont Tales* were first placed in the hands of Messrs. Gall and Inglis by Messrs. Chambers, to whom she originally sent them; and whether Messrs. Gall and Inglis have any professional connection with those Publishers, so distinguished in the field of literature. Should Messrs. Gall and Inglis not wish themselves to undertake the publication of a volume of poetry, they are at perfect liberty to submit the work to Messrs. Chambers. An early answer will oblige.'

Three months later comes another letter, still further relaxing her secrecy, and still on the subject of the 'volume of poems':—

'August 6, 1853.

'Miss C. M. Tucker presents her compliments to Mr. Inglis, and begs to acknowledge the receipt this morning of his obliging communication to Miss A. L. O. E., which *nom de guerre*, in compliance with his wish, and in reliance on his promise to preserve her incognita, she now exchanges for her own.

'Miss C. M. Tucker is now at the seaside, and is therefore unable personally to communicate with Mr. Inglis. She requests, however, that he will continue to direct any letters to S——, to the care of Miss Lanzun.

'Miss C. M. Tucker is much pleased to learn that her little work has been favourably received in America. She will be very happy to write such an addition to *The Fortress*, as may make it equal in length to its companion tales.

'As Mr. Inglis' objection to publishing *The White Shroud*, etc., seems only to rest upon the shortness of the poems, Miss C. M. Tucker would have no objection to sending a larger book of her poetry, from which Mr. Inglis might select what he thought likely to please the public. Miss C. M. Tucker has written an Epic on the eventful Life of St. Paul, and a variety of other pieces. Would Mr. Inglis wish them forwarded to Scotland, or to his present address in London? Miss C. M. Tucker herself selected *The White Shroud*, as she thought it one of those most likely to be popular, and perhaps most calculated to be useful. The *name* might attract readers, who would not glance at what appeared from its title to be exclusively religious. It would also be well adapted for illustration; but that Miss C. M. Tucker leaves entirely to the taste and judgment of Messrs. Gall and Inglis, only suggesting that perhaps the commencement of winter might be a favourable time for such a work of Fancy to make its appearance, when it might take its place among the elegant little volumes designed for Christmas remembrances.'

Others were disposed to take a different view as to the peculiar attractiveness of such a name as *The White Shroud*, and when the volume was published it came out as *Glimpses of the Unseen*.

A first interview between Charlotte and one of her Publishers, recalled by some of the family, probably took place at about this date, or not very long afterwards. She is said to have been shy on seeing him, though not commonly supposed to suffer from shyness. In any case it is to be hoped that few Authors are, at first starting, so absolutely convinced of their own powers as not to go through certain twinges of bashfulness.

One copy of *The Claremont Tales* was sent out to her brother, Mr. St. George Tucker, who was again in India, and had recently gone to Azimgurh. When the book arrived, he sat up reading it until past one o'clock in the morning; no small compliment to a young Author. He then despatched a messenger on horseback to Benares, with the volume,—a ride of sixty miles,—that his brother, Mr. Henry Carre Tucker, might with all speed enjoy the same pleasure. Charlotte, hearing this through her Mother, was not a little gratified.

Thenceforth Charlotte went steadily in for Authorship. Volume after volume flowed from her fertile pen; most of them for children; many of them exceedingly amusing; all of them definitely designed to teach something. One is rather disposed to fancy that in the writing of these books there may have been, in the beginning, something of a struggle. Charlotte was by nature ambitious; and her literary gift was considerable; and some of its potentialities appear to have been sacrificed to her ardent desire for usefulness. Whether she ever could or would have made her mark in any of the higher walks of literature is a question which could only have been decided by actual experiment; but at least she must have felt it to lie within the bounds of possibility. Some people may think that her desire for usefulness was a little too ardent in its manifestation, since it led to so extremely didactic a mode of writing as that of many among her books. No one can deny that some of the said volumes do contain a large amount of direct 'preaching'; not merely of life-lessons, interwoven with the story in such wise that the one could not be read and the other missed, but rather of little sermons so alternating with the story that a child might read the latter and skip the former. Probably, most children, when reading to themselves, did follow this plan. Directness to a fault was, however, a leading characteristic of Charlotte all through life. The same tendency,— many would say in plain terms, the same mistake—is apparent in the later years of her Indian work, in the mode of her Zenana teaching.

With respect to her writings, nothing is more impossible than to gauge correctly the amount of comparative good worked in any age, by different books or different styles of composition. That which makes the most stir, that which has the greatest apparent success, is by no means always the most wide in its influence. Some of us may be inclined to think that A. L. O. E. might have reached a larger circle, might have gained a more extensive influence, if she had less anxiously pressed so very much didactic talk into her tales,—if too she had more studiously cultivated her own dramatic instincts, and had more closely studied human nature. All this we are quite at liberty to believe. For the question as to 'doing good' through a book does not rest upon the amount of religious teaching which may be packed into a given number of printed pages, but rather upon the force with which a certain lesson is presented, with or without many words. There is no especial power in an abundance of words; rather the reverse!

But the main gist of the matter as regarded Charlotte herself lies outside all these questions. It is found in the simple fact that she determinately stamped down her own personal ambitions, and bent her powers with a most single heart to this task of 'doing good'; that she resolutely yielded herself and her gifts to the Service of her Heavenly Father, desiring only that

His Name might be honoured in what she undertook. Whether she always carried out this aim in the wisest manner is a secondary consideration. From the literary and artistic point of view, one may say that she undoubtedly did make some mistakes. From the standpoint of a simple desire to do good, one may question whether she could not have done yet more good by a different style of writing. But with regard to the purity and earnestness of her desire, with regard to the putting aside of personal ambitions, with regard to the single-heartedness of her aims, there can be no two opinions. And He who looks on the heart, He who gauges our actions not by results but by the motives which prompt them,—He, we may well believe, honoured His servant for her faithful work in His Service.

Nor must we ignore the measure of marked success which she certainly had, if one may judge from the speed with which her books came out, and the demand which apparently existed for them. Even in her most didactic tales there are keen and witty touches, and droll descriptions. For 'teaching' purposes her boys may sometimes converse together as boys never do converse; but none the less those boys are real, and they recur in after years to the memory as only living people or vivid creations ever do recur. In some of her rather higher flights, such as *Pride and his Prisoners*, are to be found stirring scenes, drawn with dramatic power.

One thing should be noted: the curiously allegorical or symbolical style of thought which was natural to her.

It did not appear in the girlish dramatic efforts,—unless in the direction of a perpetual play upon words,—but in her published books it developed speedily. This was remarkable in her; *not* because of any peculiar result from it in England, but because of its very peculiar adaptation to Indian needs. One may almost think of her authorship in England as mainly a long preparation for her Indian toil; the continuous practice in habits of imagery and allegory, by no means especially suited to our Western minds, gradually fitting her to deal with the Oriental mind, little as she yet dreamt of any such destination for herself. All these years, without knowing it, she was waiting for and was working upward to 'the Crown of her Life,' as it may be termed; those eighteen years in the Panjab. All these years she was being prepared and made ready, till she should be as a 'sharpened instrument' in the Hand of her Master, fitted for the work which He would give her to do.

Among the many volumes published during the first fifteen or twenty years of authorship were the following:—*The Giant-Killer*, *The Roby Family*, *The Young Pilgrim*, *History of a Needle*, and *Rambles of a Rat*, before 1858; *Flora*, *The Mine*, *Precepts in Practice*, *Idols in the Heart*, and *Whispering Unseen*, before

1860; *Pride and his Prisoners, The Shepherd of Bethlehem, My Neighbour's Shoes, War and Peace, Light in the Robber's Cave,* and *The Silver Casket,* before 1864. A trio of volumes appeared in succession, the first of which she wrote at her Mother's suggestion,—*Exiles in Babylon, Rescued from Egypt,* and *Triumph of Midian.* Another trio, coming in due course,—*Fairy Know-a-Bit, Parliament in the Playroom,* and *The Crown of Success,*—were bright little books, containing a good deal of useful information. Besides these were published at intervals *House Beautiful, Living Jewels, Castle of Carlmont, Hebrew Heroes, Claudia, Cyril Ashley, The Lady of Provence, The Wreath of Smoke,* and very many others.

One of the most strongly allegorical of her earlier works was *The Giant-Killer;* and in that little book she no doubt made free use of her own experiences.

It is easy to believe that she must have had many a hard battle with Giant Sloth, before she gained the habit of always rising at six o'clock in the morning, a habit persevered in through life. Again, one of her eager and impulsive temperament could not have been naturally free from a clinging to her own way, and from a certain vigorous self-seeking; and many a bitter conflict must have been gone through, before friends could, with an all but unanimous voice, speak of hers as a peculiarly unselfish character. In the struggles of Fides to get out of the Pit of Selfishness, we may read between the lines of Charlotte's girlish battlings.

Even more, in the fight with Giant Pride we seem to see her hardest tussle of all, and the mode in which victory came to her. Giant Pride's assumed name of 'High Spirit,' his hatred of Meanness, Gluttony, Cowardice, and Untruth, are all an echo of parts of herself. The polishing of the darkened gold of her Will she had long known in the small unavoidable frictions of everyday life; and the plunging of that Will into furnace-heat, and the straightening of its crookedness by means of heavy successive blows, she had begun to know in the death of her dear Father, and would soon know more fully through other sorrows coming after. But many more than three blows were needed for the shapening of Charlotte Tucker's Will. She may have dreamt when she wrote the book that three would be enough, and that the King's call to Fides might in her case be soon repeated. She little knew the long years of toil and patience which stretched far ahead.

A tiny glimpse of the daily fighting, which she like all others had to go through, may be seen in the succeeding letter, written to her sister, Laura, a year or two before the death of old Mr. Tucker:—

> 'I obeyed you in putting your note into the fire, after twice perusing it; but it seemed a shame so to destroy what was so sweet. How little you and I have been with each other lately,

yet I do not think that we love one another one particle the less,—I think that I can answer for myself at least. May God prosper your humble efforts, my sweet Laura. I enter into all your feelings....

'I do not like to overload dear Bella with advice. It appears almost presumptuous from a younger sister; but I threw in my word now and then. But what am I?... I fear that I have been peevish with — — to-day. I feel discontented with myself, and need your prayers.'

CHAPTER VIII
A.D. 1854-1857 CRIMEA, AND THE INDIAN MUTINY

In the year 1854 Mr. St. George Tucker again came home from India; and in the autumn he took his Mother and sisters for three months to The Mote, an old country house about six miles north of Tonbridge, hoping that the change would do good to Mrs. Tucker's health and spirits. Those were the terrible days of the Crimean War; and in that autumn the battles of Balaclava and Inkerman were fought. Several letters of interest belong to about this period.

TO MISS BELLA F. TUCKER. 1853.

'I have found out a much better hero for you than your friend Lord Marmion,—who, by-the-bye, had he lived in these days, would have run a great chance of being transported for fourteen years, or imprisoned for one with hard labour, for forgery. Mere courage does not make a hero.... When I was about as old as you are now, I had—besides Montrose, for whom I have a great regard still—a great hero, a pirate! About as respectable a man perhaps as Lord Marmion, and I was so fond of him, that I remember jumping out of bed one night, when one of my sisters laughed at him.

'But I have grown older, dear, and have seen so many bubbles break in my time that I am more on my guard. I look for something more solid now. If you are allowed to read *Uncle Tom's Cabin*, or any part of it, pause when you have done, and compare the old negro with Lord Marmion. You laugh at the idea. What!—"the falcon crest and morion,"—"the scar on his dark brow"—will not all this throw the poor ignorant thick-lipped hero quite into the shade? Yes,—if a sparkling bubble is more glorious than a diamond shut up in a black case. Time touches the bubble, and it breaks,—I have given up my pirate-hero,—but the diamond—never mind the black case! "Uncle Tom" is a hero, and one worthy of the name.'

TO MRS HAMILTON—(LAURA).

'The Mote, *Sept. 1, 1854.*

'Your and your dear husband's nice sunshiny notes reached me this morning.... I believe that you are wise not to come here, for the roads are very bad, and the climate not very bracing. Sweet Mother says that it suits her very well, and I thrive on it like anything, but not every one might be the better for "water, water everywhere." We have four pieces of water close by us, besides the moat just under our windows. The Mote nestles so curiously in a hollow of the hill, that when you have walked a few hundred yards from it, and naturally turn round to look at the noble mansion which you have left,—it is actually *non inventus*. You would not know that you were near the Mote at all. "What has become of our great house?" say you. It has vanished like Aladdin's fairy palace.

'I feel sure that this is the identical old place that Mrs. D'Oyly took us to see, where they said that some of the rooms had not been opened for one hundred years. This suits me exactly. As the boys say, "I am in clover." Damp hurts me no more than if I were a water-wagtail; but the same might not be the case with you....

'What a good thing it has been for your little darling being at so healthy a place during the trying time of teething. I shall expect to see her still more improved, when I have the pleasure of kissing her sweet lips again. How diverting it will be to watch her when she first runs alone!...

'Such nice letters from India! Dear Henry is having my Tales translated into Hindustani, for the poor natives. Oh, pray, my Laura, that a blessing may go with them. Dear Robin preaches to upwards of a hundred blind, and bears the hot weather wonderfully well.'

TO THE SAME.

'The Mote, *Sept. 12, 1854.*

'Many thanks for your welcome letter, your good news, and your kind invitation. I should not wonder if the last were very thankfully accepted some time next month; for it is quite uncertain whether the L——s will let us remain here beyond the six weeks, and almost quite certain that No. 3

will not be ready for us then, in which case we had better scatter. The boys indeed talk of standing a siege here, rather than give the place up; but you see we are afraid of treachery in the camp, having so many of the L— —'s servants. Then we might have difficulty about provisions, for we should all grow desperately thin upon the fish which Charlie catches. Besides which, the moat might be waded, although it is a doubtful point whether the wader could get on through the weeds and mud. I think, all things considered, that we had better *not* stand a siege.

'My heart can quite re-echo the cheerful tone of your note, love. I do indeed feel that we are loaded with blessings. I enjoy this place exceedingly, it is so pretty; just the place to "moon" about in. Don't you remember Mrs. D'Oyly taking us to see it, when we drove here in two carriages, and you were with the sprightly, and I with the sedate party? I feel sure that this was the identical old house. My room ought to be haunted, only it is not. It is such a pity that you have not the fairy carpet to come here without fatigue. But, as it is, you serve as a magnet, to help to draw me back to Middlesex without regret.

'Kind love to dear Mr. Hamilton, and twenty kisses to the Princess of babies. I can well imagine the pleasure that she is to you—a large lump of sugar in your cup!'

TO MISS BELLA F. TUCKER.

'*Dec. 12, 1854.*

'We went to St. James' Park to-day, to see Her Majesty on her way to open Parliament. I had an excellent view of our poor dear Queen; and the sight of her mournful subdued countenance, as she bowed graciously to her people, but without the shadow of a smile, quite touched my heart. This war weighs very heavily upon her; and I am anxious to know whether she was able to get through her speech without breaking down altogether. She looked to-day as though it would have taken less to make her weep than laugh.

'How England is exerting herself to send comforts to her brave sons in the Crimea! A lady was here to-day who, having seen that books were thought desirable presents to the Army, made up a box of them, which was to go to a Mr. S. who had offered to receive them. But when her intended gift was known,—"O pray do not send any more books!" was the poor receiver's cry. "We have seventy thousand volumes!" and they did not know how such a tremendous library was to be forwarded. In the lint department, parcels came in at the rate of two hundred a day! Good-bye.'

TO THE SAME.

'Jan. 13, 1855.

'It is singular in how many ways last year I seemed to be taught a lesson of patience. I was disappointed over and over and over again. In one matter in which I was greatly interested, I was so at least five times; but before the close of the year I had cause to say with much pleasure,—"I am glad that I was disappointed." Another time I had a very heavy heart from a different source of disappointment; and some months later I was grieved, even, I am half ashamed to say, to tears; and yet before December was out I was actually glad of both these disappointments, as well as the five others; and a good appeared to spring from the evil. Now, if I am inclined to be impatient,—and *very* impatient I am by nature,—I try to remember my experience, and really to get the valuable lesson by heart. I think it a good plan at the end of a year to review the whole, to try and find out what especial lesson has been set one to learn in it. I found it to be *praise* one year; last year *patience*. I know not what it will be this year. I hope that—but no, I will not write what I intended. Whatever is, is best. We have not to choose our tasks, but to learn them.'

TO MRS. HAMILTON.

'June 15, 1855.

'What news have I to give you? We have had a nice note from dear Henry to-day, saying nothing about health, except that Robin is well. St. G. and I have just come from a loiter at the Botanical Gardens, which showed us that we need be under no great concern, were hemp and flax exterminated from the vegetable world, and silkworms to leave off being spinsters, as we could dress cheaply and well on plantain fibre, have capital paper and excellent ropes, etc.'

In the August of 1855 she had the pleasure of going with her brother, Mr. St. George Tucker, to the great French Exhibition at Paris. This was the celebrated occasion of the Queen's visit to Napoleon, after the close of the Crimean War; and Paris was thronged. So full was the place that rooms in Paris itself were not to be had, and they went to an hotel in Versailles, occupying apartments which had once been occupied by Louis Napoleon. Charlotte's warlike enthusiasm showed itself in the fact that she was willing to pay twenty-five francs apiece for seats at the Champs de Mars, where they might witness the review of 45,000 French troops. When Her Majesty had quitted Paris, it became possible to obtain rooms at the Hôtel Bristol.

From Versailles she wrote to Mrs. Hamilton, on the 21st of August:—

'Dearest Wifey,[5]—You wished for a letter from France, so here is one; but if you expect a description of what I have seen, I really cannot undertake to give you even a *précis*. Paris surpasses my expectations. All in its gala dress as it is now, swarming with people, crowded with soldiers, gay with fluttering flags and triumphal arches,—it is really a sight in itself. The grand Exposition of pictures is splendid; it is only too large. I was amused at it by a lady coming up to me, and politely requesting me to inform her who Ophelia was. An old French lady, looking at a picture of the burial of Harold, and, I suppose, feeling that the subject might be painful to me as a Saxon, politely assured me of her regret at that monarch's death! "Let bygones be bygones," say I.

'Most of the French foot-soldiers are very little fellows, compared to some of our troops; but amongst the Cavalry are very fine tall men. The Zouaves are very heathenish-looking warriors. They dress something like Turks, with all about their throats so perfectly bare that they quite invite you to cut their heads off.

'St. G. and I so enjoyed this exquisite evening in the stately gardens! A fine military band was performing, the people were happily listening, little children skipping about, the glorious sunset tints illuminating a palace fit for the "grand Monarch."

'We have seen our Sovereign Lady three times, which was being in great luck. I am rather tired of writing, so will only add kindest love, and beg you to believe me your ever attached,

C. M. Tucker.

'P.S.—I told a fat funny little French baba to-day that I had a niece younger than herself, and asked her if she would not like to see her. The answer was unsatisfactory.'

The Crimean War was ended; and two years later came the outbreak of the Indian Mutiny, with its awful carnage, its heaps of slain, its tortured women and children, its heroic determination, its dauntless courage. Then was seen a Continent, lost apparently in one day, won back to the British Crown by mere handfuls of indomitable men facing armed myriads. Such a tale had never been told before.

If Charlotte's patriotism had been stirred by the Crimean struggle, this came nearer to her yet! She had five brothers, all in India, all more or less in daily peril. Mr. Henry Carre Tucker was Commissioner at Benares; Mr. St. George Tucker was at Mirzapore; Mr. William Tucker was in a less acutely unsafe position; Mr. Charlton Tucker, after seeing his Colonel shot down, was for weeks in hiding. All these escaped. But her early companion, Robert,—the father of her 'Robins,'—was among the slain; and the three children, already long half-orphaned, became now wholly orphaned.

Robert Tucker's remarkable powers, and his successes at Haileybury, have been earlier spoken about. Naturally of a serious and stern disposition, though not without lighter traits, he had been a good deal saddened by troubles, which no doubt resulted in the more complete dedication of himself and all that he possessed to the Service of his Divine Master. A short sketch of his life, written by his sister Charlotte, and published by the S.P.C.K., tells of his work at Futteypore, where for many years he was Judge.

About four years before the Mutiny he had written home about the 'extraordinary success' which was attending his Christian school, established and kept going by himself. On Sundays he was in the habit of regularly addressing a collected crowd of Natives; literally 'the poor, the maimed, the halt, the blind'; and he did not teach them only, but also ministered liberally to their bodily needs.

In her little sketch Charlotte says of him,—'Careless of his own comfort, restricting his personal expenses to a very narrow compass, he gave to the Missionary cause at the rate of forty pounds monthly, and one year even more'; adding that with 'shrinking from ostentation' he had never given his name on these occasions. And again—'It was his deep and abiding sense of the debt which he owed to his Saviour, which made the Judge devote not only his substance but his heart and his soul to the Lord. How deep was the gratitude which he expressed in these words—"If every hair upon my head were a life, it would be too little to sacrifice to the Lord Jesus Christ!"'

A clue to many things in Charlotte's own later life may be perhaps found here. There can be no doubt that the story of her brother's self-denying life and tragical death made a profound impression upon her mind. His example, long after, was closely copied by this sister, when she too 'restricted her personal expenses to a very narrow compass,' precisely as he had done, and with the same object, that she might have the more to give away. Also his energy in teaching was reflected by her own burning desire, in old age, to speak on all occasions to the Natives of their deepest needs, and never to miss an opportunity of trying to lead some poor Hindu or Muhammadan to Christ, always with the vivid sense upon her, when she met man or woman, that the call to herself might come before they could meet again, and so a second opportunity might never recur. Another eighteen years had, however, yet to elapse before she would go out to India, to follow in his steps, and to render to Hindustan a loving return for this 'year of horrors.'

In June 1857, like a thunder-clap, not indeed utterly unforeseen but practically unexpected by the majority of Englishmen, came the fearful outbreak; and for a while it did really almost seem that the British Raj in India was at an end. But those who thought so were soon to be undeceived.

When first the storm broke, Robert Tucker did not expect to be himself one of its earlier victims. His brother, Mr. St. George Tucker, says,—'Robert was in high spirits when the Mutiny broke out. He wrote to me that he had seen a magnificent horse, and that if he could buy him, he could ride from Futteypore to Delhi, and soon finish the war. Robert was the Judge, and Sherer was the Magistrate. Sherer decided that all the Europeans must leave Futteypore and fly to Banda. Robert refused to leave Futteypore, and said that his duty required him to protect the Natives. The rest of the Europeans went off to Banda.'

Many Native Christians fled also,—among others a Native Catechist, Gopi Nath. He was taken by Muhammadans, imprisoned and cruelly treated; and he it was whose sinking courage was revived by the almost dying words of the English boy-officer, Arthur Cheek, the 'Martyr of Allahabad.'

But with the spirit of a soldier, Robert Tucker, the intrepid Judge of Futteypore, remained at his post, the only European among countless Natives, bent still on doing his duty.

The night preceding the tenth of June he passed at his Cutchery or Office; and in the early morning news was brought that his own house had been set on fire. He then tried to collect some of the landholders, to protect the Natives in the town, and their houses; but not all his efforts could prevent the burning of the latter. His next step was to ride off to the Jail, in the hope of securing the prisoners; but he was too late, the prisoners having been already set at liberty. Mr. Tucker fearlessly reprimanded the Jail-Guard; whereupon the Guard, belonging to a bad Cawnpore regiment, opened fire. Though every shot missed, Mr. Tucker must then have seen that all was up. Everything was in confusion; the Native officers would not support him; and he stood absolutely alone.

He rode to the Cutcherry, no man daring to intercept him, and took up his position on the top; and for hours he remained, fearless and calm, awaiting his death. The day was intensely hot, causing him to suffer terribly from thirst; and one of his horsekeepers at length brought him some milk,—a deed of mercy, which shows that one man at least was not devoid of gratitude.

'There he remained during that fearful day,' wrote Charlotte Tucker. 'There, as evening was closing in, he made his last lion-like stand, when the fanatic Musselmans, bearing a green flag, the emblem of their faith, came in a fierce crowd to attack him.' How many he shot as they advanced is not certain; some say twenty, or even thirty; but at length one of his assailants shot him in the head, and the moment he fell, they took courage to rush up the stairs and to finish their work.

For Robert Tucker himself, cut off though he was in the very prime of life, there could be no regrets, except on the score of all that he might have done, had he lived. No man could be more ready than he was to go. But the blow fell heavily on those who loved him; and though for nine years he had not seen his children, whereby the sorrow to them was softened, yet the loss to their future could not but be great.

'So he fell,' wrote one who had escaped; 'and in his fall the constant and fervent prayer of his latter days was answered, for he fell at the post of duty. All who knew him well mourn in him the loss of a true and noble friend, generous even to prodigality, highly talented, a thorough gentleman, and an upright judge.'

Mention of this event was made at the time in the Journal Letter of Viscountess Canning,[6] worth quoting in addition to the above.

> '... The story of Futteypore is a strange one. The whole country round was gone, and there was a large Sepoy guard in the treasury, and every reason to believe they would rise, so all the Europeans took to boats, and went away to safe stations down the river, and I think to Banda. Only Mr. Tucker, the magistrate, would not stir, and remained with fifty Sepoys and the treasury. He was son to the late Director, Sir George

Tucker,[7] and was one of the four brothers whose names we hear constantly, and he was as brave as a lion. He had a deputy-magistrate—a Mohammedan—in a high position, treated as a gentleman, and in as high a place as a native could occupy, next to himself. To this man had been given a body of mounted police, and he undertook to keep the country clear between the great trunk road and the river for some distance. He did it admirably, and took delight in it, and sent in detailed reports up to the last. But when he heard of some more places being gone, he suddenly returned to the treasury, to which his position gave him access, dismissed the fifty Sepoys with a thousand rupees apiece, and then attacked Mr. Tucker with all his police force. Mr. Tucker was killed, after defending himself till he had killed with his own hand, some say sixteen, some twenty men. I suppose he had a whole battery of revolvers, and so kept his assailants at bay.'

Though Robert was gone, other brothers of Charlotte Tucker were still in hourly danger; and the pressure of anxiety went on for months, as shown by letters of the time.

TO MISS B. F. TUCKER.

'Sept. 9, 1857.

'I need not say how I long for tidings from India. Most especially do I desire news of Havelock's precious little army. Upon its success, humanly speaking, may hang the safety of all our beloved ones in India.'

TO MRS. HAMILTON.

'Sept. 19, 1857.

'We are longing for our letters, but I do not think we shall get them till Tuesday. Dearest Mother tries not to think more of India than she can help, and has, I am glad to say, given up reading the papers, so we only give her the good part of the news verbally. I could not endure to be kept in the dark myself. I go every day to fetch the papers. I half live on them, and would far rather go without a meal than not see them.... We heard from poor dear Mrs. Thornhill to-day. She hopes that Henry and his wife are in Lucknow. Such a hope is not worth much, one would think.'

TO MISS B. F. TUCKER.

'*Sept. 21, 1857.*

'God be with our brave and beloved ones! My heart feels very low—worse than before the letters arrived. We hide from dear Grandmamma that Mirzapore is threatened. She only knows that the troops are there; not why they have been sent. N—— W—— has sent his dear wife and children to Calcutta. He feels so desolate without them, but takes the separation as a lesson from his Merciful Father to set his affections more on things above.... Does not your heart sicken for Lucknow?'

All through England hearts were 'sickening for Lucknow,' at this time. But the Cawnpore-like catastrophe, dreaded for Lucknow, did not come. The rescuing party mercifully arrived in time. As months went by, the Mutiny was stamped out from end to end of India; and no second Tucker was added to the roll of England's martyrs there.

Just before the outbreak Mr. Henry Carre Tucker seems to have requested that some copies of his sister's books might be sent out to him for distribution: and an interesting letter was written by her on the subject to Messrs. Gall and Inglis.

'*July 17, 1857.*

'Sir,—I am glad to hear that the box is likely soon to be on its way to my dear brother. We have been in great anxiety on account of him and his family, as Benares, the station of which he is the head, with a population of 180,000, is one of the most wicked places in India, a "holy city," a stronghold of fanaticism. My brother has taken a bolder part in upholding Missions, and spreading religious literature, than almost any one else in the country; therefore, if Benares had followed the example of Delhi, the terrible event might have been attributed to his excess of zeal.

'The Almighty, to whom my brother attributes the glory, has hitherto watched over Benares in so marked a manner, that it remained quiet in the midst of disturbances; and my young niece has bravely ridden through it by her father's side, giving confidence to the timid by her fearlessness.... But a few lines in the telegraph, read aloud in Parliament, informs us that the troops in Benares had risen at last, and been driven out of the city with great loss. I await the next mail with intense anxiety. I have five brothers in India.'

It is interesting to know that Mr. Henry Carre Tucker devoted himself a year later to the task of helping forward in every possible way Missionary work in India, as a species of 'Christian revenge' for the death of Robert and the sufferings of his countrymen. He took a leading part in starting the 'Christian Literature Society for India,' and was for a while himself its Honorary Secretary.

CHAPTER IX
A.D. 1857-1865 LIFE'S EARLY AFTERNOON

One-half of the life of Charlotte Tucker was now over; a quiet and uneventful life thus far. If we like, we may mentally divide her story into four quarters, each about eighteen years in length, corresponding to Early Morning, Noontide, Afternoon, and Evening. The first eighteen years of her Early Morning had been, perhaps, as bright and cloudless as the existence of any girl could well be. In the succeeding Noontide hours she had known still much of brightness, though they included her first great sorrow, and ended with her second. Also, in the course of that Noontide she had entered upon her career of authorship, with all its hopes and aims, its hard work and its delights. Probably none who have not experienced it for themselves can quite understand the fascinations of authorship.

Now she had passed her Noontide, and was entering on the hours of early Afternoon. Eighteen years of that Afternoon still lay between the dark days of the Indian Mutiny and her own going out to India, for the Evening of her Life,—the fourth and last eighteen years, which were to be the fullest and the busiest of all her busy days.

We have first to do with the earlier portion of the Third Period; a period including much work, many interests, and some deep griefs. Between 1857 and 1866, however, lay a quiet stretch of everyday life, distinguished by no rocks or rapids. The river flowed on peacefully for a while.

Life at No. 3 continued much as it had been in years past. Many friends were in and out, and were always cordially welcomed. Mrs. Tucker, since her husband's death, had made one difference, in that she no longer gave dinner-parties; but luncheons were in full swing, to any extent; and Charlotte's powers of entertaining were still in abundant requisition.

No better place can well be found than this for part of a letter to A. L. O. E.'s nephew,—the Rev. W. F. T. Hamilton, son of her favourite sister,—from Sir Francis Outram, son of General Sir James Outram, of celebrated memory.

'*June 25, 1894.*

'My recollections of No. 3 Portland Place and of its typically kind inmates carry me back just half a century. But they are very clear, though, I regret to add, only of a general and intangible character.

'Mr. Tucker I recall with grave respect, unmingled with awe, as evidently one of the wisest and most influential of my Parents' proved friends. Mrs. Tucker retains an honoured place in memories of these and later days as the kindest and most liberal of "old aunts,"—so she desired me to designate her, and at once adopted me into her very large circle of favoured nephews and nieces,—the inexhaustible source of varied goodnesses, especially such as were of the most approved edible nature.

'Their sons I cannot recall, except as the genial and trusty friends of later life. But the five daughters of the house none of us who enjoyed their unselfish kindness at all stages of our youth can ever forget.

'Of the two who ere long became successively "Miss Tucker," however, you would alone wish me to speak. They cannot be dissociated in the memory of the generations of young people, whose privilege it was to be entertained and gratified by their unwearied attention throughout many a long holiday afternoon and evening, while stuffed by Mrs. Tucker *ad libitum* with all the best things of the season.

'As we grew older, we not only more fully understood the exceptional boundlessness of old-fashioned hospitality and kindness which that house and household exemplified thoroughly, but we came to understand somewhat of the heart-source whence issued that truest manifestation, of "everyday religion," which evidences itself in an absolutely unselfish consecration,—consistent, unreserved, and essentially practical,—for everyday wear, and not only under "stimulating environments." Such was the life's lesson which our association with these two now ageing sisters suggested to us.

'Miss Charlotte had, as you know, much of the Romantic in her composition.... In person she was always slight, and somewhat fragile-looking. Indeed, both she and Miss Fanny gave one the impression of being too incessantly though quietly busy about everything that promoted the happiness of other people, to ever become stout, or to cultivate dress and appearances, beyond what was consistent with the aims and duties and requirements of a fully occupied home-life.

'Mrs. Tucker could not quite keep pace with the new-fashioned unconventionalities of "young-lady work" in London; and one of the object-sermons, which most impressed me in my College days, was the beautiful self-restraint which these two sisters—no longer young—imposed upon themselves, in deference to their aged Mother's wishes, in regard to that outside work which inclination, or one might say conviction, as well as opportunity and qualifications, impelled them to participate in.

'Still the unbounded hospitality of the "open house" in Portland Place went on; and still they were content to devote their time, talents, and energies to successive generations of juveniles and elder guests, without a murmur.'

One can well believe that the self-restraint had to be severe in Charlotte's case, with her abounding energies, and her eager desires for usefulness. But she patiently abided her time; and she did not wait in vain. These were years of quiet preparation.

In appearance at this time Charlotte was, as ever, tall and thin,—decidedly tall, her height being five feet six inches, or two inches over her Mother's height, and only one inch short of her Father's. She had still as of old a peculiarly elastic and springy mode of walking; and while possessing no pretensions to actual good looks, there was much charm of manner, together with great animation. Still, as ever, she threw herself energetically into the task of entertaining others, no matter whether those 'others' were young or old, attractive or uninteresting. This at present was a main duty of her life, and she never neglected or slurred it. Still, as ever, she was guided and restrained by her Mother's wishes, yielding her own desires when the two wills, or the two judgments, happened to lie in opposite directions.

Although not really fond of work, Charlotte was a beautiful knitter. She would make most elaborate antimacassars, of delicate lace-like patterns, invented by her own busy brain; and while working thus she was able to read Shakespeare aloud. Her Father had loved Shakespeare, and Charlotte had early caught the infection of this love, never afterwards to lose it.

Visiting in the Marylebone Workhouse went on steadily; she and Fanny usually going together, until Fanny's health began to fail, which was probably not until after 1864.

Fanny was *par excellence* the gentle sister; very sweet, very unselfish; always the one who would silently take the most uncomfortable chair in the room; always the one to put others forward, yet in so quiet and unobtrusive a fashion that the fact was often not remarked until afterwards. Of Charlotte it has been said by one who knew her intimately, —'I wonder whether before the year 1850 any one has described her as "gentle."' The gentleness, which was with Fanny a natural characteristic, had to be a slow after-growth with the more vehement and resolute younger sister. Many a sharp blow upon the golden staff of her Will was needful for this result.

As an instance of Fanny's peculiar gentleness, it is told that one Sunday, when she saw a man trying to sell things, she went up and remonstrated with him, speaking very seriously, but in so mild and courteous a manner, so entirely as she would have spoken to one who was socially on her own level, that he was utterly unable to take offence. She was also very generous, giving liberally to the poor out of her limited dress-allowance, in earlier girlish days. This same generosity was a marked feature in the character of Charlotte; perhaps especially in later years.

Fanny was of middle height, and thin, with dark eyes; very neat and orderly in her ways, wherein she was the opposite of Charlotte, who was famed for untidiness in her arrangements. Charlotte was, however, methodical in plans of action, and in literary work; and later in life she seems to have struggled hard after habits of greater tidiness, as a matter of principle. But in middle life she could still speak of her drawers as—at least sometimes—supplying a succession of 'surprises.'

Her 'little Robins' were now growing up, an ever-increasing care and interest to her loving heart; and the devotion which she felt for Letitia was of a most intense nature. The two boys were of course much away at school; but Letitia was always with her,—until the year 1865, when it was decided that she should go out to her uncle, Mr. St. George Tucker, in India. Moreover, many other little nieces and nephews had a warm place in the life of 'Aunt Char,' none more so than the children of her especial sister-friend, one of whom was her own god-child.

Side by side with innumerable home-duties and home-pleasures went on the continual writing of little books for children; one or two at least appearing every year. The amount of work in one such volume is not heavy; but A. L. O. E.'s other calls were many. And she was not writing for a livelihood, or even for the increased comforts, whether of herself or of others dependent upon her; therefore it could not be placed in the front rank of home-duties. The Tuckers were sufficiently well off; and Charlotte is believed to have devoted most or all of the proceeds of her pen to charitable purposes.

To secure a certain amount of leisure for work, she accustomed herself to habits of early rising. Her Mother had always strongly objected to late hours, making the rule for her girls,—'If you can, always hear eleven o'clock strike in bed.' Charlotte is said to have made her a definite promise never to write books late at night; and through life this promise was most scrupulously adhered to.

Since she was debarred from late hours, and since in those days she could never be sure of her time through the day, early morning was all that remained to her. Punctually, therefore, at six o'clock she got up,—like her hero, Fides, conquering Giant Sloth,—and thus made sure of at least an hour's writing before breakfast. In winter months, when others had fires at night in their bedrooms, Charlotte denied herself the luxury, that she might have it in the morning instead for her work. The fire was laid over-night, and she lighted it herself when she arose; long before the maid came to call her.

Later in the day she wrote if she could and when she could. No doubt also she found many an opportunity for thinking over her stories, and planning what should come next. She usually had the tale clear in her mind before putting pen to paper; so that no time was lost when an hour for actual work could be secured.

A sitting-room behind the dining-room of No. 3, called 'the parlour,' was by common consent known as her room. Here she would sit and compose her books; but she made of it no hermitage. Here she would be invaded by nieces, nephews, children, anybody who wanted a word with 'Aunt Char.' And she was ready always for such interruptions. Writing was with her, as we have seen, not the main business of life, but merely an adjunct,—an additional means of usefulness. Since she had secured the one early uninterrupted hour, other hours might take their chance, and anybody's business might come before her own business. With all these breaks, and in spite of them, she yet managed in the course of years to accomplish a long list of children's books.

One of the said nieces, Miss Annie Tucker, writes respecting certain visits that she paid to her grandmother, Mrs. Tucker, at Portland Place:—

> 'In each of these visits it was always my beloved Aunt Charlotte who entertained me,—if I may use the word,—though I was a mere child; and she did it just as if I were a grown-up person. I could never see that she took less pains to interest me than she did to please the many grown-up people who called. She usually entertained us in her room behind the dining-room, so that my grandmother should not be wearied too much.

'How often have I gone in and out of her room, with a freedom which now almost surprises me! but she never seemed interrupted by my entrance. I have seen her put down her pen, though she was evidently preparing MS. for the press, and attend to any little thing I wanted to say, without one exclamation of vexation or annoyance, or a resigned-resignation look, that some people put on on such occasions, at her literary work being put a stop to. And yet I am sure that was not because she did not mind being interrupted.'

It is not for a moment to be implied that all hard toilers in life are bound to follow precisely here the example of A. L. O. E. Circumstances differ in different cases. Often the work itself is of supreme importance; the interruptions are unnecessary and undeserving of attention. If everybody worked as Charlotte Tucker worked at that particular period, the amount accomplished would in some cases be very small, and in other cases, where undivided attention is essential, the result would be absolute failure. In her case the literary work was of a simple description, and the home-calls appeared to be distinctly first in importance. But the spirit which she showed was well worthy of imitation. Many, whose favourite occupations are, to say the least, no whit more pressing than were her books, are exceedingly tenacious of their time, and exceedingly impatient of interruptions; and with too many the home-calls come second to all personal interests. It was far otherwise with Charlotte Tucker. Whatever had to be done, she was ready to do it,—not one iota more ready to write her books, or to visit in the Workhouse, than to teach the 'Robins,' to amuse visitors, old or young, to entertain guests at dinner or luncheon, to take her part in a family 'glee,' to join in merry games, to conduct friends on sight-seeing expeditions. No matter what it might be, she did it willingly, throwing her whole energy into the matter in hand, always at everybody's service, never allowing herself to appear worried or bored.

Despite her somewhat fragile appearance, and an appetite commonly small, there must have been a marvellous amount of underlying strength,— of the 'wiriness' which often belongs to delicate-looking people. If tired, she seldom confessed the fact, and never made a fuss about it. Her extraordinary vitality and mental vigour carried her through what would have entirely laid by many another in her place.

The following extracts are from letters ranging between 1861 and the beginning of 1866:—

TO MRS. HAMILTON.

'*Nov. 6, 1861.*

'Will you kindly tell my Letitia that I have put up her paint-box, to be sent to Somerset House, as I dare say that your dear husband will kindly take charge of the little parcel....

'The weather here has not been very choice. We had candles at luncheon yesterday. We make ourselves very happy, however, by vigorous reading. In the evening we discourse with Queen Elizabeth, Leicester, Paul Buys, and Olden Barneveldt, etc.; in the morning we go out hunting with M. Chaillu, plunging amongst hippopotami and crocodiles, demolishing big black serpents, or perhaps capturing a baby-gorilla, more troublesome than dear Edgy himself.

'We are all just now in a state of indignation about your pork! Don't suppose that it is any fault in the pork; on the contrary, it is acknowledged to be the most "refined" pork ever known; and Mother says that if she shut her eyes, she would not know that she was not eating chicken!! We had a beautiful roast of it one day at luncheon; and Mother cut off a choice bit, to be reserved for our table, cold, while the servants were indulged with the rest of that joint. To-day Mother asked for our reserved bit. Would you believe it?—those dreadfully greedy servants had eaten *our* bit as well as their own, though they had legs of mutton on Friday and Saturday, and a 22 lb. joint of roastbeef on Sunday! Do you marvel at our indignation? Mother means to call some one to account. She puts all the pathos of the question upon *me*. Miss Charlotte to be disappointed of her reserved bit of pork! I can hardly keep my countenance, but of course must not disclaim my interest in the question. These greedy servants must be kept in order. It is not for nothing that we read of valiant encounters with alligators and hippopotami.'

TO MRS. HAMILTON.

'*Dec. 3, 1862.*

'Dearest Laura,—We at last opened our piano, and your song has been thoroughly examined. The result is that some parts are much liked. Clara was so much pleased with the verse about the Rose, that after singing it over for Mother's benefit she sang it three times over for her own. The words are not worthy of the music; it ought to be sacred; and I intend to copy it out in my own little music-book as a hymn, so that its interest will not die away with that of the bridal.[8] The part next best liked is the Shamrock verse; and if I might venture a suggestion, I think that the whole of the "We hail thee" might be set to it; only the "glittering" accompaniment must be confined to the Shamrock verse. I think people often like the repetition of one air over and over, far better than a great variety.

The air is flowing and attractive, and there is no harm in its brevity. The first part, "We hail thee," has a transition, which we fear that the rules of thorough-bass might not permit; and the Thistle is hardly equal to either the Shamrock or the Rose,—of which, you see, I would make a *separate* song and hymn. If you would write out the song to the music of the former, I do not see why we should not try to get it accepted by a publisher. I hope that you will excuse my thus venturing to criticise your song and so unmercifully to cut it short.

'I will give on the next page the words which I propose putting—for my own use—to the hymn part. Very little alteration will make them go very well to the air, for I have tried them; and the repetition of the last words, which your sweet music requires, suits lines the whole emphasis of which falls on the closing words; at least I fancy so.'

The lines following are given here, not exactly as they appeared in the letter, but in the corrected and improved form which afterwards appeared in print with the music:—

> 'The Lord He is my strength and stay,
> When sorrow's cup o'erflows the brim;
> It sweetens all if we can say,
> "This is from Him!"
>
> All comfort, comfort, flows from Him.
> 'When humbly labouring for my Lord,
> Faint grows the heart and weak the limb,
> What strength and joy are in the words,
> "This is for Him!"
>
> 'Tis sweet to spend our strength for Him.
> 'I hope for ever to abide
> Where dwell the radiant Seraphim;

Delivered, pardoned, glorified;
But 'tis through Him!
All light and glory flow from Him.

'Then welcome be the hour of death,
When Nature's lamp burns low and dim,
If I can cry with dying breath,
"I go to Him!"
For Life Eternal flows from Him.'

TO MISS BELLA F. TUCKER.

'Feb. 11, 1862.

'I have read your touching account of your most sorely afflicted friend with great interest. I visit the Imbecile Ward,[9] and I fear that she must be in the Insane Ward; but I will be sure to make inquiries, and perhaps I may find that I can follow her thither. I am not timid. Very very glad should I be to impart any comfort in such a case of awful distress; but I fear that she may not understand even sympathy.'

TO THE SAME.

'Feb. 26, 1862.

'I went to our afflicted friend.... I talked to her as comfortingly as I could, and told her that I thought this sad trial might be sent that she might be like Christiana, walking on a Heavenward path, with all her children with her. I was glad to draw forth one or two tears, for tearless anguish is the most terrible. She said that she prayed the Lord to take her. I did not think that a good prayer, but suggested that she should ask the Lord to come to her, as to the disciples in the storm. She has promised to repeat the two very little prayers, "Lord, come to me"; and "Lord, make my children Thine, for Jesus' sake." It was touching to hear her repeating softly, again and again,—"Make me Thine! make me Thine!"'

TO THE SAME.

'March 25, 1862.

'Though still very low to-day, Mrs. —— did not seem to me to be inaccessible to religious comfort. I fancied that there was a little lightening of the darkness.... I do not know of anything that she wants. I have supplied her with working materials. Perhaps a little book with pictures in it is as good as anything, as amusing without fatiguing the mind.... I know the beautiful large texts that you allude to; but I do not know where they could well be fixed in the Insane Ward. They are more, I think, for the bedridden.'

TO MRS. HAMILTON.

'Gresford, *Sept. 13, 1863.*

'I thought of you as I stood on the soft green slope down to the water, and looked on the bright little stream, with its white foam sparkling in the sunlight. How much of its beauty it owes to the pebbles that fret it; and how much of its rapidity to the fall in its course. But in our lives, how we—at least I—shrink from the pebbles! How we would fain have all glassy smooth,—though Nature itself teaches us that then it would become stagnant. The "sea of glass" is for another world....

'I sometimes think that consoling is one of the most delightful employments given to God's servants. It is pleasanter than teaching; far far more so than reproving others, or struggling against evil, or examining our own hearts. You were a comfort to poor dear — —, and I dare say that the sense of being so lightened your own trial of parting. I would give a *great deal* to have your influence with — —; but the Almighty has not been pleased to grant me this. Perhaps He will some day.'

TO THE SAME.

'*July 29, 1864.*

'I want particularly to know whether, in case I see my way to gaining money by it for some religious or charitable purpose, you will make me a present of that little bit of your welcome to the Princess which I have turned into a hymn. Also whether you would mind Mrs. Hamilton's name being published on it. The hymn has been ringing so in my ears, and with such a soothing effect when I did not feel particularly cheerful, that I should like others to have the same comfort. I have made inquiries as to the cost of printing and publishing it.... Being very short, I do not think that much could be asked; and this is perhaps the gem of your music. I do not want it to be done at your expense, but at my own, and to manage everything after my own fashion,—but I cannot plunder you either of your music or your name without your leave....

'Dear Fanny is better, though still prisoner to her room. She has had a sharp attack of fever; and I am afraid it will be difficult to throw off the cough. The rest of our party are well, as I trust that I may find you and your dear circle.'

TO THE SAME.

'*Aug. 1, 1864.*

'Your and your dear husband's sweet notes quite added to the cheerfulness of our breakfast-table. Even Fanny did not appear knocked down by your tender scolding. She, for the first time since Tuesday, came to breakfast. She still needs great care, for the cold was on her chest, and even speaking is liable to make her cough. Mother highly approves of your plan of coming to town. She desires me to say that she knows that her face is before you, as yours is before her. Dear Fanny will probably not start for Brighton till Wednesday week, so she will have the pleasure of welcoming you, and I am sure that you will try not to let her be loquacious....

'Many thanks for your kind present of the music. I am going to have it printed by converted Jews, and the entire profits devoted to the Society for the Conversion of Jews; so that it will be a little offering from us both to one of the holiest of causes.... I take the expense of the edition of 500 copies. They are to be sold for 1s. apiece; so if all are sold there is a contribution of £25 clear to the Society.... I am rather hopeful that the whole edition will go off before Christmas; for one shilling is not a formidable sum, especially when people can get a new song and help a good cause at the same time.... I take great pleasure in this little piece of business. I have been quite *haunted* by the music. I am ordering the plate to be preserved, in case of a Second Edition being required. So Mrs. Hamilton is going to come out as a Composer!'

TO MISS 'LEILA' HAMILTON.[10]

'*March 31, 1865.*

'My dear God-daughter,—I shall like to think of you particularly to-morrow, because it is the Anniversary of the day when your dear parents in church solemnly presented their precious little first-born babe to God; and I stood there to answer for her. Dear Leila, may each return of that day find you drawing nearer and nearer to Him who said, "Suffer the little children to come unto Me." If we could only feel in our hearts that He really does love us, and that He deigns to care whether we love Him, what a motive it would be for doing everything as in His sight! We are too apt to think of our Saviour as very far off, and with so many to care for that we are almost beneath His notice. But this is wrong. The Sun shines and sparkles on every dewdrop in a field, as much as if it were the only dewdrop in the world. He does not pass it over, because it is little; he makes it beautiful in his light, and then draws it up towards himself.... I wish that I could come and pay you a visit; but I do not see how I am to leave Grandmamma as long as dear Aunt Fanny is an invalid. I seem wanted at home.'

It may have been somewhere about this year, or not very long before it, that Charlotte wrote the following pretty and graceful lines:—

'Each silver thread that glitters in the hair,
Is like a wayside landmark,—planted there
To show Earth's pilgrims, as they onward wend,
How nearly they approach their journey's end!'

CHAPTER X
A.D. 1864-1866 A HEAVY SHADOW

The afternoon shadows were again to darken around Charlotte Tucker; and one blow after another had to fall. Her mother was growing old, and in no long time would be called away. The health of her gentle sister, Fanny, had begun to fail, never to be entirely restored. But a yet sharper sorrow, because utterly unlooked for, was to come before the loss of either her mother or her sister, like a flash of lightning into the midst of clear sunshine.

Of all the many whom she dearly loved, none perhaps lay closer to her heart than Letitia, the only daughter of her brother Robert,—the youngest of 'the Robins.' The two boys were now out in the world, one in India, one at sea; but Letitia hitherto had never left her, except for visits here or there among relatives and friends. One who knew them both well describes the contrast between aunt and niece at this period,—Charlotte Tucker, 'so upright and animated, very thin, fair, with auburn hair, not very abundant, but which curled slightly, naturally,'—and Letitia, 'grave, with beautiful dark eyes and hair, and rather dark complexion.' Another speaks of Letitia as tall and handsome, with dark eyes, dark chestnut hair, regular features, and sweet smile.

The gravity seems to have been a marked characteristic of this gifted young girl. From very babyhood she was earnestly religious, and of a peculiarly serious temperament; though at the same time energetic and sometimes even lively. She had not her aunt's spirit of fun; but the two were alike in generosity and in determination. Perhaps Charlotte Tucker's training had especially developed these traits in her niece. A favourite proverb of Letitia's was—'Perseverance conquers difficulties';—and it would have served equally well for A. L. O. E.

Letitia was also very fond of little children, and she worked much among the poor. She was an exceedingly good and fearless rider; and at twenty years old there was already promise of a literary gift. Her passion for reading was so great that Hallam's *History* was a recreation in her eyes. She had written at least one short story, which had found its way into print, and many pretty, simple verses, chiefly of a religious character. One of her hymns, composed at the age of eighteen, may be given here:—

'My soul was dark, for o'er its sight
The shades of sorrow fell;—
In Thee alone there still was light,
Jesus, Immanuel!

'And all around me and above
There hung a gloomy spell;—
I should have died without Thy love,
Jesus, Immanuel!

'For in my sinking heart there beat
An ever-sounding knell;—
But still I knew the "promise sweet,"
Jesus, Immanuel!

'I looked to Thee through all my fears,
The pain and grief to quell;—
Thy Hand hath wiped away my tears,
Jesus, Immanuel!

'I heard a low, "a still small voice,"
Soft whisper, "It is well";—
And knew the Saviour of my choice,
Jesus, Immanuel!

'And still, o'er all life's changing sea,
In calm or stormy swell,
I'll look in faith straight up to Thee,
Jesus, Immanuel!'

On November 28, 1864, Letitia left English shores, to join her uncle, Mr. St. George Tucker and his family, in India. Letters of Charlotte Tucker, referring to the event, have not come to hand; but she must have felt the separation very keenly, whatever might have been the precise reasons which led to the move. Letitia had now been practically her child for eighteen years; and a close tie existed between the two. But no doubt Charlotte looked upon the parting as of a very temporary nature; as merely sending her child away for a longer visit than any preceding. The real anguish of separation came a year later, when suddenly the young girl was summoned to her true Home.

The few following extracts lie between these two dates,—the going of Letitia to India, and the tidings of her death.

TO MISS 'LEILA' HAMILTON.

'Jan. 3, 1865.

'Many thanks, my dear Leila, for your affectionate note.... There was another nice cheerful note from my Letitia to-day. She wrote it when on the Red Sea, which she evidently found very warm, for she described the ship as a "hothouse," and said that she and her fellow-passengers would be "fine exotics" before they arrived. There had been two Services on board on Sunday, and Letitia had heard two excellent sermons. Mary Egerton had her harmonium on board, which had been brought up from the hold, so there was nice hymn-singing too. How sweet the music must have sounded on the water! I think that, steaming over the Red Sea, one would have liked to have raised the song of the Israelites—

"Sound the loud timbrel o'er Egypt's dark sea,

Jehovah hath triumphed, His people are free!"

'My dear sailor is to leave us on the 17th or 18th for China. I believe that he is to travel part of the journey in the same vessel as the Cuthbert Thornhills, who were to have taken charge of Letitia had our first arrangements held good. They will have one Robin instead of the other. Poor dear Mrs. Thornhill, what a sad parting is before her! I had a loving note very lately from my Louis. He fears that he will not get leave to see his dear sister for a twelve-month.

'The weather here has been chilly. None of the ladies have ventured out of the house since Saturday; but Charley has in vain longed for skating. Ice forms, then melts again. Dear Grandmamma keeps wonderfully free from cold; but then she remains in the house.'

TO MRS. HAMILTON. (Undated.)

'My loved boy left us yesterday, quiet and firm, shedding no tear. We (Mamma) had a little note from him this morning,—such a simple one,—you might have fancied that he had only left us for a week. Dear boy! I trust that he is going into sunshine; above all I hope and pray that his Father's God will ever be with him. It would not have been well for him to have remained much longer in London with nothing particular to do. Active life is most wholesome to a fine strong man like my Charley....

'Dear Mother keeps well. Sweet Fan I cannot give so good an account of. I have urged Mother to have further advice; and I believe that there will be a little consultation on Friday; but perhaps you had better not write about this, except to me.'

TO THE SAME.

'*Nov. 15, 1865.*

'What a bright account you give of your dear busy young party! Tell dear Otho that I shall be charmed if he makes the discovery of a magenta-coloured caterpillar, or a mauve earwig; and that as it will be ten times as curious as the Spongmenta Padella, it ought to have a Latin name ten times as long. I don't despair of the great sea-serpent Did I tell you that dear Mrs. Thornhill had, when a girl, conversed with a Mrs. Hodgeson, wife of one of the Governors of our West Indian possessions, who had watched the movements of *two* that were fighting in the waves for about *ten minutes*?

"'Twere worth ten years of peaceful life,

One glance at such a fray!—"

I took down the particulars, as I thought them very curious....

'This is my sweet Letitia's birthday; she is just twenty.... My Letitia is going to pay Louis a visit at Moultan.'

No foreboding whisper in her heart spoke of what that visit to Moultan, so lightly mentioned, would mean to them all. When the two next letters were penned, little as Charlotte dreamt of what was coming, the blow had already fallen, and Letitia had passed away.

TO MRS. HAMILTON.

'*Jan. 2, 1866.*

'May the best blessings of the opening year rest upon my beloved Laura, and her dear circle.

'I hope that dear Leila received my *Rescued from Egypt* in the Christmas box. I put it up for her, and to the best of my knowledge it went to Bournemouth; but as neither she nor you have mentioned seeing it, I feel half afraid that in some way I cannot imagine it has missed its destination, and the dear girl has fancied that when sending little remembrances to her brothers I had forgotten her.

'Such a delightful budget of letters I had from Letitia by last Southampton mail! She writes that she is "very very happy."'

TO THE SAME.

'Jan. 3, 1866.

'I feel that I have not said half enough to your dear husband for his splendid book. I was in such a hurry to write and thank him, that I only gave myself time for a cursory glance.... Dear Fanny enjoyed looking at the pictures with me; and to-day I carried up my book to dear Mother, that she might have the pleasure also. She admires your dear husband's gift greatly, and we agree that it is just the book to take to the Cottage. It seems to be quite a treasure of curious and interesting knowledge; a volume to keep for reference as well as for perusal. Do thank dear Mr. Hamilton again for me, and tell him that I consider *Homes Without Hands* as a family acquisition.

'We are all much *in statu quo*. Our time is now passing swiftly and pleasantly. Mother looks so bright and bonny and young! We were talking together to-day of your and your dear husband's kindness to sweet Fanny. I am sure that it has not been lost.'

Then came the mournful news; and a hasty short scrawl conveyed the first intimation of it from Charlotte Tucker to her niece, 'Leila' Hamilton; a note without any formal beginning:—

'Break to your sweet Mother and Aunt Mina that God has taken my darling Letitia. His Will be done,—Your sorrowing Aunt,

'C. M. T.

'All was peace,—*smiling*!'

The illness had been short,—a severe attack of erysipelas, while Letitia was in her brother's house at Moultan. Somewhat early in the illness she had said,—'I am sure I shall die; but one ought not to mind, you know.' While delirious she was heard to say distinctly,—'Ta,'—her pet name in the past for her aunt Charlotte; but the message, if there were one, could not be distinguished.

After much wandering, she regained sufficient consciousness to assure those around that she was suffering no pain; and five or six times she repeated to her brother,—'I am very fond of you!' This was on a Wednesday. The next day, Thursday, she was too weak for speech; though in the morning, recognising her brother, she gave him a sweet smile. Thenceforward the dying girl was entirely peaceful; as said by one of those present,—'constantly smiling. Her whole face was lighted up as with extreme pleasure.' All day this continued, as she slowly sank; the face remaining perfectly calm and untroubled; till at length, when she passed away, soon after eleven o'clock at night, 'she ceased to breathe so gently that she seemed to have fallen into a deep sleep.' But the placid smile was still there, unchanged, till the sweet young face was hidden away.

Charlotte Tucker, writing to her sister, Mrs. Hamilton, about these sad particulars, which yet were not all sad, observed:—

> 'I am sure your heart has been aching, and your eyes have been weeping. Such a sudden—such an unexpected stroke! But God is Wisdom and Love....
>
> 'Darling—my own darling Letitia! Oh, when she looked so happy, did she not see the angels—or her beloved Father—or the Bedwells and old Rodman whom she had so tended,—perhaps all coming to welcome her,—or the loving Saviour Himself? I do not grudge her to Him; but oh, what a wealth of love I have (apparently) lost in that one young heart! Her *last* parcel of letters to me contained sweet commissions for her poor.... I dare say that I shall hear from you to-morrow; but it is a relief to me to write now to you, who were so kind and dear to her. I went out before breakfast this morning. A thrush was singing so sweetly. I saw the first crocus of the year. My flower,—my lovely one,—she may now be singing in joy, while we sit in sorrow.'

This letter was dated January 21; and three days later another went to Mrs. Hamilton, not from Charlotte, but from Fanny:—

> 'My own dearest Laura,—Your dear letters have been very soothing to our Charlotte, and have helped to remind her of the mercies mingled with the bereavement. The sure sweet hope that her darling is safe, and for ever happy, has been her strong consolation; and God is mercifully supporting her, I am thankful to say. Last Sunday she went both to Church and to the Workhouse.
>
> 'I am thankful to be near her, to minister to her,—but wish I were a better comforter, such as *you* would have been, dear.

'The sad tidings were most gently broken to our dear Mother by Clara. She was therefore mercifully spared the shock of the sudden intelligence.

'With kindest remembrances to dear Mr. Hamilton, and love to your dear self and your dear ones, believe me, dearest Laura, your very affectionate

'F. Tucker.'

C. M. T. TO A COUSIN.

'*Jan. 24, 1866.*

'Many thanks for your kind sympathy. My sweet consolation indeed is that my own darling girl sleeps in Jesus. When such a bright look of "extreme pleasure" lighted up the dear face of one called away in the bloom of her youth and beauty, was she not realising her own sweet lines,—

"I heard a Voice, 'a still small Voice,'

Soft whisper, 'It is well,'

And knew the Saviour of my choice,

Jesus, Immanuel"?'

TO MRS. HAMILTON.

'*Feb. 6, 1866.*

'Did I ever tell you that my darling wrote to me when she was at the Hills, saying that she did not wish me to be altogether disappointed in regard to her, and asking me whom I would wish her to try to resemble. I mentioned you,—for I thought that as her disposition was lively, it would be more easy for her to try to be like you than dear Fanny; besides she had seen you as a wife and mother, and I did not know whether the Almighty might not destine her to be such. He had something "far better" for my loved one.

'It will interest you to know that G—— (P——'s *protégée*), after winning honours at Cambridge, wishes to be baptized as a Christian. Amy H—— and her husband are to be two of his witnesses, and he is anxious that dear Henry[11] should be the third; for it was Henry's consistent character which first showed him what Christianity really is.'

TO MISS 'LEILA' HAMILTON.

'*Feb. 13, 1866.*

'I thank you lovingly, dearest Leila, for your letter. I prize your affection,—you write to me almost as my own darling used to write. If my health had broken down, so that I could not have been a comfort to dear Grandmamma and Aunt Fanny here, I should thankfully have accepted the invitation which you so affectionately press; but as I keep pretty well, I do not think that it would be well for me to leave my post at home. Dear Grandmamma seems to cling to me so,—she is so loving! I am thankful that she keeps so well. Dear Aunt Fanny was not so well for two days, but is better again....

'My darling once wrote and asked me whose character I would like her to try to copy as a pattern. I gave her your sweet Mother's. She replied that it would be difficult, but that it was well to aim high. I think that *you* will like to know this. You have the same sweet model always before you; you, dear one, have advantages that my darling had not.

'Though I have cried over this note, it has soothed me to write it; I have felt as if I were taking another dear young niece to my heart,—a sad heart, but I trust not an ungrateful one for the earthly affection which is God's gift, and of which I have been granted much.—Your affectionate Aunt and Godmother

'C. M. T.'

TO MRS. HAMILTON.

'1866.

'I send you on the other page a few lines which came into my mind yesterday in regard to my sweet Letitia:—

'A Thought.

'She travelled to the glorious East; she met the rising sun,—
And even so her day of heavenly bliss was soon begun;
I knew 'twas sunrise with my child, while night was o'er me weeping,
E'er closed my weary day, my darling was serenely sleeping.
And so Thou didst ordain, O Lord, as Thou didst deem it best,—
That hers should be the earlier dawn, and hers the earlier rest.'

TO MISS B. F. TUCKER.

'May 22, 1866.

'I have been learning a new art, and am thankful to find that I have sufficient energy left in me to do so. I sent for some reading in embossed letters for a blind man here, and amused myself by puzzling it out myself. I have succeeded in reading right through the fourteenth of St. John in two sittings of about an hour and twenty minutes each. It was an effort of memory as well as attention, as some of the letters are utterly unlike those to which we have been accustomed. The poor blind man promises well to acquire the art, I think.'

TO THE SAME.

'July 16, 1866.

'Have you seen the mysterious sky-visitor? On Friday evening our maids saw something like three stars, one red,— but they disappeared. On the following night Cousins[12] called me to look on what I would not have missed seeing for a good deal. About thirty degrees above the horizon, I should think, shone what was like a star, but more splendid than any that I had ever beheld, of a brilliant magenta colour. It was no falling star passing rapidly through the sky, but appeared quite fixed in the heavens for—perhaps ten minutes. As I gazed with something like awe on its wondrous beauty, suddenly its colour utterly changed; the magenta became white, with a greenish tinge; and then—as suddenly—the star disappeared; not as if hidden by a cloud, but as if *put out*.

'I watched for the mysterious light last night, but could not see it; the evening had been so strangely dark that we had lighted candles an hour before sunset, though our window looks to the west. No star was visible to me; but our maids had a short glimpse of a strange light. I am sitting by the window now to watch for the visitor in the north-west.... I searched *The Times* to-day to see if there were any mention of it, but could find none.'

Evidently Charlotte Tucker had been fortunate enough to see a very fine meteor; though probably the supposed duration of ten minutes was in reality a good deal shorter. The idea of watching for the same meteor next night is somewhat amusing. The maids doubtless saw what they expected to see; but Charlotte Tucker, though non-scientific, was far too practical so to indulge her powers of imagination.

In another letter written during this same July to Mrs. Hamilton occurs one little sentence well worth quoting, for it is a sentence which might serve as a motto for many a seemingly empty and even purposeless life —

>'It is sweet to be somebody's sunshine.'

In June Mrs. Tucker had written to a friend, — 'Charlotte walked twice to church, and thinks she is stronger.' And in a letter to Mrs. Hamilton, on the 23rd of July, Charlotte said of herself, — 'I am quite well now, and up to work'; — yet the following to a niece, on September 1st, does not speak of fully restored energies: —

> 'I have so much to be grateful for, I wish that I were of a more thankful spirit. It seems as if this year had aged me. When I saw a bright creature like — —, I mentally contrasted her with myself, and thought, — "She has not the gee out of her. Cheerfully and hopefully she enters on her untried sphere of work. In her place I should be taking cares!" — very wrong of me. I often take myself to task.
>
> 'I feel putting off my dark dress for *one day* on Wednesday.... My darling was to me what she was not to her other Aunts.'

To some people, or in certain states of body and mind, the afternoon is apt to be a more tired time than the evening. At this stage in Charlotte Tucker's Afternoon of life she passed through a somewhat weary spell, though never really ill; but her energies were to revive for the work of her Eventide.

On October 6th she could say, —

> 'I am not poorly, though I look thin; I think that I am stronger in health and firmer in spirit now than I have been almost all this trying year; and for this I am thankful.'

TO MISS 'LEILA' HAMILTON.

'Nov. 2, 1866.

'Your sweet Mother will wonder at not receiving the little book which I promised to send her; but our bookseller, from whom I ordered the copy, has been unable to get it yet. I will tell you something that may cause delay. Of course I looked with some interest at the illustrations which my Publisher sent me; but I was not a little surprised in the last one to find one whom I considered to be a man represented as a *bear*! He was bearish in character certainly, but still — certainly not a bear in shape.

'Of course I wrote to Mr. Inglis about it; who replied that he had been annoyed himself at the resemblance to a bear, and had sent the picture more than once to be altered, and had been at last so much provoked that he had paid off the artist altogether. Now, though I may be a little sorry for the poor man,—I never proposed his dismissal,—I confess I am rather glad that he is not to illustrate my books any more. There is no saying what creature he might turn my characters into next. Mr. Inglis is going to have the picture altered; so this may occasion delay.'

CHAPTER XI
A.D. 1867-1868 GIVING COMFORT TO OTHERS

Three more years only remained to Charlotte of life in the dear old home of her infancy. Those three years passed quietly, marked by no stirring events. On the 11th of December 1867, Otho St. George Hamilton, son of her sister Laura, died at the age of thirteen, after a long illness; and during these years Fanny continued steadily to fail. The delicacy developed into a case of decided consumption, but of a slow and lingering description. A few sentences are culled from the many letters which remain, belonging to this period.

TO MISS 'LEILA' HAMILTON.

'Feb. 1867.

'I wish my sweet Leila to receive a few lines on her birthday.... *Tempus fugit*, indeed. When you open this you will be thirteen years old. It seems to me as if each year now were growing more and more important; the stream is widening; the mind is opening; and ... may the heart be opening too to that Love which is beyond all earthly love.

'I had a pleasant childhood. My mind was very active, as well as my bodily frame; and at your age I dare say that life lay before me, a bright, hope-inspiring thing. It is well that it should be so; it is a kind arrangement of Providence that the young should be usually full of energy and hope. I like to recall how I felt, that I may enter into the feelings of others.

'Now of course I have not exactly the same kind of landscape before me as I had at thirteen. I am in my forty-sixth year, have known care and sorrow, and have at present but feeble health. And yet, dear, I don't want to exchange my landscape; I have no wish to go back. I have found that middle age has its deep joys, as well as early youth its sparkling ones. Sometimes I ask myself,—"Now, in my present position, if I had no pleasure in religion, if everything connected with that were cut off, what would be left me?—what would life be to me?" O Leila, what a tasteless, what a bitter thing! We want delights that will not grow old, that will never pall, that will be just as fresh and lovely at eighty as at eighteen. Religion is not merely, as some seem to fancy, to prepare us for death, but to be the happiness of life. It calls indeed for the sacrifice of self-will in a hundred little ways; but it repays those little sacrifices a hundred times over. Just think what it is to realise such thoughts as these,—"The Lord Jesus loves me! I am His own! I shall see Him one day, and be with Him!" How can such thoughts ever lose their sweetness?'

TO THE SAME.

'*April 28, 1867.*

'How different your still, noiseless dwelling must be to ours at present! Not that we have much noise, but sometimes so much seems going on. Yesterday M— — A— — D— — and a young cousin came in the morning; then before they had left Cousin M— — E— — and four fine children, then Uncle St. George and his wife. All this before luncheon; others came after it; and I went to the Poorhouse, and then lodging-hunting with Uncle St. George. He *is* so sweet and loving and good.... He delights Grandmamma.'

TO THE SAME.

'*July 1, 1867.*

'It is mournfully interesting to read my darling's papers, of which L— — has brought home many. Her prose is usually lively; her poetry full of tenderness, often very sad.... The two latest dated poems were, I think, written August 14. They were called "An Early Grave" and "All is Vanity." Every stanza of the first expresses desire for an early departure. The second thus beautifully closes—

"There's rest beneath the yew; I know

There's deeper Rest in realms above;

The Saviour's Arm the valley through

Will me uphold with strengthening love;

My hope His Righteousness; my buckler, faith;

Why should I fear to tread the shades of death?"

'If this really be the darling's last written stanza, what a touching interest it gives it!'

TO MISS B. F. TUCKER.

'*Sept. 9, 1867.*

'Poor little Otho has rallied again, though the doctor holds out no hope of ultimate recovery. This is a sad time for my poor Laura, though there are sorer trials than that of bereavement.'

The Hamiltons were at this time in great trouble, as they watched the long-drawn-out sufferings of their dying boy; and many letters were written by Charlotte to her favourite sister, full of intense feeling. Day by day she lived with them in their sorrow, anxiously looking out for fresh tidings, and thinking what she could say to comfort or soothe.

TO MRS. HAMILTON.

'*Oct. 30, 1867.*

'Precious Sister,—Your touching letter has quickened the spirit of Prayer; but oh, I feel as if my prayers were often so weak and worthless. I want more faith, more earnestness. I have not time to write more, but could not let *that* letter be unanswered by your loving

'C. M. T.'

TO THE SAME.

'*Nov. 9, 1867.*

'Fanny and I have been conversing to-night on the subject of your dear suffering boy. You long fervently to see him rejoicing in the prospect of departing and being with Christ. Perhaps the one obstacle to his being able to do so is the thought of parting from you. If his Mother were going with him, he may think, he would be happy to go.

'Now to me, were I in your darling's position, there would be comfort and pleasure in the idea—"Perhaps, as regards me, leaving the body will *not* be real separation from dear ones. Perhaps I may be allowed to come to them, and minister to them, and cheer them; though they cannot see me I may see them!" This idea does not appear opposed to Scripture. The rich man in the parable believed that Lazarus *could* go to Earth; and Abraham never said that he could *not*. If dear Otho thought that he might possibly be permitted to watch over his Mother, and help to make her happy, and be one of the first to welcome her to bliss,—perhaps the real bitterness of death would for him seem taken away. It seems quite possible that dear Robin was by his child's sick-bed, and that she *saw* him, when her face so lighted up with joy. "I believe in the Communion of Saints."

'Your dear boy is very young. A child's religion seems almost to begin with the Fifth Commandment. We can hardly yet expect dear Otho to love the Lord whom he has not seen *more* than the parents whom he has seen and fondly loved. Do you not think, darling, that you are almost *too* anxious on the subject of Otho's state of mind? He is only a lamb; and the Good Shepherd knows that he needs to be carried.

'I should like to know when your dear boy takes the Holy Communion, that I may be with you in thought and in prayer. Otho is an invited guest to the Great Feast above; his robe is prepared by his Lord,—don't fear, love, that it will not be very white and very fair....

'*P.S.—Nov. 10.—*I have been thinking much of your dear one in church; and I open my note to add another reason suggested to my mind, as a cause why he may be unable ... to feel joy in the thought of departure. You and I, my Laura, have known many of God's saints now in bliss; we have almost as many dear friends in the world of spirits as in this. Perhaps we are hardly aware of the influence which this has on our minds,—how it helps to make Heaven a home. Your dear boy may feel that he is going to enter amongst a great company of saints, almost every one of whom is a stranger to him. To one so reserved as Otho, this may be rather an awful thought. I wonder if it is a comfort to him to think of sweet Letitia and Christian[13] being there. Perhaps if you reminded him of that, it might remove a feeling which—if he entertains it—he might not like to mention even to you.'

TO THE SAME.

'Nov. 13, 1867.

'I thank God that He has made your darling willing to depart, even to leave you. Your note is deeply interesting; and I think you may feel that your prayers have been answered.... You must now only think of the "far more exceeding and eternal weight of glory." Probably every hour of suffering in some mysterious way enhances and increases future rapture,—rapture more intense than we can conceive.

The longer I live, the more convinced I feel that there *is* this mysterious connection—in the case of God's children—between personal pain and future delight. So that, if we could, as we fain would, shield our treasures from suffering, we might be depriving them of some rich blessing.

'*You* are in the furnace, my precious sister,—a hotter furnace, perhaps, than that which tries your child. I need not repeat that whenever you want me, you have only to send for me. You and I understand each other! How sweet is the tie between us! Dear Mother is apt to indulge hopes of your boy's recovery. I think that she hardly realises his state, and probably she scarcely knows how to write under the circumstances. She has had a cold these last few days, but is, I hope, throwing it off....

'I send you a little book,[14] which I am sure will interest you. It has been a mournful pleasure to me to prepare it. Your lamb as well as mine will probably soon "be folded above."'

TO MRS. HAMILTON.

'*Nov. 14, 1867.*

'My heart feels more with you, my Laura, in that still sick-room than here. Perhaps many angels are about you and your boy, though you see them not.

'Like your dear invalid, I am especially fond of St. Luke's account of the dying thief. There is something so touching in his looking at such a moment to the Saviour, whose Blood, shed for his salvation, was at that moment trickling down in his view; and there is something so sublime in our Lord's conferring Eternal Life,—such a gift,—at the time when He was Himself undergoing the terrible sentence of death! We may envy your dear suffering child, my Laura, when we think how soon, in human expectation, his eyes will behold the King in His beauty.

'O darling, you could hardly wish to keep him back, when the Master calls him,—calls him to His Home—His Arms!

'I feel for your dear husband; this is a time of sore trial for him; but you suffer together. May God give you both "songs in the night." Those songs are perhaps sweeter to Him than the Hallelujahs of the Angels.'

TO THE SAME.

'Nov. 21, 1867.

'How well I know that feeling which you describe,—the feeling of being unable to pray fervently,—of being scarcely able to pray at all! This is probably caused ... by fatigue of body, and overstraining of mind and nerves. Perhaps God permits it, that we should just sink in complete helplessness at our Saviour's Feet, and ask Him to pray for us, since we cannot pray for ourselves.... You may be like a very little child, that can't even *ask* for what it needs, but yet trusts and fears not.'

TO MISS LEILA HAMILTON.

'Dec. 11, 1867.

'Your very very sad account of dear Otho received this morning makes one think that, even before this reaches you, the sufferer may have been called *home*! Oh what a blessing it is that it is indeed Home.... Dear Otho has had a sorely trying journey, wintry and wearisome indeed; but there is no shadow, never can be a shadow, on the Home to which he is bound. He will never have to leave it again, to learn the lesson of patience in pain. He will, through his Lord's merits, be ready there to welcome the dear ones whom he is now leaving behind,—when they too may quit their school, and go to their Father in Heaven....

'This is a solemn time for you, my Leila. I had reached the age of thirty before I ever looked upon that which is called death, in my own home. These events make the invisible world seem nearer. They should draw us upwards; they should bring us closer to our God.'

TO MRS. HAMILTON.

'Dec. 12, 1867.

'Most precious Laura,—When Lady Catherine L——'s only son was called, she sank on her knees, and said,—"My child, I wish you joy!" so wonderfully was she enabled to realise the happiness, the ecstasy, of the freed spirit, rising up to the presence of her Saviour and God. Happy, happy Otho! No more to be pitied, but to be envied!

'"O change, O wondrous change!

Burst are the prison bars,—
One moment past—how low
In mortal pangs,—and now
Beyond the stars!"

'I will not write much to you now, darling. I am going to see your Freddie, but intend to tell him nothing.

'Express my tender sympathy to your dear husband. God support you all.—Your loving

'C. M. T.'

TO MRS. HAMILTON.

'*Jan. 14, 1868.*

'It was not with dry eyes, my beloved Laura, that I could read what was written in those volumes, to which a tenfold value is given by their being last Remembrances from your lately suffering, now blessed boy. Oh, with what a heavy heavy heart must you have put up those parcels, and written those inscriptions! It will perhaps be a long time before you can realise with calm thankfulness that it is indeed so "well with the child" that you can rejoice in his safety, his happiness.... I am now much more disposed to praise for my angel-girl than to weep for her.... I can see so clearly the Love and Wisdom that took her Home. Presently, my precious sorrowing sister, you may feel the same about your boy. Your intense love will remain, for love is immortal; your sorrow will die, for sorrow with Christ's people is *not* immortal, thank God.—Your tenderly loving

'C. M. Tucker.'

TO THE SAME.

'I have enjoyed your dear letter, and it makes me feel thankful. I have often thought that freed spirits probably lead a life of delightful activity; none of the "burdens of the flesh" to fetter them down. The idea of spirits preaching to spirits is, however, rather new to me. But there seems nothing against it, and probability rather in its favour. That verse in St. Peter, to which you refer, certainly strengthens the idea; for the disciples are permitted in so many ways to follow their Master.

'It is thus possible that, while you are weeping for your darling, if your eyes were opened, you might see him the bright, joyful centre of a little group of spirits of Indian children,[15] repeating to them the lessons which he first learned from you, but which he would now know better—oh, how much better!—than you could ever teach him. I am sure that you would not wish to take him back again to pain and weakness from such an occupation.'

TO THE SAME.

'*April 14, 1868.*

'My own sweet Laura,—I feel that this month must be full of heavy recollections to you; and oh, it is hard to have a bright face to hide a bleeding heart. I hope that you will not put any restraint upon yourself with me.... Easter has its peculiar message of hope and joy to the mourner. Nature, bursting into new life and beauty, repeats the message, gives it to us as it were in an illumination of green leaves and bright blossoms. The Church says, "Christ is risen indeed!"—and all around us joyfully adds, "And *we* shall rise again!" Your parting with your boy is over; now only the meeting is before you. The shadows fall behind; the glowing sunshine is in front.'

CHAPTER XII
A.D. 1868-1872 THE OLD HOME BROKEN UP

One letter at about this time gives particulars of how Charlotte tried to influence, not without results, a poor Roman Catholic woman, whom she came across in the Infirmary. Another makes allusion to the Ragged Schools and their work, in which she was always greatly interested. Yet another contains the answer to an inquiry from a niece about a book which should be bought, probably for a gift. The suggested choice ranges between Sir Walter Scott, Felicia Hemans, Jean Ingelow, the Author of *The Schonberg-Cotta Family*, and Miss Sewell,—a rather curious mixture.

TO MISS 'LEILA' HAMILTON.

'*July 7, 1868.*

'I met a mole the other day in a field. It did not attempt to get away, but let me stroke it; and had I chosen I could easily have taken it up in my hand. This seems quite a country for moles. I have seen them repeatedly. I take a greater interest in them, from that book, *Homes Without Hands*, which your father kindly gave me.'

TO THE SAME.

'*Aug. 11, 1868.*

'We have strange pets here. There are numbers of wasps; I never saw so many at any one time, I think. They sting our poor maids in the kitchen, but behave in such a gentlemanly way in the drawing-room, that, instead of a plague, they seem a pleasure to dear Grandmamma. She watches them, feeds them, admires their beauty, and calls them her babies. One got within Aunt C——'s jacket, which naturally rather alarmed her. She drew the jacket off, and I found the wasp in the sleeve. It had been between it and C——'s bare skin, and yet had never stung her.

'I dare say that you are rather impatient to be settled in Firlands.'

TO THE SAME.

'*Sept. 21, 1868.*

'On Saturday — — and I read my *Castle of Carlsmont* aloud to dear Grandmamma. I have been amused at — —'s little criticisms, and shall like to know how far yours agree with hers, if you read my Tragedy. — — says that "Clara is rather stupid"; that she likes Agnes best. "I have rather a sneaking likeness for Agnes," says she. She says that the ending disappoints her; she would cut off the last page and the four preceding lines, which would completely alter the whole ending. The ending stood originally just as she would have it; but years afterwards I added the page and four lines, which *I* think an improvement.

'Tell me frankly what you think, and whether you approve of the style of binding. You remember when I talked to you about the Tragedy, as we sat together in the garden. The two things that occurred to you were,—how could I get the work, when printed, *sold*; and that people would not like it in pamphlet shape. Messrs. Nelson have obviated the first difficulty; and by having covers put on by the Jewish Society, I have obviated the second. I am sure my wee book will have your good wishes, dear, that it may bring in a little sum to dear Auntie Fanny's Mission purse.

'You will wonder what has become of that work of mine, of which I read part to you last year. I can only warn you, my dear Leila, when you write a story, don't call it *On the Way*,—for it seems to be always on the way, and never to arrive.

'What a long note I have written! Pay me back by a review of my Tragedy, and be as blunt as ever you like; for if you tell me that my poor lady is "very stupid," instead of "rather stupid," you will only make me smile.'

TO THE SAME.

'*Feb. 4, 1869.*

'It is only fair that I should send you a long account of the wedding.[16] I thought that I should be the first of the party in church, for I went early; but I was mistaken. Gradually a large family party gathered.... There was a good deal of how-d'ye-doing and kissing and that kind of thing, before the word was heard, "The bride is coming."

'Dear Bella looked nice and sweet, leaning on the arm of her father. A large Honiton lace veil fell over her pure white silk dress; her lovely hair plaited, instead of made into an ugly chignon, appeared graceful under the white wreath, from which a spray drooped down her neck. I did not think the bridesmaids looking picturesque; there was too square a look about the purple trimming of their white alpacas. The bridegroom and bride stood side by side. I could see Bella's profile distinctly, and could hear every sentence, both when James and when she repeated their vows.... There was no crying that I could see.... You know that there were eight little children present, four little boys and four little girls. Some of them were given flowers from an ornamental basket, to strew in the path of the bride, as her husband led her down the aisle.'

TO MISS 'LEILA' HAMILTON.

'*June 12, 1869.*

'Sweet Grandmamma continues much the same,—serene,—without pain, not exactly ill, but so delicate that she is still carried up and down stairs, and sees none of the family but Aunt Clara and myself, and only a little of me.... Dear Grandmamma sent for me while I was writing the above; and to my surprise I found her, pen in hand, busy with a note to welcome Uncle Willy. I am much pleased that she should send him one, though I should not have thought of asking her to make so great an effort. Of course the note is very short.'

TO THE SAME.

'*July 10, 1869.*

'My heart should be full of thankfulness, for to-day dear Aunt Fanny was able to pay her first visit here to see Grandmamma. Uncle and Aunt St. George[17] drove her here in their pony-chaise; and she had quite enjoyed the drive. I thought Aunt Fanny decidedly better; but dear Grandmamma—who has scarcely realised the severity of her late illness,—said to me, with evident disappointment, "I was surprised to see my own Fanny look so pallid. I think she looks worse than I do." This is true; but then the fact is that Grandmamma's lovely pink and white complexion often makes her look stronger than she is....

'Uncle St. George has given me such a lovely piano-piece. Grandmamma likes me to play it through every day, or I should be inclined to lend it to your dearest Mother. It would remind her so of the dear Ancient Concerts, the delight of our youth, and of good old Mrs. Burrough. It is Glück's music, arranged by Calcott, from *Half-Hours with the Best Composers*, published by Lonsdale. The piece commences with the delightful chorus of Furies, Cerberus barking, etc., which your dear Mother may remember.

'I am ashamed of such an untidy scrawl as this. I do not know how that blot on the first page made its appearance. Of course the *writer* was not to blame!... I could chat much longer with you, dear one, but I have other notes to write; and my pen, or ink, or paper, or something or other, will go wrong to-night, so as to make the act of writing irksome, as well as the note untidy.'

Another heavy blow, not less heavy because sooner or later inevitable, was now drawing very near. Mrs. Tucker, who had reached the age of eighty, had of late failed steadily; and Charlotte must have seen that this dear Mother was soon to pass away from their midst. Before the close of July the call came; and already every word that she spoke was treasured up by her daughter, as may be seen in the following letter:—

TO MRS. HAMILTON.

'*July 12, 1869.*

'So many thanks to my beloved Laura for her valuable and gratifying gift, which reaches me to-day. Dear Mother has heard your sweet music twice over already, and both she and Clara admire it. So do I. I wish that your song were published, that more might benefit from it. I am pleased that you occupy yourself in composing, love. I dare say Mother will often ask for her Laura's song. "Is not she a darling?" exclaimed Mother to-day.

'I not unfrequently sing, "Hark, my soul," to sweet Mamma. It is better to go over and over the same than to give much variety, though I sometimes sing "Rock of Ages" also. I heard Mother saying to herself one day, "Jesus speaks, and speaks to me"; and she once observed of that hymn, "That takes one to heaven."

'Dear Mother is much the same; not ill; with no fever, no pain; just very delicate and weak. She was so particularly sweet yesterday, Sunday. She looked lovely sitting by the large open window, with a light gauze veil to keep off the flies. Mother said that it had been "a holy day"—"a solemn day,"—and twice asked me to read the Bible to her.... Once after waking she observed that she felt "between Heaven and earth." Mother has repeatedly alluded to her dream of being in Heaven with Mrs. Thornhill; and often talks of her father,—"such a holy man!"

'She said yesterday, "I have been dreaming." I observed, "I hope they were pleasant dreams." "Mostly prayerful," was her reply.... She is very serene and peaceful, which is such a mercy.'

TO MRS. HAMILTON.

'*July 24, 1869.*

'Beloved Laura,—So tenderly and so gently the Lord has dealt with our sweetest Mother! She woke this morning, and told Cousins that she herself had slept too long. There was a slight feeling of sickness about eight, which made Cousins call poor Clara. In about an hour she gently fell asleep.... No pain nor even consciousness at the last. I had gone to London on business, as you know. I was telegraphed to; but ere I arrived she—the sweet, the beloved—was where she had wished to be. O Laura, Laura, she has long been drinking the *dregs* of life, however sweetened by affection. I felt for her. But I seem as if I could hardly write connectedly. All the three dear brothers have been here. St. George still is here. Poor dear Fanny also,—she is to have my room, for she is so thankful to be here. We have, however, only been allowed one very brief glimpse and kiss of the revered remains. *Only* remains, my Laura. Think of her bliss! *She* is not here.... Your fond

'C. M. T.'

In Charlotte's desk, kept as one of her greatest treasures, and found there, years later, after her own death, was the last note ever written to her by Mrs. Tucker. It contained these words—'*My precious Charlotte, you have been such a comfort to me!*' No wonder the loving utterance was treasured up by the daughter through the rest of her life.

During forty-eight years Charlotte Tucker had known but one home— No. 3 Upper Portland Place. Now at length in her forty-ninth year the inevitable family break-up had come; and the dear home of her infancy, of her girlhood, of her middle age, could be hers no longer. No. 3 had to be given up; and the sisters had to go forth into fresh scenes. The trial must to all of them have been great; perhaps least so to the gentle Fanny, already on the border-land of the Life beyond.

As a first move, Charlotte and Fanny went together for about two months to Sutton. An idea had, however, arisen of a home, at least for a time, with their brother, Mr. St. George Tucker, and his wife; and the next step was to join them at Wickhill, Bracknell, in the month of September 1869. This was Fanny's last move. She was taken thither, from Sutton, most carefully by Charlotte, in a post-chaise; and the long drive does not appear to have materially affected her. Although by this time wasted to skin and bone, Fanny still kept about in the house; spending much time in her own sitting-room, yet often coming down among the rest for a short time; and during this autumn Charlotte seems to have chiefly devoted herself to Fanny. Before the close of November, however, the end of the long illness was reached.

One day, when speaking to her brother, in allusion to her earlier good health and plumpness, Fanny observed: 'My dear St. George, I have been imprudent.' She did not specify what manner of imprudence hers had been. Probably, like many another in a thoroughly healthy family, she had not soon enough read the true meaning of suspicious symptoms. During some four years past she had been steadily failing; and the end could but have been a joyous release to one so ready to go.

Thus blow upon blow had fallen between the years of thirty and fifty upon the golden staff of Charlotte Tucker's Will. Her Father's death; the death of Robert; the death of Letitia; the death of her Mother; the death of Fanny; all these one after another make a list of sorrows. Doubtless, *the* most keen and bitter losses which she had to endure were, above all, the death of her almost idolised Father, and the death of Letitia. No other pain would equal these, dearly as she loved her brother Robert, her Mother, and Fanny, until her own peculiar sister-friend, Laura Hamilton, should be summoned away. Mercifully, that blow was not allowed to fall until a very short time before her own call Home.

Charlotte was not crushed by these sorrows. This is plainly to be seen. Although the wild spirits and abounding glee of her childhood were toned down, she was still active, still buoyant, still able to enjoy life. She sorrowed, but by no means as one without hope; and if her life was shadowed, it had not lost its spring. As time went by, the spirit of fun and mirthfulness revived; and the little ones in her new home could not fail to be a fresh delight to one who so greatly loved children. Even the earlier letters after her Mother's death are not only calm but cheerful.

TO MISS 'LEILA' HAMILTON.

'*Aug. 23, 1869.*

'I cannot help hoping very sincerely that Uncle St. G. may find a house near Bracknell, large enough to hold Aunt Fanny and myself, as well as his own party. Would it not be nice? But I am rather guarded about setting my heart on anything of the sort. Aunt Fanny would like it very much.... It would be like a haven to me. I think I know one young maiden who would not be sorry to have her old godmother within reach of a walk. But I am quietly waiting to see how things are arranged for me.... I have to manage things for Aunt Fanny, as well as for myself, just as if I were her husband. It is very new work to me. I am not, like your dear Mother, accustomed to think and arrange about a mass of property.'

TO THE SAME.

'*Dec. 2, 1869.*

'I hope that my sweet Leila has not thought me unmindful of her loving sympathy because I have not thanked her before for her note. I am sure that you have heard of us from your beloved Mother, who so tenderly shared my watch by the bedside of my heart's sister. O Leila dear, does not such a peaceful, holy departure show us that our Lord has indeed taken the sting from death? Without Him, how terrible would be the dark Unknown!—with Him, how bright is the valley!

'Sweet Aunt Fanny quoted to me not long ago, I suppose in reference to departure,—"When Thou wilt; where Thou wilt; how Thou wilt!" I think that the last chapter which I read to her was Romans viii. It is such a long chapter, that I stopped at about the 25th verse, fearing to tire the dear invalid; but she made me finish the chapter.

'I went out of the drawing-room window before sunrise to-day, to gather flowers to make into wreaths. The gardener had not opened the greenhouse; but I found much more than I should have expected in the beginning of December,—even rosebuds. The ferns look lovely still. A few days ago I made a wreath of myrtle. I thought it like an emblem of my own sweet sister; sweetest when bruised; with an unfading leaf; and a white, simple-looking, yet lovely blossom.

'Good-night, my Leila. May the Almighty make you, my dear Godchild, as unselfish, conscientious, and lowly as was the loved one by whose grave I am to stand to-morrow.'

Although the plan of living with Mr. and Mrs. St. George Tucker was at no time regarded as a permanent arrangement for the remainder of Charlotte Tucker's life, yet it actually lasted six years. For about eight months from September 1869 they all remained at Wickhill. In 1870 they removed to Windlesham, in Surrey; and in the following year, 1871, they again moved to 'Woodlands,' at Binfield in Berkshire, nine miles or so from Reading, and only about two and a half miles from Mr. and Mrs. Hamilton's home, Firlands, near Bracknell. Charlotte had, therefore, from that time not only the interest of her little nephew and two little nieces in the house, but also of her sister Laura's children within three miles. The companionship of a very favourite brother and of his affectionate wife, together with these little ones, work among the poor, writing, and many other occupations, made her life still a busy and a bright one.

In one letter written to a niece from Firlands, in 1870, she describes 'the rural seclusion of this lovely place. I am charmed with Firlands, and the groves of fragrant pine in which I wander every morning.' In another letter, dated February 1871, she says: 'I hasten to give you the good news that Uncle St. George has taken "Woodlands" for seven years. I am so glad, and I am sure that you will be so also.' This was to her Godchild. Thus she entered upon the final stage of her English life. Before the close of those seven years Charlotte Tucker was in India.

The following extracts from letters belong all to the two or three years after her Mother's death:—

TO MISS LAURA V. TUCKER.[18]

'Feb. 10, 1870.

'I took Sir Frederick and Lady Abbott[19] to-day to the Infant School at Bracknell. They seemed to be much pleased, and so I am sure were the Infants, as their visitors treated them with sugar-plums and lemon-cakes, in return for a number of songs.... A translation of my *War and Peace* has been made by Madame de Lambert, and is coming out in the *Musée des Enfants,*—under the name, I believe, of *Le Soldat Aveugle.*'

TO THE SAME.

'*Dec. 12, 1870.*

'A lady was here the other day, who has a curious taste for different creatures. She has had a slow-worm round her arm as a bracelet—has kept an oyster which seemed to know her—and taught frogs to come out of the water at the sound of their names. One day, when she was quite young, she showed an old gentleman one of her dear snakes, coiled up. He thought it an imitation-one, and said something about good imitations,—when the reptile began to hiss at him.

'"O you horrid girl, it's alive!" exclaimed the poor old gentleman, forgetting his politeness in his sudden alarm and disgust.

'Baby is now thriving nicely, and getting quite fat. It is funny to see her looking at the picture of the white kittens and cherries. She gets quite excited, trying to clutch hold of the cherries with her tiny hands.'

TO MISS 'LEILA' HAMILTON.

'*May 12, 1871.*

'Many thanks, my sweet Leila, for your affectionate letter, and also for your kindness in going to see Sarah Jones.

'My darling Letitia! Notwithstanding all that has passed since she was last pressed to my heart, the sudden blow of her loss has left, I think, a deeper scar than any trial before or after it. I seldom mention her name; and now my heart seems rising into my throat as I write of her....

'I feel tired, dear one, so will not write a long letter. I had a long business walk before luncheon, and then the overland letter to Uncle Willy to write, and a great deal of proof-sheet of the *Lady of Provence* to correct.'

TO MRS. J. BOSWELL.

'*Nov. 13, 1872.*

'I am very busy, for there seems an almost endless field for work in making foreign wall-texts; quite a new occupation for me. In Italy and Spain they will now be warmly welcomed,—India, Syria, China, Labrador, all offer openings. I feel it so gracious in my dear Master to give me this little work for Him, now that the power of composing seems to be taken away. I find delight in going over and over the precious texts, which I have to copy in various tongues. I do not think that I ever before so realised their sweetness. I tried to gild my own little works with Scripture truths; but now I have pure gold to give to others,—without admixing with it any alloy of my own.'

For awhile at about this time she seems to have lost almost entirely her power of writing; the failure being no doubt due to the state of her health, or to re-action from the strain of all that she had gone through in past years. She therefore spent many an hour in painting texts in different foreign languages, on a large scale, to be sent abroad.

The sacred poem which closes this chapter was written in the summer of 1871. It appeared in a little volume, called '*Hymns and Poems*', by A. L. O. E.

A DREAM OF THE SECOND ADVENT.

'I dreamed that in the stilly hush of night—
Deep midnight—I was startled from my sleep
By a clear sound as of a trumpet! Loud
It swelled, and louder, thrilling every nerve,
Making the heart beat wildly, strangely, till
All other senses seemed in hearing lost.
Up from my couch I sprang in trembling haste,
Cast on my garments, wondering to behold
Through half-closed shutters sudden radiance gleam,
More clear, more vivid than the glare of day.
What marvel, then, that with a breathless hope
That gave me wings, forth from my home I rushed,
Though heaved the earth as if instinct with life,
Its very dust awakening. Can it be—
Is this the call, "Behold the Bridegroom comes!"
Comes He, the long-expected, long-desired?
Crowds thronged the street, with every face upturned,

Gazing into the sky,—the flaming sky—
Where every cloud was like a throne of light.
None could look back, not even to behold
If those beloved were nigh; one thrilling thought
Rapt all the multitude,—"Can HE be near?"
Then cries of terror rose—I scarcely heard;
And buildings shook and rocked, and crashing fell,—
I scarcely marked their fall; the trembling ground
Rose like the billowy sea,—I scarcely felt
The motion; such intensity of hope—
Joy—expectation—flooded all my soul;
A tide of living light, o'erwhelming all
The hopes and fears, the cares and woes of earth.
Could any doubt remain? Lo! from afar
A sound of "Hallelujah!" Ne'er before
Had mortal ear drunk in such heavenly strain,
Save when on Bethlehem's plain the shepherds heard
The music of the skies.

Behold! Behold!
Like white-winged angels rise the radiant throng
That from yon cemetery's gloomy verge
Have burst, immortal—glorious—undefiled!
Bright as the sun their crowns celestial shine,
Yet I behold them with undazzled eye.
Oh that yon glittering canopy of light
Would burst asunder, that I might behold
Him, whom so long, not seeing, I have loved!
It parted—lo! it opened—as I stood
With clasped hands stretched towards Heaven; my eager gaze
Fixed on the widening glory!

Suddenly,
As if the burden of the flesh no more

Could fetter down the aspiring soul to earth,
As if the fleshly nature were consumed—
Lost in the glowing ecstasy of love—
I soared aloft, I mounted through the air,
Free as a spirit, rose to meet my Lord,
With such a cry of rapture—that I woke!

'O misery! to wake in darkness, wake
From vision of unutterable joy;
Instead of trumpet-sound and song of Heaven,
To hear the dull clock measuring out time,
When I had seemed to touch Eternity!

In the first pang of disappointed hope,
I wept that I could wake from such a dream;
Until Faith gently whispered, "Wherefore weep
To lose the faint dim shadow of a joy
Of which the substance shall one day be thine?
Live in the hope,—that hope shall brighten life,
And sanctify it to its highest end."

'Fast roll the chariot wheels of Time. HE comes!
The Spirit and the Bride expectant wait,—
Even so come, Lord Jesus! Saviour—come!'

CHAPTER XIII
VARIOUS CHARACTERISTICS

In the last few chapters we have had glimpses of Charlotte Tucker's life rather from within than from without; chiefly in reference to her successive losses, and her own feelings connected with those losses or with passing events. Now we will try to obtain a few glimpses of her, rather from without than from within; to see her as others saw her, not so much as she saw herself. I do not for a moment mean to imply that the two views must be antagonistic. The view of a castle from within and the view of that same castle from without are totally different; yet they are not in the least antagonistic. The one is as true as the other.

In doing this it has to be remembered that A. L. O. E. was a many-sided and to some extent a complex nature. Hers was not a character to be lightly sketched in a dozen lines. Probably no character of any human being can be satisfactorily so disposed of; and there are complexities in the very simplest nature. But the main outlines of some people are more easily perceived, more 'consistent' according to popular notions of character-consistency, than the main outlines of some other people; merely because they happen to embrace fewer opposites. There were a good many opposites in the character of Charlotte Tucker.

All people did not see her exactly alike,—partly because of necessity they looked upon her with different eyes, and partly because of necessity she was not the same in her manifestations to all of them. Being a many-sided individual, one side of her became prominent to one person, another side became prominent to another person. While one friend remembers vividly her spirit of ardent devotion, and another recalls especially her work among the poor, a third pictures her sparkling conversation, a fourth her spirited games of play with children. While one has the strongest impression of her resolute sternness, her horror of evil and self-indulgence, another cannot speak warmly enough of her intense unselfishness and her unlimited kindness, and yet another smiles over the remembrance of her irrepressible fun. All these things were included in her; but naturally not all these things were equally apparent at all times, or to everybody who knew her.

Nor need it be supposed that Charlotte Tucker was a being all light, with no shadows. She was thoroughly human. There were shadows of course,—what else could one expect?—and she had many and many a hard fight, not in girlhood only, but all through life, to overcome her faults.

Again, it is not claimed for Charlotte that everybody who crossed her path loved her. We do read in certain little books, of a particular calibre, about angelic heroines who were invariably worshipped by everybody in their small world, without a single exception. This, however, is, to say the least, uncommon; and with one of Charlotte Tucker's strong personality it would be all but impossible. A very wide circle did most heartily esteem and admire her, did most dearly love her. But of course there were exceptions. In the course of her life some few with whom she was thrown failed ever to come within the grasp of her affectionate influence. But this was only natural. Everybody is not made to exactly suit everybody else.

Among some of her most marked features were an intense vigour and energy, an extraordinary force and vitality, together with great eagerness in whatever she undertook, and a burning desire to be useful in her age and generation. She was very resolute; very persevering; very affectionate; reserved, yet demonstrative; untidy, yet methodical; exceedingly anxious for the happiness of all around; apt often to think people better than they really were; generous to a fault; unselfishly ready at all times to put her own wishes aside; vehement and impulsive, yet never in a hurry or flurry; unyielding, yet tender; severe, yet frisky.

Of course there were other natural characteristics of a different kind; weaknesses not wholly mastered; faults not entirely conquered. She was not perfect,—who is? The strength of determination would occasionally run into obstinacy; the resolute manner could be a trifle dictatorial; the very wish to help and please others might be carried out in a way which did not gratify. With all her exceeding kindness, hers could hardly be described as the true sympathetic temperament. Opinions here vary a good deal among the friends that knew her best; but those who at different periods of her life lived for any length of time under the same roof, will be able to recall certain instances of an absence of tact, a lack of quick understanding of the feelings of others, which certainly never arose from want of a desire to understand. She had any amount of heart, of pity, of thought, to bestow; but while feeling fully *for* others, she could not readily so place herself in the position of others as to feel entirely *with* them, to see matters from their standpoint and not from her own. The highest form of sympathy is a rare and subtle gift; and it can scarcely be said that Charlotte possessed this gift. Still, if any one did bring a burden or a trouble to her, she would spare no pains to help and to comfort to the utmost of her power.

One direction in which she showed through life a marked deficiency was in the housekeeping line. Both early and late she had always an intense dislike and dread of housekeeping. Whatever else she undertook, that was if possible a thing to be avoided; and it seems to have been an understood matter between her friends and herself that anybody rather than Charlotte Tucker might be housekeeper. Probably she had an innate sense of want of power, an innate consciousness that she could not do the task efficiently. If compelled to attempt it as a duty, she would not refuse; but she never took to the occupation, or overcame her dislike.

Moreover, the gift of nursing was not hers. Although in a threatening case of scarlet fever she could be the first to offer herself as nurse, with entire unconcern about the infection; although she shared with others the watch beside Fanny's dying bed, and later on the watch beside Mr. Hamilton's; yet she repeatedly speaks of herself as no nurse, and alludes to her own want of experience. Experience no doubt she might have had, before the age of fifty, had her natural bent lain at all in the direction of nursing; but the necessary gifts were not hers. She had not the reposeful air, the placid voice and manner, above all, the ready tact, which for good nursing are essential. Self-indulgence, laziness, cowardliness were unknown factors in her existence, and could never have held her back; but here too there was probably an innate sense of lack of power; and here too she never through life took to the occupation, 'as to the manner born.' It is noticeable also that, frequently as she would offer her services in times of illness, these offers were seldom accepted. Others doubtless knew as well as she knew it herself that nursing was not in her line.

Somewhat late in life, when a friend, after hours of hard study, was endeavouring to rest, with a severe headache, Charlotte would bring her guitar, sit near, and sing and play to the sufferer. A gentle protestation was of no avail; for so sure was she of her remedy, that she only supposed her friend to shrink from giving her trouble, and the music went on unchecked. This—which happened repeatedly—was done with the kindest and most loving intentions. Charlotte was devotedly fond of music, and she did not herself suffer from headaches. But it is an instance of the want of tact occasionally shown in small matters. The *will* to do good and to help others was abundantly present; only she did not always find the right mode.

It must not be forgotten, however, that, whatever her natural disqualifications for the part of a nurse might have been, she did in her old age so far overcome them as often to take a share in tending the 'brown boys' of the Batala High School when ill, in a manner which won their loving gratitude, although she did not prove successful as a nurse to English invalids.

One who knew her intimately has written the following short sketch, which is well worth quoting *verbatim*:—

'I think one marked point, physical and mental, in her, was her tireless energy. Her very walk was indicative of this; the elastic springiness of every step. Also of another point in her character, stern determination,—the resolute folding in of her arms and hands, as she paced along a road or up and down a garden,—drawing herself up to her full height the while, with sparkling eye and compressed lips. She was teeming with life and energy;—whether it were over her favourite chess, when she would wait patiently but eagerly, thinking out each move; or enjoying the small-talk of society, watching faces and reading characters, to treasure them up for painting in one of her forthcoming volumes; or teaching a niece the beauties of sound and thought in the Italian of Dante; or playing at some game of thought with young people; or reading aloud one of her two favourite dearly-loved and untiringly-studied authors, Shakespeare and Boswell's *Life of Johnson*. She was very sociable, lively, and threw her whole heart into the kindly entertaining of guests of all ages. Her eldest brother used to be very much struck with the unselfish way in which she bore any interruptions and calls upon her time. Even in the midst of her literary work, she would at once rise, leave it, and give her whole attention to any subject an incomer might wish to speak to her about.

'Clever and stern, she was not one to be trifled with. Purpose seemed woven into all her liveliness; and she tried to keep others up to her level.'

Another writes, in reference to the time when A. L. O. E. was living at Birch Hall, Windlesham, with her brother and his family, in 1870:—

'I had just arrived on a visit, and she came into the drawing-room, kissed me, and said, "I am Aunt Charlotte." She was not good-looking, but was always full of life. Her ready wit and charming conversational powers made her a welcome guest everywhere, and made many a dinner-party at her brother's house go off well.... She was always thinking of others, and seemed to count time spent on herself wasted.

'I well remember a time when I longed to see Windsor and the Queen; and Aunt Charlotte immediately said she was longing for the same thing, and gladly undertook to pioneer an expedition. I was far from strong, but could not wait for lunch in my anxiety to have a good place at the railway station, to see Her Majesty arrive. Having seen me and my young cousin safely placed, Aunt C. disappeared, and after a while made her way through the crowd, laden with cakes for us all, finally producing a glass of claret for me from under her cloak, which I was obliged to take then and there. Her enthusiastic loyalty made her enjoy the sight, no novel one to her, of our dear Queen, as much as any of us.

'Our evenings owed much of their brightness to her presence. She could sing,—sometimes lively little songs, accompanying herself with the guitar. Her ear for music was so correct, that on one occasion she came downstairs from her room, to tell me I had played a wrong note in a chord of Beethoven, and the exact note I should have played.

'Sometimes she thought of games for us. One was called "Statues." We each had to pose as a statue, suggestive of some subject, such as Melancholy, Joy, Fear, etc. Whilst she, personating a visitor to the sculpture studio, would try to upset our gravity by her amusing remarks on the statues.... She also invented a geography game for us, providing us with skeleton maps, and small round counters, on which the names of towns were printed. As these were drawn and the name called out, we had to claim them and give them their places on the map. Whoever had a map filled in first was the winner.... Sometimes we read Shakespeare together, each of us taking a part....

'I think things were only a trouble to her when she had to do them for herself. Nothing was a trouble if it helped another.... Work for the Master whom she loved was her animating motive.... She was, I think, the most unselfish character I ever knew. She lived for others; whether in the great work of her life, the use of her pen, the proceeds of which went to fill her charity purse, or in the simple act of leaving her quiet room, on a dull, rainy afternoon, to play a bright country dance or Scotch reel, and set the little ones dancing to vent their superfluous spirits.'

These slight recollections are from the pen of one among her numerous adopted nieces.

Another niece, not adopted but real, says:—

> 'I think the first thought that would have occurred to any stranger, as regards her appearance, was the peculiar fashion of her dress. I remember her in the days of crinolines, standing straight and dignified in her plain dress, without the least attempt at fulness in the skirt. I should think it must have been always so; her individuality and disregard of the world's opinion were so strongly marked.'

This question of dress does not appear to have become a matter of principle with her. She was simply independent, and utterly careless of what might be said. She had not by nature the art of dressing well, and she 'thought it a bother.' As observed by one of her brothers, 'Charlotte never cared what she put on. She never had the art of amalgamating the different parts of her dress!' In plain terms, her taste in dress was not good, and she did not take trouble to improve it. Nor had she the knack of putting on to advantage what she wore. Things that would have looked well upon another did not look well upon her.

Caps were a trouble, and she was most grateful to any one who made her a present of a cap. She could not make nice ones for herself, and she disliked the style of bought caps.

One little story of middle life days at No. 3 illustrates her indifference to what she wore. A friend was staying in the house, to go to a wedding; and when the time came her bonnet had not arrived. Old Mrs. Tucker, knowing that Charlotte possessed a new bonnet, and knowing also that there was no fear of vexing Charlotte by the act, lent this new bonnet to the friend, to be worn at the wedding. Charlotte was then absent. But meeting the friend, either at the wedding or afterwards, she noticed the bonnet, failed to recognise her own property, and most innocently begged to apologise for remarking what a particularly pretty bonnet it was!

She had unconsciously a good deal of manner, and used certain gestures, which either were natural, or through long habit had become a part of herself. One trick of manner was that of clasping her hands, as an expression of certain feelings; also her head was apt very often to be slightly on one side. Seeing a young girl, upon Sunday, busily engaged in copying music, Charlotte Tucker sat down and looked earnestly, with her head a little on one side. 'People have different ideas about occupations for Sunday,' she remarked at length. 'I, for instance, would *not* copy music on a Sunday.' The hint, pleasantly given, was at once gracefully taken, and the music was put aside.

Another time this same young girl had been confessing herself very much of a coward, and regretting the fact. 'Oh, never mind,' was Charlotte Tucker's consoling reply. 'Some day, when there is real danger, you'll flash out!' Perhaps she was thinking of the scene in one of her own little books, when a timid young governess confronts an escaped panther.

Once a young girl, at table, being vexed by words said in depreciation of a near relative, showed her feelings very decisively. A. L. O. E. afterwards put her arms round the girl, and said, '*Quite* right, my dear!'

Again, she had a mode of crossing her hands upon her chest, with a meditative air. Many recall this attitude as peculiarly characteristic of her. If she were thinking deeply, her hands would instinctively take that position.

She was very warm-hearted, and, as one has said, liked 'to make you happy and pleased with yourself.' Ever eager to see the best in everybody, she wore rose-coloured spectacles which now and then would lead her into thinking of people much better than they deserved, and 'disillusionment' had to be gone through. Always endeavouring to see the best, she often saw more than the best; and small harm if she did. At least she ensured thus the making of mistakes on the right side, instead of on the wrong. The common tendency is so very much the other way. The romantic side of Charlotte's nature would interfere with her judgment, and the impulsive first view would be erroneous. When she had had time for calm thought she generally worked her way to a sensible view of a question. But the tendency to over-estimation of others continued through life, and was perhaps especially to be marked in her Indian Missionary work.

In her religious opinions she was a warm Churchwoman, belonging to the 'Evangelical' school of thought. As she grew older, however, she became more and more large-hearted towards those from whom she differed on minor points, more and more ready to hold out a kind hand of friendship on all sides. This side of her appeared more distinctly, and developed more markedly, in India, than in her secluded English home.

Both at No. 3, and in her brother's house, she was wont to read aloud her own stories to her young nephews and nieces, for the sake of their 'criticisms,' and perhaps quite as much for the sake of amusing them. Some of the then children, now grown up, recall those readings with pleasure.

Life at Binfield was quiet and regular. Charlotte kept up her habit of early rising; and from eight o'clock till half-past eight each morning she would take her 'devotional' walk in the garden,—hands folded on chest, head up, step firm and dignified. The impression left by her 'dignity' is strong, singularly so, when considered side by side with a step so springy that some describe it as even 'jerky.'

Mornings were mainly given up to writing in her own room; and little was seen of her, as a general rule, between breakfast and luncheon. In the afternoon she was always ready for callers; and if not needed for them or aught else, she would go and visit the poor. On these rounds she commonly carried with her the conventional 'bag,' full of painted texts and tracts.

Evenings were devoted to sociable enjoyments; frequently to music and dancing. Charlotte was an adept at playing dance-music for her nephews and nieces; and at Binfield she also danced a great deal with her brother and the children. It does not seem that she had lost any of her old light-footedness, whether or not she had had practice during some years past. Sir Roger de Coverley, the Lancers, and the Minuet were great favourites. When the Gavotte began, the children stopped, for they could not spring high enough; but Charlotte was able to make the most wonderful springs. This does not look as though her spirit were yet broken by all that she had gone through.

Besides playing for the children, she would plan games for them, and would superintend charades; and when they grew older she would read Shakespeare with them, often knitting busily all the while as she read. Singing too had a share in these sociable evenings. She still steadily refrained from going out to parties at other people's houses; but she never failed to be present at any party in their own house, not only making her appearance, but contributing her utmost to the entertainment of guests.

Her village work included visiting of the poor, and also, for a while, a class of big boys in the night-school. With the boys she was not successful. They were very troublesome and naughty, and she could not get hold of them at all. This failure is curious, in contrast with her after-success among the Native boys in India, those 'dear brown boys,' as she often called them. Western and Eastern boys differ considerably, however; and no doubt the explanation resides in this fact. Also, an English ploughboy requires different treatment from a high-caste Indian; but she was 'friends' with boys of all castes there.

In a letter to Mrs. Hamilton, written from Binfield, she says: 'The Curate is already a comfort to me personally, for he has taken my night-class off my hands. I have no scruple in letting him do so, for I believe it is far better for the boys. They were too much for poor old Char. I had seventeen last night, and felt my inefficiency.' And in another letter, soon after: 'We had a talk about the proposed Sunday School. I asked not to have boys. My feeling is that I am too old for them.'

She was not too old, many years later, for Batala boys; but plainly she had not the requisite gifts for managing or winning rough English village lads.

A few recollections, jotted down by three of her nieces, may close this chapter:—

I

'In 1869 she came to her house near Sutton; but that sorrowful year to her did not leave much impression upon me, probably because she was so little with us, and so much with her sister who died in our house. I remember her next in the summer of 1870, when my sister was born, coming into the nursery to announce the fact, and afterwards showing us the baby, assuring us that she was "as fragile as egg-shells." She played the organ in our little country church, and visited the poor,—on one occasion going out at night to administer a mustard plaster to one poor woman, who thought herself dying, and sent for Miss Tucker....

'As we grew older she would help us with our charades and games, planning wonderful card games herself, and ornamenting them with brush and stencil. It was she who introduced us to Shakespeare, making me love him as no one else ever could, and making us read him in parts.... On Sunday afternoons she would take us up to her room, in order that my Mother might rest in peace from the children; and there we always spent a delightful time, looking over her dressing-case with its treasures, and listening to the histories of each trinket and curiosity, or messing with her paints. I do not remember that we ever felt ourselves to be in the way in that happy room. It was during this time that she wrote *The Haunted House*, which thrilled me with so much horror, that it was not until years after that I learnt there was a spiritual meaning underlying the tale.

'She was never ill, but always felt the cold extremely in winter, though she did not complain much. One day I came down to breakfast, exclaiming, "How beautiful the snow is!"—when she told me how pleased she was that I could say so, instead of saying, "How *cold* it is!" When I was ill in the year 1872, she often came to see me, quite disregarding the infection of my throat; she would play her guitar to me, or, as I grew better, would patiently guide my little fingers to the right places on the strings. She made up a pretty letter in rhyme, and sent it in a stamped envelope to amuse me. I do not remember her ever talking to me on religious subjects;

but her untiring energy and gentle patience made much impression on me....

'My aunt would never give way to us little ones when she was convinced that we were wrong; and I well remember a prolonged struggle between her and my baby-sister, who was left in her charge one day.... My aunt regarded the sin of drunkenness with the greatest horror; she rarely mentions it in her books, and generally, where it is touched upon, she writes with the deepest pathos, as in *The Great Impostor*. She would only talk of brandy by its French name, and considered it dangerous to take Tincture of Rhubarb, on account of the spirit it contains....

'My aunt would never have expressed disapproval of others, as many of the younger generation do, who are of her own way of thinking. Where she did not approve, she was usually silent....

'But stern as she was by nature, her intense love—the love of a strong nature—made her gentle to the weaknesses of others. She could not sympathise often with the weak, but she could pity and love. Long years of home-discipline gave humility, self-control, and gentleness.'

II

'There are some lives that carry about with them an atmosphere, as it were, of influence and example.... It was thus with "Auntie Char." We used to think and say, "How she would have admired such a deed!"—"How she would have grieved at such a want of courage!" if anything mean or underhand were done. One knew beforehand what her opinion of the transaction would be; at the same time her marvellous sympathy, so readily given, was the first sought in cases of bravery or of moral courage....

'She rarely "preached" to one. I should say she rather suggested little things that somehow were never forgotten. The letter I, for example—when written with a capital letter—called for playful comment. Up to the last I would often count in a fearful manner the all too plentiful I's in my letters to her....

'My father remembers "Sister Char" as the life and soul of their nursery circle in Portland Place,—how in the gardens close by she used to lead their glees and songs.... *We* knew what a great hand Auntie Char was at games of all kinds. No one could play like her. She seemed far younger than any child present, and was quite an enthusiast in them, as in everything she undertook. No one could play half-heartedly with her....

'Auntie Char had a wonderful way of strengthening and encouraging one to open out one's heart to her, and a great and rare capacity for putting herself in "her neighbour's shoes."[20] It was during a visit to us, in the May of 1875, that she acquired the pet name of "Fairy Frisket,"—the name of one of her own works,—owing to her marvellous activity. She would come home after a long day's walking, and run lightly upstairs, faster than we young ones cared to do. In many of her letters to me from India she playfully alludes to this pet name.'

III

'She never seemed to care a bit to receive any praise for her books, and she never let writing interfere with any family duties. She was wonderfully sweet-tempered, but there was no weakness in her sweetness. If others were inconsiderate to her, I never saw her resent it.... Her unconscious influence was, I believe, much larger than she has ever dreamed. She was more utterly regardless of personal ease and comfort than any one I ever knew, but was ever ready to praise others....

'My aunt had a guitar on which she enjoyed playing as far back as I can remember, and on which she used to play to us with much animation and impressiveness, singing to her own accompaniment; but I never remember her playing to herself for her own personal amusement. One of her songs I do not remember hearing from any one else. The refrain in each verse was—"Till green leaves come again." ... Another song that she sang took my fancy,—I believe it was an old-fashioned one in MS.,—and she at once copied it for me, making time to do so amid the many things occupying her at the time. Most people would have let me copy it for myself, as I was quite a girl and had plenty of leisure; but she never seemed to do things like other people....

'Nothing that I can say would explain how beautifully unselfish she was, how utterly regardless of herself, and thoughtful for others. She was one of the few whom one could most truly call *noble*, and yet so sweetly humble. I mourn her irreparable loss all the more for the long parting since she left us for the Mission-field abroad.'

CHAPTER XIV
1875 AN UNEXPECTED RESOLVE

It is not quite easy to say at what precise date the idea first seriously presented itself to the mind of Charlotte Tucker, that she might go out to India as a Missionary. Some years earlier, after the death of her sister Fanny, she had evidently regretted that she could not do so, looking upon herself as too old. But the question again arose—Was she really too old? That question Charlotte now faced steadily.

The plan of living in her brother's house, never looked upon as entirely permanent, had lasted several years; but various causes pointed to a change before long as probably necessary. In January 1875, Mr. Hamilton, who had long been in failing health, passed away; and Charlotte seems, either in anticipation of the event, or directly after, to have had some floating ideas of making a home with her widowed favourite sister. Here also, however, there were certain difficulties in the way of an entirely permanent arrangement; and meanwhile the thought of India was becoming prominent.

Charlotte was now close upon fifty-four years old,—an age at which few women dream of making an absolutely fresh start in life. Some are and some are not elderly at that age; but as a general rule no doubt a woman's best and most vigorous days are then over, and she is more or less disposed for an easy existence. Many at that period can thoroughly enjoy travelling for pleasure. But to make a new home amid new surroundings, to learn a new language, to enter upon a new line of work,—these things after the fiftieth birthday have a somewhat alarming sound.

Not so with A.L.O.E.! For her these fifty years and more of quiet English existence had been years of preparation, of training, of patience. For her parents' sake she had dutifully held back, during the noontide and early afternoon of her history, from much that she would fain have done; and though the latter part of her 'afternoon' had been full and busy, with freedom to do what she willed, yet even this was not enough. At fifty-four she stood practically alone, with no near relative entirely dependent on her kind offices. She was absolutely necessary to none. Had she been, she would not have gone to India. But finding herself thus unfettered, the thought came up,—Why not devote the Evening of her life to Missionary work? Why not set an example to others who, like herself, might with advancing years be left free of ties? Or at least, why not put the matter to the test of actual trial, and prove whether or not elderly women, and not younger ones only, might go forth to work among the Heathen?

There was the question of health. Could she stand the trying climate of India? Would she not be a mere burden on others?—an additional care instead of a help?

Well, at least she could try. If her health failed to stand the climate, she could but return home. If she succeeded, she might be the Pioneer of many more, who would perhaps venture to tread in her footsteps.

Had it been a question of going out at the expense of the Society's funds, the Society might rightly have hesitated; but Charlotte Tucker had enough of her own. While placing herself under the authority of the Zenana Society, and obeying orders, she would pay her own way; therefore, no risking of Missionary funds was involved.

No doubt she was peculiarly well adapted for the attempt. Although thin and delicate-looking, she was distinctly wiry, with much underlying strength, and an immense amount of vigour and vitality. A woman of fifty, who can lightly dance the gavotte, with springs which a child cannot emulate, is not quite an ordinary specimen of advancing years. The failure of power which had followed upon the death of Letitia, lasting more or less during some years, had now pretty well passed off; and there seemed to be good promise of a healthy old age.

She was generally sound, with no especial delicacy; she did not suffer from any tendency to headache; she was not fussy, or self-indulgent, or dainty as to her eating, or particular as to personal comforts, or squeamish as to her surroundings, or shy in making new friends, or afraid of toil and trouble. All these things were in her favour. She was in fact no timid shrinking Miss Toosey,—dear little old lady that Miss Toosey was!—but a fine spirited specimen of A middle-aged Lady of England,—well fitted, it might be, to become even then A Lady of India. Those who think of following the example of A. L. O. E. ought to possess at least some of her qualifications. Had a Miss Toosey, instead of a Miss Tucker, been the Pioneer of elderly ladies in the Mission-field, the attempt would have been a disastrous failure.

Although the matter was not definitely settled until the spring of 1875, it had plainly been for some time in Charlotte's mind as something more than a bare possibility; for during many weeks she had been studying Hindustani. She had, however, said not a word about it to any of her relatives, beyond privately consulting her elder brother, Mr. Henry Carre Tucker. She thought much, prayed much, and waited to be shown her right path: meanwhile beginning to prepare for what might be her duty.

When at length she gave out her intention, as a matter already decided, the announcement fell among friends and relatives like the bursting of a bomb. Nobody had dreamt of such a career for 'Auntie Char.'

LAURA

About the Year 1871

The following letter contains her first intimation of what was coming to her sister, Mrs. Hamilton:—

'*March 24, 1875.*

'My beloved Laura,—I do not know when I shall send this, for I hardly hope that when you know my plans for the future you will say, as Henry did, a month ago, "Selfishly I should be delighted,"—but I hope that when you have quietly thought and prayed over the subject, you will not let your tender affection make you wish to keep me back from the work for our dear Lord for which I have for some time been preparing myself by hard study.

'Years ago I said that if I were not too old to learn a new language I should probably—after sweet Fanny had departed—have gone out as a Missionary. This year the question came to my mind, *Am* I really unable to learn a new language? I find that I can learn, and the only real objection to my going is taken away. Yes, sweet Laura, the *only real* objection; for I can leave you rich in the devoted love of your children. Thank God, *you* are not lonely; and circumstances might easily arise to make it undesirable that I should make a third or fourth lady in—perhaps—a Curate's dear little home.

'I have not come to my present decision in a hurried moment. In the second week of February I made my Missionary project a subject of special prayer; on the 24th I had an important interview with Henry, with whom I had corresponded on the subject. He had no fears as to my health standing the climate, or as to my being able to learn the language. I began to learn it on the 14th February, and by many hours of diligent study have nearly gone through St. Matthew in Hindustani, besides making a vocabulary of more than three hundred words, learning by heart, etc. I have thrown my soul into the work, thankful and happy in the hope that the Lord would open my lips, that my mouth should show forth His praise to the poor Zenana prisoners in India. The enclosed, being the two last letters which I have received from the Secretary of the Zenana Mission, will show you how graciously God has smoothed the way for me, providing an escort all the way to the place which I now think of as my home—Amritsar.

'But you will say—"Why choose India? Why at your age be not content to work in England?"

'I will give you a few reasons for my thinking it desirable for me to go to the East:—

'1. In that corner of the Vineyard the labourers are indeed fearfully few; scarcely *one* to many, many thousands of perishing heathen.

'2. Not one Englishwoman in ten is so well suited to bear heat as myself.

'3. Not one woman in a hundred at least is so free from home-ties as myself.

'4. There is a terrible want of suitable literature for Indian women. If God enabled me still to use my pen, intimate knowledge of even *one* Zenana might be an immense help to me in writing for my Indian sisters.

'Do not grudge me, dear one, to the work for which my soul yearns. You see by the enclosed that my arrangements are made, and that expostulation would but pain me. I would have told you of my plan some time ago, only I feared to distress you when you have had so much of trial. But why should you expostulate, or why should you be distressed? Is not Missionary work of all work the highest? I only fear that I am presumptuous in coming forward; but it seems as if my dear Lord were calling me to it; and my heart says,—"Here am I; send me." I own with shame that much that is unworthy mingles with my desire to serve the Lord in India; but the desire itself has, I trust, been put into my mind by Him.

'Cheer and encourage and pray for me, my Laura, that my Autumn may be better than my Spring and Summer—that the richest harvest come in the latter days. Ask the Lord to give me Indian gems in the crown which He has bought for His servants.

'On the 28th February, at Holy Communion, I devoted myself to the Zenana Mission. But I am bound by no vows. I go out *free*, an honorary Agent of the Society.—Your loving

'C. M. Tucker.'

Writing again on the 7th of May, she said: 'I have been formally presented to the Committee of my own Society, who were very courteous.' The Society was then known under the cumbrous name of 'The Indian Female Normal School and Instruction Society.' A few years later it separated into two distinct Societies; one of which, 'The Church of England Zenana Society,' Charlotte Tucker joined.

As was to be expected, her new plan met with some opposition. Many who dearly loved her were most sincerely grieved at the thought of such a parting; and others were disposed to look upon the scheme at her age as somewhat crazy. Small marvel if they did. Such an attempt had not been made before; and the untried always contains unmeasured elements of danger and difficulty. Probably her unusual fitness for the undertaking was hardly realised as yet even by many of those who knew her best. She had not, however, the pain of opposition from her best-loved sister, Mrs. Hamilton. 'It will be a sore pang to her to part with me,' she wrote to her niece, Mrs. Boswell; 'but her feeling will be that she gives me to God. And to my great comfort she does not attempt to stay me.'

Before going to India, she resolved to take another voyage—a trip to Canada, for a farewell sight of her nephew, 'Charley'; the youngest of 'The Robins.' She would have his brother, her other nephew, Louis Tucker, for a companion on this preliminary journey. Of its perils and pleasures Charlotte Tucker's own pen can best tell the tale.

TO MRS. J. BOSWELL.

'*May 24.*

'I had more than an hour to wait at Paddington, but — —, who was with me, gave me a little lesson in Hindustani. P. E. did the same yesterday; he let me repeat and read from the Testament to him, and then he read a little to me. I generally understood what he was reading when he went slowly. I am so thankful to snatch lessons in pronunciation.... Louis and I are, if all be well, to start in the *Nova Scotia* on Thursday, at one o'clock.... What a beautiful hymn there is in *Hymns Ancient and Modern*, "for those at sea"! Not that I consider drowning a worse way of going Home than any other. As a lady said, "We cannot sink lower than into our Father's Hand"; for it is written, "He holdeth the deep in the hollow of His Hand."'

TO MRS. HAMILTON.

'Gresford, *May 26, 1875.*

'I am almost packed, ready for my start to-morrow morning; but I have a nice quiet time for a little chat with precious Laura. Loving thanks for your sweet letter....

'You wished me to see Dr. Griffith. I have seen him to-day, though not in the character of a patient, I am thankful to say.... The dear old man appeared to feel real gratification at hearing of my going to India as a Zenana visitor, inquired with interest about the language,—health did not appear to enter his medical mind,—and really affectionately gave me his blessing. I am glad to have it. I told him that I am fifty-four, and Dr. Griffith made nothing of it. Dear Aunt is so loving and motherlike; but she sympathises in the cause, which is a comfort to me. It would have been very painful had she disapproved,—almost as painful as if my favourite sister had disapproved. Dr. G.'s visit really refreshed me.'

TO THE SAME.

'On board the Nova Scotia,
May 27, 1875.

'I did not think that I should have had an opportunity of having a letter posted from Derry, but it appears that I shall. I am now quietly scudding over the Atlantic. There is not much motion in the vessel, which seems to me to be a very large one. There are a great many emigrants, but I doubt whether it will be easy for me to communicate with them.

'You who are so kindly anxious about my comfort will be pleased to know that I have a very fair amount of wraps, and am more likely to suffer from heat than cold, seeing that my cabin port-hole is never opened, and that the only way of ventilating it is by leaving the door open,—a thing not to be thought of at night, as ladies' and gentlemen's cabins are not at all in separate parts of the vessel. By-the-by, the latter part of that long sentence will not please you. I should have broken the paragraph into two. I have at present the luxury of having the cabin all to myself, and only hope that when we touch at the Irish port, we will take in no fair passenger to share it.

'Now I think I will go on deck.... I am perfectly well at present. The only thing I fear is using up my oxygen at night. I have had such a nice letter of welcome from Mrs. Elmslie.'[21]

CIRCULAR LETTER TO SEVERAL OF THE FAMILY.

'June 5, 1875.

'"Yes, you will see icebergs, plenty, more than enough," said the Captain to me on the 3rd. "This is an exceptional year for ice." He spoke so quietly that I did not at the time give full significance to his words.

'But on the next day, the 4th, we beheld icebergs indeed,—I believe more than a hundred, and some, O how glorious! Our eyes were satiated with beauty. Now a bold iceberg rose before us, reminding me of pictures of Gibraltar; but this berg was all of snow,[22] and, as well as we could guess, about 150 feet high. Then another, most graceful in shape, appeared, like a sculptured piece of alabaster, wearing a huge jewel of pale greenish blue; this, from its pure beauty, Louis called "The Maiden." We turned from its softer loveliness, to gaze on that which I thought the finest iceberg of all, the ruins of some huge amphitheatre.

'As we gazed, some of the bergs changed greatly in shape. The "Maiden" split quite in two. Fancy these glorious wanderers from Greenland or Labrador, with the sea-spray dashing against their sides, showing that they were aground; for, as you are aware, the mass of ice below water is far greater than that which is visible above it. One could not but think, "What a mercy it is that we did not pass those large icebergs in the night!" Had our great emigrant-ship, freighted with 2000 tons of iron, dashed up against one of them, we should have gone to the bottom like lead. Nothing more would have been heard of the *Nova Scotia*, and the more than 600 mortals on board.

'But the day was clear, and it was easy to give the bergs a wide berth. Every one's spirits rose. There was nothing but enjoyment of the beautiful scene, admiration at the strange sights before us. The sun at length sank; but a few icebergs loomed in the distance, and I had an idea that we had almost come to the end of the ice-tract. We had delightful music in the saloon, and all appeared cheerfulness and peace. Even when my attention was directed to strange dark objects on the ocean, which I could see through the round saloon window, no thought of danger came into my mind.

'At the invitation of another lady I went on deck, where I was able better to watch the strange scene before me. Out of the ice-tract, indeed! Why, we were in the very midst of *thousands* upon *thousands* of masses of floating ice, through which the vessel very, very cautiously as it were felt her way, sometimes stopping altogether. Strange to say, even when I heard the keel *grate* over ice, it was very, very slowly that I received the impression of danger. The night was exquisitely lovely, the stars shining gloriously. I could hardly have supposed that any star would have cast such a reflection on the smoothest water as Mars threw on the still ocean.

'The brightness of the starlight, the quietness of the water, greatly added to our chance of safety. One felt that a watchful and skilful captain was cautiously piloting us, avoiding the larger masses of ice, though our vessel passed right over some of the little ones. I watched the tiny globes of phosphoric light which sometimes gleamed on the water, and the dark objects which I knew to be pieces of floating ice. There was pleasure in watching them; for though reason at last convinced one that danger there must be under the circumstances, a touch of fear, or rather sense of danger, rather enhances enjoyment.

'I was tired, but lingered on deck, till a lady came up to me, and suggested that we had better go below, as she believed that lights were put out at eleven, and if we did not go we might have to retire to bed in the dark. Down I descended to my cabin in the lower part of the vessel. Some of the passengers on deck had been considering the possibility, on so fair a night, and with Newfoundland near,—for we had sighted the light on shore,—of our being saved by the boats, even should the vessel be lost. But we remembered that there were more than 600 persons on board. The Captain would do well, if he could manage to place half the number in the boats. It was clear that all could not expect to be saved.

'When I went to my cabin, I was not disposed at once to go to rest. I knelt on my sofa, so as to be able to look out from my port-hole on the ocean and its numerous floating fragments of ice, seen in the starlight. Not only was the sense of sight exercised, but that of hearing. Nine times I thought that I heard the keel grate against the ice. I may possibly be mistaken in the number of times; but the noise was distinct, and its nature not to be mistaken. At a short distance—it did not look a hundred yards—the clear, smooth sea appeared to be skirted by a tall hedge. It was not *land*, for occasionally I saw a light gleam through it. I asked a seaman afterwards what it was,—it was, as I suspected, a bank of fog between us and the coast of Newfoundland.

'I watched till my cabin-light went out, and I was left in darkness, save that my port-hole looked like a pale moon in the dark cabin. I turned into my berth, but not at once to sleep. I lay thinking, reflecting on the possibility of feeling the vessel going down, down,—and reflecting on what an easy death drowning would be. Still, I did *not* really expect to be drowned.

'The vessel stopped dead still,—I listened for the sound of pumping, or of preparing boats. I heard one—to me—strange noise, I can hardly describe it, between a blast and a bellow. I thought that it must be a signal, and I was not wrong; for I hear this morning that it was the fog-whistle from the shore. It seemed to me that it was useless for me to rise; if there were any use in my returning to the deck, dear Louis would call me. He would be sure to think of my life before his own.

'After a while I went fast asleep, and did not awake till the bright, clear morning, when there could no longer be the shadow of danger. I rose, dressed, and went on deck. The sea was beautifully smooth, blue, and clear from ice, except a few bergs in the distance. I had a happy, thankful heart.

'One lady had remained on deck till past three. She told me of a field of ice, and great masses of ice, through and beside which we had passed; and she had seen the Northern Lights, which I am sorry to have missed. The Captain never slept till the drift-ice was passed. He was at breakfast, however, this morning, and I doubt not felt very thankful. I believe that he has had three anxious, wakeful nights; but the change in the weather must have been a very great help to him. We had had such miserable dull weather, and such heavy rolling seas. Last night all was so clear; and I saw the stars, I think, for the first time since our starting. Please pass this letter on; for I cannot write over the same thing to all dear ones.'

TO MRS. J. BOSWELL.

'On board a huge River Steamer,
June 9, 1875.

'Here we are steaming up the St. Lawrence to Montreal.... Quebec is a wondrously fair city.... We went this morning to see the Montmorency Fall, a cascade where a great volume of water churned into foam dashes down a precipice 300 feet high....

'June 10.

'I finish this off in Montreal, a very handsome, thriving-looking city, with far grander buildings than Quebec: but it wants the dreamlike, exquisite beauty of its sister. More kindness meets us here.... Have you seen the account of the loss of the *Vicksburg* in the ice, just three days before we encountered the ice off the same coast? Only five sailors saved; not one passenger! We should have gone down faster than the poor *Vicksburg*, because of our heavier cargo. I should not have had a chance; and my gallant Louis would probably have lost his (life), because he would never have deserted me.'

Although Charlotte Tucker's Indian life lay still in the future, this seems to be the right place for quoting a few words from her pen, written after years of toil in the East. Her mind was plainly reverting to the voyage above described:—

'It seems strange that the idea of an ice-bound vessel should suggest itself to a Missionary, working in the "glowing East"; yet it is so. We, in Batala, seem for years to have been labouring to cut a passage through hard, cold ice, with the chilly bergs of Muhammadanism and Hinduism towering on either hand. But though channels which had been laboriously opened may be closed, *the crew are by no means disheartened.* The worst of the winter is now, we hope, over. We see on various sides cracks in the ice. A Brahmin convert, brave and true, has been like a bright fragment broken from the berg, helping somewhat to throw it off its balance. The way is becoming more open, and there are tokens of melting below the surface of the ice. We know that one day of God's bright sunshine can do more to make a clear way than our little picks can accomplish.'

CHAPTER XV
1875 BESIDE NIAGARA

There can be no mistake about Charlotte Tucker's enjoyment of fresh sights and scenes across the Atlantic, or about the fact that increasing years had at least not dimmed her appreciation of beauty. Most kind and warm hospitality was shown to her at Quebec, at Montreal, and at Toronto. She was met at Oakville Station by her younger nephew, Charles Tucker,—the latter in 'a state of joyous expectation' which had kept him awake through three previous nights. Then followed a welcome from his wife, in their 'pretty little home,' elsewhere described by her as 'a Canadian settler's little farmhouse.'

While there, finding the life quiet, and plenty of time on her hands, she 'took to Persian characters,' as 'an interesting riddle to solve,' and also worked hard at her Hindustani, spending many hours over both.

Also she insisted on doing in Canada as Canadians do,—making her own bed, and even essaying to accomplish some ironing. Perhaps the last attempt did not meet with brilliant success. She wrote home about it:—

'"Though seldom sure if e'er before

That hand had ironed linen o'er ..."

the great matter is that the things are *clean*; but I own I am glad that I shall have a *dhobi* in India.'

Another day she wrote to Mrs. Hamilton: 'The little maid here amuses me. She is very fond of music, and likes me to sing for her. She asked me—kindly—if I would like my boots cleaned, and as I thought that I should, the little dear cleaned them, and brought them to me to show off her work,—as a six-year-old child of the house might have done. She looks such an innocent duck!'

An expedition to Niagara was achieved with much success; after which she wrote to one of her aunts in England: 'My nephews think me amazingly strong, and yet I have become almost a teetotaller. Except your little bottle of sherry, I have only tasted wine twice since I left you. How I did enjoy your lemon-juice!'

Her glowing description of the Falls themselves, sent to Mrs. Hamilton, must be at least in part quoted. Though an oft-related tale, it may perhaps gain some freshness from her mode of telling it:—

'Clifton House, Niagara Falls,
'June 22, 1875.

'I must write to some dear one while the sound of Niagara is in my ears, whilst the impression of Niagara is fresh in my mind; and I direct my letter to you, sweet Laura, knowing that you will let others see it....

'I have looked on the most glorious scene, I believe, that is to be seen on this planet. How can I attempt to describe Niagara? When I gaze on what is called "The American Fall," I ask myself a dozen times, "Is it possible that there can be anything more beautiful?" ... though I have only to turn my head a little to behold the "Horse-Shoe Fall," which is even *more* gloriously beautiful. The American Fall would make in itself twenty or thirty cascades that would delight us in England. O the sparkling rush of diamonds,— the white misty foam breaking on the picturesque rocks beneath,—the accessories so beautiful,—the cloud-like veil so transparently lovely!

'Earth here is so fair, with bold crags draperied with the richest foliage, that one could imagine her contending for the palm with water; but water carries the victory at Niagara; Earth but serves to frame and set off her magnificence. If Earth be green, so is water. Where Niagara plunges over her Horse-Shoe-shaped rocks, the colour of the water is often brilliant, crystal-like green. Then as the river emerges from its veil of spray,—spray sometimes rising pyramid-like for hundreds of feet,—it assumes a deeper green, more blue than that of the surrounding foliage, but pure in tint.

'A lovely, most verdant island, Goat Island, divides the two grand Falls,—or, I may rather say, three, for one glorious cascade is called Central Fall. In this exquisite island, and other smaller ones, you wander amongst silent shady woods, or stand so close to the rushing waters, that one or two steps would send you over the brink into the cloudy chasm below. Perhaps, Laura, nothing can better convey to you the impression left on me, than to tell you what was my repeatedly recurring thought. "If I had to suffer martyrdom, in no form could it appear more attractive than by being thrown over Niagara!" To be launched into eternity, shrouded in that cascade of diamonds, would rouse such a thrilling sense of the beautiful and the sublime, that half one's fears would be swallowed up in something almost like joy. It would seem ten times more horrible to be flung from a high tower on to the hard, cold earth. This is not a mere fancy of my own. I find that I am not alone in thinking that death would appear less repulsive at Niagara than elsewhere.[23]

'I have seen the many beauties of this place well.... I have looked on the rapids above the Falls. They seemed to me an emblem of human life. Such a rushing,—such a hurry,—chafing against obstacles,—impatience, passion, excitement. Then comes the grand leap—boldly, almost joyously, taken,—the leap into cloud and mystery,—and below, the river emerges from froth and foam, comparatively calm. One wonders that it is as quiet as it appears to be after such a plunge!

'Yes, I shall never see such a sight again, till I behold the Great White Throne, and the Sea of Glass, like unto crystal.

'We all wandered about yesterday, till we were too much tired to wander more. We had intended to sit up to see moonlight on Niagara; but instead of so doing we separated at 9. I soon fell asleep, but I woke in the dim twilight, I suppose at about 3 a.m. The opportunity was not to be lost. I washed and dressed, as much by feeling as by sight, opened my venetian shutters, and walked out into the verandah which commands a fine view of both Falls.

'I was in utter solitude, under the light of the moon. Not in silence, for the sound of many waters is unceasing. I suppose that for thousands of years Niagara has been praising her Creator, as she does now. The sound is not at all *noisy*; on the contrary, it does not disturb conversation, which surprises me.

'I sang snatches of the Hallelujah Chorus, as I looked on the waterfall by moonlight. There was no distinct play of moonbeams on the water; there was an immense amount of mist,—one felt as if looking down on clouds. Presently the clouds in the sky flushed rosy in the dawn; the moon grew pale; Niagara with her emerald green more distinct. I waited till I had seen the sunrise—it was not a very bright one—

and then I retired to my room, and went to sleep again.... Solitude is congenial at Niagara.... I do not care to write on trifling themes now....

'A thought came to my mind as I was resting just now. As photographs, however faithful, convey but a very inadequate idea of the real Niagara, so must our highest conceptions of Heaven fall short of Heaven itself. Who that has merely seen a photograph, or many photographs, of the Falls, can drink in the beauty of the living, bounding, changing, glorious miracle of Nature, which is beheld here? Yet Niagara itself is but a bubble, compared with "the glory which shall be revealed."'

Towards the end of July she returned home, to spend a few last weeks with her dear ones before bidding them a long farewell and going forth to her Indian campaign. Through all these weeks she does not seem to have relaxed in her persevering study of Hindustani, or in her struggle with the difficult gutturals which had to be mastered. Apart from this she must have had enough to occupy her time. Among lesser employments, she is said to have spent hours at a time in looking through her papers and letters—the collection of a literary lifetime—and consigning masses of the same to destruction. One cannot but wish that the destruction had been less wholesale.

The Dismissal Meeting of Missionaries was on the 11th of October; and two or three days later the *Strathclyde* sailed.

To most of her relatives the parting was a good deal softened by the conviction that Charlotte Tucker would surely soon find herself compelled to give in, and to return to England. One of her nieces can say: 'We all thought, when she left us for India, that she would fail in health, and be obliged to come home again. And so I could stand at the doorway, and watch her as she turned round in our carriage to wave her last good-bye, without any misgiving that it was indeed the last time that I should see that bright smile.'

But her sister, Mrs. Hamilton, the loved Laura of early days, had a truer prescience of how things would be. Speaking afterwards to a friend about that day of parting, and about the intense, loving devotion which had always existed between them, she said: 'When my sister and I parted from one another, it was a parting for ever on Earth. My sister will not return to England on furlough, as other Missionaries do, for the reason that she could not again go through the pain of separation.'

At the time little was said in letters about that heart-rending pain. It had to be endured, and it was endured courageously.

So ended the fifty-four years of Charlotte Maria Tucker's English Life. She turned herself now, with a smile of good cheer, to the eighteen years of her Indian Life—the Evening of her days. Three-quarters of her tale is told, counting by years. Only one-quarter remains to be told.

Fifty-four years of preparation; and then the Evening of hard toil. Fifty-four years given to slow perfecting of the instrument; and then eighteen years of use for that instrument. This was what it came to. Not that her English life had been without its uses and its fruits; but the long, quiet home-existence had doubtless been mainly a making ready—or rather, a being made ready—for that which was to come after. The first was subordinate to the second.

Was it very long preparation for comparatively short work? But the worth of work done does not depend upon the length of time occupied in the doing. We may better understand this if we think of our Blessed Lord's Life,—the Thirty Years of silent preparation and waiting; and then the Three Years' Ministry. Each moment of His Life upon Earth bore fruit; but none the less, those Thirty Years were mainly of preparation for what should follow.

There are some who would not agree with Charlotte Tucker in considering 'Missionary work of all work the highest'; yet in one sense, if not in all senses, it certainly is so. The soldier who goes on a forlorn-hope expedition ranks higher in the minds of men than the soldier who remains in camp; and the pioneer is counted worthy of more honour than the settler.

We hear in these days many a careless sneer levelled at attempts to convert the Heathen, at the uselessness and fruitlessness of such efforts. Nothing is easier than for a man, sitting at home in his luxurious arm-chair, to flout those who go forth into heathen lands. And there is a certain trick of seeming common-sense in the arguments used, which sounds convincing. So much money spent, and so many lives sacrificed,—and for what? Half-a-dozen converts, perhaps, in a dozen years, some of whom prove in the end to be faithless, while others are very far from being faultless saints. Is the result worth the outlay?

As for the characters of some of the converts, we only have to look at home, and to see for ourselves what the average civilised and well-taught and highly-trained Englishman is—how very far in a large majority of cases from being either blameless, or saintly, or entirely faithful to his Baptismal vows. After that glance, one may feel less surprised to hear of failures among young and untrained converts, the whole *pull* of whose previous lives has been utterly adverse to Christianity; not to speak of the baneful effects of a surrounding heathen atmosphere, always present after conversion.

But as to the main argument, — whether the result is worth the outlay, — I should be disposed to say at once frankly that, from a purely mercantile point of view, it certainly is *not*. Very often indeed the immediate results, seen to follow upon Missionary work, are not at all commensurate with the amount of money spent. Many a Missionary has given his time, his income, his life, his all, for the sake of no apparent results in his own lifetime. There have been grand men, who have toiled steadily on through ten years, twenty years, thirty years; and at the close, if they have had any converts at all to show for their labours, those converts could be counted on their fingers.

It may well be that one man brought out of the darkness of heathendom is a prize worth fifty times — or five thousand times — the money expended in bringing him. But this would not be seen from the mercantile point of view. Neither does it touch the true gist of the question.

A little story told of the great Duke of Wellington, so ardently admired by Charlotte Tucker, shall supply us with a clue here. Whether or no the tale itself be genuine hardly affects its value as bearing on the subject. A young clergyman is stated to have one day, in the presence of the Duke, spoken about foreign Missions in the disparaging terms often affected by a particular class of young men. One can exactly picture how he did it, — the supercilious contempt of one who knew little about the matter; and the careless looking down upon all who did not agree with himself. But the Iron Duke is said to have responded sternly: —

'Sir, you forget your marching orders, — "Go ye into all the world, and preach the Gospel to every creature!"'

If the Duke did not speak the words, they sound very like what he would have spoken. It is a soldier's view of the matter, and it is the view which all true 'soldiers and servants of Christ' ought to take. For this is no question of mercantile views, of business arrangements, of what will or will not repay, of so many converts more or less, of success and failure. This is not in any wise a question of results. It is purely and simply a question of Obedience. The Church generally is commanded to preach the Gospel throughout the world; whether men will hear, or whether they will not. Individuals are bound to go, *if called*, — and if not themselves called, they are bound to send others.

All of us who are Baptized in the Name of the Father, and of the Son, and of the Holy Spirit, are bound to His Service who is our Royal Master; and His orders we have unquestioningly to obey. Whether or no we can see the wisdom, the necessity, of what He commands to be done, makes no difference. We are but privates in His Army; and a private has no business with an opinion of his own as to where he shall go or what he shall do in the time of war.

When the 'noble six hundred' of Balaclava were ordered to charge the Russian guns, they knew the uselessness of the act, the certainty of a blunder; but with that they had no concern.

> 'Their's not to make reply,
> Their's not to reason why,
> Their's but to do and die!'

And though with our Royal Master we have no fear of mistakes, the same spirit of absolute obedience must be ours, whether or no we fully see the reasons for each command. What would be thought of an English soldier who, on being ordered to some lonely and difficult post, were, instead of going at once, to begin to calculate whether it were worth while, — whether the cost and trouble of his going would be sufficiently repaid by results? Yet such is the spirit in which certain soldiers of the Cross — somewhat faithless soldiers, surely! — are disposed to regard this great Marching Order of our Captain and King.

Another way of looking upon the question is embodied in certain popular ideas that, on the whole, the Heathen may be hardly worse off as Heathen than they would be as Christians. The less knowledge, the less responsibility, we are told; and a good deal of cant is talked on this subject. Those who have seen how things verily are in heathen lands, those who have witnessed the awful and desperate cruelties which there prevail, know what the argument is worth as to the present life. While as to the future, — let it be fully granted that ignorance means few stripes, that every excuse will be made for those who did not and could not know better, that increase of knowledge must of necessity mean increase of responsibility. But there again we come back to our 'marching orders.' If Christ died for the heathen, if God wills that they shall know the Truth and shall at least have it in their power to rise thereby to higher levels, what are we to dare to decide that they shall be left in darkness?

The whole question of our duty as Christians, on this point as on all others, hinges here, — Are we doing, or are we not doing, that which God wills us to do? All theories respecting outlays, values, results, sink into utter insignificance beside this question. If we are called to go, it is not for the sake of honour, it is not for the sake even of success, but it is simply for the doing of the Will of God. If we are bidden to remain at home, it is still for the doing of His Will,—and that Will includes the spreading of the Church of Christ throughout the world. Those who stay at home can at least help those who go on this mission.

In the matter of results very unreasonable expectations are often formed. The best results do not commonly appear at once, and may not appear for a lifetime. A farmer ploughs his land, then sows his seed, and then waits months for the harvest. The Church too frequently scratches the hard ground with an impatient hand, drops in a few seeds, and immediately breaks into lamentations, because no instantaneous harvest springs forth.

It may take twenty years merely to plough the hard ground in some heathen spot, and to sow the seed; and years more may pass before the first tokens of a harvest are seen. Sometimes the fuller results are the longer delayed. Mustard-seeds spring up a good deal faster than acorns.

The main work of Charlotte Tucker's eighteen years was to be that of ploughing. And whether few or many converts rewarded her toil is an entirely secondary consideration. They would have been very gratifying to her own feelings, no doubt; and that said, all is said. Results there were; but not all kinds of results can be reckoned upon one's fingers. Charlotte Tucker went out in obedience to what she felt to be the Divine call, the Divine command. So long as she was steadily endeavouring to do the Will of God, results might very well be left in His Hand. The Word of God does not return to Him void; but naturally its working is not always apparent to us.

PART II
LIFE IN INDIA

'O Spirit of the Lord, prepare
All the round Earth her God to meet;
Breathe Thou abroad like morning air,
Till hearts of stone begin to beat.

'Baptize the Nations; far and nigh
The triumphs of the Cross record;
The Name of Jesus glorify
Till every kindred call Him Lord.'

CHAPTER I
A.D. 1875 FIRST ARRIVAL IN INDIA

In the second week of October 1875, Miss Tucker left English shores, never to return. The voyage was uneventful, differing therein from her trip to Canada. On its very next voyage the good ship *Strathclyde*, which carried her to the East, went down within sight of Dover. But no threatenings of such a catastrophe disturbed A. L. O. E. on her way out.

A fellow-passenger on board the *Strathclyde* wrote long afterwards:—

'My first introduction to A. L. O. E. was when I was lying in all the helplessness of the first days of my first voyage, quite unable to stir from the deck. I became conscious of a grey-haired lady stooping over me, offering some *eau de cologne*, and with a winning smile asking if she could do anything for me. She was a good sailor, and in those miserable days moved about amongst the sea-sick passengers like an angel of mercy. Even then dear Miss Tucker looked very frail and delicate; and one could scarcely have expected that she would be spared for eighteen years to work in all the heat and discomfort of India. One thing remarkable about her on that voyage was the influence she had over the men on board,—some of them quite indifferent, if not hostile, to religion. No one could withstand her genial, loving ways; and it was a sight to be remembered, to see her gathering the young fellows round the piano, while she led off in some old English ditty.'

Her own letters to Mrs. Hamilton, while on board, are cheery as usual, and speak no word of pain or longing for all that she had left behind; indeed the very first ends merrily: 'Please give my kindest love to your dearest girl, and tell her that I have already hung up her famous bag. I hope that no ayah will *bag* it! I could not resist the pun, bad as it is.'

There were five ayahs on board, and she soon struck up an acquaintance with one of them,—a Christian ayah,—reading aloud her Hindustani Bible, and delighted to find that the ayah could understand what was read. 'I am bribing one to teach me,' she wrote. 'The ayahs ought to be glad to help; for they, at least two or three of them, seem to regard me as a kind of supplementary nurse, and if they want to go to work make over the baby to me.' In the same letter she states: 'We have a strong Missionary force on board; two Scotchmen, the wife of one of them, and six Missionary ladies. We have not quarrelled at all; but then, most of us have been seasick!'—again a little glimmer of fun. 'We lady Missionaries get on very well together,' she says in another letter. 'Very gentle and modest are the Misses A., "your pretty girls," as Lady I. called them to-day.'

As to amusements on board, she wrote:—

'Lady I. has started a game which dear Leila and Fred may add to their store at Christmas. She wrote something, missing out all adjectives. A gentleman went round and collected adjectives haphazard from the passengers, inserting them in the places left blank. The piece was then read out. It was a description of the voyage and many of the passengers. Of course nobody could be offended, because the adjectives came haphazard. But how your young folk would have laughed when, amongst other personages described, came—"Miss Tucker, of a *grandiloquent* disposition, with other *bouncing* Missionary ladies."'

About a fortnight later she wrote:—

'A contrast to —— is Mr. S., the competition-wallah, probably the most highly educated man in the ship. I look upon him as the Squire of the Mission ladies. In his most quiet, proper fashion, he is ever ready to do our behests; and he never seems to tire of hymn-singing.... He has evidently plenty of moral courage. The very funniest thing was that Mr. S. was actually present at the solemn conclave held by us six M. L.[24] to decide whether we could conscientiously attend a second theatrical amateur performance, *Mr. S. having been the principal actor* in the first one, which we did attend. It was as if Garrick had been present at a Clapham conference on the subject of whether it were right to go to see him act!!! Mr. S. was very amiable and good: he had taken a great deal of trouble to amuse the passengers, and *his* part was perfectly unexceptionable; but if we all absent ourselves next time I do not think that he will take any offence. I proposed that we should all sleep over the matter, one of my reasons being that I could not but feel Mr. S.'s presence a *little* embarrassing. On the following day we met without him, and decided that the question is to be an open one; each M. L. is to judge according to her own conscience. I believe that we shall divide; but this is not, we have agreed, to disturb the harmony between the M. L.'

After a few days spent in 'bright, beautiful Bombay'—these are her own words—she proceeded by rail with one companion to Allahabad. A pause at Jabalpur had been planned, but this fell through; and they accomplished the whole long journey of 845 miles without a break. Wisely, her friends had insisted on first-class, and she was none the worse for the fatigue. On the very morning of her arrival at Allahabad she could say: 'I had a nice warm bath, and then a good breakfast, and I feel almost as fresh as if I had not travelled 845 miles at a stretch, but merely taken a little drive. Think how strong I must be!'

Later in the same letter, a long and cheery one, bearing no signs of fatigue, she speaks of Mr. George Bowen, an American Missionary, who had 'laboured without intermission for twenty-eight years' in the East, and who was known among Natives as 'the English Faqir,' on account of his wandering and self-denying life.

'He will take no salary,' she wrote, 'but has earned his own living, I hear, by teaching, supporting himself on the merest trifle. I esteem it a great honour that I sat beside him at breakfast at the Zenana Mission House last Thursday. Mr. Bowen looks quite skin and bone, wondrously thin, but not in the least unhealthy, but as if there were plenty of work in him still. He told me that he does not "believe in age." He seems to feel as fresh as he did twenty-eight years ago; and yet at the beginning of his career he was so fearfully ill that his life was given up, and he wrote his farewell to his mother. As India has agreed so splendidly with Mr. Bowen, I asked him—as I generally do those who thrive in the climate—whether he drank only water. "Tea," he replied, smiling. He gave his opinion that to take stimulant here is "the way to have to leave the country." Almost all the Missionaries whom I have met appear to be water-drinkers. I am particularly delighted with the American Missionaries whom I have seen.... I am ashamed of ever having had a prejudice against Yankees. I am attracted also by Native Christian ladies.'

On her way up-country she came in for the wedding of a Missionary lady, and after her usual fashion she was most active in helping; working hard at the making of wreaths and at the decoration of the Ludhiana Church porch. As the married pair were about to drive off, rice was brought to be thrown; but somebody present objected to the custom for India, as originally heathen, and liable to be misunderstood.' Then the horses shall have it!' declared Miss Tucker; and with two hands well filled she went to the horse's heads, and fed them, amid much laughter, in which she heartily joined. Her own description of the event is overflowing with spirit and enjoyment. It is dated November 30.

'I have just come in to rest a bit, and wash my soiled hands,—for what do you think that I have been about?—at the express request of the bride, helping to decorate the church for her wedding, which is to come off to-day. This house is jammed full—that is to say, a good deal more full than is comfortable; but the kind folk would not hear of my leaving till after the wedding, so I do not go to my home till to-morrow morning. Indian railways are regardless of convenient hours. I, who was up this morning soon after five, must be up to-morrow morning soon after three. Of course I had to arrive here by starlight; and on the same night there had been another arrival at one a.m. ... There is a grand tamasha[25] about the wedding. Every one seems pleased. It is Missionary wedding Missionary, and—perhaps I had better go and make myself useful....

'*Later.* Oh, such a pretty wedding! The little church fresh white-washed within, clean as a wedding-cake. The porch almost like a bower. A border of flowers on either side up the centre made a kind of path. Then the presence of the school-girls in their white chaddahs; the number of Natives in their picturesque costumes,—both Christians and heathen, inside the church and looking in from the outside,—all made a charming scene.

'But before we went to church, a Begum, a royal lady, granddaughter of Shah-Soojah, came to see the fun. And only fancy, Laura, I was left for perhaps a quarter of an hour to entertain the fine old lady. Would not your Fred and Leila have laughed to have seen me, making gallant efforts to keep up conversation with my dreadfully bad Hindustani. I dashed at it, tried to explain why I wore a black dress when I had lilac and blue ones at Amritsar, told her that I had never been married, answered questions regarding my family, etc. The Begum laughed, and I laughed, for I knew that my Hindustani was very bad; but I did remember always to use the respectful "Ap"[26] to the princess.

'Presently the dear old Missionary, Mr. Rudolph, appeared. The "pardah"[27] lady, on seeing a man, hid behind an arm-chair. But when I told her that it was "Rudolph Sahib," the old lady said that he was her father, and that she would make her salaam to him. I hear that the Begum is almost a Christian, and she can read. Wrapped in her chaddah, she walked with me to church, and stayed through the service. I was close behind her. When it was over, I managed to say a little sentence to her in rather better Hindustani, "The Lord Jesus Christ is here; He gives blessing." The Begum gave a sound of assent.'

Next day, the first of December, Charlotte Tucker reached Amritsar,—the spot which she fully expected to be her home for many a year to come. But Amritsar was only a stage on the road to Batala, where her Indian work really lay.

All who know aught of India know the name of 'The Panjab';[28] that province to the far north, a land of five great rivers, where in Mutiny days so much was done for the preservation of our Indian Empire. Amritsar[29] is one of the larger cities of the Panjab, containing a population of about 135,000 inhabitants,—Hindus, Muhammadans, and Sikhs. It is the Holy City of the Sikhs, and has their 'golden temple,' wherein they worship, and wherein also is kept their sacred book, the 'Granth.'

Missionary work has been mainly carried on in the Panjab by the Church Missionary Society; just as, in many parts of Bengal, Missionary work has been mainly carried on by the Society for the Propagation of the Gospel. Where the one great Church Society has obtained a footing, the other great Church Society does not interfere in either case, but goes elsewhere in the Mission field. It is greatly to be wished that this spirit of courtesy were more widely seen in the working of Missions generally among the heathen. During late years the ladies of the Church Zenana Society have come in as an additional help to the Societies above-named,—as true 'handmaids,' alike in the Panjab and in other parts of India.

The Mission premises are about half-a-mile distant from the City of Amritsar. A. L. O. E.'s first Indian home was here; in a bungalow, surrounded by a large compound or garden which was part of the Mission premises. When she arrived, in the beginning of December, roses were in full bloom, as well as abundantly-flowering shrubs and creepers. The great banyan-tree, which grew and still grows in front of the bungalow, was soon named by Miss Tucker 'The Mission Tree.'

A warm welcome was given to her by the Missionary ladies living there:—Miss Emily Wauton, who still labours on in the same spot, though nearly twenty years have passed since that day; Mrs. Elmslie, widow of Dr. Elmslie, the Pioneer of Missionary work in Cashmere; Miss Florence Swainson; and Miss Ada Smith;—not to speak of the C.M.S. Missionary gentleman living close by.

After her wont, Miss Tucker was very eager, very bright, very anxious to become immediately one of the little circle. That first evening, as they sat round the table, she said: 'I don't want to be "Miss Tucker" here. Can't you all call me "Charlotte Maria"?' The ladies naturally demurred. 'We could not possibly,' they said. Miss Tucker's face fell a little; then came a happy thought, and she brightened up. 'Call me "Auntie,"' she said. 'So many call me "Auntie." All of you must do so.'

'But we cannot directly. We don't know you yet,' objected the others again.

She was very much delighted when Mr. Rowland Bateman, one of the Missionaries, began the same evening, without hesitation, to speak to her as 'Auntie.'

Soon after, news came of the death of her brother, Mr. Henry Carre Tucker. It was needful to arrange for her mourning; and pending the arrival of other things, one of the younger ladies offered to alter for her an old black silk dress which she had. Going to her room, the young lady knocked and said, 'Miss Tucker, may I have the dress now?' No answer. Another attempt;—and 'No Miss Tucker here!' was the result. 'Unless you call me "Auntie," you will not have it.' 'But how can I so soon? I don't know you yet,' was once more the unavailing plea. Miss Tucker had her way, however; and thenceforward she became 'Auntie' to an ever-increasing circle of nephews and nieces in India.

Some extracts from her own letters, written to Mrs. Hamilton in the December of 1875, will give, far better than words of mine can do, the impressions received in her new position.

'December 2, 1875.

'It is early morning, before 6 a.m., my first morning in my new home. A cock has been crowing, otherwise everything is profoundly still. I hear a cart in the distance. You will like to hear something of my surroundings.

'Mrs. Elmslie came to meet me at the station; also Mr. Clark and Mr. Baring. It was slightly bewildering, for, says Mr. Clark, "the Bishop wants to see you; he and Miss Milman are to go off by this train." Now the thought most in my mind was, "I won't let poor dear Miss F.[30] think that I desert her for new acquaintances." She also was going on by the train; but there was a pause at Amritsar station for perhaps a quarter of an hour. So I had to be agreeable to the Bishop, Miss F., and all,—and keep Mrs. Elmslie waiting besides.

'This is a splendid room of mine ... about twenty-four feet each way, and so lofty. I am surprised at the elegance of these Indian bungalows. Please put from your mind all idea of *hardship*.[31] I have now lived in four bungalows, and all have elegant rooms, and there is such an air of refinement that I have great doubts whether it would be the correct thing to put out my hand and take a slice of bread off a plate. Mrs. Elmslie is a lovely lady, tall, slight, fair; but however tall, a lady every inch of her; she might be a Countess with her meek dignity....'

'December 9.

'I directed *via Brindisi* my sad letters to the almost broken-hearted mourners, and I thought, "I will write no more by this mail. I should only write on one theme, my precious, noble Henry." But I have since thought that I was wrong in this determination. My own sweet Laura will be closing a heavy year.... If I can turn the channel of sad thoughts, it is better that I should write, and not only on one theme. She will like to hear of my home and my work, and I ought to write to the darling!...

'What shall I say of Mrs. Elmslie? She is one of a million. I never met with any woman in my life so like an angel without wings. Tall, fair, elegant, graceful, with a face that Ary Scheffer might have chosen to paint for a seraph,—her soul seems to correspond to her external appearance. Saintly as she is, she is not in the *least* gloomy; she tries to make all happy, and is business-like and practical. Fitted to grace a drawing-room, she throws her heart into school-work, and seems to manage the house beautifully. It will give you an idea how winning she is, when I tell you that Miss Wauton and Miss Hasell call Mrs. Elmslie "Mother," "Mother dear," though the name seems strange from one who looks quite as old as herself. You should see Mrs. Elmslie with a black baby in her arms, looking at it with such loving tenderness and pleasure too, just as its guardian angel might....

'I must not fill up all my letter with my sweet friend, and it is nearly time that I should take my morning walk. I always take a rapid one in the compound, which is large, with a good many trees and nice flowering shrubs in it. I hope always to keep up the habit, which is so very conducive to health; but of course I shall not walk so *fast* when the hot weather comes.

'It may give you a little idea of life here, if I describe yesterday's occupations.

'I rose about six, dressed, and wrote a little. My Ayah brought me early breakfast. I went out and took my walk, then returned and prepared for my Munshi.[32] He is a convert, and was baptized last month, with his two little children. The Maulvi, as we call him, is a dear good man, but too indulgent for a teacher. He is not particular enough in correcting my faults. I have an hour with him before breakfast; and after the meal comes family worship—the morning hymn, prayer, and chapter, always in Urdu.

'After prayers yesterday I returned for a short time to my room and occupations. I was engaged to go to "the city"— within the walls of Amritsar—with Mrs. Elmslie; for it is desirable that I should see work going on. The conveyance is a kind of large box of a carriage, contrived to let in air and keep out sun. Yesterday we went to four native houses; Mrs.

Elmslie went to a fifth, but went alone. Such strange narrow lanes one has to go through; sometimes on foot where the gari could not go, mounting up to the first floor of the houses by very steep steps....

'We returned home after our city visits, and had dinner. Yesterday being Wednesday, after dinner we went to church; we always attend the *Native* church. As the prayers are a translation of our own Liturgy, I can join in them well enough, but I can yet make very little of the sermon....

'I find it a good plan to go to Mrs. Elmslie's Orphanage, and sit and listen to the lessons, and thus learn myself. The girls in their white chaddars[33] look, generally speaking, well and happy. I was to have amused some of the younger ones last Sunday with Bible pictures; but when I had had the sad letters I gave up my intention of helping sweet Mrs. Elmslie in this way. I hope to do so another time.'

'*December 13.*

'I have so much to interest me here, and every one is so kind.... I call this bungalow "House Beautiful," on account of the dwellers within it. It is also a nice refined place, with an extensive compound, and plenty of trees and flowers. If I were not so busy I should like to send you a sketch of it; but daylight seems too short for what I want to do; and when once my mouth is really opened, I shall feel as if I never could get through all the interesting work that is to be done. The ladies here have a kind of general superintendence of twenty-two schools—*not* Christian—but where they are allowed to teach the Bible. Fancy what an opening!'

TO MISS 'LEILA' HAMILTON.

'*Dec. 13.*

'There are some things in Indian life which would strike you as curious. For instance, I have *five* glass doors to my bedroom. One alone is never opened ... but through all the others people, especially my Ayah, come in; and she never knocks.... Folk can walk in from the outside of the house through two of my glass doors. It is a very public sort of living, but it is Indian fashion. The great thing is to let in abundance of air; and where air comes in other things come in too. I have, however, "chick" blinds to my outer doors; these are made of thin split bamboos; and if I let them down, no one can see in. Of course they would not keep out my dear little Ayah; she can always pop in by lifting the chicks. She is the only one who really laughs at my bad Urdu.... My Munshi laughs a little, but not in the same way. He is gentle and pleasing.'

TO MRS. HAMILTON.

'*Dec. 21.*

'I have been waiting to write to you till the tardy mail should come in. But why wait any longer, when I have always so much to say to my Laura now?—only I lack time—and light—for this is the shortest day, and the houses are built to keep out light, which comes in underneath a heavy verandah, so that I am sometimes obliged to feel rather than to see....

'I did not open my picture-box for some time after my arrival, but when it was opened it would have pleased you to have seen the pleasure given by its contents, including your lovely tidies. Mrs. Elmslie was eager as a girl, settling where the different pictures were to be hung, jumping up on chairs, and keeping us up beyond our usual hour for retiring, for she could not bear to leave the picture-question unsettled. We had consultation, trying this place and that place on the walls, trying to balance sides and keep all things straight. For the angel-lady likes to have everything pretty.... It seems to me as if both England and America had sent their cream to India. But then Amritsar is a specially favoured place.... As is natural where the Missionaries are first-rate, there is a great deal of leaven working amongst the heathen.'

TO MISS 'LEILA' HAMILTON.

'*Dec. 23.*

'Though I posted a letter to your sweet Mother only yesterday, perhaps I had better tell you of my visit to the Zenana of —— whilst it is fresh in my mind. Dear C., Miss H., and myself went to-day to visit this Muhammadan house. It is a handsome one, in the midst of fine park-like grounds; and from the lofty verandah we had a better view of part of our city than I have seen before.

'The Muhammadan Sahib has three wives. I suppose that they were the three middle-aged or elderly native women who sat on a bed; the other five women present, old or young, may have been servants; but one of them, a handsome girl, with very dashing nose-ring, and eyelids blackened on the edges, native-fashion, shook hands with us as well as served us. There were a fair number of free-and-easy little dark children playing about. The eldest is C.'s pupil; and one of the first things done was to hear her repeat her part in a kind of catechism—Christian, of course.

'One of the ladies smoked a hookah; had it been even invisible, we should have been made sensible of its presence by an occasional bubble-bubble sound, and then a perfume— to our minds by no means odoriferous. Another lady had her teeth horridly blackened by what she had been chewing; but, generally speaking, the natives' teeth are very nice and white.... I showed off my beautiful chatelaine, your dear Father's gift, which I think pleased; and Miss H. showed hers, which is quite different in style. You must not suppose that this was a mere visit of amusement.... No, we had Bible-reading and hymn-singing; and afterwards C. was evidently holding a religious discussion with the elder lady.

'*Dec. 24.*—I find that only two of the ladies were wives of the Sahib; the third was somebody's relation.

'Mr. Clark[34] approves of my Oriental tale, only he wishes some names altered. He is going to give me a list of names, Muhammadan and Hindu.'

TO MRS. HAMILTON.

'*Christmas Day 1875.*

'I was awakened in the night by the Indian Waits, children singing in the language of the Sikhs ... one of their native airs. My little Ayah came up to me and shook hands when she entered my room early in the morning,—is not this the great Day, and is not she a Christian?—so she may indeed rejoice and be glad in it. I have prepared little presents for the dear ladies here, except C., to whom I gave a wedding-present yesterday. I will pause now, and go on later in the day, when I may better describe our Indian Christmas. 6½ a.m. Orphans singing hymns at the top of their voices. They are evidently very happy. They are to have a Christmas tree.

'*Later.*—I have come home from church, from receiving the Holy Communion. Thank God, the sheaves *are* being gathered in! What would dear Henry Martyn not have given to have seen what I saw to-day? So many Natives remained to share the holy Feast, men and women, young and old,—in our little church there must have been nearly if not quite fifty communicants. I received the Cup from the hand of a Native. I felt the scene quite affecting. It is a great privilege to be in India, and specially now, when the blades are ripening,—though, oh, how few in number, compared with the Muhammadans and heathen!

'After church and luncheon I went to the Orphanage Garden, to help sweet Margaret[35] to deck the Christmas Tree. In less than half an hour the little guests are to be summoned to receive their dolls, tops, books, etc. I expect a charming scene.'

CHAPTER II
A.D. 1875-1876 A HOME IN AMRITSAR

In the previous spring, when first Charlotte Tucker decided to go out, she wrote in one letter a statement of the financial plan to be followed. 'I have arranged with the Society,' she said, 'to pay 200 rupees a quarter for my board and lodging, exclusive of Munshi[36] and conveyance.' For this she had been told to expect a bedroom and a bathroom; meals being taken with the other Missionaries. She had also been told that she would require an Ayah and 'half a tailor.' 'I do not want superfluities,' she wrote; 'for mine is a modest income, and I should not like to spend it all on myself.'

Modest though it might be, she gave away largely, restricting herself to a limited amount, and practising great economy. After being for a while in India, she seems to have been strongly impressed with a dread of needless luxuries, and to have become eager to set an example of extreme simplicity in the Missionary life. The rigid simplicity which she cultivated was, no doubt, partly a matter of pure economy, that she might have the more to give away,—partly a matter of her innate generosity; but partly also it arose from a deep-rooted desire to remove the reproach, which has of late been often levelled at the ease and luxury, real or supposed, of many Missionaries in India or elsewhere.

It is always a difficult question to decide in such cases what does or does not constitute luxury. For example, the number of servants kept, which often startles an Englishman, is unavoidable to some extent, arising from the very low wages given, and the small amount of work which each servant will undertake. Indian servants sleep often in the verandah or in outside huts, and provide their own food out of their small wages; so, keeping several of them is a very different matter from keeping many English servants. Moreover, an Englishman, still more an Englishwoman, labouring in such a climate as that of India, *must* as a matter of simple safety have many things which in England would be entirely needless. To walk any distance under the heat of the Indian sun would for the ordinary European often mean death. To 'rough it,' to brave the climate, to be reckless of hardships, would in the majority of instances be tantamount to suicide. Yet, on the other hand, it may well be that under the guise of necessity some things not necessary have here and there crept in. A story has been told of an officer, himself a hearty supporter of Missions, who received a very unfavourable impression of one particular Missionary from observing the large amount of comfortable furniture which arrived at the said Missionary's bungalow, for the latter's use. The officer felt at once, as he said, that the Missionary 'was not made of the right stuff.' He may have judged hastily, and he may have been mistaken. It is by no means impossible that the Missionary *may* have been 'of the right stuff,' despite his superabundance of home-comforts. Nevertheless, such judgments will be passed, and it is well if Missionaries can live a life that shall render them uncalled for.

The more closely modern Missionaries can approximate to Early Church Missionaries, the better. One can hardly picture S. Paul as settling down in a very luxurious bungalow, with a very huge amount of luggage; and though the conditions of life are greatly changed, and allowance has to be made for the change, yet the principle and spirit of Missionary work remain the same. Things harmless may become harmful, if they prove an actual hindrance to success in the work, if they cause an actual lessening of influence. The question should be,—not, How much may I allow myself?—but, How little can I do with? This was the question asked by Miss Tucker, and she set herself bravely, as the years went on, to test and to prove how much or how little was truly needed.

On first arriving she had of course to do simply as she was told,—not always even that, without protest. When the first Sunday came, she was informed that they would all drive to church. Miss Tucker objected. She did not like horses to be made to work on Sunday. She was told that it was a necessity, but she was not convinced. She would put her large thick shawl over her head, and walk. Nothing could hurt her through that shawl! Others had to yield to her will; not without fears of consequences; and Miss Tucker trudged off alone, with the thick shawl well over her head—heroically half-suffocated. When they all came out of church, she would not wait to be driven, but again severely marched off alone. However, the result of this was so bad a headache—though in general she never suffered at all from headache—that she was once and for all convinced. Evidently she could *not* do in India precisely as in England; and from that time she consented, when it was necessary, to be driven to church like the rest. Of course this question of walking or driving depends largely on the time of year, as well as upon the hour at which the Service is held. As will be seen later, Miss Tucker never lost her habits of good walking until quite late in life; and when the hour of Service or the time of year rendered walking safe, she always preferred it to being driven.

Some friends who knew her best in India have been requested to jot down their recollections, and have most kindly responded. Certain 'sidelights' upon what she was will be best thrown by quotations from two of these papers as to the beginning of her Indian career.

Miss Wauton writes:—

'I have been asked to put down a few reminiscences of A. L. O. E. in her Missionary life in India. But how shall I do it? It seems like being asked to help in painting a rainbow. We can hardly compare her to anything else; so varied, so harmonious, so lovely were the rays of light which she reflected. Spirit and mind were as a clear prism, through which the light of Heaven fell, irradiating the atmosphere in which she lived, and which shone out all the more brightly when seen against the dark clouds of heathendom.

'The first mention of her intention to come out to India reached us in May 1875. Well do I remember the evening when Mr. Clark, coming to our Bungalow, with a letter in his hand, said, 'Who do you think is coming to join you here as a Missionary?—A. L. O. E.!' The title instantly brought to mind books such as *The Young Pilgrim*, *The Shepherd of Bethlehem*, which had delighted us in our childhood's days. And now we were to welcome the well-known and gifted authoress into our house! This *was* a privilege; and earnestly did we look forward to the pleasure of receiving her; though at the same time we were perhaps conscious of a slight shadow of doubt crossing our minds, as to how far one of Miss Tucker's age would be able to accommodate herself to the new surroundings, and bear the trials incident to life and work in a tropical climate.

'If such doubts did occur to us, they were soon dispelled by a closer acquaintance with the object of them. The letters received during the following months by her future fellow-Missionaries showed with what whole-heartedness she was coming forth, prepared from thenceforth to make her *home* in the land of her adoption, and to devote all she was and all she had to the grand work of winning the people of India to Christ....

'Miss Tucker reached Amritsar on the 1st Nov. 1875. The warm kiss with which she greeted her sister-Missionaries showed the affectionate nature; and it was not long before we felt that we had in her, not only a fellow-worker, but a loving and true friend. At her own request the formal "Miss" was soon dropped, and she was always addressed as "Auntie." The family of adopted nephews and nieces, beginning with three or four, gradually widened, till it finally embraced more than twenty members. Nor was this relationship a mere formality. It represented on her part a very special share in the sympathetic interest extended to all fellow-Missionaries, and on their side a reverential love and esteem, which in many cases could not have been deeper, had the tie been one of natural kinship.

'She soon became known amongst the members of the Indian Church as the "Buzurg," or "Honourable" Miss Sahib; and the title of "Firishta" or "angel" was not unseldom heard in connection with her name. And indeed they might well call her so. Every time she spent even a few hours under our roof we felt that we had entertained an angel, though not unawares, so bright were the memories she left behind in loving words and deeds....

'She was so considerate for servants, that she would, during the first hot weather, often stop her pankah-walas at two or three o'clock in the morning, for fear of tiring them. Her face and hands covered with mosquito-bites showed what she endured in practising this self-denial. It took a long time to convince her that there was no hardship in employing these men in night-work, seeing they had plenty of time to rest during the day.

'A. L. O. E. lost no time in beginning to use her pen in the service of India. I think it was the very day after her arrival that she came to us with the MS. in her hand of a little book she had written on her way up-country. It was called *The Church built out of One Brick*; its object being to stir up the Christians of this land to give more liberally, and to work more heartily, for their own Churches. We were amazed, on hearing the little story read, at the wonderful knowledge which Miss Tucker had even then gained, or rather, which she seemed to have intuitively, of the people amongst whom she had come to live. She said, "I want to Orientalise my mind"; but she seemed to have been born with an Oriental mind. Parable, allegory, and metaphor were the very language in which she thought; and her thoughts always seemed naturally to clothe themselves in those figures of speech in which the children of the East are wont to express themselves.

'She always wrote her books in English, as there was never any difficulty in getting them translated into the vernaculars. Many thought that, on this account, she would not care to study the language; but she had no idea of reaching the people only through her pen. She was determined, as far as it was possible, to use her own lips in telling out the message of salvation she had come to bring.

'Accordingly, she was soon hard at work with primer, grammar, and dictionary. At the end of a year she passed the Hindustani Language Examination, and then began Panjabi. She learnt to express herself intelligibly in both these tongues, though the acquisition of them cost her many an hour of hard labour.

'How she did toil over them! I remember, when sharing a room with her once, waking about four o'clock on a cold winter's morning, to see her, already dressed, with a book before her, in which she had herself written in very large printed characters, that she might the more easily read them, a long list of Hindustani and Panjabi words, which she was busily learning off by heart. By this incessant industry she acquired a large vocabulary, and was also soon able to read intelligently many vernacular books, which gave her an insight into the religious life of the people.'

The Rev. Robert Clark writes:—

'I remember well her arrival, when she was received by Mrs. Elmslie and Miss Wauton in the Mission House.... We felt that a spiritual as well as an intellectual power had come amongst us.... Like the great Missionary Swartz, she never went home on furlough; and she never took more than a month's[37] holiday in the year, but remained at her post, hot weather and cold weather, sometimes eleven months, sometimes twelve months in the year, during her whole service....

'Her first endeavour on her arrival in India, as she said, was to seek to "Orientalise her mind." She noticed everything, watched everything around her, sought intercourse with the people, and tried to think with their thoughts and feel with their feelings, and to realise their position and circumstances, in order that she might bring God's Word to bear on them *as they were*. It was in this way only that she could hope to do them good....'

During the greater part of 1876 Miss Tucker remained at Amritsar, cementing her friendship with the ladies there, learning the Hindustani and Panjabi languages, studying the ways of the people, and writing little books for translation into the Native tongues. At her age it was by no means so easy to master a new language as for a younger person;—indeed, hard as she toiled, she never did absolutely master any Indian language colloquially, though for a time she became thorough mistress of the Hindustani grammar and construction. In later years much that she had conquered, with such hard and persevering toil, slipped from her again.

Also, it was less easy for her, than for a younger person, to fall in with *modes* of work, so entirely unlike aught to which she had been accustomed. Her very warm-heartedness and impetuosity were now and then somewhat of a hindrance,—as when, on her first arrival, going into a Zenana, she pressed forward and eagerly shook hands with a bibi,—an Indian lady,—forgetting the difference of Indian customs and English ones. Had it been a Christian bibi, this would not have mattered. As it was, the mistake was so serious, that it might have resulted, and very nearly did result, in the closing of that particular Zenana to all further efforts.

The letters home from this time are so full and so abundant, that the only difficulty lies in selection. By far the larger number are of course to her much-loved sister, Mrs. Hamilton. For the saving of space, it may be understood in the future that letters not especially stated to have been written to any one else, were written to her.

> '*Jan. 8, 1876.*—My expenses have been less than I expected. I think that Margaret must be a very good manager.... I can now form a rough idea of my expenses, and I think my sweet Laura will like to see a rude estimate.[38] As rupees and annas may puzzle you, I write in English fashion—
>
> | | | |
> |---|---|---|
> | Board and Servants (there will be pankahs to pay for), say— | per annum, | £80 |
> | Carriage | " | 15 |
> | Travelling | " | 25 |
> | Munshi, say | " | 10 |
> | Postage, say | " | 5 |
> | Dress, etc., etc. | " | 20 |
> | | | £155 |
>
> 'As I allow myself £270 in India, you see that I have a nice balance to spend; so you may be quite easy, and I quite

thankful, regarding finances. One ought to thank God for independent means; and I am very grateful to my honoured father also.'

FROM MRS. ELMSLIE TO MRS. HAMILTON.

'*Jan. 13.*

'I am sorry to have been unable to write to you sooner, as I should have wished to tell you how much we love your dear sister, and how truly she has already become an honoured and trusted member of our Mission circle. You know her gentle, loving, winning ways too well to doubt our soon learning to love and cherish her; but I dare say you also know her unselfish character so well, that you will often feel anxious lest she should suffer on that account. She had not been one hour with us before I found out that it is her delight to be giving to others the comforts and honours which are due to herself; and it shall be my endeavour that she shall not lose one iota of anything that should help her, or of anything that is truly good for her. Being the housekeeper here, I can manage this....

'Her understanding of the language and character of the people is quite wonderful. I hardly think any one ever read character so clearly and truly as she does,—or so charitably. She sees good in all. And when she must acknowledge some blemishes, she finds some kind excuse for them. "Thinketh no evil" seems written on her brow. I believe she will do much for India, if spared; she sees where teaching is needed, and her ready mind so cleverly weaves the lessons into sweet stories which, when read by the people, will do wonders in opening their minds. I hope she will be persuaded to go to the hills in summer, for this work, which is so peculiarly her own, can be carried on there as well as here, and at one-thousandth part of the expense to physical strength.'

C. M. T. TO MISS 'LEILA' HAMILTON.

'*Feb. 1, 1876.*

'I feel as if one of my chief works here must be to try and keep up the spirits of my poor, anxious, overworked companions. I cannot possibly take much work off their hands; but my loving, clinging Margaret seems to feel it such a comfort to have an *elderly* friend to lean on.'

Towards the end of February Miss Tucker went, with Mrs. Elmslie and two Bible-women, on her first itinerating expedition,—not, as she herself said, to use her lips, but to use her eyes. Writing while away, she says:—

> 'Behold us here, my Queen Lily[39] and I, encamped in the midst of a Sikh village, and living in a tent, without lock or key, with as little sensation of danger as I had at Woodlands or Firlands....
>
> 'It was indeed romantic to travel along that wild path by starlight.... Do you remember the well-known engraving of Una with her lion entering a witch's cave? Now, as I jogged along in my duli,[40] while Margaret rode on her white pony, she made me think of that picture of Una. She is so fair, so graceful, so pure-looking, with her chiselled profile and her sweet expression; I could not make out, however, anything that would do for the lion.
>
> 'Dear Leila's most useful bag is now fastened up in our tent.... Poor Sarah Jones' night-bag is on my bed; please ask dear Leila to tell her so, when she sees her, with my kind remembrances.
>
> 'Oh, a Sikh village is a curious place; built of mud, and pretty thickly populated, it reminds me of an ant-hill. I wonder how such houses stand the rains. The people are not very dark, and they seem to be very friendly. It is not from rudeness that they crowd about one, and examine one's dress.
>
> 'It would have amused you to have seen Margaret and me perambulating the village, going through its muddy lanes; sometimes so narrow that one could have touched the walls on either hand,—or nearly so. Do not suppose that we walked alone. We had wished to take a quiet stroll together, but this was out of the question. We carried a train with us; and when we had entered a tiny court, inhabited by four families, when I raised my eyes I saw a set of spectators perched on the wall above, like so many sparrows, gazing down on the English ladies. One had not in the least the feeling of being amongst enemies,—only once or twice I saw a man look sternly at us. I concluded that these men were Muhammadans, of whom there are, I believe, a few in this village. The Sikhs seem to be a good-humoured, friendly set, who have not the slightest objection to our speaking as much

about our religion as we like. Some of the people here—like the Pandit[41]—know Urdu, but by no means all of them.

'But, Laura, you who have an eye for the picturesque, and a soul for the romantic, you should have had a glimpse of us yesterday in the Pandit's house, at evening prayer! The long mud-built room looked strange enough by day; but at night seen by the gleam of one lamp, it looked—like the entrance to a cave or a catacomb.

'There sat the Pandit on his large mat, and at a little distance his wife on a very small one, the dull lamp throwing their black shadows on the mud wall behind them. A black buffalo calf was at one end of the apartment; but the place was too dark for us to see much of it. The Pandit bending over his book was a study for an artist, with his white turban and his extraordinary spectacles. I was asked to choose the chapter; I chose Romans xii. The Pandit had such difficulty in finding the place, that it seemed evident that he is not familiar with the Epistles. But he must have been pleased with the chapter, when he did find it; for he not only read it, but the one which followed it. Then came a long Sanscrit prayer.'

'*March 7.*—One of the things most admired has been a prism, which I have as a letter-weight. The splendid colours which through it an Indian sun casts on the walls excite much admiration and pleasure. My little Ayah to-day asked me what my Zouave had cost. I should hardly call her *my* Ayah, as, luckily for me, I have only one-third part of the little woman. To have a whole Ayah would be too much of a good thing.

'I took your *Illustrated* yesterday to show to the Mother-in-law of the German Missionary.... I tried as I walked to the house to get up a little German; but, O Laura, the Urdu had driven it almost all out of my head. If I wished to call up a German word, up would come an Urdu one! I did indeed remember "wunderbar," and "shrecklich," so that helped me with the *Illustrated*, but they would not have been very useful in a lengthy conversation.

'If I had had time to write yesterday, I might have given you such an interesting account of the Panjabi Munshi, which I heard from Mr. H. This Munshi, I forget his name, is the son of one of the four priests of the Golden Temple, and a man of character, some talent, and influence. Mr. H., who is translating some of the Bible into Panjabi, wanted — —'s assistance. The Munshi courteously declined, as he feared that the Bible would be contrary to the "Granth," the Sikh Scriptures. These Scriptures, so far as they go, Mr. H. says, are not bad at all; and true Sikhs detest idolatry. "Well," says Mr. H., "both you and I worship the Great God. We will make a bargain. If in the Bible we meet with anything against the Great God, we will close the book at once." The Munshi instantly closed with the offer; and the result is that at last he has told Mr. H. that there is no book in the world like the Bible. When the Munshi's sister lay dying, he nursed her night and day, and used to carry to her what he had been reading with Mr. H.

'The Munshi's father, the priest, seemed to have had rather a natural fear of his son's imbibing what he would consider wrong doctrine. He therefore, with two friends, made the Munshi read over to them what he had been busy about with the Christian Sahib. After a while the priest observed, "At first I listened as a critic; now I listen with interest."

'What an honest, conscientious man the Munshi is, was shown by his conduct to a rich tradesman in the city. This rich man paid the Munshi to come and read the "Granth" to him,—I suppose for amusement, as he himself is a Hindu and idolater. When — — came to read, he saw an idol in front of the Hindu, and the Sikh positively refused to open the "Granth"—his sacred book—in presence of the idol. "Why," says the Hindu, "you worship the picture of your saint, so you need not object to my image." But — — positively denied that he worshipped the picture. "Bring one here," he said; "and in the presence of witnesses, I will tear it in pieces. Will you do the same with your idol?"'

The following letter to one of her aunts, dated May 8, 1876, refers to the above expedition:—

'I see you have an impression that we Missionary ladies dress oddly, behave strangely, and undergo all kinds of hardships. You think that I slept on the ground when I went to O— —. Not a bit of it! Margaret and I took beds with us, and a table and seats and cooking utensils, and a stock of provisions—and *Common sense*!!! We were never the worse for our adventure. The Missionaries scold each other more for imprudence about health than any other thing, and I am the scold of the party, so that as I preach I must practise.

'2ndly. As regards dress, I consider that we dress rather prettily than otherwise. Of course in England it would look funny to see a lady of my age all in white, with a topi and pugri and white parasol; but it does not look funny in India. Why, the very soldiers look like figures in plaster of Paris. As for the natives thinking us "Chinese," there is no fear of their doing that. I believe that we Missionaries are much respected; we are treated with courtesy; and one of us may walk alone through crowds of hundreds of natives, and never have a disrespectful word....

'Then you so kindly take a little anxiety about my health; but I do not know that I was ever better in my life. I fancy that I am even a trifle fatter. Thank God, I have not had a touch of fever or headache yet; and though my pankah has been up for days, I have not cared to have it worked. Of course the greatest heat is to come; ... but heat, except of course exposure to the sun, does not seem to injure me; and I am more afraid of December cold than of July heat.'

In April she went to Lahore for a visit, as companion to a Missionary, left alone. Writing from there, she observes: 'Visits to Missionary stations are a part of my education; and one which Dr. Murdoch strongly recommended for me. He would have me running about the country; but really I am too old to be a comet like my nephew.'[42] And again, speaking of a walk through the narrow streets of Lahore: 'Presently we met a cart drawn by buffaloes, which filled up the greater part of the width of the road,—of course one does not expect pavements for foot-passengers. Miss H. was a bit frightened, and seemed to think that the big ugly creatures would leave us no room to pass; but I could see that there was plenty of room, if we went single file. And as for being afraid of a stolid buffalo, that looks as if it never would dream of goring any one, even if its horns were not so set on that it *could* not do such a thing, there would be small excuse for that. Why, Margaret one day, when she was in Cashmere, saw a big black bear only a few yards from her, with just a little icy stream between, and she was not terrified. One bear would be equal to a hundred black buffaloes. I am rather struck by the amount of *dash* amongst Missionaries! Miss —— is perhaps an exception, but then hers is merely school-work. I think that Margaret is a gallant lady, and that Emily[43] would be true as steel. As for some of the gentlemen, I feel sure that there is plenty of real heroism in them.' In almost her next letter she says of one of these Missionaries: 'I do hope that your cheque may make my nephew take a *little* more care of his health. He is so careful of Mission money, that he almost provokes us by travelling in ways likely to make him ill. I believe that he has seriously injured himself by economising in his own comforts. He ought not to be knocked about, for he is very fragile indeed.'

'*April 20.*—The weather is gradually getting warmer. The thermometer in my verandah to-day, where it had been in the shade all the day, was about 107°, that is more than twenty degrees hotter than I have ever seen it in the most sultry day in England. But do not suppose that I mind the heat, or that it has hitherto done me the slightest harm. Thank God, I am in perfect health, not in the slightest degree feverish. I charmed Margaret at dinner to-day. "You are better in the hot weather than the cold," she cried. "I never knew you ask for a second help in the cold weather." And the two poor dear girls opposite me sat with plates sadly clean; neither of them would touch a bit of meat.... Of course we shall have the weather a good deal hotter presently, but then pankahs will be up.'

'*May 8.*—There is a little romance going on here. A little native maiden was betrothed to a native lad. Before the marriage came off, the destined bridegroom and his parents became Christians. The girl's parents wanted to break off the match, and unite the girl to a heathen. But *her* heart was set on her young bridegroom. The case came before court,—Emily thinks about a year ago. It was adjudged that the maiden was too young to fix her own fate. But she is old enough now, and she has kept true to her lover. The final decision must be made in twenty-one days. The young girl—she looks such a child—wants, I hear, to become a Christian. Emily fain would ascertain whether she does so from love of religion, or only from love for her boy. I hope to be at her baptism,—and her wedding too, if all be well.'

'*May 29.*—I have done so few lessons to-day, I had better set to them bravely. I have written out, large and black, so that I may easily read in dim light, more than 1300 words, to go over regularly every fortnight, masculine separated from feminine nouns. I know others that I have not written down. But, Laura dear, all these words—rather a tax on an old lady's memory—take one on but a small way in speaking this difficult language.'

Early in June she yielded very reluctantly to Mrs. Elmslie's pressure, and consented to go for a short time to Dalhousie; and the letter following was written at an inn on the way:—

'Dâk Bungalow, *June 13, 1876*.

'I have been giving dear Leila an account of the first part of my journey; now I will go on with you. I slept a good deal in the gari. I dreamed that I was talking with you about Margaret....

'Well, I reached the dâk bungalow (kind of inn) early in the morning, took early breakfast, and started in my duli (kind of palanquin) at about 6.15. I wanted to start earlier, knowing that I had a nineteen miles stage before me, and that the day would probably be hot. I had nine men to carry me and my luggage. They made little of it, but went at the rate of nearly four miles an hour, including brief stoppages. Three times the poor fellows asked for leave to stop and drink water. This of course I granted. Twice I was asked for bakhshish; but I declined giving any until I should arrive, and then if they carried me nicely I promised them something.

'They did carry me very nicely. When they had gone about ten miles, and might be supposed to have grown pretty tired, then they began to be lively, laughing and chatting together, I suppose to beguile the way. It would be well if we took life's journey as patiently and cheerfully as these poor half-clad mountaineers. *Note inserted.* Oh, doubtless it was a relay!...

'The thunder has been grumbling. Perhaps I may take a little walk before I start on my long night expedition. This seems to be a lovely place, but of course I shall not walk in the heat of the day....

'It is indeed a miracle how a mere handful of Englishmen rule such a country as this. Since I left Amritsar I have seen but one English face, and that was the face of some one lying full length in a duli which I passed. He was very likely ill. Yet one feels oneself under a *very strong* wing of the law,— far more so than one does in England. There have I been travelling with a band of natives to whom threepence is a good present ... my language, my religion, are strange, and yet I neither receive nor fear the slightest disrespect. Is not this like a miracle?

'Thunder again! If I have a storm to-night in the mountains, how sublime it will look!'

But though she enjoyed her time in the mountains, she was eager to return to work; and even from Dalhousie her letters contain chiefly details of what was being done, there or at Amritsar, in her absence. On the 18th of July she was on the road; and again she wrote from an inn:—

'I have bidden farewell to Dalhousie. The skies were weeping violently when I started; so was not I!... Dalhousie is grandly beautiful; but I have been asking myself why I have not been in raptures with its beauties. I think that two things are wanting to its perfection;—first, the soft blue haze which one connects with distant mountains. High and hard, some snow-crowned peak cuts the sky. You are told that it is a hundred miles off. You don't believe it! It is as clear and sharp as if only two. Then water is a very great want, at least to me. Certainly, there is the Ravi, one of the five famous rivers of the Panjab; but at Dalhousie it looks, at least in June, first cousin to a swamp. One wants waterfalls. One-hundredth part—one-thousandth part—of Niagara, glorious Niagara, would be a boon at Dalhousie....

'It is a curious thing, dear Laura, that kind of *instinct* which one acquires in India! I have often and often thought on the subject. One feels as if one belonged to such a lordly race. It is that odd kind of impression upon one that, though one may *personally* be weak as water, one forms a part of a mysterious power. There is a kind of instinctive persuasion that neither man nor beast would dare to attack one,—except perhaps a vicious horse. One travels by night, without the slightest protection, surrounded by half-clad, ignorant semi-savages; one never dreams of fearing them. One takes one's early walk in a lonely place, where the cheetah or snake may lurk, without the smallest alarm. They would not surely attack one of the English!...'

CHAPTER III
A.D. 1876 CURIOUS WAYS

More than half of Charlotte Tucker's first year in India was now over; and still no thought of work for herself in Batala had arisen. She knew about Batala, and was interested in the place, no doubt, as in all other outlying parts where Missionary work had been even fitfully attempted. But Amritsar was thus far her home; and there she expected to remain. She continued to study hard and perseveringly, in preparation for fuller work, often lamenting her own slowness in learning to speak; and already she was making herself known and beloved by a few Indians,—either Christian, or disposed towards Christianity.

After her return from Dalhousie she wrote in joyous strains: 'Here I am at dear Amritsar again, which I much prefer to the abode amongst the clouds.' There was some idea that she might have to go all the way back to Dalhousie, to nurse a sick Missionary there; and she was perfectly willing to do so, without hesitation on the score of fatigue, without a thought of the long, troublesome journey. No one else could be so well spared at that period from Amritsar as herself; and this she fully realised. 'If however dear Florrie rallies nicely,' she wrote, 'I have not the slightest intention of going to cloudland again. Pankah-land suits my taste better.' Happily, it was not necessary for her to go.

It was in the spring or summer of this year that she began to name her various new friends after certain jewels, according to her estimate of their respective gifts and characters. She possessed, in imagination, a jewelled bracelet, representing the different Missionary gentlemen of her acquaintance,—Diamond, Opal, Amethyst, etc. A companion bracelet was supposed to represent the Missionary ladies,—consisting of Diamond, Sardonix, Onyx, etc. Also she had in mind 'an extraordinary necklace, Oriental pattern, formed of Native friends,'—those Indian Christians, whom she had begun to know and to love, many of whom repaid her love, and did not disappoint her trust in the coming years.

A little later, in the letter describing this favourite idea, she adds: 'Now we come to my yellow girdle, studded with gems. This is composed of dear ones in Old England; my own Laura being the Pearl nearest the heart.'

A more prosaic and less romantic nature can perhaps hardly understand, much less sympathise with, the delight afforded to her curiously symbol-loving mind by this manner of regarding those whom she loved.

In July a letter speaks of 'seeing more of the lights and shadows of Missionary life' than before. A certain young Muhammadan, in whom they were greatly interested, after long inquiry and hesitation, at length made up his mind to come boldly forward, and to be baptized. Arrangements were made for his Baptism in the Church by a Native clergyman; the matter being kept as quiet as possible, for avoidance of the opposition which was sure to arise. Miss Tucker was told only on the morning of the day what was about to happen; and great was her delight, as well as her fear that some hindrance might intervene.

'I had a kind of intuitive feeling,' she said, 'that something might come to prevent the Convert from openly confessing his Lord. I knew not how great the danger was.'

One hour remained before the time fixed for the Baptism, when the young man—Babu G. he may be called—came in, troubled and pale. His Mother had somehow divined his intention, and was doing her utmost to prevent its being carried out. She flung a brick at the head of one Christian Native, who had had a hand in influencing the young Muhammadan; she raved and beat her breast; she cursed and tore her hair; she declared to her son that if he became a Christian she would die.

Babu G. believed all this, and was sorely shaken. His Mother was brought to the Mission-house, and a vehement scene followed. The old lady sat upon the ground, pouring out threats and curses, beating her breast and tearing her hair anew,—only, as A. L. O. E. somewhat drily observed afterwards, she very cleverly avoided hurting herself by her blows, and none of her hair seemed to come out with all the apparent 'tearing.' But the young man could hardly be expected to see this as a stranger would! He wavered—hesitated—and at last gave way. The Baptism did not take place; and the unhappy young fellow, convinced of the truth of Christianity, willing in heart to be a servant of Christ, had not courage to take his own decision, but remained a Muhammadan. Bitter tears were shed over his defection by gentle Mrs. Elmslie; the first that Miss Tucker had ever seen her shed.

Such stories as this show conclusively that *the* work which most of all needs to be done in India is to transform the Mothers,—to educate a generation of Christian Mothers. Their sons then will be Christian too. No power in the world surpasses that of a mother over her children, whether she be English or Hindu or Muhammadan.

Charlotte Tucker's stern side seems to have come out in this stormy interview with the furious old lady. 'Are you not *afraid*,' she demanded, 'that God's anger is on you? You have been your son's enemy. When affliction comes, remember,—*remember*,—remember!'

Side by side, however, with this great disappointment, were other more hopeful aspects of the work. Light and shade naturally go together. A few days later she wrote:—

> 'The mother still holds her unhappy son in bonds, and forbids him even to breathe the air of our compound.... But even about her we need not despair. I was reading the Gospel to-day with the sweetest-looking elderly woman that I have seen in India. All beauty generally departs with youth, but this woman is really attractive still. She was in bitter grief at the baptism of her eldest son; when the next was baptized she blessed him; and now she is quite ready for baptism herself. Such a sweet expression came over her face yesterday when I reminded her of her former grief and her present joy!'

On August 8th she wrote:—

> 'The old Chaukidar[44] made us laugh the other evening by his earnest, emphatic warning against our ladies driving out at night. He uses sometimes almost frantic gesticulations. He told us that there is danger of meeting at night a dreadful being, in appearance somewhat like Mr. H.—a tall, fair, blue-eyed handsome young friend of ours!—whose object is to *cut off English heads*. I have heard of a similar superstition in the Hills; but there I fancy that Native heads, not English, were in requisition. You can imagine from this what a funny fellow the old Chaukidar is; but we look on him as true as steel. One day Mrs. E. found him most good-naturedly pulling Iman's pankah for him. She was so much pleased that she gave him four pomegranates. The old fellow was delighted, and at once gave three of them away, keeping only one for himself. His friend, our half-blind Iman, was one to benefit by his generosity.'

The name 'Iman,' meaning 'Faith,' was bestowed by Miss Tucker upon a poor pankah-wala, whose affectionate disposition made a strong impression upon her. The poor fellow, although half-blind, volunteered one day to walk the whole twenty-four miles to Batala and back in three days, to carry medicine to a sick woman there,—the wife of the young

Muhammadan, Babu G., above mentioned. Iman himself was, to say the least, disposed to be a Christian. These little side facts all serve to show the manner of influence which was acting gradually in all directions.

In another letter, belonging to August, are the words: 'We are rather on the tiptoe of expectation about our Bishop that is to be. There is a rumour that good Mr. —— is the man; but surely it is impossible that such a shy, boy-like Missionary should be turned into a Right Reverend Father!' The appointment when made proved to be that of Bishop French, well known in Mutiny days as Mr. French of Agra, who utterly refused to allow the Christian Natives to be banished from the town, as was proposed by some faint-hearted people there. If they went, Mr. French said, he would go with them; and he undertook to answer for their faithfulness. His resolution prevailed; and the little band of Indian Christians were faithful to the end of the Siege.

About this time a change took place, which A. L. O. E. 'quite approved,' but which she did not 'like.' Mrs. Elmslie left the Mission Bungalow, to live at the neighbouring Orphan House, taking charge of the orphans. A superintendent under her had hitherto done the work, but had proved inefficient; and the new plan was not only better in itself, but promised to save money—always a prime consideration where Missionary funds have to be considered.

On August 23rd comes a letter of some importance, respecting the kind of Missionaries wanted out there. This subject will recur from time to time in the course of the correspondence; but even at so early a stage as this Miss Tucker seems to have clearly grasped what was and what was not required.

> 'It is very kind in you to send me the *Illustrated*. After it has been seen here, and at the Orphanage, and by the dear, good Germans, off it starts for Dalhousie, and Florrie probably makes it over to the soldiers after she has done with it; so you see that you benefit many by your kindness.
>
> 'I do not think that my Margaret at all enjoys being away from us in the schoolhouse, though she keeps bright and brave. "The Mother is as home-sick as can be," was the description given by one of our ladies, this house being the "home" meant. Of course, we go over and pet her, and get her here when we can. I hear that her room was leaking so last night; that must be looked to at once. But rooms had a fair excuse for leaking; we had such a storm!...
>
> 'It was amusing when Emily, Ada, and I were talking over our youth the other day. Dashing, energetic games had been

the delight of my companions; and I begin to imagine that cricket, rounders, and bolstering form no bad preparation for Missionary life. Dash and energy and physical strength are very desirable. We want ladies who fear nothing, grumble at nothing, and are ready to carry the Holy War into the enemy's camp. One of Emily's many advantages is that she is a fearless rider. I am rather alarmed at hearing that an extremely delicate lady is coming out to us. We want hearty, strong ladies, not sickly ones. The Missionaries are too short of hands to be able to undertake much sick-nursing. If I were to require to be nursed at night—which, thank God, I have not done—I should feel inclined to run off somewhere or other, so as not to tax the strength of my nieces.'

Only two days later we have mention of the first Baptism in Batala, her future home during so many years. She writes: 'A deeply interesting event took place yesterday at Batala; the baptism of a Brahmin, a man in a very influential position, and in Government employ. Dear Sadiq[45] and I believe other Christians went to Batala on Wednesday for the Baptism, which was to be as public as possible—in a tank.' This was written August 25; and on the 29th she gave more particulars.

'The jackals treated us to their varied music last night; but one does not mind them a bit, for they never seem to attack people, or intrude into houses. I wish that they would teach their good manners to the sparrows. The cheetah also is a modest creature. There was an account very lately of a cheetah going into a verandah at Dalhousie; nothing between it and the interior of the house but a chick blind; but it was too polite to intrude. It would be rather exciting to look at a cheetah through a chick blind; you can see through it quite well, as the light is outside.

'But, O Laura, I ought not to waste my space on cheetahs or jackals, when I can write of things so *much* more interesting. I had such an interesting account of the Baptism of B—n, the Brahmin at Batala, from Mr. Beutel,[46] supplemented by one from Sadiq. They were both present.... Mr. Beutel observed that he (B—n) had had to go through more than many do in a campaign. Why, except the Catechist and his wife, he is the only Christian that we know of in that fierce, bigoted Batala. As the Muhammadans did not know of the time fixed for the baptism, at the beginning of the Service by the tank not many people gathered; but seeing that something was going on, gradually a crowd collected. At last the crowd grew large—and excited also—and the police authority had to be called in for protection.

'Perhaps the worst of all was the Christian's reception at his home; his wife came with her three little ones to meet him, beating her breast, etc. Sadiq had intended to carry B—n back to Amritsar with him, to let the first fury of the storm blow over; but poor B—n preferred remaining at Batala, because if he left his wife, he did not know what she might do with his children. So there the brave fellow remains. We ought to pray earnestly for this our brother.'

In a letter to her niece, Mrs. Boswell, on September 1st, Charlotte Tucker spoke of herself as 'heart-sick with anxiety' about the convert, regretting much that he had not come to Amritsar.

'Would that he could have carried wife and children off with him! but I suppose that this was impossible, against the woman's will. Dear Sadiq soon went again to Batala;—alas! he was not suffered to see the convert, who is surrounded by enemies, and seems to be quite in their power. B—n's wife, after starving herself for three days from grief at his baptism, has died, it is said from an attack of cholera.

'Our fear is that the heathen are starving B—n and his three children to death! One poor lamb is but a few months old. If I were a man, I would be off to Batala. My friend Mr. H. has written a strong note to an English official at no great distance from Batala,—there *not one* Englishman resides,—and I feel little doubt that he will bring the strong arm of the law to protect B—n. But the note will not reach till this evening. For eight days B—n will have been in the fiery furnace. How long can he hold out?'

Reports, happily false, of the retractation of the convert came to distress them at Amritsar; and Mr. Beutel, leaving his wife and mother dangerously ill, went over to Batala to inquire how matters stood. He found B—n, though much tried and sorely pressed, still standing firm.

It is melancholy to read of Charlotte Tucker's eager delight in carrying the good news to her favourite Maulvi Z.,—of whom at that time she thought so well and hopefully as an established Christian, and who in later years was to grieve her most bitterly by himself becoming an apostate.

Letters at this time show her steadily growing interest in Batala, her ever-increasing desire for systematic work there.

'*Sept. 14, 1876.*—I have been delaying writing till I could give you news from Batala,—that place towards which Missionary eyes longingly turn, as those of the Germans did towards Strasburg. May Batala be given to us, as Strasburg was to them.'

'*Sept. 20.*—As regards my little Indian tales, I have sent a good many to Nelson, who has accepted them; and consequently I suppose intends to publish them. It is very likely that they have been appearing in the *Family Treasury*.... Sadiq had just come from Batala, where he had seen B—n. Dear Sadiq! I think that he must have gone altogether seven or eight times to Batala. He is a friend worth having. B—n expressed his willingness to bring his little girls to Amritsar; but his baby was so very, very ill, that he feared she could not be moved.... The little lamb appeared to be sinking fast. My surprise is how she has been kept alive so long. The last account was that the baby was "not fit to be picked off the charpai";[47] she seemed dying. Dear little martyred innocent,—dying because her father gave himself to Christ! B—n intends to bring his two elder children; but of course nothing can be done while baby is dying....

'O Laura, I feel as if these two deaths in Batala marked the place as *our own*. So much cannot have been suffered in vain.'

TO MISS 'LEILA' HAMILTON.

'*Sept. 26, 1876.*

'Those rogues of sparrows have fairly driven me out of my room this morning. They make such a chatter. I intend to request Mr. H. benevolently to shoot a few; just to show the rest that really they must not expect to be allowed to build, and gossip, and make themselves disagreeable in every possible way in the room of a Buzurg Miss Sahiba....

'It is much cooler. These two last nights I have needed no pankah, and was able to bear a blanket. I have resumed wearing a merino vest by day, and it is very comfortable. The darzi,[48] who squats in the verandah, is busy on a magnificent dressing-gown, which I have ordered. I brought out flannel from England, but not a flannel dressing-gown, so I have bought a rich shawl-pattern, and the flannel will line it, and I shall look like a Maliká[49] and feel—almost as comfortable as a sparrow.... It seemed to be a question with the darzi whether the white flannel was to be inside or outside! The matter appeared to interest some of the servants. One lives in such a public way in India. Whatever one gives to be made or mended is made or mended in the verandah; and the darzi, as he cuts out, clips, and sews, talks—perhaps with the pankah-wala, perhaps a stranger, perhaps the munshi (tutor) whose pupil is not quite ready to take her lesson.... There is no shutting the world out; and the Indian world is such a curious world.

'Then people's characters are so public; no one seems to think it worth while to wear thick cloaks over them. Everybody seems to know about everybody else. The very public papers seem personal. ... O yes, India is a very curious place,—people curious,—ways curious,—insects curious,—dress curious, etc. The very Anglo-Saxon character appears in a new and curious aspect. India is a place to develop an instinct to command, and to carry things with a high hand. Weakness does almost as much harm as wickedness. But I feel myself too old to learn the zabardast[50] way of going on. I am not fitted to grasp reins of government, and drive a team of twenty-two Indian servants, syces, pankah-walas, bearer, khitmatgar, ayah, etc., see that the horses are not cheated of grain, that pankah-walas pull, that kahars don't take French leave, etc. etc. I hope that Florrie[51] will hold the reins, if she and I go off together.'

'*Oct. 5.*—We had a visit from our good Pastor Sadiq yesterday. I was the one to receive him. You know that I am not strong in the language yet. I knew that Sadiq was speaking about sickness, castor-oil, and quinine, and people going about to look after the sufferers; but I could not get at his full meaning; and as he was clearly on business, I thought it better to call in C. to my aid. It was well that I did! Sadiq's heart was full of Batala—our Strasburg—where people are dying of fever, faster than even in Amritsar. Sadiq wanted a subscription to be made instanter to send off quinine and castor-oil. The Christian lawyer, R., would go on to-day or to-morrow, and Sadiq himself would follow on Monday. Talk of languid, apathetic Hindus! Sadiq, when he takes a thing into his head, goes at it like a battering-ram....

'To-day I had what seemed to poor me a long *tête-à-tête* with the Pandit from O——, that village which you will remember I visited with Margaret. O dear! it was a bit of a mental effort. He is a learned man! I longed for C. to come to my rescue, but battled with verbs and genders as well as I could.

'I was determined to do the polite, so I boldly asked the Pandit to stay to dinner. I could do so, as, oddly enough, I am now the senior Missionary at Amritsar,[52] though I feel such a child in the language. Rather to my surprise, the Pandit accepted my invitation at once. He would not eat with us when he was here before, nor when at O— —, for he is a curious half-and-half sort of Christian,[53] leading such a lonely life amongst heathen. The Pandit shared our meal, but only took vegetables and bread-and-butter.

'Do you not laugh at the notion of poor Char, sitting at the head of a table, and entertaining a Pandit, and feeling her ignorance, and plunging about in a bog of Urdu? I did not, however, attempt to talk much after C. came in, as she has been nearly four years in India, and speaks the language well.'

When the next letter was written, on October 14, the Batala plan was under discussion. Padri Sadiq seems to have first suggested the idea that Miss Tucker should proceed thither with Miss Swainson, and open a Mission in the place. Miss Tucker does not appear to have at first viewed the scheme with any great enthusiasm.

'Such a merry breakfast we had this morning! Our three dear ladies, Margaret, Emily, and Florrie, arrived at about 9 a.m. after nine hours of raft,—very tiring, for it involved much walking, and it was raining away,—and twelve of dâk-gari. Margaret looked young and lovely; Florrie much improved.... She is delighted with the Batala scheme; but Margaret tells me that it cannot be carried out till December at earliest, and I have my doubts about its being carried out at all. At any rate, the difficulties will not have come from *me*. I am quite willing to go; but of course a new station would involve the Committee in expenses, and it is not easy to procure a suitable house, etc., so it is likely enough that Sadiq's plan will be disapproved of in high quarters. I quietly wait to see what direction is taken by "the fiery, cloudy pillar." ...

'Last night I had to chaperon to our noisy, bustling station after dark a young Missionary, who looks to me quite unfledged. There I met the school-teacher, Miss — —, with her young sister, yet more unfledged, bound on the same errand.... I think that the stations at Indian cities are more noisy and bustling than the worst London ones. It almost shocks my sense of propriety, young girls travelling at night,—it is funny even to an old lady, hurrying up and down a bustling platform amongst Natives. I think that I managed pretty well for *my* charge, for I got her into a carriage with a lady and children, so she was safe enough; she was not to cross the Sutlej till daylight. Poor little Miss — — was put by her sister into an empty carriage; but who knows whether some drunken, low European may not have got into it at the next station? And the poor, simple little thing was to cross the Sutlej at midnight, with her baggage to look after!!! We would hardly do such things in England. I have slept a night here, *with not a soul in the house but myself*, and the house seems so strangely open; but I was not a bit afraid.'

'Oct. 20, 1876.—When this reaches you, perhaps you will be feeling the first pinch of winter. We do not escape it here in our bright, glowing Panjab. I cherish a fond hope that if we go to Batala, we shall find it warmer than Amritsar.... Emily, Florrie, and Sadiq have gone off to-day on a house-hunting expedition to Batala. It is considered a very healthy place; except, of course, at present—an exceptional season. If I go, I do not expect to have much to do at first except learn the language. I leave school-work to Florrie; she is well up to it; and I hear that Zenanas are likely to be very slow in opening....

'My Munshi ... asked me to give him leave of absence on the next day, or that following it, as it would be the Muhammadans' *great day*. He could not tell me which of the two days it would be, because all would depend on the moon. If the moon were seen on the night after the 18th, then the 19th would be the feast day, the end of the long Muhammadan fast. If the moon were not seen, the poor people must wait till the 20th. "Suppose," said I, "that the people at Lahore see the moon, and that those at Amritsar do not, will the Lahore folk have a feast and you a fast?" A. answered in the affirmative....

'I talked with A. a little about the fasting. He told me with gusto that he had once gone to the house of a Muhammadan friend, who happened to have a little hole in his door, on one of the days of the fast. A., the old rogue, peeped through the hole, and detected his friend in the act of eating. A. then knocked at the door. His friend—it made me think of Friar Tuck!—popped the food into a box, wiped his mouth, and was ready to receive his visitor. "What were you doing?" asked A. "Reading," was the reply. Then A. opened the box, and showed the discomfited hypocrite the food, and—according to his own account—gave the man a lecture. I have my doubts about the latter part of the story—I mean the lecture.'

'*Oct. 26.*—Our poor city has been bearing some resemblance to a hospital. Some think that not one of her inhabitants—120,000—has altogether escaped the fever, and many have died; but I am thankful to write that the sickness is on the decrease.... I cannot, however, go to dear Louis, for the Beutels, who have been very ill, are going to Ludhiana; and their mother, too ill to be moved, must have some one to look after her a little during their absence. I am the only lady available, being well, and with no pressure of work. I am almost astonished at having been so exempted from suffering, when thousands and thousands have been so ill. I have not spent a day in bed ... since leaving England. It is a cause for much thankfulness. Of course I had a little fever, but it has left no dregs. The weather is so nice, that one hardly understands why any one should be ill....

'The Batala plan is rather hanging fire at present. Day after day passes, and no reply is received to the letter asking permission for us to occupy apartments in the palace. No other place in or near Batala seems to be available. Even in the palace considerable alterations would be needed, to make the rooms at all suitable for English ladies.'

'*Nov. 16.*—Sadiq does not quite approve of our selection of a house. He would have liked one right in the city; but it is far pleasanter to us to be a little out of it.... I asked him if he had any news of B—n. Sadiq told me that he had seen him at Batala, the beginning of last week. Our brave Brahmin convert had been very ill, and had written—or caused to be written—a paper stating that he wished his body to be buried by Christians, his children brought up by Christians, and his property taken care of by the Mission. I am thankful to say that B—n did not die; but as Sadiq said, he has had affliction upon affliction.... In a few months this convert has lost wife, babe, and only brother. Sadiq said that B—n's regret about the babe was that it had not been baptized. But when I remarked that I thought the babe had been a kind of martyr, like the little ones killed by Herod, Sadiq looked pleased.'

'*Dec. 1.*—I suppose that my next letter will be addressed to you from my new home in Batala. My nieces are very anxious to make arrangements for my comfort. I am not to have the trouble of helping to put the new house into order. Two ladies go before to make everything nice....

'I went to dear S. Begum to-day,—the one who was lately baptized with her young daughter,—to speak to her about Holy Communion. I am glad that I shall have the First Sunday in Advent in Amritsar. It will seem strange to reside in a place where there is no church! I suppose that we shall go over to the Catechist's house, and have Urdu service there....

'It was very interesting to hear Mr. Wade's account of the opening of a little church in the village of G. The peculiar and very interesting feature of the affair is that in this Rajput village a little flock has been gathered just by *Native* agency. And the way for the Native evangelist, the excellent C., was wondrously prepared.

'In old Runjit's time a kind of Native prophet declared that our Lord was greater than all others. This Pandit was succeeded by another, who declared that all the people would become the Lord's followers. They who came first would receive *honour*; they who came next, a mere *subsistence*; they who came last would be *driven* in! Then a third teacher arose—the present one. He said that a shepherd pushes one sheep after another into the fold, and when all are in follows himself; and that so *he* would get the people into the Christian fold, and then follow them.

'It seems to us a most extraordinary way of evangelising; but when the Rev. C. came to the village, he found that these strange teachers had really ploughed up the ground to receive the good seed; and the third teacher *has* come himself into the fold with four of his relatives. His wife still holds out.

'The opening of the tiny church was a delightful scene. There are only 14 or 15 baptized Christians; but the people, men and women, flocked in, till there was hardly room to sit on the ground. In the thoroughly Oriental church there are no seats.'

'*Dec. 4, 1876.*—I have this morning read your loving expostulation to Margaret and myself regarding Batala. You think that your strong point is my unfitness for an out-station. But, sweet one, you forget that I am so specially fitted, by age, for the post, that if I were to draw back, the whole promising plan might fall to the ground. The Natives reverence grey hairs; and I dare say that some of them will pet me. As for the language, I manage to get on after a fashion, and smiles go a good way.

'I assure you that I have never felt my heart lighter than I have done lately, fond as I am of those I leave. It seems as if the way were so plain. If I were perfectly dumb, I should still be useful as a chaperon. But I am not quite dumb.

'I had such a golden First Sunday in Advent yesterday.... Fancy the encouragement of seeing B—n, the one Christian convert residing in Batala, and sharing the Cup with him in our dear Amritsar Church. I shook hands with him after afternoon service. I am sorry that when I uttered the two words, "Hamara bhai,"[54] I should have said "Hamare," instead of "Hamara." It was a pity that my first word should have been incorrect; but I could not think of grammar at such a moment.... Then I have had such an encouraging note from dear Emily, who is making things straight for me at Batala....—Your happy

Char.'

CHAPTER IV
A.D. 1876 A PALACE FOR A HOME

In December 1876 Charlotte Maria Tucker entered upon the final stage of her earthly career. Final in a sense; for though more than once Batala had to be temporarily deserted, the place was never given up. Thenceforward, Batala became in very truth her home; Batala work was essentially her work; and the remaining years of her life were devoted to Batala.

Having once made up her mind that she was definitely called to this particular post, nothing could withhold her. Difficulties, oppositions, hindrances, prospects of loneliness, imperfect knowledge of Indian languages, increasing age,—all these were as nothing in the way. If she was called, she would go! And Miss Tucker believed that she *was* called.

Others were not so sure. Mrs. Elmslie wrote on the 8th of December to Mrs. Hamilton: 'I agree with you that your beloved sister's power lies in gifts which can be used to perhaps greater influence here than in an out-station. This isolation from European society is not what I should have chosen for one who can exercise so much influence for good among her own countrymen; and whose pen can do more for India than perhaps the lives of many others.' No doubt this view of the question weighed greatly in the judgment of many. For one who can write books suitable to Indian requirements, there are scores of Missionaries who can with ease learn the Native languages, and who can visit and teach in Zenanas, perhaps far more effectually than A.L.O.E. did.

To lookers-on it may seem that she judged wrongly here; that her eagerness for personal work was a mistake; that she might have done more by following the advice of her friends, and remaining at Amritsar. Advice she had; for Mrs. Elmslie says in the same letter: 'We have one and all of us tried to dissuade her from going; but she sees the Pillar going straight on before her. And who are we that we should gainsay it?'

Suppose she only *fancied* that she 'saw the Pillar,'—in other words, that she was called or led or ordered to Batala? A mistake of this description is not impossible, especially in the case of an ardent and impulsive nature. If so, it was the mistake of burning love and self-devotion; and one can well believe that such a mistake must be dearer to the Heart of our Lord than the correct attitude of those who always decide on the safe and comfortable side.

But why should we imagine it to have been a mistake? The true gist of the matter is not, after all, to be found in the question as to which particular type of work she might be best fitted for intellectually. The main question was rather—to which especial work was she bidden by her Master? One can hardly live many years on Earth, with observant eyes, and believe that people are always or generally given exactly that work to do, for which they are by natural powers best adapted. Things often seem, indeed, just the other way; people being put to work for which they appear to be least well adapted, and simply having to do their best. To us it may seem that A.L.O.E.'s pen was worth more to India than all her heroic struggles to conquer the languages and to teach in Zenanas. But if, as with her whole heart she believed, God had called her to work in Batala,—'who are we,' to say that she should have remained away? The Commander-in-Chief of an army has a perfect right to place his soldiers where he will; and so long as the soldier who is ordered to any particular post hears the word of command, it matters very little whether anybody else hears it also.

Suppose A.L.O.E. had *not* gone to Batala, but had taken the advice of others, and had remained at Amritsar! Possibly she might, by devoting herself to writing alone, have accomplished treble or quadruple the number of little books and tracts for India which she did accomplish. But then a very heroic example of courage and self-devotion would have been lost to the Church. At Amritsar she would have had plenty of loving friends, and would have been altogether more comfortable, altogether in easier circumstances. Easy and comfortable examples, however, are not rare. Even the writing of a good many more little books might not have made up to us for what we should have lost in other respects.

Besides,—she believed that she had her 'marching orders.' Even if, by any possibility, she were mistaken in that belief, she could not disobey. A soldier always instantly obeys what he *believes* to be the order given.

Yet it could have been no light matter,—this going forth alone, with only one young companion, into a very fastness of Muhammadanism and Heathenism. Miss Tucker herself was no longer young. Though marvellously strong and spirited for her time of life, she was now in her fifty-sixth year; hardly an age when, at the best, a woman is commonly willing to undertake great responsibilities in a new and untried direction. It was, however, true, as she said, that if she did not go, the Mission in Batala could not be at once started—as a resident Mission. No two young women could have gone there alone. They must have waited for a married Missionary and his wife to head the effort.

In this step of Miss Tucker's a clue may perhaps be found for some lives, here or there, where a vocation is earnestly sought and not yet found. Why should not other middle-aged ladies go out, as she went out?—not necessarily always to attempt full Zenana work; but to be protectors, housekeepers, nurses, to younger and more active ladies? Whether it would be right to use any portion of Mission-funds for such a purpose may be doubted; and in many a case Mission *rooms* could not be spared; but there are exceptions as to the latter. And as to the money part of the question, doubtless many a warm-hearted lady, over fifty years of age, free from home-ties, with a spirit full of love and self-devotion, could afford to spend £150 or £200 a year on such an object. Much might be done by her to cheer up the workers, to leave them more free for all that needed most to be done,—and indirectly she might help forward the work of evangelisation by the mere force of a fair Christian example in a dark land. There can be no question that Miss Tucker's *life* worked far more effectually than her words. What she said may have been long ago forgotten. What she was will never be forgotten. Her spoken words doubtless had at the time some power; her written words perhaps had much more; her life had by far the most of all.

For any such line of life as is above suggested, however, only that type of woman is fit which has been already described in some of A.L.O.E.'s letters. Thin-skinned, anxious, feeble-spirited ladies, easily worried and easily vexed, will not do; and angular, managing, argumentative ladies would be quite as unsuitable. Those alone may venture who are not only fairly strong in health, vigorous in spirit, fearless as to difficulties, and careless as to discomforts, but who are also gentle, kind-hearted, sympathetic, willing to yield to the judgment of others, ready to please and not to rule. Almost above everything else, there should be a freedom from grumbling tendencies. If *such* elderly ladies of England are willing to tread in A.L.O.E.'s footsteps, and to give the Evenings of their lives to Mission-work, openings enough for them might be found.

The closing words of Mrs. Elmslie's letter to Mrs. Hamilton on December 8, show what Miss Tucker's presence in the Amritsar bungalow had been: 'I shall miss my darling Charlotte much. She has been sunshine to me ever since she came; and I am accustomed to think of her as a very precious gift from a loving Father Who knows our need. I hope to have her again at Christmas. Please feel assured that we shall tenderly watch over your dear one, even though not so closely together as formerly.' Miss Wauton also, speaking of that time, says: 'Her general presence was a great cheer to her fellow-workers there.'

Mention has been made of the Mission-tree,—a large banyan, in front of the Amritsar bungalow, where Miss Tucker had now spent so many months. The central trunk had received the name of Amritsar, and other slender trunks around, already rooted, had received the names of various out-stations, where occasional work had been begun, but where no Missionaries yet resided. One slender shoot was called after Batala. It had then just reached the ground, but was not firmly rooted. Now, in 1895, it is 'a thick, substantial trunk.'

Batala, a walled town, about a mile across, has a population of some 25,000 people, and is twenty-four miles to the east of Amritsar. The Dalhousie range of the mighty Himalayas lies about fifty miles off; but the mountains, when snow-capped, look very much nearer. In those days there was not, as there is now, a line of rail connecting Amritsar with Batala. The journey from one to the other had commonly to be accomplished, either by *tum-tum*, a light cart, with two or three changes of horses; or else by *ekka*, a country cart, which last mode of conveyance was very often used by Miss Tucker in coming years. It was a peculiarly rough and wearisome mode of travelling, the ekka having no springs; but very early she took to doing as far as possible what the Indians do in such cases. Anything that would tend to make her one with them was eagerly attempted. For instance, she began speedily to sit upon the floor as Natives do; and at Indian gatherings or feasts she would not only sit as they sat, but would share their food. She must have been singularly supple-jointed for her years, to be able to adopt this position without any serious inconvenience. The Rev. Robert Clark writes, with reference to her Batala mode of life:—

> 'No conveyance was kept. Miss Tucker always travelled in her little dhoolie (or bird's-nest carriage), or in an ekka, a native conveyance without springs, where a seat about a yard square was perched on wooden wheels. On this she spread her bedding, which is always carried about by Missionaries. She was so well accustomed to sit on the ground, that her legs in this conveyance never were in the way. She gracefully folded them before or under her—we never could tell how— in a position which was very painful to most English people, but which seemed quite natural to her. She often used to trot over in this way, in an ekka, to Amritsar, on a road which caused many bumps and aches to most people's heads and arms and bodies; but she would never allow that the shaking of twenty-four miles of such travelling as this ever did her

any harm. I think she wished to be an example to us all. We used to travel then in tum-tums or buggies, or other vehicles with springs. But ekkas have much more become the fashion in our Missionary circles.'

One idea Miss Tucker had, on first going to Batala, which the other Missionaries dissuaded her with great difficulty from putting into execution. This was to *dress* as the Indians do! It was not considered a wise or desirable plan, from any point of view; but Charlotte Tucker had gone so far, in her enthusiasm, as to provide herself with a Native dress, and her heart was very much set upon wearing it. To make her give up this favourite idea was no easy matter.

Batala is a picturesque old town, with fine banyan-trees, and many old mango-tree gardens towards the north, enclosed either by walls or by aloe hedges, curiously appropriate for A. L. O. E. It is said that in her younger days a review of some of her books spoke of them as being 'bitter, like the name of their Author.' Did Miss Tucker ever recall this little notice when she looked upon the aloe hedges of Batala?

There is also a large lake-like tank close to the house in which Miss Tucker lived, and other tanks lie further off. This nearer tank has an ornamental pleasure-house in the middle; and the tomb of the man who dug the tank is on its bank. Many handsome old tombs are to be seen in the place. The town itself is old, with exceedingly crooked and narrow streets; so narrow, that a duli when carried through often touches the walls on both sides. The Batala people have the character of being particularly bigoted, hard-natured, quarrelsome, and difficult to deal with.

Early in 1876 Miss Wauton had written in the Society's Report: 'I think we may consider the Batala Mission now thoroughly established.' This meant that about five Girls' Schools had been opened for Hindu, Sikh, and Muhammadan scholars, under the superintendence of the Catechist's wife, being from time to time visited by the Amritsar Missionary ladies. The children were taught elementary Christian truths; they learned to sing simple hymns; and books were given to them. The work, however, was hardly more than begun, when A. L. O. E. decided to make Batala her home. One Native Catechist and his wife were there; one Batala man had been baptized; and a certain number of children had begun to learn a few simple truths. For the rest, Batala was 'a stronghold of bigoted Muhammadanism.'

And the first thing which had to be done was *not* to reap a harvest, *not* to begin looking for results, but simply to plough the hard ground, and thus to make seed-sowing a matter of possibility. When the ground was broken and softened, then the seed might be sown; after that, the sown seed could be watered, and the harvest patiently waited for.

Almost every letter at this time contains something of interest. To quote half of what might be quoted is impossible, for lack of space. It seems, however, worth while to give fuller records of these early days, when all was fresh, and when Miss Tucker's interests were keenly awake to her novel surroundings, even though more fulness here means some curtailing later.

A certain change in the style of her letters is observable after she reached India, especially in the long series to Mrs. Hamilton. Personal matters are pushed very much into the background; while tendencies to introspection or to moralisings are almost non-existent. The letters fall naturally into a simple record of the work being done. She is far too fully occupied with things and people around to have any leisure to bestow upon her own feelings. Moreover, the mode of expression gains a terseness and vigour, not always characteristic of the earlier correspondence.

To write the life of A. L. O. E. at this period is hardly possible, without at the same time writing the life of the Infant Church at Batala. The one is almost identical with the other.

The house in which their first start was to be made is described by Miss Tucker, as will be seen, in somewhat glowing terms. She was resolutely bent upon making the best of everything, and upon seeing all around through her rose-coloured spectacles. There were, however, two sides to the question. The 'house,' so called, was in reality an old Sikh palace, 'used by Sher Singh, son of Maharajah Singh, as a hunting-box.' Sher Singh is said to have spent no more than one night in it. The building was very substantial, and two-storied. A central room below was over thirty feet in length, and another exactly over it was of the same size. Other smaller rooms lay around, and of these one was chosen for Miss Tucker's bedroom. The great, ponderous, creaking doors were difficult to close; and the wind would sweep through them in a manner suggestive of chill and rheumatism. In the winter months they were very cold and comfortless apartments. The name of the old palace was 'Anarkalli.'[55]

'When we first used these rooms, during occasional visits to Batala,' writes Miss Wauton, 'they were largely haunted by owls, bats, and rats; and it was a long time before these occupants understood that they had notice to quit the premises. Then it seemed impossible ever to make those huge, weird, gloomy-looking rooms at all cosy and home-like. However, we did our best with matting, screens, and furniture, to make it look habitable. And in Miss Tucker's eyes the very strangeness and romance of the place made up for its deficiency in warmth and comfort.' Mr. Clark also, referring to this large and somewhat dreary palace, says of it: 'The winds blew through many chinks in the uncurtained doors; and the house was once likened to Eden, because four streams flowed through it.'

Two days after her arrival she wrote to her favourite sister:—

'Batala, *Dec. 8, 1876.*

'Do not connect Batala with any idea of self-sacrifice. I am astonished to find myself in such a beautiful home. It is more suited for an Earl and Countess than for two lowly Missionaries; and yet our rent is only a little more than £20 a year! Certainly, we have had to make that very necessary article, a fireplace, and to build servants' huts; but the house is grand! It seems unnatural to be the lady of it.

'We do not intend to furnish the room in which I am now sitting,—till the fireplace is finished in our smaller room we use this fine apartment,—but its length is about thirty-six feet. Poor Shere Singh! little he guessed, when he built the fair mansion, that he was but to sleep in it for *one* night, and then be murdered at Lahore! He never dreamed of Mission-books, Bibles, etc., being stored up in those most convenient presses in the walls, which add exceedingly to one's comfort. For really the native house is not only stately, but wondrously comfortable. It seems to me to be decidedly warmer than Amritsar bungalow—a matter of real importance to me. It is a great deal lighter, and I suspect that in summer it will be cooler also, at least in this room, which is splendidly protected from the sun.

'Another advantage as regards both health and cheerfulness is that we live on the first floor, and this first floor is a good height from the ground. One first ascends five steps to the substantial platform on which the house is built, and then twenty-nine steps to our apartments. Florrie and I have each a nice, light, airy bedroom, with bathroom attached. We shall soon have a pleasant sitting-room, to which this splendid unfurnished apartment will serve as a vestibule.'

'*Dec. 9.*—I have just come from the City,—we live more than half-a-mile out of it. O, my Laura, a wide door is open before us. I was told that Batala is a place where we could not read the Bible: but I have copied a great deal into my

Bible picture-book; and there is no let or hindrance that I can see in showing the pictures, and reading the descriptions, which are God's own Word.... I find that a good way to begin, when I enter a house, is by showing off my Zouave. [56] ... Every one is delighted with it. A good large group of women and children assemble.... It is harder for me to understand the women, than it is for them to understand me,—they sometimes jabber so; and if they mix Panjabi, I am all at sea. In the evenings I intend to do a little Panjabi with Florrie; and in return I teach her to play the guitar. I have begun to learn the alphabet, which has thirty-five letters. We hope next week to have an Urdu Munshi; but I only intend to have one hour and a half with him [*i.e.* daily]....

'In nine days we hope to make a day's itinerating tour to two villages. There are little schools in them,—not of course Christian. The poor women here seem inclined to like me, for which I am thankful. Florrie told me to-day that she thought she would have gone into fits of laughter at what was said of me. My being elderly and unmarried seemed to be giving an impression that I was a kind of saint or faqir,—perhaps my being thin and wearing my faithful old green dress added to the impression. One woman asked me whether I had eaten anything that day. Florrie thinks that it was from a courteous wish to feed me, if I had not.

'I arrived here on Thursday,—-this is Saturday. Yesterday I saw poor, dear B—n at the house of the Catechist. He looked sad; not as he looked in the Amritsar church. I suspect that his Cross is still very heavy....

'I am in excellent health, thank God, and Florrie seems to be getting all right again. She and I "pull well together, when yoked twain and twain." I have not seen a single white face but hers—not even in travelling here—since I left the dear Amritsar bungalow. I think that I shall improve more rapidly in the language here than if I had remained at my first station.

'What an extraordinary and somewhat romantic position I am in, for an elderly lady, who in her youth hardly ever stirred from a London home! How amazed we should have been when we were girls, if we could have known that I was to find my home in an Oriental palace—afar from all Europeans—and itinerate a little in heathen villages! How good God has been to your loving sister!'

TO MRS. J. BOSWELL.

'*Dec. 11, 1876.*

'I have not been many days in this my new home, but I could fill pages and pages with Batala. My time, however, is precious, and I must not waste too much even in writing to dear ones.... I was much struck by an incident which occurred to-day. Four workmen are still engaged in making a fireplace for us. This morning, as I sat reading, waiting for my Munshi, one of the men stood near, as if silently watching me. I thought this strange; but, as he was not rude, I made no remark but read on. Presently the man said to me, "Is that the Gospel?" I said, "Would you like to hear the Gospel?" He assented. I read part of Matthew v.; and the three other men came and listened. Afterwards at morning prayer I sat very near the open door leading to the room where two of these men were working at the fireplace. Two of our Muhammadan servants come now regularly to family prayers. The men at the fireplace were so perfectly still that I am sure they were listening to God's Word.... Of course, it is quite optional with the servants to attend or not; and the workmen could easily have drowned my voice, if they had chosen to do so....

'I find my walking Zouave so very useful in opening a way, that I much wish for five or six clever clockwork toys, such as would take the fancy of natives.... The toys should be rather small, and such as I could easily show off. The floors are so rough, that I am obliged to make my Zouave walk on the top of his own tin box, short as it is. I feel the toys, if really clever, so important....'

TO MRS. E— —.

'*Dec. 14, 1876.*

'I dare say that you will be rather curious to know how I like my new home. I like it very much indeed. I cannot tell you what the city is like; for though I have been into it every day but to-day, I cannot say that I know anything of its general appearance, except that the streets are extremely narrow, and that the houses appear to be made of brick. The fact is that I never go into the city, except shut up in a duli, a kind of box with no window. Unless I push the curtain a little back, I see nothing, and nobody can see me. I am rather careful about the proprieties; and to be carried in a box is the correct thing. My duli is red; Florrie's moderately white.

'Now fancy yourself at my side, dearest Aunt. I will give you a kind of rough idea of what is said and done, after my duli has stopped at the door of one of the four Zenanas now open to us at Batala. I will suppose C. M. T. alone, as she sometimes is.

'C. M. T. gets out of her box, and enters,—perhaps mounting a small, rather dark staircase. Presently she finds herself in a place where there are perhaps a dozen or twenty women and children.

'C. M. T. smiles, says, "Salaam," and informs her who seems the chief woman that she is happy to see her. A bed or perhaps an arm-chair is politely put for C. M. T. to sit down on.... C. M. T. begins by showing off a clockwork figure that can walk. Women and children look on with curiosity and pleasure. Says C. M. T., "The doll is cleverer than the idols; it can walk." The house being Muhammadan, the observation is approved of; and C. M. T. amuses the good folk by a few lively remarks as to the doll being weak or tired, etc.

'Then C. M. T. says, "I have made a very long journey from Europe by sea. I have come thousands of miles. Why have I come?" Silence amongst my auditors. "I have come to give good news." They listen with interest. "Jesus Christ came into the world to save sinners. This is good news. We are all sinners. He died for us," etc. None look angry; some look pleased; some look tenderly at me, as if they thought me very kind to come such a long way to give them good news.

'Then a Bible picture-book is opened; perhaps the story of the Fall read. Muhammadans believe a great deal of the Old Testament; one can talk to them of "Father Adam," and "Mother Eve," without shocking them in the least. I cannot talk much,—very little indeed,—but I can say such things as I have written above, and tell the dear women that I am happy, that I do not fear death at all, because I believe that the Lord bore the punishment of my sins on the Cross.

'I have not met with any discourtesy. There are three things in my favour—my age; my family being of the Sarkar-log;[57] and my receiving no salary.... Another thing which seems to awaken a sort of interest is the fact of my being unmarried. I have met with the idea that there is some merit in celibacy. I repudiated it, and said that in our Book marriage is spoken of as an honourable thing.'

TO MRS. HAMILTON.

'*Dec. 16, 1876.*

'We never drive *in* Batala, but on the roads outside. Of course we often meet Natives. Some of them salaam to us, and I make a point of bowing with marked courtesy when they do so. One feels the salaam a breaking of the ice. Those who have exchanged greetings on the road with us are less likely to shut their doors against the polite strangers. Florrie has been admitted into a fifth Zenana to-day. The Catechist thinks that after a while there will be more work than we can overtake.'

TO MRS. J. BOSWELL.

'*Christmas Day, 1876.*

'Is not this a curious life for me? What a contrast Batala is to Marylebone! But I stand up for Batala. This is a capital house, in spite of rats. You should see Florrie and me in our tam-tam driving along kachcha roads,[58] the odd-looking conveyance plunging up and down or from side to side, like a boat on a rough sea. Or fancy me seated in my red duli starting for the city. I remember how I looked on the picture of such a red duli, painted on talc, and pitied native ladies for having to travel in a box. It really, however, is not bad, and it is the only practicable conveyance for the narrow streets of Batala.'

CHAPTER V
A.D. 1877 DISAPPOINTMENTS AND DELAYS

The year 1877 dawned full of work and full of hope, in Batala. Fresh openings were appearing on all sides; and to the four Zenanas which at first could alone be entered, others had been already added. Then suddenly came a check. Miss Tucker's hard-working companion, who had all through suffered much from the Panjab climate, broke down, and was ordered off to England. For Miss Tucker to remain alone at Batala, without a single European companion, could not be thought of; and so many Missionaries had been invalided during the past unhealthy year, that no one else could possibly be spared. She had perforce to return to Amritsar.

The great disappointment—and very great it was—she took patiently, even cheerily. Some considered a few months more at Amritsar no bad thing for her or for her future work. She had freedom from responsibility, and more leisure in consequence for study and for writing. Many a short story went forth from her busy pen that winter for India's millions. But her eyes were still bent longingly upon Batala; and her whole desire and prayer were that she might soon return there again.

Nor had she to wait long before the granting of her wish. Mr. and Mrs. Beutel, then resident at Amritsar, were appointed C.M.S. Missionaries at Batala; and when they went she could go also. Mr. Beutel describes as follows the course of events:—

> 'One day—it was early in 1877—after returning from a preaching-place in the city (Amritsar), I met Miss Tucker on my way home. She was glad to see me, and then told me of her intention of going to settle at Batala, provided that my wife and I were willing and prepared to go with her. After a while this was sanctioned, and consequently we left Amritsar for Batala in April, and settled in the old house ... which is still used for the Christian Boarding School. It then looked like a haunted house, inhabited by owls,—which regularly had a dance in the loft almost every night!—bats and wasps, etc. Miss Tucker occupied the one wing of the

upper story, and we the other. The centre-hall served as a dining-room. She was our daily boarder.

'As a rule she rose very early in the morning. After her morning walk, service, and breakfast, she regularly went out into the city, to see and teach some women in their houses, occasionally accompanied by my wife. Now and then she also paid visits, like myself, to the villages in the neighbourhood. As a rule the afternoons were filled up by her with the study of the language, reading and writing, etc.

'But, alas! not quite two months had passed, when both Miss Tucker and my wife were laid up with fever. The chief cause of this, as the Doctor afterwards explained, seemed to be the stagnant water almost all around the house; and he ordered them both away as quickly as possible. Consequently we all returned to Amritsar by the end of May 1877, and settled again in our old quarters.

'As soon as the hot season was over, we all went back to Batala, a second time. The condition of the house was as bad as before; but Miss Tucker immediately offered her help, and I set about fifty people to work. The ground near the house was soon raised about two feet or more; and consequently the place became more healthy, so that this time we could stay there all the winter, doing our work as before.'

After a few months, however, came a renewed check. Mr. Beutel was required for work in Amritsar; and when he and his wife left Batala, Miss Tucker had to leave also. Once more she was obliged to settle down for a term of patient waiting and study at Amritsar.

Not till the spring of 1878 was any really permanent arrangement made. Then a school of Panjabi boys was removed from Amritsar to the old palace, under the presidency of the Rev. Francis Baring; and Miss Tucker went to live under the same roof, to carry on the work among women of Batala. Thenceforward her home was at Batala to the end. Throughout the year 1877 she had much of doubt and disappointment to endure; but her brave trustfulness never broke down under the strain. Charlotte Tucker was a thoroughly loyal soldier of the Cross,—willing to go, or willing to stay, as her Master might dictate. Her heart's desire was to live and toil in Batala; but a yet deeper desire of her whole being was to carry out His Will, whatever that Will might be. The Centurion's words, 'I am a man under authority,' may be cited as peculiarly applicable to her. If God's Will for her were Amritsar, not Batala, she would be content.

For a short time, seemingly, things were so; but not for long. Fresh plans in 1878 would make all clear. Meanwhile some months of change and uncertainty did no harm. They were but part of the polishing of the golden staff of her Will,—to revert to her own allegory of earlier days.

The history of these months, beginning with the time when she was first at Batala with Miss Swainson, will best be told by occasional extracts from the abundance of letters remaining.

TO MISS 'LEILA' HAMILTON.

'Batala, *Jan. 4, 1877.*

'Here we are in a regular "fix," as the boys would say,—no bread nor butter in the house, and with the probability of a grand lady, a Commissioner's wife, coming to-day, perhaps to stop the night. Pity the sorrows of—of ladies twenty miles from civilised life. I'm not housekeeper, so I can laugh; but poor dear Florrie!! You can feel for her. This is how we got into the fix.

'We settled on to-day, Thursday, for a general giving of prizes in the six City schools. Several pounds have been spent on prizes, and Florrie and I were for hours yesterday ticketing and preparing them. The prize-giving is of real importance; for we give prizes *instead* of money, as the Government gives. To throw *éclat* on the affair, we asked Mrs. T. to give the prizes away, which she kindly consented to do. A note was sent to her on Tuesday morning by a kahar,[59] to tell her the day, and the kahar was to bring back bread and butter, which we have always to get from Amritsar, twenty-four miles off.

'Thursday morning, the grand morning, has arrived,—nay, it is nearly eleven o'clock, and the children of six schools, their teachers and their mothers, and perhaps scores of women besides, will be on the tiptoe of expectation,—and our *kahar has never returned*!!! We don't know whether Mrs. T. is coming; we don't know whether she is sticking half-way on the road, waiting for the horse which we offered to send twelve miles, *if* she required it! Like the famous little pig, we have eaten all the bread and butter; and if the grand lady arrives—without that faithless kahar—what shall we give her to eat? I urged Florrie at least to send to the city for meat; but she fears that in the absence of the cook the guest may arrive.

'O dear! O dear! Why did we trust that *sust* [60] kahar,—or eat up all the bread? O how shall the bari Bibi ever be fed? I must go and try to cheer up poor Florrie, who suffers from her head, in addition to being in this "fix." I must tell you how the matter ends afterwards.

'Don't fancy we're starving! Oh, nothing like it! We had a famous breakfast, chapatties,[61] eggs, etc. We don't starve!

'*Later.*—No one has appeared. No tidings either of lady or kahar; but Florrie has sent for meat. She told me that the poor children had said that they would be ready at 7 a.m. If so, they must be rather tired by this time, nearly 11½ a.m. ...

'*Later.*—The kahar came at last, and brought the provisions, and a note from Mrs. T. to say that she is coming to-morrow.

'*Jan. 6.*—I was rather glad when yesterday's grand affair was over. As we had two dulis for three ladies, we had to manage by Florrie always going first,—*i.e.* she proceeded to School 2, while we lingered at No. 1—to School 3, while we stopped at 2, etc. I had to try to amuse and show off the children to Mrs. T. during the waiting time, which sometimes seemed rather long, especially where the girls would *not* sing. In vain I started even a bhajan[62] in one of the schools.

TO MR. AND MRS. CHARLES TUCKER.

'Batala, *Jan. 6, 1877.*

'How well I can fancy you in your home, with the wide blue expanse of Ontario stretching in front. I suppose the world looks very white with you just now; with us it is pretty green. We have no garden, but our large house stands in the country, without any enclosure. Herds of goats or strings of camels could pass near to our mansion. There is certainly not much noise of carriages. Here the sight of a dâk-gari is somewhat rare; and in the city I have never seen any wheel vehicle, except bullock-carts in the wider streets. We can sometimes hardly get through the narrow streets in our duli; and I am not aware that there are any other dulis in Batala except that of the Catechist's wife.

'Very funny things we hear of ourselves; and I dare say many funny things are said that we do not hear. In one place which my companion visited, in company with E., the Catechist's wife, she overheard the remark that she—-Miss Swainson—was the husband, and E. her bibi. I think that I excite more curiosity than my companion on account of my age. On account, I suppose, of an Englishwoman with any silver hair being a rarity in India, I seem to be sometimes considered wonderfully old. Florrie told me that she had heard the women talking as they might have done had I been a hundred years old.

'One day I wore brown kid gloves. My hands were looked at with surprise. I suppose that the women wondered why I should have brown hands and a white face. I pulled off my gloves, and this seemed a new cause for surprise. Natives are very curious. One ... young man of good family acts as my Munshi. He told me to-day that his aunt wished to know whether I have any salary. How astonished we should be if French or drawing masters asked such questions in England! I have been asked what salary my nephew receives. My being unmarried makes me doubly an object of curiosity to the Hindu women.

'A poor woman came the other day to see us, and brought us some common yellow flowers. I did not at all admire them, but I thought it only courteous to accept so small a present graciously. Miss Swainson did not like to accept the flowers—I did not know why.... She told me afterwards that she was afraid they were brought as religious offerings,—flowers are what are used for such offerings,—and she had heard repeatedly that we are 'devi.'[63] What gross, fearful ignorance! I heard on good authority that in one place in India, not the Panjab, offerings are actually made to a dead European, who was a special object of dread to the Natives, and whom they therefore wish to propitiate as a kind of *demon*! Do not the poor, deluded creatures want teachers? I find the women in general very gentle and courteous, and quite willing to listen when they are spoken to on the subject of religion. With the men—except of course the servants—we have little to do.'

TO MRS. HAMILTON.

'Batala, *Jan.* 9.

'Florrie and I hired four extra kahars, took earlier breakfast, and started this morning for O——, the village in which, as you may remember, I encamped for two or three days with my Margaret, about ten or twelve months ago.

'We started on foot, as it was not at all too hot for a walk; and though we never walk in the city, we have no objection to doing so in the country. Our dulis, white and red, with eight kahars, followed us. When we had walked about a mile, whom should we meet but the postman, with the English letters! I popped the rest of the things into the duli, but read my Laura's despatch as I walked along the dusty lane. Very many thanks both to you and to dearest Leila. *The* bonnet has not yet arrived,—I dare say it will be very elegant,—and yet, as well as the bag, owe its chief value to the love sewn up in it. Your lovely tidies ornament my Batala home.

'When F. and I returned from the village, being rather tired of going about twelve miles in a canvas box,—of course there is no seat in it; one sits half-Oriental style on a kind of coarse carpet,—I got out to walk the last mile home.'

'Amritsar, *Jan. 13*.—My note to dear Leila will tell you of the change which now a good deal engrosses my mind. You did not like my going to Batala; and as far as we can see, our Heavenly Father does not intend us to remain there. He is Wisdom; and what to us seems mysterious and trying must in the end be seen to be right....

'Ah, well, it is doubtless good to have the branches shaken, on which we perch; and happily I have built no elaborate nest.'

TO MISS 'LEILA' HAMILTON.

'Batala, *Jan. 20*.

'I am writing in such a dismantled room, making a table of a chair, and sitting on the floor. My luggage went off yesterday—such a quantity! My big boxes and little boxes, chairs, tables, almira, sofa, etc. I do not intend to unpack more than I can help, for I rather hope to have another move before long,—a move back to dear Batala....

'I have been round to the six schools and three Zenanas, explaining the sad cause of our sudden departure. I have found sympathy and kindness. On three faces at least there were tears. Facts are often more eloquent than words! The Batala people have seen B—n suffering keen anguish for Christ's sake; they see that the property which was — —'s is his no more, for Christ's sake. They have seen two ladies going fearlessly, trustingly, amongst them, one of them old, and the other so ill that she has fairly broken down in her work—for Christ's sake! These things may tell more even than preaching.... With God's blessing Batala will yet be ours.

'Strange to say, the Mission has just bought a house in the midst of the City; not hired, but bought it out and out. I went over it yesterday.... There is room on that ground to build a church on. And, please God, we shall have a church there some day. *Nil desperandum.*'

To another she wrote on the same day: 'It seems very sad, when there had been such a promising beginning; a new and interesting Zenana opened to me only yesterday; and I must quit Batala to-day, for one lady cannot stay by herself. But I am not in the least discouraged. I believe that the Almighty will not suffer the Mission to be permanently broken up. He will send some one to take poor Florrie's place; and then I am ready, at twenty-four hours' notice, to return to my post. I hear that the women are very sorry for our going. I have myself seen tears on brown faces.' Her confident hope was soon to come true.

'Mission Bungalow, *Jan. 29.*—Here I am, back again in my nice large room. My nieces would have it so, and made all arrangements during my absence.... I must tell dear Leila what C. H. said one day, absurd as it sounds; but it was a compliment to *her* work, therefore I repeat it. "How bonny the Auntie looks in her new bonnet!" There is a bit of flattery, spoken for once by one who is particularly plain-spoken! But it was the bonnet that was bonny, not your loving old sister.'

TO MISS 'LEILA' HAMILTON.

'March 5, 1877.

'Many thanks to you and your sweet Mother for your loving notes and the *Illustrated*. I am glad that I have not been sent *Froggy's Brother*. Not only am I afraid of shedding one useless tear; but I seem to have scarcely any time for reading what is unconnected with my work. I have begun the Koran, which will be rather a tedious task,—only in English,—but I think it well to read it, and a few books of manners and customs. Then I have two Munshis; and with my imperfect memory, I must be perpetually going over and over what I learn, so as not to lose it. Then I ought to write, whenever I can, and visit Natives a little; and we have so many interruptions. The day passes so fast; and perhaps at the end one feels—"What has been done?—how little!" But as for sitting down to amuse oneself with an English story-book,—how can that be done by your attached old Missionary Auntie?'

TO W. F. T. HAMILTON.

'*March 9, 1877.*

'I am about a very tedious work, reading through the Koran in English. I think that it may be very desirable for me to be able to say—"I have read your Koran right through." But, oh, how sleepy one gets over the book! It is so full of repetitions; the same ideas and stories over and over again. I am perfectly well, and the weather is now charming,—such a comfort to get rid of the cold!—but I believe that I twice this forenoon went to sleep, simply from reading the Koran. I read and read, then leant back in my comfortable chair, and took a nap!

'The poor Muhammadans must get a painful idea of the Almighty from their book. It seems almost a mockery to head almost every "Sura" with "In the Name of God the Compassionate, the Merciful." One is so perpetually reading of the torments of unbelievers, the fires of Gehenna, etc.! Our Lord is written of with great respect, and His Birth regarded as quite miraculous; but the Muhammadans will not believe Him to be the "Son of God." There is a great deal about Abraham, Moses, Joseph, etc., in the Koran; Old Testament stories altered and enlarged upon, to suit Muhammadan tastes. I have met with no reference to the Blood of Atonement; in the account of the Exodus, given over and over, there is no allusion to the Paschal Lamb; Muhammadanism appears as a religion of works.

'It would seem to me to be a dreary kind of religion, and well suited to make men hard and stern. Of the three religions in the Panjab, I think Sikhism by far the best; but then the race of those who profess it in purity seems to be dying away.... The Enemy would not leave poor Man even the scraps of Truth bequeathed by the noble Guru Nanak. It is a sad pity. Hearts which had only known *pure* Sikhism might have formed a rich soil to receive the seed of the Gospel.'

Early in March it was arranged, to her great joy, that before the close of the month she might expect to be back in Batala again, living there with Mr. and Mrs. Beutel. When the time came, the roads being especially bad with the heavy rains, Miss Tucker performed her journey from Amritsar to Batala in what she called 'a most luxurious conveyance,—the big, heavy Government dâk gari,[64] in which one can recline at ease, as if in a bed.' The twenty-four miles' drive proved, however, to be not altogether luxurious; for on the worst and roughest part of the road the whole gari went over on its side,—'one big wheel aloft, another big wheel below.' Miss Tucker being entirely unhurt, thought mainly of the safety of her desks and of her 'dear travelling clock.' She found them, to her great relief, 'quite serene,' as serene as she was herself in her 'funny position,'—the clock ticking placidly on, undisturbed by the jar. Describing the scene afterwards, she continued:

> 'A number of men came to the aid of our forlorn conveyance, down in the mud. The horses were of course released from the traces. Many hands make light work; so, with a good deal of pushing and shouting and tamasha, the carriage was set up again on its wheels. I got out, thinking that I should have to trudge through the mud on foot, carrying my clock in my hand. But I was not obliged to make my entry into my palace in so humble a fashion. I was able to re-enter the gari. Of course, I presented the natives with a reward.'

> '*April 14, 1877.*—I wrote to our Commissioner to ask his permission for fish to be caught in the large tank, close to which our mansion is built. He politely replied that we were welcome to fish with hook and line, but that a net is prohibited. I am rather amused to find that our dear, kind-hearted Germans cannot bear to give to the fish the suffering which a hook would inflict. I think that we shall do without fish.

> 'Such stormy—oh, such stormy weather as we have had, night after night! There have been such thunder and lightning, and rushing blast, and banging of doors and windows, as if in this great echoing house there were pistol practice.... Those Indian unmanageable doors and windows are the worst of it, particularly if any inmate of the house has headache or fever. One wanders about in the dark,— perhaps helped by the lightning,—to find the region of a door that is the chief offender. The one which I managed to shut in the night, for the first time since my coming chose to shut itself in the morning, so that neither I nor my Ayah could open it. Some one had to go round by another route to lift the latch, which had gone down without being touched.'

In the same letter, speaking of a young Indian, who had eagerly said to her that 'the Bible is the light of our eyes, and the root of our faith,' she sadly remarked that it was 'almost sickening' to think what the young Muhammadan 'would have to endure, did he openly confess Christ,'—even while earnestly hoping that he *would* be constrained 'by the cords of love' to leave all and come forward.

TO MISS LAURA V. TUCKER.

'*May 2, 1877.*

'Thanks many, darling Laura, for your dear, sweet letter. You speak of the flowers. Ah, if I could but give you a sight of the glorious pink water-lilies or lotuses out of our nice tank! I am not sure, however, whether I would not change them for—cabbages; certainly I would for cauliflowers. It is not very easy to get our vegetables, twenty miles away from an English garden. However, V. brought two cucumbers to-day,—a welcome sight,—and a Native presented us with some kelas,[65]—more welcome still. My experience is that fruit and vegetables are particularly conducive to health in India.

'You may rejoice to hear that we have got rid of our very wicked cook.... But it is funny to have no cook at all!! Mrs. Beutel's old mother does all the cooking; perhaps Mrs. Beutel helps a little; and it puts her quite into spirits. If we were not likely to go into Amritsar in ten or eleven days, I think that we should be obliged to procure a cook. It is a most unusual thing for Europeans to cook in a Panjab *May*; every day likely to get warmer and warmer! And if Mrs. J. fell ill, as she did last year—her daughter is constantly off and on with fever—where should we be? In a laughable dilemma, I should say; for I don't think that Mr. Beutel could cook; and I am sure that *I* can't! I forget—"can't" is not a Missionary word! But I really don't see what I could do, except boil eggs; we have plenty of them. You know that Fairy Frisket did not fancy a kitchen!

'We have bread brought in regularly; for I did not think the heavy, solid German home-made bread suitable for India. The bread we get is so beautifully light. I do not know exactly where it comes from,—I fancy from Gurdaspur or Amritsar. I am not housekeeper.

'What a greedy letter this seems! so much about eatables! But it may help you to picture to yourself life at Batala. I am very happy here.'

The end of May found her back again in Amritsar, but by no means downhearted. The fresh check was evidently regarded by Miss Tucker as only temporary.

'*May 30.*—It does my heart good to see Emily walking off to her work, perhaps at 6 a.m., so brave and bright, with firm, elastic tread.... Sweet Margaret has been very unwell. She looks too much like the statue of an angel in white marble. But she is better again; and if we can coax her back to her old quarters here, and pet her to any extent—her medicine—I think that she may weather the hot weather well.

'As I have little need of a separate kahar here, I was advised to part with V. I tried to do so, but I really could not. The poor fellow pleaded,—it was so hard to get work,—and I remember how miserable he looked when out of situation before. Then he is a married man, and such an intelligent, faithful creature.[66] So I gave in! It seems to me very hard to cast off good servants, just because the perpetual changing about makes one rather a supernumerary. V. is invaluable to me at Batala; and I hope to return to Batala. I was rather pleased at C.'s pleading for his companion. He seemed quite eloquent; but I confess that I did not understand much of his eloquence; only he evidently did not want poor V. to be cut adrift. I would at any time, if troubles arose, trust my life either to C. or V. I get quite interested in some of the servants, and they seem to be really affectionate. They are much like children.'

'Amritsar, *June 11, 1877.*—Emily said quietly to me yesterday, "You certainly have wonderful health." Not that I was well during my last trying time at Batala; but I have surprised my friends by getting all right again so very rapidly. The heat is very moderate as yet. I have only once this year had the thermometer in my sleeping room up to 90°. It seldom rises above 85° or 86°, which is nothing.'

'*June 22.*—The banyan-tree has dropped its brown leaves at last. Fancy a tree waiting till May or June before it will put off its old dress! It waits till all its new leaves are well out; and in midsummer throws off the withered ones. It is a grand tree; the one here is a fine one, but not to be compared to the one at Batala.

'The quite new school at Batala, the first *Boys'* School in which Christianity is taught, has already risen to 175 pupils. The house is too small, and I. D.[67] is going to give up his for it, and take another. The religious instruction has been given by three natives.'

'*June 30.*—Dear Emily is done up. She actually asked me for an amusing book, feeling evidently fit for little but to lie on the sofa and read. She overworks, and the season tells on her. When dear Leila happens to be writing to Bella Frances, would she kindly ask her to send me by post "Fairy Know-a-bit," and "Fairy Frisket," and "Pride and his Prisoners," my funniest tales. We have three trying months at least to come; and I want to keep my ladies as cheerful as I can. They have not much time for reading, except when poorly, and then a laugh is medicine.'

'*July 2.*—The work is going on at Batala, love, though we are absent. The Bible-woman, lately sent, who was here to-day, has access into nearly double the number of zenanas that Florrie and I had. There is also daily bazaar-preaching; and I. D. tells me that he has great hopes from the new Batala Boys' School, where the little lads listen readily to daily religious instruction. The women, I hear, want me back; but I do not see my way to returning till the rains are over. It would not do to dwell in a house which might be surrounded by water.'

'*July 14.*—It was so nice last Wednesday welcoming my dharm-nephew[68] back to Amritsar. Dharm is a good word to distinguish my Missionary relatives from my relatives by birth. A Godmother is a *Dharm*-mai. The Natives themselves have put me up to adopting the distinction. One of them asked Emily after me as her "dharm-poti," (religion-aunt). My dharm-nephew was only two days in Amritsar; he is off to Dhamsala, to be out of the heat of the plains. He looked better than I had hoped to see him, and just his own bright self.'

TO —— ——

'*July 20, 1877.*

'Mr. Clark told us the other evening that he had had an hour's interview with a Brahmin, who has come from beyond Benares. This man's views remind one of the Brahmo Somaj; but God grant that this Hindu may find more light than those Hindu Unitarians ever found. He is a man of great courage; he has flung aside the prejudices of his caste; he vehemently opposes idol-worship, and will readily eat with Christians. One of his special difficulties in regard to our faith is, I believe, the difficulty of reconciling God's justice with the punishment of the Innocent. The Brahmin is a gifted, eloquent man, and many go to hear him.

'Margaret and I were taking a moonlight drive after the heat of the day, with lightning flickering in the sky, when we passed a house in which I knew that the Brahmin has taken up his abode. It is some little way out of the city, and is a European bungalow. I pointed out to Margaret a little crowd in the compound, in the picturesque white Oriental costume, and told her that it was formed of those who were listening to the preacher.

'Margaret stopped the carriage, and we tried to catch the words which could reach us at the distance. They were, however, few; so we got out of the carriage, and without going near the crowd drew a little nearer and nearer to the place where the Brahmin was addressing his audience. We were still too far off to hear much, and there was too much of Hindi mixed with his Urdu to make his language clear; but we could see the man's eloquent, animated gestures, and hear the rich tones of his voice.

'It was a very picturesque scene; the mingled torchlight, moonlight, and heat-lightning,—the quaint, white-robed crowd,—the man who has dared to break through so much, who calls himself a Luther, telling idolaters of the folly of idol-worship. I should think that it would be wise to place in communication with this remarkable man some of our most talented converts from Hinduism—not Muhammadanism.'

TO MRS. HAMILTON.

'*Aug. 11, 1877.*—I missed a grand opportunity the other day of killing a centipede. It lay so quiet, as if to invite me to make myself illustrious. But I hate crunching creatures, so called out for some one to kill my centipede.... It is not fear of being bitten, but dislike of killing. The ladies think that it would not do for me to keep house, for that I should spoil the servants. I *did* give C. a decided rebuke the other day for beating his wife. He promised me to be kind in future.'

'*Aug. 13.*—I have this morning received my precious Laura's letter, with a request for a certain prayer—which I shall certainly remember. If a feeling of fear comes over my Laura, it must surely be as regards the *act* of departure, not what follows; for there is "no condemnation" to Christ's people, no death in the real sense of the word.

'But why, love, should we fear the act of departing? How many, many, pass Jordan, as it were, dry-shod? Remember how peacefully sweet Fanny sank to rest,—dearest Mother,—how my Letitia's face was lighted up with a smile,—how our Bible-woman at Batala sang aloud a happy hymn within a few hours of her going! To me it seems such a simple thing for the—I had almost said *imprisoned* soul, to leave its "cottage of clay,"—for the bird, as soon as fledged, to spread its wings! We are winged creatures, and it seems a humiliation to be creeping on earth so long. Only think what the first sight of the Lord will be! I am not sure whether some departing ones do not see Him before the last breath is drawn.'

CHAPTER VI
A.D. 1877-1878 A BROWN AND WHITE 'HAPPY FAMILY'

Though Miss Tucker had by no means fallen in love with Dalhousie during her former visit to the Hills, she was again this August to be, as she said, 'almost trapped' into going there. Mrs. Elmslie, albeit in need of rest, could not leave a child in the Orphanage who was dangerously ill, perhaps dying; and Miss Wauton, worn out with heavy toil through the very hot weather, imperatively needed change, yet was in no condition to manage the long distance alone. Miss Tucker therefore resolved to go with her; and the two started off in company, Miss Tucker in her duli, Miss Wauton on a pony. They travelled slowly, with frequent rests by the way, so as to extend the usual two days' hard journeying into six days of easy advance. On August 22, before leaving Amritsar, Miss Tucker wrote:—

> 'Man has been described as a "laughing animal," "a cooking animal," to distinguish him from the lower creation. I would suggest "a packing animal," for neither birds nor beasts—except the elephant—have anything to do with filling trunks! What an amount of packing I have had in the last two and a half years! Of course, these thoughts are suggested by my present business of packing for the Hills.
>
> 'One must be prepared for all sorts of weather, for burning heat, bitter cold, or furious rain. One may have all three in the course of a week. Then one must prepare—as for an attack of cavalry—for a dinner-invitation from the Commissioner's wife. One is pretty certain that one will meet some worldly folk, who are inclined to think Natives "niggers," Converts hypocrites, and Missionaries half-rogues and half-fools; so that one must not "appear as a scrub." I do not wonder that the weary Emily wants to keep in the jungle as long as she can. Ah! if we could but keep in the jungle *all* the time, I need not pack up my "Conference Cream,"[69] nor my faithful moire antique. There would be some fun in meeting with

a cheetah or a hyena,—I should not like a bear unless there were a kud[70] between us,—but I shrink from the world and his wife. However, Missionaries, like sailors, are bound for all weathers....

'If it won't shock dear — —, I think that I must give you a laugh over a funny little story, which was told me the other day as a true one. A very attractive Scotch clergyman was teased in the same way that the Energetic used to be. At last a—one can't call her *lady*, actually wrote to offer him "her purse, her hand, and her heart." The cream of the story is the clergyman's reply. He wrote to his silly sheep: "I advise you to give your heart to God, your purse to the poor, and your hand to him who asks for it." Was it not clever? I hope that the lady profited by the pastoral rebuke, though she can hardly have enjoyed it....

'Thanks for the paper about the Telephone. But I hope that we may *not* hear our Queen's voice by it, if it is to sound like a trombone.'

From Dinaira, a place some twenty-two miles short of Dalhousie, she wrote:—

'There is something more soothing to the eye in the softly wooded mountains in which we are now cradled, than in the cold, stern white peaks, seen higher up. The great want is water. One sees the rough, almost precipitous, channels of mountain torrents, but there is not a drop trickling in them. The land suffers sorely from drought. The early crops were partly spoilt by furious storms, the second crops are threatened with destruction by the failure of the rains. A peasant saw me yesterday very slowly getting down rather a rough bit, and with kindly courtesy came and offered me the help of his brown hand. He almost immediately afterwards began to speak of the want of rain; it is the uppermost thought amongst the poor, dear people....

'I feel that I was rather ungrateful last year about Dalhousie. Though I do not like the place much, it is a very great blessing to have it.'

'Dalhousie, *Sept. 3, 1877.*—This ought to be a good day for letter-writing; for it is like an exaggerated November day in England: rain more violent; wind more furious.... I amuse our ladies by my indignation at one of our best hands, Miss

H. of J— —, deserting us for matrimony. Merrily laughed the bonny blue-bell at my proposition that, in addition to the fine of £100 imposed on Mission Miss Sahibas who marry within three years of coming out, it should be part of the contract that they should have all their hair shaved off on the day before the wedding. Don't you approve, dear? In the Strathclyde, beside Miss F. and myself, there were four Mission Miss Sahibas going out for the first time. One of the four has gone home, invalided; two have married; only my noble Miss G. remains in the field! It is a great deal worse when experienced Missionaries marry; we do not know how to supply their places....

'You must not fancy that we have always weather like this in the hills. When we first arrived, and for days afterwards, the weather was lovely, July in the middle of the day, October at night. The scenery was glorious. I hope, however, that I may get back next week. I intend to travel rapidly, as I travel alone.'

A few days afterwards saw Miss Tucker back in Amritsar; and later in the same month she went all the long journey to Murree, giving herself only six days of absence, to be present at the wedding of her nephew, Louis Tucker. Thence she again returned to Amritsar. Exciting events had happened at Amritsar during even that absence, in the shape of fresh Baptisms and fresh persecutions. In October she was once more off on a short itinerating tour through villages. A letter written on the first of October refers to the Batala work, of which her heart was full.

'Mr. Beutel told me with regret that Mr. Baring, on account of low funds, had desired him on Nov. 1st to stop two village-schools near Batala, in which 50 or 60 boys are receiving instruction. I had my Laura's £5—grown to £5, 10s.—half of her handsome gift, of which Margaret has the other half. This will keep the village schools going till April; and by that time, please God, others may send help.... People do not seem to care for *village* schools. Government does not. And the people—our dear Natives—are so anxious to have them. The nicest boys seem the village ones.'

An undated letter belongs, probably, to about this time.

'I think I mentioned to you that a troop of guests invaded my poor Margaret almost in the middle of the night, 3 a.m. She had too much bustle, too much discomfort. She fell ill, as was almost to be expected; but I left her up again, and going to work. When she was lying on her sick-bed,—lovely she looked, with her soft pink cheeks, and her long golden hair hanging loose,—I went and had a chat with her. She has had too few chats with those whom she loves since going to live at the Orphanage.... Says Margaret, "What caps are you going to take to your nephew's?" "Oh, killing caps," said I. Perhaps they would look killing if Margaret wore them! She would not believe me,—her playful banter, her arch smile, so reminded me *of my Laura*! Margaret went on exactly as you would have done. She was certain that my velvet cap must want a new ruche; would I send over a whole set of caps for her to improve? It would amuse her, she said. The Doctor came in, when I was having one of my playful chats with Margaret; and he highly approved of my giving her a little laugh.... She called me "sparkling champagne." There is a fine name for a Missionary Miss Sahiba! Fancy my discovering one day that, in her crowded little dwelling, she had so emptied herself of needful comforts, that she had not so much as a basin to wash in. If she wished to wash her hands, she must stoop or kneel to perform the ablution in her bath! Off went I to the city, and procured a toilette-set for our house in Batala, which Margaret has the use of till we go,—when I hope that she will return to the Bungalow.'

The above must have been written before her visit to Murree, already mentioned. By the middle of October she was on the point of again starting for Batala; and she wrote cheerily beforehand, on the 15th:—

'Many, many thanks to my own sweet Laura for the pretty sketch of what was once to me a very happy home. I am so pleased that your hand has not lost its skill. I am in great hopes that, like myself, you may have renewed vigour as you walk down the incline of life's hill. My companions here wonder at me. In another month I shall have been two years in India,—only two months, journeys included, spent in the Hills; all the remaining twenty-two in the Plains, with one peculiarly unhealthy season, and another of unusually prolonged heat;—and yet I am just as strong and well as if I had been just sauntering about an English garden all the time....

'I am considered to have a wonderful constitution; and as my Laura is my own sister, I always hope that she has one also....

'Take no fears about Batala. Fear is another thing with which Missionaries should have nothing to do. It seems to me that English folk in India rather change in character. I never imagined the effect of being in a land like this, where you belong to a conquering race. I must not just say that no one seems afraid of anything, for that would be an exaggeration; but physical courage seems to come quite naturally. Those who might be timid girls in England fearlessly travel at night, quite alone—save for the company of wild-looking natives,—through lonely mountain-passes, perhaps through lightning and storm, with the possibility of meeting cheetahs, bears, and snakes. I feel no more afraid of being at Batala, with or *without* Mr. Beutel, than you would of sleeping in a London hotel.'

FROM MRS. ELMSLIE TO MRS. HAMILTON.

'Oct. 18, 1877.

'I have just returned from seeing our darling off to Batala. I know you will be sorry to hear she has gone there again; and Miss Wauton, Mr. Clark, and I have tried hard to prevent it,—in vain! She thinks it her duty to go, and she makes it her pleasure. How we miss her here, I cannot tell you. She is beloved and honoured by rich and poor, young and old. She is our Sunshine. Her bright fancies, her quick perceptions, her wise suggestions, are invaluable to all of us in the Mission.

'While she frets over her want of power in speaking Urdu and Panjabi, we are rejoicing, not only in her power of writing for the people, but in her wonderful perception of the national character, her insight into the weaknesses and also into the virtues of our Native friends, Christian and heathen. Her loving, unselfish ways are wonderfully soothing and sustaining; and life has seemed to me a different thing since God brought her to us.

'She has been wonderfully free of fever during the past year; and the excitability which used to make me anxious has quite passed away. I think she has been looking quite lovely of late; the expression of her dear face has been so restful, so sweet, so angel-like. She has been a little less thin too, and has been wearing more becoming caps and bonnets. We find it necessary to look after her in such sublunary things; and many a laugh she has at our anxiety about her appearance. You asked me to tell you of anything she ever needs; and I think you may like to know that she has no intermediate dress for everyday use; nothing between the dark green cashmere and a very pale kind of Chinese silk.

'A light material of a rather dark grey colour, nicely made up with a tunic bodice and belt, would be very useful to her. But what would she say to me, if she thought I had written this? Another thing is a *feather* pillow. Such a thing is not to be had in India; and her dear head is, I am sure, often tired. We put our only one into her gari just now, hoping she would not notice it. Off went her coach, and we were so pleased to think it was with her, but she found it out before reaching the end of the Avenue, and sent it back. If you could send one with a coloured cover, it could do either on bed or sofa; and I think it might be well to put her name on it in indelible ink, for she is so very likely to give away such a desirable thing....'

C. M. T. TO MRS. E— —.

'Batala, *Nov. 15, 1877*

'Where do you think the gay Mission Miss Sahiba has been to-day? Never consider mine a monotonous life! Why, I have been to a fair, a *mela*, as they call it here. I had never thought of a lady's going to a heathen fair; but two of our Mission ladies are here for ten days, to conduct examinations in the schools. Our valuable Miss Wauton said that she would like to go to the mela. Of course, I would not let her go without a lady companion; so we both accompanied Mr. Beutel in his light covered cart, plunging over ruts in the kachcha road in fine style.

'It was a pretty sight. The weather was delicious. Numbers of people in their picturesque costumes were threading their way to the village of A— —, white being the prevailing colour of the men's costumes, gay red that of the women's, with a fair sprinkling of green, a touch of yellow and blue, and here and there a grand display of glittering gold. But we did not go just to look at the folk, or to buy fairings either. Emily and I went armed with books and pictures, to try and sow a little good seed amongst the women, whilst Mr. Beutel and the two Catechists preached to the men.

'Mr. Beutel found a shady place for us, and Emily and I tried to gather women around us. The men were curious, and wanted to see and hear also. We could not secure an exclusively feminine audience. It was a Hindu mela; and not many Muhammadans seemed to be present, which made matters easier for us.... No one objected to hearing as much about the Blessed Saviour as we could tell them. Emily speaks Punjabi famously; I have only about a thimble-full of it; so I chiefly listened to Emily, and held the umbrella to shield her from the sun.

'It was interesting to look at the faces, when Emily, with admirable fluency, told the story of the Prodigal Son. At this time her audience seemed to be principally Sikh men. They crouched upon the ground around us, and listened with hearty interest. Nowhere, either from men or women, did we meet with any rudeness; nor did any one seem vexed with our describing what our Lord had done for us....

'The way in which Batala is opening out is marvellous. I go from Zenana to Zenana, and have not by any means finished paying all my *first* visits!! Our Bible-woman thinks that about *thirty* Zenanas are open to her. I doubt that nearly so many are open in the large mother-stations of Amritsar or Lahore. We ought to have two or three clever, active, strong Miss Sahibas here, instead of one elderly lady, who is slow at both learning and teaching.

'The two ladies from Amritsar are delighted with Batala. To-day is, I think, the anniversary of my arrival in India; so I have entered upon my third year! My Missionary life has, on the whole, been a very happy one....'

TO MRS. HAMILTON.

'*Dec. 13, 1877.*—The overland mail was particularly long in arriving this time. I hoped that it would bring me something particularly nice; and what should come to-day but your dear loving letter, and the first halves of your munificent contribution to our schools! How very kind and liberal my Laura is! I had been speaking to Mr. Beutel but yesterday of those two village schools, which would—from the lowness of funds—have been dropped, but for your last handsome gift. I was asking Mr. Beutel how far your Rs.55 would carry them on. He replied—till past the beginning of March. Beyond that there was no provision for them at all.

'How delighted Mr. Beutel will be, on his return from Amritsar, to hear that a bountiful supply has come in! I think it better to apply your gift to the village schools, than to the girls' schools in Batala. The latter, I think, excite more interest, and are not so likely to be in want of funds. These poor village schools—since for retrenchment sake they were cast off—are like waifs and strays. Government does not care for village schools; the School Society cannot afford to keep up half the desirable number. Mr. Beutel often receives applications for new village schools, and is so much interested in them that he and our Catechist have one between them....

'We are to have a grand tamasha here at Christmas-time. Mr. Beutel is going to gather, not only the boys of our Batala Mission School, but boys from village schools. Of course, this is not merely to give enjoyment, though the enjoyment will probably be great, but to bring more forcibly before the lads the tidings of great gladness. We are a little puzzled about the poor little girls; as their cruel and absurd pardah rules prevent the possibility of gathering them all together, even in the Bible-woman's house.'

The beginning of 1878 found Miss Tucker at Batala; and though once more for a short time her work there was to be broken through, the spring of this same year, as explained earlier, would see an end of the difficulty which had attended her permanent residence in the place. The letter to her sister, written on January 5th, is all through a particularly characteristic one. A large amount will bear quotation.

'The warm dress which you have so very kindly procured for me has not yet arrived; but I should not wonder if it were here on Monday or Tuesday.... We have been guessing of what colour it will be. Mrs. J. and I both fixed upon grey, Mrs. Beutel purple, and Mr. Beutel brown. Perhaps after all it will turn out to be blue. I hope that I may have it in time to wear at B.'s baptism, which I do hope may take place to-morrow week, if some clergyman will only come from Amritsar. To this baptism I look forward with joyful interest. B.'s white dress is probably ready now. We like converts to wear pure white at baptism. I intend to give J., the Bible-woman, a new skirt to wear on the occasion; and I should like to wear something perfectly fresh too....

'I was in a Zenana to-day, which it is always a mental effort to visit; but it is very interesting. Instead of talking to the women there, I am certain to have one or two men, descendants of the famous Guru Nanak, who engross the conversation with me almost entirely.

'The religion of the fine old fellow who is the principal talker is a regular puzzle. He talks Panjabi; so you may imagine how very difficult it is for me to understand him; and he *wants to make me understand*. I do my best to do so. This is what I gather of his views. S. is *not* a Muhammadan; he says that he is a Hindu; though by his birth he ought to be a Sikh. He reverences Guru Nanak,[71] very properly, but thinks that Guru Nanak has given religious tenets such as I am certain that he never did. We have no reason to suppose that the excellent Guru had ever heard of our Saviour. But S. propounds doctrines that are amazing from the lips of a *Hindu*. He believes in the one true God. He believes that a time of great war and trouble will come; and that then Isa Masih (Jesus Christ) will come like a flash of lightning, and become the Ishar (Divine Lord) of all the Earth.

'I had taken a Gurmukhi Testament with me. Neither of the men seemed disposed to read it. I thought that perhaps neither of them *could*; so I opened it myself, and chose a pretty easy place. I had never read the Gurmukhi character in a Zenana before. My old Sikh—for I cannot help considering him one—listened very attentively, correcting my pronunciation now and then. I did not venture to read much. Then he took the Testament himself, and began to read it in regular Sikh fashion, in a kind of measured chant, as if it were poetry. It was clear that he *could* read; so I left the precious Volume as a loan in that house. May God bless it!...'

'*Jan. 9, 1878.*—Hurrah! the box has come! It is in process of being opened.

'Was I not a real witch? Did I not guess a grey dress? What an elegant, ladylike, quiet costume! And so warm and comfortable!... When I opened my tempting box, I thought of the dear fingers which had been employed in putting it up! How very, very kind you have been! So many, many thanks! And what loves of cushions! You have remembered my weakness for cushions. Soft, warm, and so pretty!... I am obliged to go to Amritsar, just for a few days, as Mr. Clark and Margaret cannot come here; and we must have a serious, prayerful discussion about what is really very important, and too complicated for letters.... I see my *own* path clearly. I intend, please God, to stick by Batala. My friends will not hear of my staying alone.... May God guide us! Batala should NOT be abandoned.'

'*Jan. 23.*—I have come back from Amritsar, with nothing settled, except that the Beutels are to go to Amritsar about the middle of March. The Batala affairs have been much talked over.... I earnestly hope that I may not have a third time to retreat from Batala, for lack of a companion. We are beating about for one, but it seems a hard thing to find, we are so undermanned. Every one seems to acknowledge the great importance of Batala....

'As for its being unhealthy, I regard it as *more* healthy than either Amritsar or Lahore. The tank is a lovely tank, with no bad smell; and when it is very full I can *see* the current of water flowing in on one side and out at the other. Fishes live and jump about in it; and birds delight in its bright waters. I have a better chance of keeping well through the hot weather here than at the bungalow at Amritsar. This house is far better built, with thick walls, lofty rooms, etc. But none of my Missionary friends at Amritsar will listen to my staying here alone. So I must just wait, and see what is God's Will. He can send me a companion, if He sees right to do so.'

'*Feb. 7.*—Perhaps you will be glad to hear that all our attempts to find a companion for me at Batala have failed. Poor — — must go back to England; it was a mistake ever to have sent out so delicate a lady. Miss — — with whom I was in treaty, is going home too. Mrs. — — has been secured for another station.... Perhaps I have been too ready to say to myself, "There is no place on earth where I can be so useful as at Batala." I must come down a little, which is wholesome. But I have not any sense of defeat; no, thank God,—every visit to Batala, it seems as if fresh ground had been gained. The waves retreat again and again, while the tide is advancing.... I believe that a far better spirit, a spirit of kindness towards us, a lessening of prejudice, a most encouraging readiness to listen, is now spreading in Batala.[72] Maulvi Z. felt the difference. B—n feels the difference. I believe that there will be *real* regret at our leaving Batala. Dear B—n!... I had brought for B—n's children two gay little coverlets.... B—n took them and wrapped them round the plump little girls as chaddahs. I think that he was quite pleased....

'Oh, did I tell you—I told somebody—about my other Brahmin; the elderly man who prays by the side of our tank? I have repeatedly spoken to him in my indifferent Panjabi; and I spoke to my nephew, R. Bateman, about him, when he was here for two days. So on one of the mornings I see my nephew seated beside my Brahmin close to the tank, with only a handkerchief round his delicate head. His old Auntie soon supplied him with an umbrella. R. Bateman gave me afterwards an account of the Brahmin's strange view of religion. One can hardly imagine a mind in which the whole visible creation is regarded as God. The Brahmin had no idea of *sin*; he had *never seen it*, he said,—as if it were a thing like a stone or a tree!

'I saw the poor fellow by the tank yesterday morning, and went out and spoke to him. I invited him to come to morning prayers. Rather to my surprise, the dear man really did come. He must be a wondrously meek Brahmin; for he seated himself on the floor amongst the servants, labourers, etc., apparently quite forgetful of the tremendous difference between their castes and his own. Mr. Beutel makes morning family prayers almost like a regular service. He not only reads the Bible, but expounds. I had asked him, for my Brahmin's sake, to make his address as Punjabish as possible; so he stuck in Punjabi words where he could. My Brahmin looked very attentive. He has a sort of childlike readiness to listen, looking full at you when you speak; and his face quite brightening as if with pleasure when you talk of a Saviour. It must be all so strangely new to him! I wonder if he will come again....

'To-day I went to two new houses,—I have such a number to go to! When I sang of the Saviour's invitation, to a Hindu, not only did she seem to listen attentively, but I saw her wiping moist eyes.

'Margaret and E. Clay intend coming here the day after to-morrow for two days.... I must not dwell on parting with Margaret.[73] I rejoice in the happiness which I hope she will enjoy. She has worked long and very hard.... No doubt there are some wise and merciful reasons for sending me away from Batala.'

'Batala, *Feb. 14.*—Another curious phase in my strange, strange life! I told you or dear Leila of the idea of the Boys' Orphanage being brought here. That idea was knocked on the head; but another is taking such shape that it is likely enough that I shall find myself, not exactly planted in, but on the top of—and underneath also—*another* boys' school! The Rev. F. Baring, the Bishop of Durham's son, has fallen in love with Batala, and has set his heart on buying this house from Government, for a Boarding-school for Christian Native Boys.

'We have no wish, however, to lose our hold of our beautiful palace as a station for the Zenana Mission; so it is likely that, if Mr. Baring succeed in buying Anarkalli, he will allow our Mission to rent from him, on easy terms, that part of the house which we now occupy (by we I mean myself), with the addition of the drawing-room and part at least of the grand dining-room. Dear, good Babu Singha and his wife and family will probably live in another part of the palace, he being Under-Superintendent of the School!!

'Here's a brown and white Happy Family for you! Natives and Europeans can hardly chum together; yet it would be absurd to have *three* cooks for us. The present idea is for Mr. Baring and me to chum, *till* I am joined by any young lady. Mr. Baring ... is quite happy with me, because of my venerable age, which I have found such an advantage in India. He asked me to-day to have him as a nephew! How rich I am in these dharm-nephews,—to say nothing of the real ones! Now I have *five*; one of them being my Afghan, and the others four of the most valuable clergymen in the Panjab Mission.[74] Henry, my Afghan boy,[75] you must know. He is the youngest of all my dharm-nephews.

'Now, what does my sweet Laura say to my plans—and my family? I like you to know all my nephews.... I have more nieces even than nephews; but you have had enough of my dharm-family for the present. Mr. Clark wanted me to take him in too. If he had asked to be a *brother*, I should have welcomed him; but I really could not have as a nephew one to whom we look up as a head-pastor, a kind of bishop! I don't think that my nephews should be more than forty years old.'

'Amritsar, *Feb. 23, 1878.*—Here I am again in dear old Amritsar.... I know that you will be curious to hear how the Batala school plan progresses. Well, we are waiting to hear what our saintly new Bishop says to it. In a matter of such importance it is right to wait for the advice of such an Apostolic man.... I wait passively. There is plenty of work for me at Amritsar, more than I can do at all properly....

'You see, Laura darling, there are quantities of Aunts in England; but an old Auntie is a rare bird in India, and therefore in request. I am like a hen with such a large brood!

'Dearest Margaret will be much missed. Many, many, both English and Natives, love her.... The Native Christians have quietly subscribed for a shawl for her Mother, as a token of their grateful love. I think the Natives very affectionate. People talk of their being ungrateful; but those who talk so have perhaps never *earned* their gratitude. If you love them, they love you! They are very sensitive, both to kindness and to unkindness....'

TO MISS 'LEILA' HAMILTON.

'*March 4, 1878.*

' ... Missionary work can be just as truly done in England as in India; but only a few of the dear workers *can*—without forsaking other duties—come out so far as the Panjab. Those who come here should be strong also, physically as well as mentally suited for the peculiar work and trying climate....

'There are plenty of poor in Amritsar, as well as Batala. I went to Mrs. Clark's yesterday, at the large Mission House. In her garden were quantities of poor folk; between three and four hundred, counting children. A Catechist preached to them first; and then a great number of chapatties, a kind of thick flat cake, of very simple make, with a small quantity of dal,[76] was handed round and distributed. Adults had two chapatties each; children one. Mr. Clark had had a Brahmin to cook, for Hindu beggars would not otherwise have liked the food, and Muhammadans do not object to a Brahmin's cooking. Station-people subscribe to help in the distribution of this food....

'Mr. Clark and my new nephew, Mr. Baring, have gone to Lahore to see our new Bishop.[77] He is known to be such a saint, that thanksgivings have been offered again and again for his appointment.'

TO MRS. J. BOSWELL.

'*March 4, 1878.*

'Is poor, dear — — going to remain in the same house, so full to her of sad memories? People feel so differently on this subject. Some cling to the spot where they have loved and sorrowed,—others fly from it. I should never like to cross the threshold of No. 3 again. I am rather pleased that it has another number now. There is *no* 3 Upper Portland Place now.'

TO MRS. HAMILTON.

'*March 8.*—I can fancy the request to have my letters directed to Batala has excited a little curiosity. It really seems likely that our comical arrangement will be carried out; and that I and my nephew will find ourselves chumming together in the midst of a Boys' School!!

'The Panjab is eager to have a boys' school for young Christian Native gentlemen. The Bishop approves. Our boys are to pay Rs.5 a month. This may cover food expenses, but of course not the expense of first-class teaching. Batala is to have this, the nucleus of a future Panjabi Eton or Harrow (if it please God to prosper it), the training-place for our clergymen, lawyers, and merchants. I am *not* to be Matron. I am the sole representative—European—of our Ladies' Zenana Society; but it would be strange if I lived in the same building with the dear boys, and took no interest in them. It is probable enough that I shall find myself playing at Oxford or Cambridge, or giving a music-lesson to young Panjabis. A comical idea suggests itself. I have a large family of new Nephews and Nieces in India. Am I to have a whole troop of brown Grandnephews in perspective!!! Don't fancy them ugly savages. Many will probably be winsome enough,— bright, attractive, and courteous.

'Good Babu Singha and his excellent wife will probably be in the house, but not chum with Europeans....

'Only imagine my darling Laura dreaming of coming to Egypt to meet me!! But I doubt her being up to such a journey; and mine would be about as formidable a one. But the dream is one of "old," not "young Love"!'

'*March 15.*—Now, darling, to answer your objections to my spending the hot season at Batala.... I doubt that the risk to health from climate will be at all greater at Batala than at damp Amritsar. Always remember, love, that at the former place I am high above the ground, while at the latter I am on it. This makes an immense difference. The large inner room at Batala would be cooler than any room here....

'I intend to take my large harmonium to Batala. It may be of immense use there. I suppose that I shall have charge of all the music; for I do not believe that either my Bhatija (nephew) or the Singhas know anything about it. It is of *immense* importance. Mr. R. told me yesterday that the Rev. C., perhaps the most valuable convert in all the Panjab (he is a Bengali), was first brought to Christ by listening to Church music. It carried his soul away! I wish that I were more competent for the charge; but I must hope and pray that God may bless my little attempts to serve Him by music. I am so thankful that age has not affected my voice; at least, it does not seem to me to have done so.'

The latter fact would tell little. People in advancing years are seldom able to judge of their own voices. Others, however, speak of the unusual manner in which Miss Tucker's voice lasted. It had never been one of much power or sweetness; but she had always had a sensitive ear, and had sung well; and to the end she still sang in tune, even when the voice itself became cracked with age.

One other point in the above may be noted. Miss Tucker was throughout anxious to make the best of her beloved Batala; and undoubtedly this was a case of 'making the best.' If Amritsar was damp, so also must Batala have been,—at all events, in the seasons of heavy floods, when it was often impossible to get about, from the state of the roads. There were times when Anarkalli was all but a veritable island, in the midst of a kind of lake. This could hardly be regarded as healthy, while it lasted.

TO MISS 'LEILA' HAMILTON.

March 28, 1878.

'I am to have my "pen," about which my dharm-nieces joke a great deal. Mera Bhatija[78] is going to cut a slice off his magnificent dining-room, to make a cool retreat for the Auntie. As a bamboo-screen right across would be very unsightly, if seen in its bareness, I am going to have mine covered on both sides. Fancy a screen, twenty feet long and six feet high! I have been very fortunate in securing a most suitable cloth for the cover. A bedroom chintz would have looked quite out of character, but I have bought a native cloth, with an Oriental pattern, very tapestry-like, old-fashioned conventional flowers and birds on a blue ground. It is such a pattern as one might see in a picture, and will not destroy the effect of the Oriental hall. Every one who saw it at once fixed upon it as *the* thing....

'Emily has ordered eight chairs for my rooms,—I had two of my own,—and your beloved Mother knows that I am splendidly supplied with cushions; such dainty cushions! I like my rooms to look rather nice, as young Panjab may get an extra polish, if admitted to an English lady's drawing-room.'

CHAPTER VII
A.D. 1878 PERSECUTIONS

Once more Miss Tucker settled down in Batala—for life! She would only leave the place again for her short and well-earned holidays; and at the last for her passing away.

During many years her home was still to be in the quaint old palace, described by others as draughty, weird, forlorn, desolate; though she herself so resolutely looked upon the discomforts of the old building through rose-tinted glasses. But its dreary aspect was soon to be changed. The bright faces of Panjabi lads, the merry voices of Panjabi scholars, were to fill with fresh life those big and empty rooms. 'The Baring High School,' as it was called, had its first existence in the shape of a small boarding-school at Amritsar, which Mr. Baring decided to remove to the palace at Batala. About fifteen boys were, in the beginning, at Anarkalli,—described by A. L. O. E. as 'our choicest young Natives, converts or descendants of converts; one is the grandson of a martyr!' These boys or their friends paid fees, when they could, which was not always; and the fees, though perhaps sufficient to cover their food, were by no means sufficient to cover the cost of a good education.

From the spring of 1878 Mr. Baring resided there, as C.M.S. Honorary Missionary, with control of the Boys' School, which indeed had been started mainly at his own expense; while Babu Singha worked under him as the Master of the School. Miss Tucker, as she stated in her letters, held no such post as that of Matron. Her position was entirely independent, being that of Honorary Zenana Missionary. She paid for her own rooms and her own board in the Palace, and regarded Zenana visiting, and the writing of small books for Indian readers, as her prime occupations. But for Charlotte Tucker to live under the same roof with all those boys, and not to give them loving interest, not to attempt to teach or influence them, would have been a sheer impossibility.

Another Boys' School had been started in Batala, which must not be confounded with the above. The Baring High School was—and is—distinctly for the education of Indian Christian boys. The Mission School, known later as 'The Plough,'—Miss Tucker recognising strongly that this early stage of work in Batala could only be compared to a farmer's ploughing of his fields,—was for Indian boys, not yet Christian. They received Christian teaching; and when a boy in the Plough School became a convert, he was passed on usually to the High School. The very starting of this 'Plough School' was due to Miss Tucker's liberality. Out of her own purse she generously paid the main part of its expenses.

We must turn again to her letters, with all their curiously fresh, *young* eagerness and enjoyment, to realise what her life was at this time. Charlotte Tucker might call herself 'old,'—she was very fond of doing so on every possible occasion; but certainly none of the weight of age had as yet descended upon her spirits.

TO SIR W. HILL.[79]

'Batala, *April 13, 1878.*

'We hope next Sunday to have a Baptism in our lovely little lake; and we have been practising baptismal hymns to sing on the joyful occasion. We had some anxiety about our young convert.... He went to Amritsar on business; and at the time when we expected his return he did not come back.

'What could have happened? Had the dear youth been seized by his Muhammadan relations? Such things do happen; the danger is a very real one. It is often no easy matter to confess Christ in India. Mr. B., who was here, wrote off a note to a Christian Maulvi in Amritsar to search for the lad. He did so, and found him, and brought him here in safety last night; but not before — — had had a painful time of it in Amritsar.

'I looked with interest on that Christian Maulvi, as he sat in our drawing-room, conversing with the English Missionaries.... *He* has known well enough to what dangers a convert may be exposed; for he has experienced them.... He was the first of his family to take up the Cross. His Muhammadan neighbours formed the fiendish design of *burning him alive in his house.* They piled up his clothes, etc., in an under room. He was sleeping above. The Muhammadans set fire to the pile; and the clothes, etc., were quickly consumed; but the fire did not, as was intended, set the whole house in a blaze. The ceiling was charred; that was all; and the Christian slept unharmed, watched over by the Eye that never slumbers nor sleeps.'

About this time A. L. O. E. wrote home to another quarter:—

'Yesterday a letter arrived from the schoolmaster of O— — with tidings that a lad of fifteen has had the courage to declare to his friends his desire to become a Christian. The natural result of such a declaration has followed,—the young confessor has been beaten. It is no small matter to stand up thus openly for Christ in a heathen village. The lad may have to endure much. I have seen one who was made to stand in boiling oil by his own father, to hinder him from going to the Christians. Whether the O— — boy's conversion has been the result of the Good Friday expedition we know not; but whether it be so or not, the lad claims our sympathy and interest. We shall try to bring him here, to the Batala Boarding-School, where he may at least receive food and protection. "It is a refuge," said our Christian Maulvi to me yesterday, glancing up at the goodly building raised by the Maharajah Shere Singh, who little dreamed that he was preparing in it a home for a Christian Natives' Boarding-School, and also for the ladies of a Zenana Mission. I am at present the sole English Agent of the latter Society here.'

TO MRS. E— —.

'*May 10, 1878.*

'You may like to hear a little more about our School of young Panjabis, as it is rather a curiosity.

'My nephew, Mr. Baring, has succeeded in making these young Natives like not only cricket, but gardening. We are to have a Horticultural Exhibition in August, when prizes are to be given for the best flowers and fruit. Considering that the gardens are all on ground *redeemed from the lake this year*, it will hardly be expected that the show will equal one in the Botanical Gardens. But oh, you should see our glorious pink water-lilies! They grow wild in the water, and would be a sight anywhere.

'I want the boys also to take to intellectual games. I am much pleased at having succeeded in making one nice lad compose two Sunday enigmas. I by no means despise this small beginning of authorship. Sunday enigmas greatly increase knowledge of Scripture, and also help to make the holy day pass pleasantly. There is a great deal of singing here also; and such a lovely text for our Chapel wall is now almost ready.... Our dear lads cannot, as — — did, give a beautiful pulpit, but I think that they take a pride and pleasure in their Chapel.

'It will look rather pretty, I hope, with its white walls, and striped pardahs of red and white, and the pretty blue ecclesiastical-looking carpet which is promised for it. A *Baptismal Register Book* is ordered. I want a large one! God grant that it may fill up rapidly. We shall require a cemetery too, and have rather set our hearts on a pretty mango tope[80] at a suitable distance from, but not quite in sight of, the house.'

'Batala; *my beloved Laura's Birthday, May 20, 1878.*

'On this day of all days in the year I could not but write to my own precious sister, even if I had not such a nice, long, interesting letter to thank her for, as I received yesterday....

'Like you, I earnestly hope that the Almighty will preserve our dear land from the fearful evil of war. You and I would scarcely now care to sing—

'"In the proud battle-fields

Bounding with glee."

'How little realisation the juvenile writer had of what war is!... *We* are in another kind of warfare here. This living in the First Century, instead of the Nineteenth, seems to give a more vivid colour to life. I suspect that I should find some Missionary stations so dull after one like this! Such as those where year after year passes without an adult baptism being witnessed,—hardly expected,—perhaps in some instances hardly *hoped* for!... The fact is that it needs some moral courage in the Missionary, as well as all sorts of courage in the Convert, to face the storm that may follow a baptism.

'One feels almost ashamed of remaining in such perfect security,[81] when encouraging a poor brown brother or sister to go up, as it were, to the cannon's mouth. I was thinking to-day what would be the *most* painful sacrifice which one could make. It seemed to me that of the *love and esteem of all our dear ones.* And that is just the sacrifice which some of our brethren have to make! No wonder that they hesitate, weep, shrink from the flood of sorrow before them; but the true-hearted ones make the plunge at last. "The love of Christ constraineth."

'The enclosed to —— will give you an idea of some people's trials; but ever and anon new cases seem to crop up. I expect that our fair Batala will be a kind of harbour of refuge to hunted ones. Mera Bhatija has been telling me that a Missionary—I forget where—is about to have a Baptism, and wants to send the new Christian over to us for a week, to let the storm blow over a little. Another lad was all packed ready to come, but he was caught. He means to take the opportunity of escaping when he can....

'Mera Bhatija and I are curious to see the Rainbow glass. Perhaps, if it be small, I may show it off in the Zenanas. New and curious things give much pleasure. From a little round pin-cushion of mine the pretty glass picture of a Cathedral came off. I often take it with me, and show it, and say, "This is an English Church, in which God is praised every day!" Mere prints do not take with the Natives. They like coloured things that glitter.'

TO MRS. J. BOSWELL.

'*May 21, 1878.*

'It is wonderful to me how an English lady can go without fear or danger all about Batala, meeting with so much respect and courtesy. I do not feel it the slightest risk. Into narrow lanes, up dark staircases,—amongst women, amongst men,—I go without the smallest excuse for being alarmed. The people, too, generally listen very quietly, though what is said may be dead against their views. I make the slender concession of calling Muhammad "Mr. Muhammad"—"Muhammad Sahib"—but no one could object to so common a title. He is never called "Hasrat"—Saint—like Moses and David.'

TO THE SAME.

'*May 29, 1878.*

'Three new boys have arrived to-day. I am glad that they did not come till I had pretty well learned up the first seventeen, tacking the right names to the right faces. It took me a good while to do this, for I have a difficulty in remembering faces....

'The Natives who send their boys to this upper-class school are of course anxious that the lads should be good English scholars. At this time of high-pressure education it is necessary that they should be so. Mr. Baring drudges day after day at the English classes; but it occurred to me that I could give a little help in play-hours. I have written an English charade for our young Panjabis to recite; and the idea has, I think, taken with them. It needed a little management to give a separate part to every one of seventeen boys, apportioning it to the individual's capacity. Pretty little P. (five years) could not be expected to manage more than a line and a half; but it would never have done to have left him out. Into each of the three divisions of the charade I have introduced a lively chorus, in which all can join. The song that takes most is—

'"I am a brisk and sprightly lad,

But newly come from sea, sir!"

'This is rather curious, as none of our Punjabis have ever seen the sea. The chorus will be first-rate practice for rapid, clear pronunciation; for

'"When the boatswain pipes 'All hands aloft!'"

would not be an easy line even for some English boys. If the lads manage tolerably well, the charade will be great fun. Who would ever have dreamt that part of a Missionary's work should be to set boys to learn a lively charade!

'I pity the City boys. I suspect that there is a sort of wistful longing raised in many a young heart, "I wish I were one of those Christian boys!" If there could be a blind ballot of Batala boys, as to whether the whole town should become Christian, I am by no means sure whether the votes would not be in our favour. I do not mean that the poor, dear lads are *converts*, but that they use their eyes and ears,—and think that ours must be a very pleasant, genial kind of religion, connected in some sort of way with singing, and cricket, and kindness.'

Another short English play, written by Miss Tucker for the boys, was called *The Bee and the Butterfly*. Miss Mulvany, a Missionary, went one day, somewhere about this time, to Batala for a few hours; and in the course of her visit she was sent upstairs, while Charlotte Tucker gave the boys a lesson in acting the said little play. Miss Mulvany has never lost the impression made upon her by the peals and shouts of laughter which came up from the merry company below.

TO MRS. HAMILTON.

'June 19, 1878.

'I am reading the Granth,[82] the sacred book of the Sikhs. Like the Koran, it is very long,—I think more than 600 quarto pages,—and with an immense deal of repetition in it. But it leaves on the mind a very different impression from the Koran. As far as I have read, it is wonderfully pure and spiritual. If you could substitute the name "Almighty" for "Hari," and "Lord Jesus" for "Guru,"[83] it might almost seem the composition of hermits in the early centuries, except that celibacy is not enjoined. Woman seems to be given her proper place. Many exhortations are addressed to women....

'There is something touching in the longing—the yearning—after God,—the intense love of His Name! The Sikh idea of God is not that of the Hindus, with their fiend-like deities. The Creator is light, and goodness, and happiness. There is indeed the ridiculous idea of people having to pass through 840,000 states of existence,—unless the probation be shortened by meditation, purity, and the repetition of God's name,—but this fearful number of births is regarded as very tiresome indeed.

'One might call the Granth "the book of yearning," and I feel humiliated that I, with Gospel light, should in spiritual contemplation and longing for closest communion with the Deity come so far behind these poor Sikhs. Unfortunately, the Sikh religion has been so much corrupted that it is almost dying out. I suppose that it was too pure to please the Enemy; he knew that the Granth would offer no strong opposition to the Bible. Here, in Batala, his stronghold seems to me to be Muhammadanism. It shocks me to find how that invention of Satan darkens the moral sense. What would be thought sin in another, is by some openly defended as no sin *if committed by Muhammad*!!

'The Muhammadans too are so ready to stand up for their false faith; far more inclined to defend it than the Hindus are to defend theirs. Mera Bhatija was saying to-day that no book has been written against Christianity by a Hindu. I have myself, however, seen a very bitter article in a paper. But, generally speaking, the Muhammadans seem to be much sterner opponents of Truth than the Hindus. I feel it in the Zenanas.

'Now, my own Laura, I am going to my long task of reading the Granth. It puts me on vantage-ground when I can tell the Natives that I have read their Scriptures.'

The High School was not to have broken up before the middle of August; but circumstances caused Mr. Baring to fix upon a fortnight earlier, and this decided Miss Tucker to go to Amritsar on July 28. She at once planned that two of the hard-worked ladies at the Mission bungalow should then take their holiday, while she remained as a companion to the third. It does not appear that she had any idea of the Hills for herself. No doubt the change to Amritsar would mean pleasure, if not rest; and she was still able to speak of herself as 'wonderfully well'; but the unselfish thought for every one else, rather than of her own needs, is not the less remarkable.

To one of her correspondents she wrote from Batala on the 6th of July: 'You know that I am the only Englishwoman within twenty miles. Now and then friends pass a night here; but in the hot weather not often.... The 29th will, if I stay till then, complete sixteen weeks of steady residence, during which I have only twice seen English ladies,—for less than twenty-four hours. I doubt whether any European has ever stopped in Batala so long before without a single night's absence.... Once from Friday evening to Monday morning I saw no white face. There is a nice brown lady in the house.'[84]

At Amritsar she found herself as usual in the midst of engrossing interests. Fresh Baptisms were taking place; and about these she wrote to Mrs. Hamilton on the 21st of August, describing one just past:—

> 'There was a sweet-looking woman, D., a convert from Hinduism, and her two dear little girls. Her husband, who is not brave enough, or perhaps not sufficiently led towards Christianity, to follow her example, saw her depart for church. "You know that she is going to be baptized," said Emily. "Yes, yes," was the reply. "You must be kind to her, and receive her back." The man made no objection,—even to his two children being baptized; though he had formerly put obstacles in the way. There was a fourth, a convert from Muhammadanism, T., whose baptism was the most interesting of all.... The clergyman subjected the poor girl to the ordeal of a severe examination. She had never probably spoken to an Englishman before; and it would have been no wonder had she flinched or faltered. But she, who has

already been beaten at home for Christ's sake, showed no sign of weakness. Her answers came clear and firm. "Is it because of Miss Wauton's speaking that you come?" "No, it is because of my heart's speaking."

'The miseries and persecutions that may be coming upon her were almost, I think, *too* faithfully set before her. "If they were even to kill me, as they did M.'s father, what fear?" said the dauntless girl....

'I remarked to ——, on my return from the baptism, that I thought that the Indian women were braver than the men. He quite agreed; he knows that *he* dare not come forward like D. and T. Our noble N. is, we believe, a Christian at heart, and we know other men of whom we think that the same might be said, but they linger and linger, and *dare* not yet ask for baptism. Here this year in Amritsar we have had five women, and last year two, who, in the face of what we might have considered almost insurmountable obstacles, have bravely confessed Christ in baptism. It must be much harder for them than for the men, but they seem to have more courage, or more faith.'

Several weeks later another reference in home-letters is found to the brave girl, mentioned above: 'By last accounts dear T. is holding out nobly. We are not allowed to see her; but I hear that one or more Maulvis[85] have been brought to try to argue the young maiden out of her faith. But she tells them that they may read to her all day long, but they never will change her. They say that Christianity is 'written on her heart,'—what a testimony from Muhammadans!—and that the ladies must have bewitched her. It reminds me of Lady Jane Grey in prison; for dear T. *is* a prisoner.'

Plans did not fit in as Miss Tucker had intended. Once more she found herself called upon to act escort to a sick Missionary, who had to go to the Hills, and was not well enough to travel alone. Miss Wauton could not just then be spared from Amritsar, and she appealed to the 'Auntie,' whose readiness to help in any emergency was by this time well understood. 'It seems as if by some fatality I must go each year to Dalhousie,' Charlotte Tucker said in one letter, adding, 'But I hope to return back in a few days.' Then, in allusion to a scheme that she should join her nephew at Murree in September, 'I do not propose staying long. After sixteen weeks of unbroken residence at Batala, behold me rushing up and down hills like a comet.'

TO MISS L.V. TUCKER.

'*Aug. 14, 1878.*

'We are to have a Confirmation here on the 3rd of November. I should be much tempted to come up from Batala to witness it, particularly if any Batala Christians are confirmed. I am afraid that — —'s wife will shrink from breaking pardah,—that nonsensical pardah, which is a real snare to some baptized bibis.... There is one dear baptized young bride in Batala, whom I have not seen, but hope to search out on my return. The brave girl dared to be baptized in Amritsar, but was then carried off by her husband to Batala, and we know not in what part she is. She is likely to be having a hard time of it, but it is quite right in her to be with her husband....'

Writing home, she described drolly her absence from Batala as—'this strange episode of my life;—seven weeks acting Superintendent of the Orphanage,—three of those weeks sole Missionary at Amritsar,—and—oh, bathos! ten days an ayah—for I had none other.' Still her health seemed to keep good. She could stand the plains in hot weather as scarcely another Missionary was able to do. While one and another broke down, and had to be off to the Hills, Miss Tucker kept about, much the same as usual, filling up as far as possible the gaps left by others.

She was full of ardent sympathy at this time for certain converts from Muhammadanism, undergoing severe persecutions, and was much distressed at the difficulty of doing anything for them. She even formed a daring plan for carrying off one brave young girl from her relatives, and taking her to a safe distance; and Miss Tucker was with difficulty dissuaded from a scheme which others of longer experience knew too well might lead to serious complications.

Another, a wife, and also her daughter, were at this time in frequent peril, because they had become Christians in heart, and were earnestly desiring Baptism. The husband, a Muhammadan, would sometimes sit between the two, sharpening a knife, and threatening to stab them. Once he violently seized the daughter by her throat. Life with them must have been one long unhappiness; yet Miss Tucker, after an interview with the poor wife, could describe her as looking '*worn*, but so bright and brave.'

In September she was at Murree, helping to nurse her niece, and to take care of the tiny baby,—which latter occupation, she wrote, was 'more formidable to an old maiden Aunt than conversing in Urdu with a learned Maulvi, or doing the agreeable to a Rajah, would be.'

Of the place itself she said: 'Murree is not a cheering place to a Missionary.... One sees numbers of Natives; but how is one to tell the glad tidings? I feel like a doctor with multitudes of sick around him,—and he cannot get at his medicine-chest. I have brought Urdu religious books; I find no good opportunity of giving even one away.'

October saw her once more in the spot where she loved to be, writing joyously home—

> 'Here I am, in my own Station again, and glad to be back. I find that our little Christian flock has been increasing in a very encouraging way during my absence. There was a nice little round of visits to pay to Christian families.[86] Those who had been last baptized I had never seen before to my knowledge. A man of some forty or fifty years of age, employed in the Government — —, who has been thinking on the subject of religion for about nine years. For about two years he has been going to some quiet place, when he had leisure, to weep and pray. He appears now to be a very earnest and bold Christian. At his own desire he was baptized in the middle of the city, in a room set apart in the school.'

Very soon after Miss Tucker's return came the death of a little Christian Native baby; and the quiet Christian funeral was in marked contrast with the wild wailings usual at Muhammadan funerals,—though some Muhammadan lamentings were heard from one visitor present.

> 'We decked the little sleeping form with flowers; a rose was placed in each hand, a fragrant white Cross on the breast.... I attended the funeral; so did a good band of Native Christians, including our schoolboys. The cemetery was a Muhammadan one. We must buy one for ourselves, as we are, thank God, a growing body. I hope that in another month we may number fifty baptized persons in Batala; and I have lately been writing out the heading for a Subscription for a *Church* at our dear Batala. We have now only schoolrooms turned into Chapels. My list is to lie on our table for visitors to see. Perhaps it will be one or two years before we have collected enough; and by that time, please God, the flock may have doubled or quadrupled.
>
> 'It will be so—and more—if we go on at the rate at which the Church has been growing. The bringing the Boys' School here has been a grand thing. The dear fellows, on the whole, set such a nice example, and they seem so happy.
>
> '*Nov. 4, 1878.*—I have come to Amritsar for a few days, for the Confirmation, and had the pleasure of receiving your

dear letter of October 1st yesterday.... How can beloved St. George send me such bad advice? I like his example better than his counsel. What did *he* do in time of trouble? Stick to his post like a Tucker! Those of our Missionary family, with whom I have spoken on the subject,[87] all agree with me that we should never desert our flocks. What sort of army would that be, in which all the officers ran away at sight of an enemy?... But take no thought about me, dear one. Unless we meet with serious reverses in Afghanistan, I do not see danger of a rising, especially in the Panjab, where, on the whole, I think that we are considered tolerable rulers.

'And if there *were* troubles, I suspect that we Missionaries would run a better chance than other Europeans, we have such numbers of friends amongst the heathen.... Just fancy — our Bible-woman and her husband are actually collecting money from Hindus and Muhammadans for our Church! A poor woman gave some barley. If you were to hear all the polite little speeches, and see all the smiles that pass between Missionary and Natives, you would not expect us to be afraid. A Missionary in any case should have nothing to do with fear, — it is dishonouring to the Master.

'My love, how can you think of sending me another dress for winter? Do you think me so careless and extravagant as to have worn out the graceful Grey already? I never take it into a duli; I keep my faithful Green for such rough work. But if a new winter dress is actually in hand, let me send you even before seeing it a thousand thanks for it.'

FROM AN INDIAN CHRISTIAN, CONVERT FROM MUHAMMADANISM, 1878

'My dear Miss Tucker, — I received your kind letter, dated 13th instant, and the newspaper yesterday. I am very thankful to you. I read it many times, and it truly made me brave. I like the piece of poetry you quoted very much. Every day I pray to God to lead me in the right way. I think my prayer is heard, for I do not feel so lonely as I did at first; but I get fever nearly every day. I had gone over to Lahore on Friday, and stayed there for Saturday and Sunday.... I remember you in my prayers, and I hope you do the same. Now I will not feel lonely. Please do not be anxious....'

C. M. T. TO MRS. HAMILTON.

'*Nov. 8.*—If I were not a Mission Miss Sahiba, who should never complain, I might give a groan or a grumble to the mice and rats. They get into my almira, and what is even worse, into my harmonium. I had a tin plate made for the pedal part, expressly to keep creatures out; but they managed to pass it. I have now had a second large one made, and hope that it may prove more effectual. The creatures have bitten almost all the red Persian away; to-day I found lumps of wadding in my harmonium. "How could they have come there?" I asked of my sharp kahar, V. I suspected the rats, but did not know where they could have got the wadding from,—when V. suggested the beautiful padded cover of my harmonium. Sure enough, the rogues had bitten holes in that, and pulled out wadding to stuff into my harmonium, doubtless to make a comfortable nest for a family of young mice or rats. I tried a Batala trap; it was of no use: I have bought an Amritsar one, and Mera Bhatija has bought another; but the rats, I fear, will not be much thinned in numbers. We try to get a weasel, but have not succeeded yet. But things might have been much worse. The rats never try to eat *us*!'

'*Nov. 14.*—I do not think that I told you of two Christian fakirs, to whom I was introduced at Amritsar. They were very badly clothed, fakir-like, but—especially one of them—had pleasing, sensible faces. I suppose that they wander about, and lead a kind of John the Baptist life. How curious such a style of Christian would appear in old England!'

'*Nov. 20.*—I have been wanting—wanting—my English letters, expecting them these four days. At last here they are, and such nice dear ones....

'I shall much like to hear what you think of my sweet Margaret. I doubt whether she will be in good looks, she has been so sorely tried by her dear Mother's illness, and the struggle in her own mind,—longing to come to our help, yet unable to do so! I feel for her.

'I think that dear Emily benefited little or not at all by her trip to the Hills. She *ought* to go home in the spring,—after more than six years' work,—so ought Miss Fuller; but neither can leave till they fairly break down; for there is no one to take their place....

'You think, love, that by September 4th "the most dangerous season was over." Far from it! September is, I think, the most dangerous month in all the year in the Panjab. Very hot, and full of fever. My hardest pull up-hill since I came to India was, I think, in September. You have had the heat then for so long, you have less vigour, and the air is so unwholesome. Sickness all around.

'How good you are to send me another dress! My graceful Grey still looks very well. I consider it rather a company dress, and have my Green for the Zenanas, which are sometimes *so* dirty! I am wearing it now, for the weather is becoming very cold. It is rather amusing to see our Panjabis come in for Morning Prayers, about sunrise on a sharp morning. There is P. with a red comforter round *head* and neck; J. is wrapped in his white blanket. Poor Babu Singha, with a cold of course, is wondering how the big room below is ever to be kept warm. Mera Bhatija and I are going to change our drawing-room. The northern room is far the best in summer; but in winter we escape to the southern, and what was our guest-room becomes our sitting-room. There is actually a fireplace in it!—and the sunbeams stream in....

'Instead of spending the long winter evenings in solitary grandeur upstairs, I now come down and make one of the cheerful party in the schoolroom. It is much less distracting to be amongst a score of boys than you would suppose. I and some of them have been trying the vitre-manie (?) for our Chapel-window. Yesterday I brought down my chess-board and challenged the boys, and fought P., R., and I. C., one after the other....

'On Sunday evening we sing hymns for ever so long together, just like one huge family. The boys never seem to quarrel, or say one spiteful word of each other. We have just had two new boys; one is an Afghan; so we shall have the sons of Christian, Muhammadan, Hindu, and Afghan, (by race,) parents all together.'

TO MISS 'LEILA' HAMILTON.

'Dec. 13, 1878.

'This evening as Mera Bhatija has gone to Amritsar, I asked three of our lads to tea.... After tea I taught the lads "Cross Questions and Crooked Answers," and showed them my splendid bubbles and my chatelaine, which were greatly admired, and my photograph-book, a great treasure to me.

But what gave perhaps more amusement than anything was the Beaconsfield handkerchief. I was so glad to get some photos at last.... My visits in the city were interesting. Dear B—n's troubles have re-opened his mother's Zenana to me. She even paid me a visit here. I do not see any inclination in her to become a Christian, however; she says that I shall go to Heaven my way, and she hers. I suggested the disagreeableness of 840,000 transmigrations; but she did not seem troubled. Perhaps she hopes that she has passed through a few hundreds of millions already.'

TO MRS. HAMILTON.

'*Dec. 23, 1878.*—"I shall go to rest to-night nestling under my Laura's love, and I shall rise very early to thank her," was my thought last night, as I got into my nice comfortable bed, with her soft, light, warm quilt above me. And here I am sitting by my blazing wood fire, long ere dawn, with that same quilt like a shawl round my shoulders,—so comfy! Luxurious Char! But, after all, I have not begun my thanks, and where am I to end them?

'Your wonderfully packed parcel reached me in perfect safety yesterday. It was something like a nut, for it was rather difficult to get at the kernel. So much careful stitching by dear fingers. At last, however, the beautifully warm skirt and quilt, and most exquisite cards, were fully displayed to view. A thousand, thousand thanks! I have so *many* things, such goodly gifts, to remember my Laura by!...

'Our Christmas festivities have already begun. Our house is pretty full with Native friends. Perhaps the most interesting is dear B., the once Muhammadan wife of a Christian Catechist, and mother of Christian children, who was so sturdily bigoted that she held out for thirteen years, before she would give herself to the Saviour. But then she did so in her honest way. B. was never a hypocrite; we respected her when she vexed us. It was something for her to remain with her husband; for, by Muhammadan law, baptism of husband or wife constitutes divorce. Mera Bhatija told me of a curious case, which excited much interest,—to Europeans it would excite much surprise. A Muhammadan, who had, I suppose, read Christian books, was travelling with some other Muhammadans, and was imprudent enough to say that Muhammad wrought no miracles, and expressed doubts as to his being really a prophet. The poor man happened to have a rich wife, who, we may believe, did not care for him. To *speak against* the Prophet is enough to constitute a divorce! The companions of the man did not let their chance go of half ruining him. The case was brought into Court, and an English judge was obliged to give a verdict against the unfortunate fellow, who had expressed an honest opinion. He lost his wife and her rich dowry....'

'Amritsar, *Dec. 28, 1878.*—I am sitting with my sweet Laura's delicious quilt wrapped closely round my shoulders, for it is warmer than a shawl; and I am up before the fire-lighting period. Not being at home, I do not know how to light the fire myself.

'Our Christmas at Batala went off beautifully, and has, I think, left a feeling of thankfulness on both Mera Bhatija's mind and my own. The following day we both came to Amritsar. Yesterday was the grand opening of the Alexandra School. Mr. Clark asked me to write an account of it for his report. I did not like the task; it makes one feel so penny-a-linerish; and one is afraid of writing to please this or that person, etc.; but I could not well refuse, so I have been scribbling something in pencil in the cold, which I mean to submit to dear Emily's criticism....

'Oh, I must tell you what a boon your Beaconsfield handkerchief is! It gave much amusement at Batala, both to Europeans and Natives; it is giving much here at Amritsar. I am engaged to dine with the Clarks this evening; so I dare say that the good Bishop, Archdeacon, and all will have a laugh over my puzzle. On Monday I am to go to Lahore, and sleep a night at Government House. I mean to take my handkerchief with me....

'Batala will present rather a contrast to bustling Amritsar and Lahore. When I return, there will probably be no European but myself there for days, as Mera Bhatija must be absent at the Conference till the 6th.'

So ended the third year of Miss Tucker's life in India. She had now thoroughly settled down to her own especial work in Batala.

CHAPTER VIII
A.D. 1878-1879 EARLY CHRISTIAN DAYS IN THE 19TH CENTURY

It is clear that Charlotte Tucker was profoundly impressed with the sense of living, as she said, in the First Century, instead of the Nineteenth. In another letter, soon to be quoted, she describes her Batala experience as 'being carried back to the days of the Apostles.'

For in Batala the complex conditions of modern life, the intricacies of Nineteenth Century Christianity, were absent. Here in England it is more or less the correct thing to be in some measure religious, to be at least nominally a Christian. People are on the whole expected to go to Church, — or, if Dissenters, just as much to go to Chapel, — and though the going to Church, as a matter of course, does not at all indicate the lack of deeper reasons, of purer motives underlying, it does make the going a very easy matter. So, also, a mother takes her little one to Church for Baptism, again almost as a matter of course; often indeed with heartfelt prayer and longing, but with no question of danger involved in the act. It is a perfectly simple thing to do. More attention would in fact be drawn by *not* doing it than by doing it.

At Batala, as in thousands of other Heathen and Muhammadan cities, things are widely different. Sharp lines of demarcation are drawn between the Christian and the non-Christian, — between the Church and the heathen world around. It was so most markedly when Charlotte Tucker lived in Batala. There, as in Early Christian days, was the great mass of those who neither knew nor cared for the Names of God and Christ; and in their midst was the Infant Church, a tiny body of brave men and women, who had come out from amongst the Heathen and Muhammadans, to be known as the servants of Christ.[88]

And the step which led from the one to the other stood clear and defined, with no possibility of a mistake. The marching-orders which our Lord and Master issued were not *only* to go forth and teach. Here is the fuller version: 'Go ye therefore, and teach' (*Rev. Ver.* 'make disciples of') 'all nations, baptizing them in the Name of the Father, and of the Son, and of the Holy Ghost; teaching them to observe all things whatsoever I have commanded you.'

That was the great order given; that was the command which had to be obeyed, whether at Batala or elsewhere. And however easy a matter Baptism in England may be, it is no easy matter in the Panjab for Converts from Heathenism or from Muhammadanism. It is a step of overwhelming importance. It means leaving the world of idolatry, ignorance, superstition, behind, and entering the Church of Christ. It also means too often leaving all things earthly that have most been loved. It means persecution, beating, cruelty, hard words and harsher deeds. It means wives separated from husbands, mothers separated from children, loss of money, loss of the means of livelihood, danger not seldom to life itself. It is the passing of the Rubicon.

Again, in that Infant Church at Batala,—or, one may equally say, in the Church at Amritsar, and throughout the Panjab,—we find reproduced the various elements which existed in Early Church days. There are strong Christians and weak Christians; there are whole-hearted ones and wavering ones; there are the true and the false. What wonder?—when the very foundation-stones of the Church of Christ included a Judas. Wheat and tares will grow together until the end; and bad fish as well as good will be caught in the net. The Church planted in a new place is seldom long without her Demas, who loves this present heathen world, and goes back to it again.

But for one who is unfaithful, for one who turns his back upon the Light, after seeming to be indeed a Convert, there are many who stand firm, persevering to the end, despite difficulties, discouragements, and bitter oppositions. These brave brown brothers and sisters of ours, who are still in the fires of persecution, from which England has been so long delivered, deserve our warmest sympathy.

In giving the story of Charlotte Tucker, and of the growth of the Church at Batala, with which she was so intimately associated, it is of very real importance to show frankly both sides of the picture,—the dark side, as well as the bright; the cloudy as well as the sunshiny. There were of course disappointments as well as encouragements. There were goings backward as well as pressings forward. Missionary life is no more one of unbroken success, even at its best, than any other kind of hard-working life, with a high aim before it; and to present it as such, by omitting to describe failure side by side with success, would—and often does—produce only a sense of unreality. The story of the Church throughout the ages has always been a chequered tale.

Hard as Miss Tucker toiled, she had not the delight of seeing many individuals won to Christianity through her own efforts. Results of what she did, still more of what she was, were visible enough to others,—but rather in the shape of a general and widespread influence than in the shape of conversions directly due to her labours. The worth of any work can never be truly gauged by the amount of success which may appear to follow within a given time; and to measure the extent or the effects of her loving influence, alike among younger Missionaries and among Indian Christians, especially among the boys in the Baring High School, is utterly impossible.

No less impossible is it to measure the results of her years of toilsome work in Zenanas. Some here are disposed to assert freely that she accomplished very little. One Native Christian, sending a few slight memoranda, goes so far as to say: 'I feel sorry to have to add that she signally failed as a Missionary, if by that term is meant the preaching of the Gospel to the heathen of India.' A very great deal more than mere preaching is, of course, meant by the term; but in any case this would be a most rash judgment for any man to venture to pass, were he English or Indian. No *man* could have entrance into the scores upon scores of Zenanas which she visited, to test for himself the effects of her work; and we all know what hearsay evidence is worth. Even if he could find entrance, he would have no Divine power to see into the hearts of the people there. The fact that she herself saw few results says nothing; for the best results are often slowest in appearing. Judging from apparent results is always a defective and a shallow proceeding.

From beginning to end she never so far conquered the languages of North India as to speak them with ease. Grammar and construction she might and did to a considerable extent master, but colloquial fluency was not in her case attainable. Still, though she never became actually fluent, it is a matter of unquestionable fact that she did both understand and make herself understood, despite occasional verbal mistakes. There are testimonies from all sides which abundantly prove this.

Her mode of working in Zenanas was peculiar to herself; and though she always held to it, she did not put it forward as a model for every one else to imitate. She made no attempt at systematic instruction, probably feeling her knowledge of the languages unequal to the task; and this in itself was a drawback. 'In point of fact,' as one says who was associated with her, 'she never considered herself as a teacher, but rather, like St. John the Baptist, as a "voice crying in the wilderness." Her visits were almost always short,'— though to this rule there were evidently exceptions,—'she seems to have gone in, greeted the people, given her message, and taken courteous leave. She always deprecated any attempt to judge of her work by the number of Zenanas on her visiting list; and indeed it would not be fair to do so, as she did not undertake regular teaching in them.'

Zenana-visiting was only one portion of her work; regarded by herself as the more important portion, but not necessarily the more important because she thought so. We ourselves are poor judges of the comparative worth of the different things which we have to do. She was also a warm and true friend to the Indian Christians, entering into their trials and difficulties, throwing herself into their interests, doing her utmost to help them onward, to lift them upward. In this direction she had a remarkable degree of influence; and in her intercourse with them she was absolutely without pride, she was full of kindliness, consideration, and affection.

With the schoolboys, as already seen, she was in her element. The old spirit of fun, the old devotion to games, were invaluable here; neither having faded with increasing age. One of her dharm-nephews, Dr. Weitbrecht, writing about the High School in Batala, says:—

> 'From this time for years to come Miss Tucker was a mainstay of the Boys' Boarding School, teaching the elder boys the English language and history, taking a motherly interest in all their pursuits, writing for them Batala School songs, inviting them in the evenings to little social entertainments, enlivened by parlour games; visiting the sick, comforting the home-sick new boy; mothering the young convert, who had been sent to Batala not less for spiritual shelter than for instruction; and upholding the hands of workers in the School and Mission generally; besides carrying on without fail her regular visits to the town and villages, and her literary work for publication, both in England and India.'

One of the former schoolboys, now a Native surgeon in India, Dr. I. U. Nasir, writes on the same subject:—

> 'Her good influence on the young minds cannot be overrated. Her Bible Classes were eagerly looked for and well attended,—it may be, for the sake of lozenges and bits of cake which she distributed at the end, but also for the interest she made everybody feel in the meeting. She would begin by asking the verse and subject of the morning sermon, and the various points of interest worth remembering. This led to the habit of closely attending to the sermon.... Then every one had a choice of a hymn to be practised for the evening services of the week; a short verse of the Bible was repeated; and Sunday enigmas from the Bible were solved.'

And also with reference to social week-day evenings:—

'She amused us with stories, comic songs, historical anecdotes, making anagrams, giving riddles to be solved, and several amusements of the kind. Many an evening was spent in Miss Tucker's drawing-room, playing various indoor games, of which chess and word-making and word-taking were her favourites. In the latter game she would consider it a great triumph to have made such long words as "Jerusalem artichoke." But she took particular delight in showing her old scrap-album to any one who desired to see it. Many an interesting incident was dropped in connection with her relatives, as she turned leaf after leaf with her old slender fingers. She never got tired of this. Then she would select good scenes from Shakespeare, whom she called "The Poet of Conscience," and give us lessons in recitation and acting.'

Charlotte Tucker had a profound belief in the good *moral* influence of Shakespeare. She is said to have greatly wished that the Indians could have the benefit of Shakespeare translated into their Native languages.

In addition to the Baring School boys, she had a never-failing interest in the lads of the Mission Plough School, started mainly by herself, and afterwards endowed by her with the sum of £50 a year. She constantly visited there, and taught the scholars, knowing many of the older boys by name, and asking them from time to time to pay her Sunday afternoon visits.

Moreover, outside all these occupations, A. L. O. E. was still an Author. For some years, indeed, after her arrival in India she wrote for India only, and not especially for England. When, however, it became gradually clear that books suitable for Indian readers were not adapted for England, she found time to accomplish separate volumes for home publication. Some would say that her writings for the Native population of Hindustan are by far the most important part of her whole Missionary work. By her pen she could reach thousands, even tens of thousands, where by her voice she could reach at most only dozens. Her tiny Indian booklets, published by the Christian Literature Society at very low prices, are among the most widely selling of the Society's productions.

It was only by an exceedingly systematic mode of life and endless toil that Miss Tucker could get through what she did. She was always up very early,—at 6 a.m. in winter, at 4½ or 5 a.m. in summer,—and her day was carefully apportioned out. Six weeks' holiday in the year was permitted by the Society under which she worked, and she would seldom take more than a month of this in the hottest weather, that she might be able to get away for a few days at some other time, without infringing on her full ten months and a half of work. Often part of her so-called holiday was spent in looking after or in acting as companion to somebody else,—or in undertaking work during the absence of other Missionaries from their posts. The marvel is, not that after a few years she should have grown to look older than she was, but that her health could in any degree have stood so great and constant a strain. Few people in the prime of life could have done and endured what she did and endured in the evening of her days.

Very early after her arrival in India, as stated in a previous chapter, the Natives seemed disposed to credit Miss Tucker with an astonishing number of years; but too much must not be thought of this. It arose from the fact that a grey-haired English lady out there is a complete *rara avis*—a sight seldom to be seen. Miss Wauton's first impressions of her, jotted down as follows, do not give the impression of a very old lady, dearly as Charlotte Tucker loved to describe herself in those terms: 'Tall, slight, with lofty brow, sparkling eye, face constantly beaming with love and intelligence; genius in every look; figure frail and fairy-like, agile and graceful; very brisk movements and light tread.' Hardly like a hundred years old! After a few years had passed she did no doubt age rapidly.

Mention has several times been made of Miss Tucker's readiness to give; and when one recalls the abounding generosity of her father, not to speak of the story of her grandmother on the Boswell side giving away to a beggar the last coin in the house, one can hardly be surprised at the generous tendencies of Charlotte Tucker's character. She had the gift of liberality by inheritance; and she cultivated her gift as a matter of principle. Giving was at all times a real delight to her. A quotation on this subject from Mr. Beutel may well come in here:—

> 'Miss Tucker was always very liberal. Wheresoever there was need or distress that she heard of, she gave substantial help immediately. I well remember, for instance, after I had taken over charge of the Boys' Orphanage, one time there were between thirty and forty boys to be fed and clothed, and no money left in hand. As soon as Miss Tucker heard of it, she immediately sent me £10; and I must confess such a blessing rested on that money, that I never came into similar straits during the twelve years that I had charge of the Boys' Orphanage.
>
> 'And again, before we settled at Clarkabad, there was a great scarcity of grain, in consequence of the failure of crops

among the Zamindars. They had very little to eat, and no seed-corn to sow. All wanted some help, and I had no money in hand.... When Miss Tucker heard of it, immediately she sent us Rs.300; and our greatest need was at an end.

'Again, in 1889, when a dear friend of mine, Pastor and Teacher in the United States of North America, with whom I had come out to India in 1869, had decided to return to India as a Missionary, in order to join and to help me in the multifarious work at Clarkabad, and he found that the money in hand was insufficient to pay for his and his family's voyage from Germany, and Miss Tucker heard of it, she immediately sent me £100, with the direction to forward that sum to him, on condition that he had not left Germany again for America. This, however, had already taken place in the meantime, and the money was returned to her.

'Again, in 1892, after we had returned to Kotgur, where there was a great scarcity in the district, and many poor people had hardly one meal a day to eat, and Miss Tucker heard that I gave relief work to some forty or fifty people, she sent me another Rs.100.'

These are merely a few among innumerable instances which might be quoted; though generally the gifts were so quietly bestowed that few or none except the recipient knew about the matter. It was not, however, only in money that she was generous. The very necessaries sent for her own use, the very clothes sent for her own wear, would be given freely away to the first person who seemed in need of them. Mrs. Hamilton, learning something of this, at one time tried in despair calling her gifts 'loans,' in the hope that they might be thus secured for Charlotte Tucker's own benefit. In later years, when a parcel arrived from England, Miss Tucker would sometimes not allow her Missionary companions to see what it contained, that she might feel more free to give away as she felt disposed.

The Rev. Robert Clark speaks of Miss Tucker as 'an English Christian Faqir,'—a curious use of the term, which he applies also to one or two other Missionaries. The original idea of 'Christian Faqirs,' sometimes referred to in Miss Tucker's own letters, was of Native Faqirs, who, on becoming Christians, kept still to their old mode of life, going about as before, teaching Christianity instead of false religions, and not begging any longer, but receiving a small sum for their support from Englishmen. Mr. Clark, in speaking of A. L. O. E., doubtless uses the word in reference to her peculiar mode of entering into Indian ways, Indian customs, Indian thoughts,—as, for instance, sitting on the floor among them, instead of on a chair, travelling in an ekka like them, and so far as she was able living their life,—as well as to the rigid simplicity and self-denial which she cultivated.

After alluding to the manner of her earlier English life, and contrasting it with the manner of her existence at Batala, where 'two chairs were placed on two sides of a table in a large and almost unfurnished room,' Mr. Clark continues: 'Miss Tucker ate very little. She always told us to tell her beforehand if we were going to see her, in order that she might have something to place before us. There was then no railway; and everything had to be brought from Amritsar once or twice a week. The bread often became *very* hard. She sometimes said, "Do try this piece; it seems a little softer." Her guests were thinking all the time of her tender gums, and of her teeth which were no longer young.'

On first going to Batala Charlotte Tucker had had the idea in her mind of inaugurating there a sort of 'Zenana' of maiden Missionary ladies,—a close retreat, from which the foot of Man should be utterly and always excluded. Probably this was part of her desire to imitate the ways of Natives. Some judicious combating was needed to break her loose from it; though when once a gentleman-Missionary had actually arrived, theories went down before the spirit of hospitality.

Once again it should be noted, that when in her letters she writes home enthusiastically about all her comforts and luxuries, these descriptions must be taken *cum grano salis*. She had not the slightest intention of misleading anybody; but she was very anxious to put a brave face on the matter; moreover, she was a Missionary Miss Sahiba, and she might not grumble. Everything was for her right just as it was. But another side to the question did exist.

In the year 1879 Mrs. Elmslie, being at home, paid a visit to Mrs. Hamilton; and one day she could not help remarking, 'When I see how comfortable you are here, and think of your sister, it makes me sad.' Her tone was almost reproachful; for she was mentally comparing A. L. O. E.'s barely furnished rooms with the abundance of comforts in this home. Evidently she thought Miss Tucker badly off, and wondered why her friends did not assist her more. Explanations naturally followed; and when she learnt the true state of the case, when she heard the amount of Charlotte Tucker's comfortable little income, she was astonished. The manner of life steadily followed out was, in fact, no matter of necessity, but purely a matter of principle. Miss Tucker counted a life of rigid simplicity worthier her vocation as a Missionary than one of greater ease could have been. She therefore kept to a certain sum of money yearly for her own expenses, while giving much away in addition; she made her clothes last as long as it was possible for them to hold together;

she had hardly any furniture in her rooms; and she refused all luxuries, including some things which in India are commonly reckoned *not* luxuries, but absolute necessaries.

The following particulars have been kindly supplied to me by Miss Wauton and others.

Her style of living, at all times extremely simple, was particularly so at the time that she shared a home with Mr. Baring. She scarcely, indeed, allowed herself even the most ordinary comforts. Her bedroom furniture consisted of a native bedstead, a small table, a wardrobe and two chairs, with a piece of thin matting on the floor, and one or two thin 'durries.'[89] Always an early riser, Miss Tucker never liked her Ayah to find her still in bed. When she first got up, she used to heat a cup of cocoa with her little etna, for her 'chhoti hazari.'[90] Miss Tucker always disliked very much being waited on, and preferred to do things for herself. She treated the servants very courteously, always addressing the Ayah as 'Bibi ji'; and any little thing offered to her at table was accepted with a 'Thank you,' or declined with a 'No, thank you,' spoken in English, as there is in Hindustani no equivalent for the expression of gratitude.

Together with her marvellous activity of mind and of body was seen a wonderful amount of patience under suffering or discomfort. In the very hot weather she would say to her companions, 'Let me be the first to complain of the heat';—and of course she never did complain. She used to ascribe her good health in Batala to the absence there of three things, generally counted indispensable by Europeans in India. She had, first, no *doctor*; she had, second, no *gari*; she had, third, no *ice*. The want of the latter must have been a serious deprivation. The lack of a gari, or carriage, was supplied by her duli, by the native ekka, and by her own walking-powers. As for doctors,—she had, when ill, to go to them, like other people, and to be grateful for their help. Doctors were not, however, favourites with A. L. O. E. She was perhaps a little hard upon them; since, on the one hand, she professed not to trust their skill; and on the other hand, she looked upon them as rather cruel than kind, in trying to keep her longer upon Earth, away from the Home where she wished to be.

Miss Wauton says:—

> 'All she had was put at the disposal of others. Every book sent out was lent round to the different Mission circles, or in any place where it might give pleasure or profit. She always had some interesting book on hand, and kept her mind richly stored with knowledge, being specially fond of history. She allowed me once to be present when giving

an English History lesson to a class of Baring High School boys. I could have wished myself one of them, to have had such teaching constantly! She was very independent of intercourse with other minds, yet thoroughly enjoyed social pleasures. I never saw any one so carry out the precept—"Rejoice with them that do rejoice." Nowhere did she seem so much at home as at the wedding-feast; and no wedding-party seemed complete without her.'

But though she could be the life and soul of a wedding feast—perhaps especially of a Native wedding feast,—Miss Tucker was not in all cases an advocate of marriage. The Rev. Robert Clark speaks of her as—'jealous of the marriage of any of our Lady Missionaries, especially to those gentlemen who were, as she said, "outside of the family."' He adds: 'In her verses on the duties and qualifications of ladies for Missionary work in India, the last couplet was, I think, as follows:—

"The Mission Miss Sahiba must single remain,

Or else she'll step out of her proper domain."

A friend who married one of our Missionary ladies, and who was nominally outside the Mission family, but who was and still is one of us, added the words—

"And never will be a Miss Sahiba again!"'

This quotation from Mr. Clark lands us in another subject, and one of no small importance. Charlotte Tucker, going as she did to India when well on in middle life, looked upon herself as a possible Pioneer, a possible example to others, and hoped that many more might be led to do the same. But she was never under the delusion that anybody and everybody is fitted for a Missionary life,—even granting the spiritual adaptedness. There must be of course whole-hearted devotion to Christ, whole-hearted love to man, and whole-hearted self-abnegation; but there must also be certain natural capabilities, certain conditions of health and vigour. Beyond all, there must be the Divine call to work in the Mission-fields. All this Charlotte Tucker felt with increasing earnestness as years went on; and she was often at pains to explain the kind of workers wanted out there, to warn against the kind of workers *not* wanted.

Before giving extracts from the correspondence of 1879, two or three quotations of different dates shall be given on this subject, beginning with a letter written to a lady who had thoughts of offering herself:—

'Batala, *Dec. 3, 1878.*

'My dear Madam,—Hearing that you have some idea of giving yourself to Mission work in India, I think that you may like to hear the impressions of one who—after dear ones no longer required her care—gave herself to that work.

'I have now been for three years in India, and I have never for one minute regretted coming. I do sometimes feel that there is need of patience; one has a number of petty inconveniences and annoyances, from which we are guarded in England. Whoever comes out as a Missionary should pray for a brave, patient, cheerful spirit, and a submissive will. But if these be granted, I should say that the Missionary life is a very happy one.

'There is a great charm in being carried back to the days of the Apostles; for in an isolated station, like Batala or Kulu, there is much to remind one of the First Century. Then there is joy in the hope that one is putting out the intrusted talents—be they few or many—to the best interest. One's time, one's money, one's efforts, seem to go further here. I have often thought, "India is the place to make the One talent—Ten." The work is so very great, the labourers so few!

'There is another thing which has intensely sweetened my Missionary life. It is finding myself a member of the Missionary Family. It has been said that there are no friendships like those made in youth. It has not been *my* experience. I have no dearer friendships than those made in advanced years. God has given me a number of new Relatives (I call them dharm nephews and nieces), and the tie is as real as that made by blood-relationship....

'In coming out as a Missionary, one has to devote oneself to duties which are sometimes what would be called drudgery, and leave the care of one's happiness to the Divine Master, whom we attempt to serve. He takes far better care of our happiness than we can.

'Allow me, dear Madam, to add another word. If you come out, you should start *soon*, to avoid the heat of the Red Sea. As regards outfit, you would find a tin-bath, in a basket-case, to be used in travelling as a trunk, a great comfort here. It is well to bring out a few pictures and pretty things; and, if you are musical, your instrument. Medicines are very useful. Warm clothes are requisite, as well as light ones. Cotton gloves are a comfort in the season when kid shrivels and dries.

'Not without a hope that I may one day welcome you as a Sister-worker, I remain, dear Madam, yours very sincerely,

C. M. Tucker.'

In a paper written some few years later by A. L. O. E., containing a list of things needed to make a good and serviceable Missionary, the following are enumerated—as usual, symbolically expressed:—

> 'We need not dwell on the necessity of Faith and Love, which may be represented as Gold. To start without these would be presumption worse than folly.... And so with the only less valuable metal, Silver—Knowledge. It is self-evident that such is required....
>
> 'And a great deal of Steel is needed ... some physical, and, above all, *moral* Courage is required. Nervous weakness of character is undesirable at home; it would be a grievous misfortune in India.... A Missionary should claim the Christian's privilege of fearing no evil....
>
> 'The old saying is, *Nothing like leather*.... What I would symbolise by Leather is a capacity for encountering *drudgery*, something that will bear the strain of daily and often monotonous work.... Give us tough leather, such as harness and straps are made of; no romantic sentimentality, but steady, resolute Perseverance.
>
> 'Another useful article is a *Letter-weigher*, by which I would represent Sound Judgment.... There is special experience required for work in a foreign land. It has often occurred to my mind what a blessing in disguise it is that Missionaries have to toil to acquire a new language; such delay giving them time to learn something of Native character, manners, and ideas. If language came by intuition, we should make many more blunders in other things than we do now; and such blunders are numerous enough already....
>
> 'Another necessary must not be forgotten—a *White-covered Umbrella*, representing Prudence regarding health. The white cover is specially mentioned, symbolising the pure desire to economise health for the sake of God's cause, without which mere prudence would be of very minor value....

'Only one more necessary I would mention, and it may provoke a smile: Be sure to bring a box of *Salve*, and not a very small one either. When maidens of different antecedents, rank, age, temperament, and—in minor matters—opinions, are brought together in closest proximity, in a climate which tries the temper, there is at least a possibility of some slight rubs, which without the soothing ointment brought by the Peacemaker may even develop into sores.'

TO — — — —

'Feb. 19, 1879.

'I hope that good Miss — — will *not* leave her present field of great usefulness for India. It is a sad mistake for those with her delicacy of head to come out to the Panjab. "Panjab heads" are proverbial. Our band is too small for any to be told off as nurses. Very delicate workers should not come out to this trying climate. For those whose constitutions are fitted for it, the Panjab is a glorious field. It is a place where the one talent may become ten. All sorts of gifts come into use; aptitude in buying and selling; engineering skill; love of music; a mechanical turn, etc., may be turned to such valuable account.

'It is *not* a mere matter of preaching to the heathen. An Infant Church has to be built up; openings are to be made for converts, that they may earn their bread; churches have to be raised with small funds and no architects, etc. A man who can carpenter, garden, or put in panes of glass, may find his knowledge most useful. A bold rider, a good shot, is at an advantage here.

'Missionary life is not just like what one fancies it in England. We do not want bookworms so much as active, intelligent, devoted men, who can turn their hands to anything, and who, in addition to Missionary zeal, have plenty of *common sense*. God grant that Cambridge may send us many such! Mr. — — is one; a very valuable man, though not gifted with eloquence, nor quick at learning languages. He has a clear sound judgment, and a power of adapting himself to varying circumstances, and of undergoing drudgery.'

TO MISS 'LEILA' HAMILTON.

'March 24, 1879.

'No, my dearest Leila, I could not in conscience urge poor dear —— to come out here. It would be cruel. Any one who in England suffers from headache, liver, back, and uneven spirits, I would rather entreat to avoid the Panjab.... She would be one of the choice delicate palfreys, yoked to artillery, who break down and give extra work to the already fully-taxed horses. If you only knew what the illnesses of those *who ought never to have come out* have cost others as well as themselves!... The Lord does not call *all* His children to India. There ought to be a certain fitness of constitution to dwell in a fever-land. I am so thankful that I am not constitutionally liable to headache, and that fever does not naturally cling to me. But I walk warily, as one in an enemy's country.'

TO W. F. T. HAMILTON.

'*May 20 (probably 1879)*.

'Your dear Mother sends me delightful accounts of the devotion of some of the Cambridge men, and their readiness to engage in Missionary work, if they saw the way clear. Now, dearest Fred, could there be a clearer opening than at Batala for an earnest Christian man, whether in Orders or not? I am not thinking of you, for I would not have any one subject to headaches come to this feverish land; but I am thinking of your brother collegians. Batala, for evangelisation, is a very central point; no end of work might be done; and it is a hopeful place....

'But I will be more minute in particulars.... I am not writing of one who wishes to become one of the regular salaried Missionaries of our Society; but of one who has the means to be an Honorary worker. Say he has an income of £100. He would find at Batala a *home*,—not a very luxurious one, but quite enough so for a Missionary. His £100 would be enough for all his personal wants, unless he travelled much; and he might keep a little horse, unless, like ——, he preferred spending his extra rupees on something else. He could at once help with English classes, if he chose to do so, and in the meantime learn the language.... If he had a taste for shooting and fishing, he would find means of gratifying it; and if he were a good cricketer, it would add to his influence over our boys. If he had any architectural skill, he would help us to build our church. If he were musical, it would be a great advantage. He might lead a very happy life, and an exceedingly useful one. We are in such want of *men*; not mere bookworms, but earnest, devoted, bright, active Christians, who can turn their hands to everything, and help to mould the minds of our rising generation. We want more St. Pauls!'

This chapter can hardly be better closed than by quoting Miss Tucker's descriptive lines as to the necessary qualifications for a 'Mission Miss Sahiba,' already alluded to. They were written at Amritsar, as early as the year 1876:—

RULES AND REGULATIONS

'The Mission Miss Sahibas must never complain;
The Mission Miss Sahibas must temper restrain—
When "sust"[91] pankah-wala won't pull at the cane;
Must never be fanciful, foolish, or vain.

'The Mission Miss Sahiba in dress must be plain;
The Mission Miss Sahibas must furnish their brain,—
Of two or three languages knowledge obtain,—
When weary and puzzled, must try, try again;
We cannot learn grammar by *leger de main*.

'The Mission Miss Sahiba must know every lane,
Climb ladder-like stairs, without fearing a sprain;
The Mission Miss Sahibas must speak very plain,
Must rebuke and encourage, must teach and explain;
The Mission Miss Sahibas must grasp well the rein;
The Mission Miss Sahibas must not look for gain,
Though doctoring sick folk, like Jenner or Quain.

'Let Mission Miss Sahibas from late hours refrain,
For they must rise early, and bear a hard strain,
Like vigorous cart-horses, drawing a wain,
That pull well together, when yoked twain and twain.
The Mission Miss Sahibas must work might and main,
And therefore good nourishment should not disdain,—
Or danger is great of their going insane.

'The Mission Miss Sahibas must topis[92] retain,
Must guard against sunstroke, to health such a bane;
And midst frogs and mosquitoes must patient remain,
Yes, e'en when tormented, must smile through their pain;
And, with courage like that of the knights of Charlemagne,
By Mission Miss Sahibas snakes should be slain.

'The Mission Miss Sahibas should sow well the grain,
Dark babies should fondle, dark women should train,
And Bibis and Begums at times entertain;
Should smile and should soothe, but not flatter or feign;
And to usefulness thus they may hope to attain.

'N.B.—Let all Mission Miss Sahibas single remain,—
If they don't, they step out of their proper domain,—
And can never be Mission Miss Sahibas again!'

CHAPTER IX
A.D. 1879 THE CHURCH AT BATALA

The annals of 1879 are as usual very abundant, and space can only be found for a limited selection of extracts. Miss Tucker was much distressed about the Afghan war; not because of any possible peril or discomfort to herself, but because her judgment disapproved of it as a whole, and also because of the sufferings which she knew it must entail upon the soldiers.

While the larger number of extracts given are, throughout her Indian career, in reference to the work going on round about her, it must not be supposed that her love for relatives and old friends, or her interest in all that concerned them, ever for a moment waned. The letters teem with loving words and messages; and every item of news from England is received with delight. Her affections seem to have grown stronger rather than weaker, through long separation.

'Batala, *Jan. 16, 1879.*—Mine own Laura, how could you write regarding the little meeting, at which you and sweet Margaret were, "Would you not like to be in my shoes at the time, and hold your darling friend in your arms?" I would much rather have been in *Margaret's shoes*, and have held some one else in my arms,—only for the wrench that would have followed! But O love, we are travelling in the same train, only in different carriages; and I am thankful that though we cannot see each other, we can as it were talk to each other out of the windows. What a blessing the Post is!'

TO MISS 'LEILA' HAMILTON.

'Jan. 20, 1879.

'Ours is not to be a village church, dear, but one in a city of more than 25,000 inhabitants, where there are graceful mosques, a large idol-temple, etc. A mere mud shed would be quite out of character; our present room in a schoolhouse would be better than that. There is considerable difficulty and expense in buying a site. It ought to be *in* the city. I have written to dear — — about one which Mr. Baring has seen, but it is very doubtful whether the place can be purchased.

'My nephew and I are both economical, and I think that you and dear Fred may depend on money not being wasted in useless decorations. But the sacred edifice ought to be of brick, and pretty strong, not only to endure for years, but also to keep out the heat. A tiny church would not cost much; one so small that beams could reach from side to side. But if our Church is to go on growing, as we hope and pray that it may, what would be the advantage of having a tiny chapel, which would not comfortably accommodate ourselves in a fiery climate, and in which there would be no room at all for heathen spectators? We should be wanting a *second*; and how could we procure a second clergyman? Please thank dear Fred very, very much for his kindness in collecting, and assure him that we wish to make the money go as far as possible.'

TO MRS. HAMILTON.

'*Jan. 31.*—I sometimes think that it is well for me that I have no one to carry cushions after me,—as the dear A——s made the boys do in George Square,—or to watch my face to see if I look pale. I have been enabled to make efforts, for which I might not have thought my frame capable, and have kept my health wonderfully.

'This is the eighth day that I have not seen an English person! Mera Bhatija has been away on duty; but I hope to have him back to-morrow. I shall not be sorry to see him again; we are becoming more and more like *real* Aunt and Nephew. He wanted me to go to Amritsar during his needful absence; but there were strong reasons against that....

'As regards health, we are between Scylla and Charybdis. People in India cannot help thinking a great deal about it, because five minutes' carelessness may wreck health for life; yet it is a great matter for us, if possible, to keep from sinking to the languid "cannot-do-anything" point. To rest there is something like letting the head go under water. I often think of dear Uncle Tom's expression,—"Never say die!"'

TO MRS. E——

'*Feb. 4, 1879.*

'My nephew, the Rev. F. Baring, has organised little relief works; for, owing to drought, and partly to the war, there is much distress in Batala. If you were here, dear Aunt, it would interest you to walk about, leaning on my arm, and see poor men in their rags, women and children, carrying baskets of earth on their heads, to fill up that part of the tank which is nearest to the house. It is a good thing for us, but a better thing for the poor folk, who are thankful to earn their pice. Mr. Baring intends also to give poor women in the city employment in spinning, and to get a Christian native weaver to make the cotton into towels or napkins....

'Both my nephews, Mr. Bateman and Mr. Baring, are very clever in finding ways to start the Converts in life, giving them means of earning an honest livelihood. One fine lad has a place in the Woods and Forests Department; another is learning work in the Press; a third is to be employed in a religious book-shop; a fourth convert is doing profitable business as a small wood-merchant. Another, who has a little money of his own, intends to set up a small shop in his own village. This is rather brave, as, only a month or two ago, he was driven forth by his own family with threats and curses. It seems to me that a very important part of a Missionary's work is to watch over converts after Baptism, both as regards body and soul. In the Church, in the time of the Apostles, converts were not left to starve. They must not be idle, but they must have the means of earning their bread. We also greatly wish that every Native convert should feel it to be his or her work to bring in others to Christ....

'We intend to have a Fancy Fair in April, for the Church which we hope to build; but the great puzzle will be to find buyers,—Mr. Baring and myself being the only white folk in Batala, and Natives generally disliking to spend money, except on marriages, funerals, jewels, and sweetmeats.'

TO MRS. HAMILTON.

'*March* 3.—I have another dear letter, to-day received, to thank you for. You need take no thought, love, about where I sit. We have benches in chapel; and as for my duli—to sit on its flat floor does not hurt me in the least. I dare say that dear E. never got into the way of it; but I take to it as a duck to the water. The only difficulty is the scrambling out of the box; but this does me no harm; it is wholesome exercise. As for a carriage, it would be useless in Batala. I was regularly blocked in to-day, even in my tiny duli. The streets are so narrow and so crowded....'

TO W. F. T. HAMILTON.

'*March 17.*

'Our saintly Bishop, Dr. French, is now our guest.... We are having such an interesting time, a heart-warming time! There is to be a Confirmation to-morrow; and oh, through what fiery trials some of the dear candidates have come! There is B—n, ... the first man who dared to be baptized in bigoted Batala. His Baptism cost him wife and child. There is the thin, worn B. D., with his hair turning grey; the only Christian in his village, he whom his own mother has reviled.... There is the aged Faqir and his stalwart sons,—but I need not enumerate all. I have told you enough to show what peculiar features of interest may attend a Confirmation in India,—especially perhaps in so thoroughly Oriental a place as this, where there are no Europeans at all but my nephew and myself.

'Ours is such a dear little Church,—I am not aware that there is one really black sheep in it, though there are some infirm ones. Ten women are to receive Confirmation. I think that all but perhaps one have been converts from Muhammadanism or Hinduism. I do not mean to say that they are all Batala people; but Batala is a genial place to which converts seem drawn.

'To-morrow, after Confirmation, we hope to spread, not the *board* but the *floor*, for a goodly number of welcome guests, more even than we had at Christmas. One feels very thankful to see such a nice large Christian family.... Of course some Stations are more trying to faith; some of God's servants have to toil for years, and apparently catch nothing; but about here in various directions one hears of converts and inquirers. There is feeling of *life* stirring among the dry bones.'

TO MISS 'LEILA' HAMILTON.

'*April 1, 1879.*

'Do you ever enter Trinity Church?[93] Probably not, it is so far from you. To your sweet Mother and myself many memories are connected with it. Weddings and Christenings,—the overflowing pew,—the corner of it where we used to see the dear bald head of our venerated Father!...

'We have a dear young convert from a village, who, like others, finds in Batala a refuge. A simple guileless lad, who likes to come, as dear U. did, to sit at one's feet, and have a talk about God's Word.... He does not know much, but enough to have enabled the lad to resist temptation and endure persecution.... I wish that dear —— would take up the subject of *portable* Bibles in Persian Urdu. Even the children of clever Christian parents are apt to be sadly ignorant of Old Testament Scriptures. How much would English school-children know of them, if they could only buy Bibles in three (Persian Urdu) large volumes,—or in one (Arabic Urdu), very large and heavy?

'It is not only the expense but the extreme inconvenience of such bulky books that must be considered. Mera Bhatija has English Urdu Bibles for his boys, but some read them with difficulty; and we cannot expect a *nation* to adopt a new type utterly different from its own. There is a beautifully written New Testament in Persian Urdu ... light, easily carried about, and costing only half a rupee. This is a great boon; but we want the Old Testament Scriptures.... They are at present almost shut out from the people. Our great want is a complete Bible, as delicately written out, and on as fine light paper, as the New Testament, and not very expensive. Most of the Natives are so very poor. I can scarcely imagine how they manage to live.'

TO MRS. HAMILTON.

'Batala, *April 20, 1879*

'Your dear, sweet letter received to-day was like a nice little visit to me in my comparative loneliness. Mera Bhatija and Babu Singha are both away at Amritsar.... If, when proposing to come out, I could have been told that I should be all alone in a house with thirteen Native boys,—my Ayah is absent from late illness,—I should have been startled, perhaps half-frightened. But these dear fellows do not worry me at all. I asked one of them yesterday: "If I were ill, which of you would nurse me?" "All of us," was the reply. I thought that thirteen boys would be too much for a sick-room; so—"We would take it in turns," was the second answer....

'Many thanks, love, for the two copies of the nice work on Prophecies in the Old Testament. It ought to convince any candid mind.... It might be valuable to English-reading Muhammadans. But it is not at all necessary with them to avoid the Blessed Saviour's Name. Yesterday, in a Zenana a bright-looking young woman exclaimed, not particularly apropos to anything that I was saying: "Jesus Christ is the Son of God." "Beshakh!" (Without doubt!) instantly rejoined an older Bibi.

'Not that the offence of the Cross has ceased. The persecution which dear —— is enduring shows this. He has been beaten five or six times; and I think that we shall have to try to get his enemies bound over to keep the peace. Personally, I am courteously, sometimes affectionately, treated. The poor converts are those who have to endure hardness!'

'*April 27.*—I know that some of my dear ones think that I must be very lonesome, with no white woman near me. But there are three things to prevent this:—1st, The Presence of the Master. 2nd, The feeling that separation of body is nothing compared to separation of soul. My ties to loved ones in England are *not*, thank God, broken! They do not depend on mere space. 3rd, Real loneliness, as regards even this world, is the want of love and sympathy. Some count my brown friends for nothing in this way. I do not do so. They draw out one's affections, and respond to them. The heart does not shrivel up in India, even when one lives in such an out-of-the-way place as Batala.'

TO MISS 'LEILA' HAMILTON.

'*May 1, 1879.*

I am sure that your dear Mother and you would peruse with interest Keshab Sen's lecture, or rather the review of it in the *Statesman* which I sent home.... Keshab Sen was a brave man, not only as regards the Hindus, but the English officials, to say what he did. To aver that it is Christ's Religion—not our superior strength, wisdom, intelligence—that holds India for us, is likely to give great offence in high quarters. To say what this Hindu did of despised Missionaries, a band of weak-minded amiable enthusiasts, if not something more contemptible,—as the world thinks them,—showed moral courage.... He has probably made a good many people, both white and brown, angry. His cry, "Jesus alone!—Jesus alone! India for Christ!" would find no echo in the large majority of hearts....

'I suspect that there is an impression amongst some Europeans, as well as Natives, that Auntie is very old. I have three times heard the latter say that I am a hundred; and I notice that in the last *Female Evangelist* I am pronounced "advanced in years." To my mind that means at least seventy!!! I was guessed to-day as eighty in a Zenana. But I must be thought a pretty active old dame, to get up such steep stairs as I do.'

TO MRS. HAMILTON.

'*June 2, 1879.*—Of course I cannot tell what God wills for me. I do not intend to do anything foolish. I do not even let my mind dwell *much* on the joy of going to a Heavenly Home, because it would seem selfish at present to wish to desert others. I realise more the value of life below than I used to do, and am thankful that at former periods God did *not* fulfil my wish to leave this Earth for a better. He is a poor soldier who is always pining for the end of the campaign!'

'*June 14.*—I never felt so that the Word of God in my hand was rejected, as in a Zenana to-day. When I came out, V., my kahar, said, "You should not go to that house again. I was outside, but I heard words that grieved me." But I had two nice Zenanas and a nice Native Christian home to balance. One of the nice Zenanas was N.'s. He spoke almost like a Christian, before his mother, grandmother, and handsome young bride. They all seemed quite friendly.'

'*June 20.*—Darling Laura, your sweet letter has arrived since I wrote the first note. Would you fairly *kill* me with kindness? You have already done too much. No, my sweet sister, I would never like to take your money for needless luxuries,—of comforts I have many. Ice is not to be had, is *not* needed, and I hardly ever even think of it. We are much better without a carriage; walking is more wholesome, and to me more pleasant. I kissed the signature on the cheque—and then—destroyed it! Forgive me! In about two years I have had *three* cheques declined; so you see that I have enough and to spare. I am quite easy-handed, love; not at all in straits, thank God.'

TO MISS 'LEILA' HAMILTON.

(Probably July 1879.)

'I am engaged in a matrimonial affair. B., Mera Bhatija's Christian servant, having just been rejected by one woman, solicits, through my Ayah, my good offices to find him a wife. He bears a first-rate character, and would make an excellent husband, but he has the single disadvantage of having only one leg. I know that Mera Bhatija wishes B. to have a nice wife; so—after consultation with one who knows the Orphanage maidens well, and has an excellent judgment,—I have fixed on a jolly, good-tempered girl, ... able to cook and scrub, and have written a note to the Lady Superintendent, requesting her permission for B. to pay court to C. C. is to be told of the lameness, etc., and then if she too be willing, B. will be allowed to have an interview with her. This interview decides the affair. Both parties have a negative voice; both must be pleased; and if so—the banns are published! This is the compromise between European and Oriental ways of arranging marriages. I think that Mera Bhatija takes a lively interest in the matter; and if the marriage comes off, we should both like to have the wedding at Batala. The people here ought to have the opportunity of seeing a Christian wedding.'

TO MRS. HAMILTON.

'July 29, 1879.

'I will give you another of my little Batala sketches. I am sitting reading. Enters M., the tall one-armed Faqir (religious beggar), who has been acting as Mera Bhatija's pankah-wala. He evidently wants to talk with me; so, seeing me willing to listen, the tall fellow seats himself on the floor, and begins....

'The poor fellow had been thinking how he could earn his livelihood,—he has a wife and four children, and of course religious begging would be for a convert both improper and unprofitable. "Pankah-pulling will last for but a short time," he very truly observed. His plan was to start a little school in his own village.

'"But could you get pupils?" I asked, knowing that the humble converts are not kindly treated by their neighbours.

'"I think that I could from the hamlets round."

'Then I inquired as to the poor Faqir's qualifications for a teacher. "I can read the Gospel well," was the simple reply.

'"Can you write?"

'He was weak in that, poor fellow. Having only one arm increases the difficulty.

'"Do you know accounts?"

'"No," he frankly owned; but he could learn; he would take pains.

'"You had better speak to the Padri Sahib; he makes all the bandobast (arrangements); he is wise and kind."

'If *I* would speak to the Padri Sahib,—he could tell *me*; but with the Padri Sahib he was shy, etc.

'It is rather refreshing to see a Native Christian, especially one brought up to regard idleness rather as a virtue, turning over in his mind what he can do to earn his living. If we help poor M. to a little better education, perhaps his little village school may prove not a bad idea, for the scholars would learn what is good from him, though they could only have elementary teaching. I do not see why rustics should want high education. The Government are educating thousands of clever infidels, who cannot all find employment as clerks, etc., and who will despise manual labour. We want simple pious *labourers* to mind the plough, spell out their Testaments, and try to obey God's commands.'

August and September this year saw Miss Tucker, not at Dalhousie, but at Dilur, 3000 feet above the sea, with forest-clothed Himalayan slopes below, and snow above. She went there, partly for the change, but more for the sake of staying with a young married couple, to whom her companionship was a boon. The snow appears to have soon vanished, as in one letter, written in September, she observes: 'The mountains are quite high and bold enough for beauty, though to my comfort there is not a soupçon of snow upon any of them.' From the budget of Dilur letters, only two quotations can be given. The first is rare in style at this period of Charlotte Tucker's life. She seldom found time for written 'cogitations.'

TO MISS 'LEILA' HAMILTON.

'Dilur, *Aug.* 25

'This is a very quiet place ... so I have plenty of time for thinking. I have been musing to-day why it is so very much more easy to love some Christians than others. You and every other servant of God must feel this, I think. It is not quite easy to get at the bottom of the matter. I ought to have particular facilities for judging; for, thank God, I find it easy to love a good many.

'I have been considering to-day that simile of the four different circles round Him Who is the Centre of light, holiness, and beauty. Those who live nearest to Him, I do believe, actually catch something, however faint, of His likeness.... Christ is the All-attractive; and in the degree that His redeemed ones reflect His Image, it seems to me that they unconsciously attract. If I be not mistaken in this idea, one sees why anything of littleness or meanness repulses. Those possessing such qualities may be sincere servants of Christ; but these qualities *spoil all likeness*! So, love, here is the result of my cogitations, as I reclined on the sofa to rest myself after rather a tiring little expedition.

'But oh, what a solemnising thought it is!—The likeness to Him, which we *know* will be apparent in another world, to begin in this! The glass of our souls, so spotted and dusty,— spotted with sin, and dusty with pettiness,—to be cleansed and polished, so as to receive such an Image! But you and I, love, have caught a glimpse of that Image in those whom we have been privileged to know; have we not?'

TO MRS. HAMILTON.

'*Sept. 29.*

'Yes, precious Laura, you might be sure that Char does not forget you in prayer any day; but your last dear letter from Ilfracombe made me more inclined to praise. It seemed as if God had granted just what I wished for you; that spiritual joy which is His special gift. Why should the Children of Light tread the pilgrim way in heaviness? "Light is sown for the righteous," and the crop begins to show itself even here....'

Later, in the same letter, when speaking of two young converts, she says of one of them:—

'He is a Mullah's (Muhammadan religious teacher's) son, and has been brought up in a fine school for bigotry. He told me what a merit it is considered to kill infidels; and that, when a child, he had intended to acquire this merit. "Do you mean that, if they could, the Muhammadans would think it right to kill all the Europeans and Native Christians?" I asked. "Beshakh!" (Without doubt!) replied the lad simply. Happily all Muhammadans are not Mullahs' sons!'

'Batala, *Oct. 31, 1879.*—What shall I say for the splendid box, which reached me in perfect condition to-night? I am almost bewildered by the multitude of my possessions, and have hardly yet quite realised their amount.... What shall I begin with?—not the medicine, surely,—and yet quinine is such a treasure in India, so often required, asked for! It is *the* medicine in a fever-land. And it is dreadfully expensive. I think that I once paid more than a guinea for a bottle, not a large one. But the cretonne—yes, that must have a principal place in my letter of thanks; such a splendid supply!...

'I hope that my Laura will forgive me if I do not gobble up all the groceries myself!! Of the chocolate and biscuit I shall probably largely partake; they are such a comfort on winter mornings....'

'*Nov. 13.*—I think that this is the fourth Anniversary of my landing at Bombay,—my Indian birthday! Oh, how much I have to be thankful for! Surely goodness and mercy have followed me!

'Shall I give you a sketch of this my Indian birthday? Up early—for I went to bed early. Ate two or three of my Laura's biscuits, and enjoyed them. Wrote till dear good R. brought the hot water for my bath. Then came breakfast No. 2—tea and an egg. At 7 a.m., or thereabouts, the prayer-bell rings, and we all assemble in chapel. After chapel comes my delightful walk in the fresh morning air. A little more writing and reading, and—breakfast No. 3 with Mera Bhatija at 9. After that, off to the city on foot, my kahars carrying my duli behind me.

'In the city I visited first a Muhammadan Zenana, then paid my weekly visit to our Brahmin convert, B.'s wife.... Then went to G. R.'s Zenana, where are four generations of the family. I can read the Gospel there, without let or hindrance. The sweet young Bibi looked as if she would like me to kiss her,—so I did! Then to Sadiq's mother. After this I returned home, noted down where I had been, and then—did *not* set to my lessons. I had something else to do. The cloth of our large screen was dirty; so Mera Bhatija suggested our putting the pictures on a nice clean one, and having the first white-washed. So I got in my Ayah to help me, and we were stitching away like anything, when I was interrupted by a visitor.

'No fashionable lady,—no insipid individual, such as you must talk to about weather, etc., but a fine, thoughtful young Man,—who had been given a New Testament, which he is reading every day, and who sat down on the floor, and quietly, gravely, asked me to explain difficulties which he had met with in his reading, such as Daniel's "abomination of desolation," the two women grinding, etc.... When he left, I returned to my beauty screen, but was interrupted by dear good Bibi M., who came to read her report. She also wanted quinine,—I am *rich*, my Laura knows. This brought me up to 3 o'clock dinner.

'Poor N. N. is not well, so I had no afternoon lesson from a Munshi, but I did a little by myself. Then out into the bright, pleasant air, where I had a nice talk with dear I. and P. After I came in, Mera Bhatija and I had tea,—now I am writing to my Laura by lamplight; and when I lay down my pen, I intend to do a little lessons. I have written out my vocabulary very large, so as not to injure my eyes. At 8½ I shall hear the bell ring for prayers; and that almost closes the day.

'Now is not this a very nice Indian birthday? I feel quite well and hearty now; much stronger than when in the Salt range.'

'*Nov. 22.*—Cold having set in pretty sharply, I have taken my "graceful Grey" and faithful old Green out of their safe summer quarters, and have prepared them for immediate service, putting in lace to the sleeves, etc. The Episcopal Purple, my grand new dress, I reserve for grand occasions. My dress must be well fastened up, and decidedly more than clear the ground, when I go to Zenanas. See me, in fancy, climbing slowly up a dirty steep outside staircase. I have the indispensable umbrella in one hand,—though it be winter, the sun may be blazing,—my large books in the other. Unless I had a third hand, I could not hold up my dress; and the steps may be of mud. Trains, elegant in the house, would never do in Zenanas.... I hope that you and dear Leila will be interested to hear that our one-legged B., in search of a wife, has succeeded in finding one. I think that their banns have been called twice; and we shall probably see the happy pair next week.'

TO MISS 'LEILA' HAMILTON.

'*Nov. 29, 1879.*

'Yesterday, at last, the cricket-match between our School and the big Government School came off. We challenged the Government School long ago; but they took no notice. Yesterday, however, a match was arranged between our Christian School and the Government one, which is about ten or twelve times as large. We were much the first on the ground, and were kept waiting for more than an hour. Most of our Eleven wore red-checked flannel vests, but R. the captain had a becoming grey one.... At last the match commenced; but it was hardly worth calling one. The Government lads could not hold their own in the least! The whole Eleven only made 5 runs between them!

'It was a very different thing when our boys took the batting. It does one good to hear the thud from R.'s bat when he sends the ball flying ever so far. He and S. made, I think, 87 runs, and were never bowled out. The rest of our boys had no turns at all; for the sun went down, and still R. and S., tired, but unconquered, held their wickets. What is most pleasing is that our boys did not crow as they might have done,—their opponents were too utterly smashed. Had the contest been a close one, there would have been plenty of cheering.

'I really hope that it may do good for it to be known through Batala that, in a manly game, the Hindus and Muhammadans "cannot hold a candle" to the Christian boys, who go preaching and singing hymns on Sunday! Piety is all the more attractive from union with manliness.

'*Dec. 8.*—Mera Bhatija intends to start a reading-room in the city in 1880, with Bibles in various languages, books, and some Native periodicals. The *Illustrated*—if you think of continuing it—will form one of the baits. Many lads now can read a little English; and the pictures will form an attraction.'

CHAPTER X
A.D. 1880-1881 LOYAL AND TRUE

The series of extracts from letters, through the year 1879, given in the last chapter, will convey a fair general idea of how many succeeding years were passed. To quote with equal fulness from each year would mean—not one comparatively small volume, but two large ones; and, however interesting the subject-matter in itself, readers might be expected to grow weary.

Year after year Charlotte Tucker lived on in the old palace, which had so strangely become her home, surrounded by the brown boys, whom she loved; and by the spring of 1880 they had grown to forty in number. Year after year she wrote little booklets for the Natives of India. Year after year she persisted in her steady round of Zenana visits; not, like the average district-visitor of England, going once a fortnight or once a week into her district,—which was the whole city of Batala,—but day after day giving hours to the work, never daunted because results seemed small, never apparently even tempted to throw up her arduous task in despair. She had to *plough* for the Master of the harvest; and she was content to leave results with Him.

It must have been a monotonous life, viewed from ordinary standpoints. Charlotte Tucker had had plenty of society in the past; and though she might laugh at stiff dinner-parties or dull morning calls, she had fully enjoyed intercourse with superior and cultivated minds. Some amount of such intercourse she had still in the Panjab; but for months together, as time went on, she was thrown mainly upon her own resources, was left with absolutely no European companions. It is hardly within the bounds of possibility that she should not have suffered from the deprivation, cheerily as she received it.

'Missionaries in work are usually rather "yoked two and two,"' she wrote to an Aunt, in the beginning of 1880. Then after a slight allusion to her successive 'yoke-fellows' at Batala, she adds brightly: 'And I look forward for the greater part of 1880 to going side by side with Babu Singha, the converted Hindu Head-master,'—with kind mention also of his wife and children.

Friends might say what they would. Miss Tucker had advanced far beyond the stage when it was possible to convince her that she 'could not stay alone' in Batala. Mr. Baring had decided to go to England for eight months; and no one else was free to join her in Anarkalli; but she refused to desert her post. In fact, she would not be 'alone' there now, as she would have been two years earlier. She loved and was loved by the little circle of Indian Christians in the place; and the merry boys of the household were very dear to her. None the less, her position was a singularly solitary one.

The frequent arrival of boxes from England afforded her never-failing delight; partly on her own account, and yet more for the additional facilities afforded thereby for giving away. Pages each year might be filled with quotations on this subject alone.

Also month by month fresh indications appeared of the reality of the work going on,—an inquirer here; a convert there; an abusive Muhammadan softened into gentleness; an ignorant Heathen enlightened; a bigot persuaded; and now and again one coming forward, bravely resolute to undergo Baptism, willing to face the almost inevitable persecution following. All these things were of perpetual occurrence, and they lay very near to Charlotte Tucker's heart.

On the 30th of January 1880 comes a pungent little sentence:—

> 'What fearful people the Nihilists are! When one reads of them, one seems to see Satan let loose! There is some similarity between India and Russia. Perhaps some years hence a Nihilist crop may rise from tens of thousands of sharp conceited lads whom the Government so carefully educate *without God*! They cannot possibly all get the prizes in life which they look for; they *won't* dig,—so will naturally swell the dangerous classes. Such dear lads as we have here will be, we trust, as the salt in the mass. But they may have a difficult work before them.'

Two letters in February to two nieces must not be passed over. In the first we have a glimpse of the dark as well as of the hopeful side:—

> '*Feb. 2.*—That most unhappy lad, — —, seems to be a thorough hypocrite. Only a day or so after professing himself a true penitent, and kneeling in seeming prayer at my side, he has, we hear, been actually preaching in the bazaar here against the Christians.... The subject is too sad to dwell upon; but it is better that I should let you know at once, as I sent home so hopeful a letter.

'Fancy poor E. Bibi actually paying me a visit here yesterday evening. The delicate creature longed to come. I told her to ask her husband's leave, and suggested that he had better come with her. She asked me to send my kahar in the morning, and she would send a message by him as to whether her "Sahib" consented or not. The answer was favourable; so I made arrangements to have two dulis at her door after dark, for E., her mother, and her two little girls. I warned our boys to keep out of the chapel, into which I first introduced the Bibis. I went to the harmonium, and sang to it, "Jesus lives," and two or three verses of the Advent hymn, etc. While we were in the chapel the husband joined us, sat down, and quietly listened. He was very silent, which I think showed good manners.

'We then all proceeded up our long staircase.... I offered tea, but no one drank it; the children ate some pudding, and I presented each of them with one of the dolls which your dear Mother sent out, which I have had dressed.... I think the party were pleased. I wonder what thoughts were passing in the mind of that silent husband. He knows perfectly well what I visit his wife for; for in Batala we do not hide our colours at all. I sometimes think that dear M.[94] dashes right at the enemy almost too boldly; but as she is a supposed descendant of Muhammad, I dare say that her dauntless intrepidity has a good effect. I do not find the women made angry even by what must startle them. Of course one's manner must be gentle and conciliating, even when meeting the question, "Do you think that Muhammad told lies?" with a simple straightforward, "Yes."

'I think that not a few Batala women do now believe that our religion is the right one, and that our Blessed Lord is the Saviour of sinners. But this belief may exist for years before there is any desire for Baptism.'

'*Feb. 6.*—One visit which I paid in the former place (Amritsar) would have warmed your heart. In a cottage in the Mission compound, occupied by one of the Bible-women, I found three who doubtless will inherit the blessing promised to all who are persecuted for righteousness' sake. There was dear faithful Begum J., and her daughter, K. (now a Bible-woman). These are the two who, as you may remember, were threatened with a razor by Begum J.'s husband, and fled, and were afterwards baptized. They had come to see another brave Convert, who had been baptized on the previous day.

'A fierce crowd had attacked her, tore the jewels from her ears, beat her on the head, threatened to cut off her nose! How she escaped she cannot tell; she was bewildered. Perhaps some unseen Angel took her by the hand. She reached *somehow* a duli, which was in waiting for her, and was baptized the same day.'

The school was so growing, that by March 1880 a good many of the boys had to sleep on the floor which formerly had been reserved entirely for Europeans. This Miss Tucker did not mind.

Before the end of March she had to bid good-bye to her dharm-nephew, who was starting for England. It must have given her a strange feeling, thus to see one and another leave for the dear old country, which she so loved, and yet which she had resolved never of her own free will to see again.

The previous day a feast was given in Mr. Baring's honour, the boys 'subscribing to buy the little dainties'; and 'speeches of love and gratitude' being made. Then, in the early morning, long before dawn, Miss Tucker felt her way down the dark staircase, to see the traveller off. 'The babies,' as she called some of the tinier brown boys, were there also; one small orphan looking 'sad and thoughtful' over the farewell. Bigger boys also came down, and they waited in the Chapel till the Principal appeared. Shakings of hands were followed by cheers, as Mr. Baring drove away in the dâk-gari,— 'probably with mingled feelings,' writes Miss Tucker. One is disposed to wonder what *her* feelings were, as she turned back into the palace; alone among her companions; the only European in that Eastern city! Yet no signs of heart-quailing can be seen in the letter to her sister, written on the same day.

In this spring of 1880 came another event of importance,—the 'Disruption' of the older Zenana Society, under which Charlotte Tucker had worked as an Honorary Member.

There is no necessity to enter fully here into the causes which led to that disruption. To some of us it may seem to have been, sooner or later, almost inevitable. Until that date the attempt had been made to work on what are sometimes called 'un-denominational lines,'—which meant that the Missionaries might be either Churchwomen or Dissenters, each teaching according to her own convictions. A difficult programme to carry out, one is disposed to imagine! After a while friction arose in the Governing Body at home. Since by far the larger majority of workers in the field belonged to the

Anglican Church, it was rightly considered that the Governing Body ought to consist of an equally large majority of Church people; and on this point the split took place. The Society broke into two parts. The one part remained more or less Dissenting; the other part became distinctly and exclusively Church of England. Each Missionary had to make her own decision as to which she would join; and Charlotte Tucker at least had no hesitation in the matter. On the 12th of May she wrote:—

> 'Here I am at home again, after my strange little visit to Amritsar; short, but by no means unimportant. All our five ladies have crossed the Rubicon; they have sent in their resignations, with the usual six months' notice. It remains to be seen whether the new "Church of England Zenana Society" will or *can* take them all on! We know not what the state of their funds will be, as they begin on nothing. Our ladies, with Mr. Weitbrecht the Secretary, seemed to have no hesitation as to what course to pursue,—that of resignation.... I am very desirous to know what dear Margaret Elmslie and Emily will do.... How the complicated machinery of the Mission will work during the strange interregnum I know not.... One expects a sort of little—not exactly chaos, but— struggling along in a fog, for the next six months; and then we shall probably see our way clearly.'

On the following day she sent in her own resignation. Little more appears about the subject in later letters. As an Honorary Worker her own position was not affected, nor was her income placed in jeopardy; and soon the new 'Church of England Zenana Society,' being warmly taken up, was in full working order. Amongst those who joined it were her friends, Mrs. Elmslie and Miss Wauton.

At this time she was becoming very anxious for the return of Mrs. Elmslie, who had been detained in England far longer than was at first intended, by family claims. Sometimes a fear was expressed that Mrs. Elmslie might never return; and no one else could fill her place. Charlotte Tucker did not dream of the happy consummation ahead. Two or three references to her earlier days occur in June and July, as if some cause had sent her thoughts backward.

> '*June 4, 1880.*—I think, love, that one gets into a kind of social fetters. When we were young we had the worry of a footboy at our heels,—it was thought suitable for our position. (Do you remember dear Fanny's lovely definition of that word?) When I was in Edinburgh, dear —— was surprised, and I

think a little shocked, at "my father's daughter" going in omnibuses. As if it were any disgrace to my father's middle-aged daughter to do what her precious princely Sire had done a hundred times! O Laura, when one throws aside these trammels of social position, one feels like a horse taken out of harness, and set free in a nice green meadow. Our honoured Father! what true dignity was his,—but how he shook off the trammels!

'To be mean and miserly is quite another thing. That dishonours our profession. One should be ready to entertain hospitably, and to pay for work done handsomely; there is a free hand and a generous spirit quite consistent with economy.'

'*July 13.*—Yes, love, we did intensely enjoy those concerts in H. Square. I want you to enjoy more concerts. It is curious how useful I have found my little music in the evening of my days. I sometimes think of dear Mother's words to me,—"Do not give up your music."'

In July, when Miss Tucker was congratulating herself that half the time of Mr. Baring's absence was over, a letter arrived speaking of lengthened furlough. She was much distressed, fearing harm to the school, and for a while was assailed by fears that perhaps he and also Mrs. Elmslie might never return. Happily these fears were groundless; but plans were afloat for some temporary arrangement while the Principal remained away. Miss Wauton too was at this time taking her well-earned furlough in England, and workers were sorely needed in the Panjab; while new untrained Missionaries on first going out could do little. 'We want Margaret,' was the burden of her cry; to which was now added, 'We want Mr. Baring.'

For herself she had no thought of a furlough. Friends thought of it for her; and she put the idea resolutely aside. Writing to Mrs. Hamilton on September 6, she said: 'And now for a more important subject, broached in your sweet letter. I do not feel that it would be either wise as regards myself, or right as regards my work, to go home next year. The great fatigue of two journeys, the excitement of meeting loved ones, and the wrench of parting again,—I doubt how my health could stand it. As regards the work—I need not expatiate. It would look as if I thought much of the little that I could do; but little is better than nothing. It seems to me that one of the most useful things about me is that—hitherto—I have stuck pretty close to my Station. If I were a Native Christian, I think that I should be tempted to hate the very word "going home," and to regard Europe as a trap for my Missionaries. Let them, if possible, have a *restful* feeling in regard to at least one old woman, whom they are ready to love.'

And a few days later to Miss Hamilton, on September 14:—

'Your sweet Mother threw out a suggestion about my going home next year; but it seems to me, love, that if I did so,— unless circumstances change,—I should deserve to be shot as a deserter. Even if I were to become blind or paralytic, I believe that it would be well to stick to Batala. I am the only apology for a European Missionary here; and, curiously enough, my very *age* is an advantage. What might be a great hindrance elsewhere is rather a help here.'

In a letter of September 14 occurs a passage about apparent success or non-success in work. She had perhaps comforted herself from time to time with such thoughts as follow.

Speaking about a certain American religious book, which had been lent to her by one who greatly admired it, and about Mr. Bateman's opinion of the same volume, she observes: 'What Rowland most objected to was the American affirming that if you take certain means to effect conversions, the result is as sure as harvest following breaking up the ground. As Rowland says, we cannot even break up the ground without God.... Are we to conclude that — — and — — are truer workers than dear — — spending his strength in breaking stones at K., while the sheaves almost drop into the reapers' arms at D.? Did our Blessed Lord Himself, Who was always sowing golden seed, reap a very large harvest during His Ministry? St. Peter's first sermon drew in a far greater number than all the disciples of the Blessed Lord before His Resurrection put together.'

It was evident that, although she must have felt her lonely position, she was gradually becoming used to it; even so far as not at all to wish for a strange young lady as a companion. Mrs. Hamilton had made strong representations to the Society at home of the need of a helper at Batala; and the letters given next seem to have been written partly in consequence of this.

As early as the spring of 1880 Miss Tucker could say: 'I used to think it rather tiresome when business took both my English companions for a few days away; now I am quite serene if I do not see a white face for months.' And in November of the same year: 'As to earthly blessings, they abound; the Natives are my real friends. The Lord gives abundant grace, and cheers me with His Presence; and I have such joy in the companionship of my Bible, that I do not miss the society I should otherwise value. Do not send a helper to me, when many other parts of India need it so much more.'

Again, on September 27:—

> 'It is very loving in you to be so anxious for me to have a lady-companion. But, unless a Missionary's wife, one might far from add either to my comfort or usefulness. To put aside the possibility of her being eloquent,—a late sitter-up,—of a melancholy or nervous temperament, or often ailing,—I really have no spare space for a lady companion. She must share my bath-room, if not my bedroom; and in India this would be very uncomfortable.
>
> 'But why, you may say, should there be more room for a married pair than for one maiden lady? The answer is simple enough. If a *gentleman* were here, the large family of the Singhas would give up their rooms and move to the Banyans. We *must* have a gentleman Superintendent.'

Later in the same letter comes a reference to one of the Heroes of her enthusiastic girlhood. Lady Outram and her gallant husband had been intimate friends of the Tucker family; and many a loving message in these later years was sent home by Charlotte Tucker to the former.

> 'I have been reading much of the noble Outram's Memoir to-day. As far as I have gone, I think that the Biographer has done his work well. The Outram of the book is just the Outram who was the admiration of our girlhood,—generous, chivalrous, noble! One feels how much pain that fine spirit would have been saved, had he realised how little it really matters whether good service be appreciated or not by man, if the great Leader accept it,—if all be done as to Him Who never overlooks or misunderstands! To our own Master we stand or fall; let earthly superiors say what they will.'

> '*Oct. 16.*—Dear, excellent —— thinks that my not having a "Revival" in Batala is because I do not study his favourite author. You can hardly have a *Revival* unless there has been some life before.... Our work is more like clearing in backwoods,—there are huge trees and boulders cumbering the ground; not just weeds overspreading a garden that once was a little cultivated. Then here women cannot read, and do not choose to learn.... I like Miss Havergal's *Kept for the Master's Use* so much. It is beautiful. But I do not feel with her that it is possible on Earth to have our *will* exactly *one* with God's. Even the Blessed Saviour made a distinction between "My Will" and "Thy Will." Dear C. T. T., for

instance, submitted sweetly to her heavy trials; but it could not be her *will*, it was her *cross*, to lose all her nearest and dearest, and see her father ill for so many years.'

'*Dec. 15, 1880.*—Dear Mr. Clark's return has caused so much joy. The Native Christians have had a loving address to him printed in letters of gold. I fancy that a general feeling is, "Now there is a hand on the reins." ... Mr. Clark is an experienced and skilful driver. True, he is very weak, but he brings *brains*, and a power of organisation. If he were a prisoner to his room he might be very valuable still.... He was sadly missed....'

'*Dec. 17.*—*Please*, love, make no plans for bringing ladies to Batala. It is so awkward to me to have to explain to nice enthusiastic ladies that they cannot come. This is not a place except for elderly or married ladies. If Mera Bhatija would bring out a nice wife, it would give much pleasure; at present plans and propositions only—I must not say burden me—but they do not help me. I do very well as I am; I have had, through God's goodness, a happy year; and if I were to be ill, I would *rather* be doctored by our Sikh, and nursed by our Natives. As for visitors, we have hardly any except in the cooler weather; and a little packing then does no harm.'

Of the following extracts to Mrs. E——, only two of which are fully dated, all probably belong to about this period:—

'*July 23.*—I saw to-day a sight which perhaps never met your eyes in India, and which I never wish to see again; though it was not without something of melancholy beauty. On Sunday towards dusk I was with some of the boys, and they called out "Locusts!" I looked up into the sky, and saw what my old eyes would have considered harmless clouds high above me; but the young eyes must have detected the motion of countless wings. To-day there was no possibility of mistake. I was in a Zenana, in the full light of day, gazing up at myriads and myriads,—dark against white clouds, light against the blue sky,—passing over Batala. They looked to me like God's terrible army; so strong; so vigorous; not one amongst the millions appeared to be weary; not one did I see drop down as if faint from long flight. They flew as if they had a purpose; our fair green fields did not appear to tempt the destroyers,—only I saw a comparatively small number in one,—but they were clearly intent on going somewhere else. Alas for the land where they alight! A Native told me that they would probably come back again. How helpless is man against such a foe! We can only ask for mercy, as Pharaoh did.'

'Kangra, *Aug. 21.*—I paid a visit to Kangra fort yesterday; a grand picturesque place, holding a commanding position. The officer in command had prepared tea and cake for me, and the dear kind soldiers lemonade, so I was treated with much hospitality. They do not often see a lady up there. I have often thought of your dear M.'s words about the soldiers, and her wondering at my feeling shy with them. They are some of the pleasantest people in the world to have to do with.... While I was taking tea with the Commander, the soldiers were concocting a letter to say that they had collected *ten rupees* to pay my expenses, and hoped that I would soon come again. I certainly do not want their money, poor dear fellows; and I mean to go again on Monday. Soldiers' money seems to jump out of their purses of its own accord. In this the Natives are far behind them. Four soldiers—I think in Afghanistan—are uniting to support a little girl at the Amritsar Orphanage. They are charmed with the idea. I had nothing to do with it, except giving the Superintendent's address. I have over and over again received help for the Mission from English soldiers, and I never ask them for it. Fine fellows!—and to think what they have to suffer!'

'Batala, *Oct. 1, 1880.*—I was amused to-day at what my kahar called out. I am quite accustomed, as I am borne along in my little duli, to hear my bearers shout, "Posh! posh!" (Hide! hide!), which is absurd enough, as if all must flee from my approach. But to-day was too absurd. I was, according to custom, walking to the city, with my kahars carrying my duli behind. There was a rider in front, mounted on a horse inclined to back. My attentive kahar, careful that the animal should not hurt me, cried out, "Save the horse!"—as if, instead of its kicking *me*, the danger was that a mild old lady approaching on foot should demolish the unfortunate animal!'

'Batala, *Jan. 31, 1881.*—As I was engaged yesterday with a party of our boys, I was interrupted by hearing that my poor dear Ayah had been stung—bitten, as the people incorrectly say—by a scorpion. I thought what could be done. I had happily by me some ipecacuanha, sent to me in 1879 by my dear kind sister, Laura, in case of such an emergency, and also pain-killer, which she forwarded to me more recently. Armed with these and a bit of tape, probably her present also, I hastened to the compound, and found my Ayah crying with the violent pain. She had already sucked the poor finger. I tied my tape round it, anointed it with a mixture of ipecacuanha and pain-killer, and gave some of the latter also internally. My Hannah appeared to derive some relief, but had much pain in the night. To-day, however, she is much better. I have never seen either scorpion or centipede in Batala; but then my long staircase would present a formidable difficulty to such reptiles.'

About this time, hearing the boys one day singing *The Vicar of Bray*, Miss Tucker wrote fresh words to suit the old tune, and taught them to her young companions. The second verse was curiously characteristic of herself.

'The rushing torrent bears along
The straw on its surface thrown, Sir;
But the rock in its midst stands firm and strong,
Although it stand alone, Sir.
Oh, may our steadfast courage so
In danger's hour be seen, Sir;
And let the tide flow,
And let the world go,
We 'll be true to our Faith and our Queen, Sir!'

CHAPTER XI
A.D. 1881-1882 CLOUDS AFTER SUNSHINE

The greater part of 1881 passed much as 1880 had passed; Miss Tucker continuing to live in the old palace, busy and happy among her Indian friends, and cheery with the boys, having no second European within easy reach. But in the spring came an unexpected joy. News arrived that her dharm-nephew, the Rev. Francis Baring, was engaged to be married to her dearly-loved friend, Mrs. Elmslie, and that the two might be expected in Batala before the close of the year. Could Charlotte Tucker have had the shaping of events for herself, for her friends, and for Batala, one can well imagine that this is precisely what she would have chosen to take place. In the opening of the year, however, she had no idea of what would soon come.

> '*Jan. 5, 1881.*—In looking over my records of 1880, I find that in the nine, or rather eight months, of Mera Bhatija's absence,—as I was away myself for a month,—I have given nearer seven hundred than six hundred teas to boys or young men. The expense is trifling; it seems as if a couple of pounds of tea lasted for ever; but all these little marks in my book represent a good deal of innocent enjoyment, not, I hope, unmixed with profit. All the boys, save two lately come, have again and again sat at my table, chatted or played with me.'
>
> '*Jan. 11.*—I was with a poor weeping Bibi yesterday. Her heart was very heavy. She told me that her husband had forsaken her; he has gone away and married another. When I asked her in the presence of her companions who Christ is, she replied, "God's Son." "Why did He come from Heaven?" "To save us." I wish that this forlorn one would throw herself on His love, and come into the Church. I read God's Word to another Bibi to-day, who is in the same position,—desolate, forsaken, ready to listen. A third case is somewhat similar. You would think it comparatively easy for these forsaken ones to come out; but even to them the

difficulties are immense. Where the husband is tolerably kind, the difficulty is next to insuperable; for marriage by Muhammadan law,—and I have lately been shocked to hear, by English law also,—is *dissolved* by Baptism. This is dead against St. Paul's directions as to the duty of believing wives towards unbelieving husbands; and you can imagine how it complicates the difficulties of Zenana visitors!... If one would express in one word the Missionary's worst perplexity, I think that I would put down the word "marriage."'

'*Feb. 5, 1881.*—I went to a wedding yesterday, one of the silly child-marrying affairs, with which the Hindus delight to ruin themselves and run into debt. Poor — — quite agreed with me that it is very foolish; but he and his relatives cannot resist dastur,[95] so both my kahars receive next to nothing for five months, to work out their debt to me. I had to do rather a difficult thing for an old lady, in order to get to the wedding-party, climb a real ladder—not very good—of eight rounds. I am not as agile as I used to be, and had to go up and up, and then down and down, very slowly and cautiously. To parody Byron's lines—

'"The feat performed I—boots it well or ill,

Since not to tumble down is something still...."

'*May 10.*

'I thought that my birthday would pass over very quietly and silently, as it fell on a Sunday.... But my Native friends would not let me go without my birthday tamasha, merely delaying it till the Monday. I could not regret it, for certainly it was one of the most gratifying evenings that I have ever enjoyed. We had our feast, given by the Singhas, on the top of their house, with the glorious dark-blue sky as our ceiling, and our lamp the beautiful moon.... I was presented with a Batala scarf or chaddah, for which my dear boys had subscribed. A wonderful chaddah it is, with borders of red and gold. I thought by moonlight that the colour was grey.... In the morning I saw the exceedingly gay *green*, of which I enclose a thread.... It is precious to me, as a token of affection.

'The Native Christians not unfrequently subscribe to give a parting gift to a Missionary whom they love, when starting for England; but I suppose they thought that, in my case, if they waited for that they would never give me anything, and that it was no harm to present me with something for *not* going away! Mr. K. was rather astonished at the wild bhajans, which he declares are all on one note—but that is a mistake—but he says that they helped to cure his earache; a very curious and novel effect, which I never knew before to belong to a bhajan!...

'I think, love, that these little particulars will amuse you. I write playfully, but the real undermost feeling in my heart is that of humble gratitude to Him from Whom all blessings flow,—the love of true and God-fearing hearts being one of the most precious of those blessings.'

TO MRS. J. BOSWELL.

'*March 17, 1881.*

'The Hindus appear to be particularly silly at this time of the year. They throw about coloured water, so as to make almost all the white dresses of their companions look dirty and disreputable. My poor —— came particularly badly off, for he not only had three times his raiment dirtied, but his hand rather severely hurt. Said I to him, "Do you think such a religion is from God?" "It is devilish," he frankly assented. "A devilish religion; a devilish deed." "Why do you not leave it?" The poor fellow was silent. It is not faith in his nonsensical religion that holds him back, but love of social ties and surroundings.'

TO MRS. HAMILTON.

'*April 13.*

'Our good pastor Sadiq and I had a long talk together to-day. We two almost, as it were, form a little party by ourselves; we are regular old-fashioned Panjabis, something like Saxons after the Norman Conquest. Sadiq highly approves of this school, because we don't Anglicise the boys.... But the Anglicising tide runs too fast for Sadiq and me. We get spoilt by Batala, where there are no Europeans or Eurasians.... This is a grand transition time in India; and the Conservatism, which I drank in at old No. 3, remains in me like an instinct now. I would keep everything unchanged that is not wrong or foolish—and there is such a fearful amount of things that *are* wrong and foolish, that one might think that to get rid of them would give all occupation sufficient. But I know that

I am old-fashioned, and live too much in one groove to be able to judge correctly.'

TO MRS. E— —

'*July 29, 1881.*

'You have perhaps heard that I am to have a charming lady to be with me; for my adopted nephew, the Rev. F. H. Baring, is bringing out a lovely bride, one whom I know well, and whom I have been accustomed to call my Queen-Lily, because she is so tall and fair. I expect her to do Mission-work much better than I can; and will not our boys love her! They seem to have made up their minds that she is to be their mother; so she will have a fine large family to look after, thirty-seven boys, or more; some of them really not boys, but men. Rowland Bateman is to perform, or rather, I believe, has performed, the marriage service for his friend. We expect to have grand rejoicings here on the arrival of the happy pair. It was a feast to see the way in which the news of their Principal's engagement was received by his boys.... There was such clapping and delight, that you might have thought all the boys were going to be married themselves!'

TO MRS. HAMILTON.

'*Sept. 4, 1881.*

'I visited to-day a poor mother who has lost a fine little boy. I seated myself amongst the mourners, and talked with the mother. What she said gave me a gleam of hope regarding the child of ten. He had till lately attended our Mission School, so of course had received religious instruction. He had the opportunity also of learning something in the Zenana, and knew Christian Hymns. His illness was *very* short; and what he said no one could understand; but, as his mother assured me more than once, "*he smiled twice.*" This seems but a sunbeam to build upon; yet as I have never known or heard of Muhammadans or Heathen smiling when about to die,— the death-smile seems exclusively Christian!—I cannot but hope that the dear little fellow *had* looked to the Saviour. I told the mother of the hope in my mind, and spoke to the weeping little brother also.'

'*Oct. 3.*—It is a real pleasure to look forward to, that of welcoming the Barings back, and placing the reins in younger and stronger hands than my own. Not a giving up of work, please God, but a lightening of responsibility. How often we say or think, "Oh, we'll leave that till the Padri Sahib comes." He is to do the thinking and ordering and arrangement in his little bishopric. As for sweet, lovely Margaret, I expect to see her gentle influence bearing on all sides. We are not likely to disagree, unless it be on the subject of who is to sing first, and who is to take the coveted second part.'

'Peshawar, Oct. 18, 1881.—A large military station like Peshawar is rather a contrast to Batala. But, poor India! Where one sees less of the enemy attacking in one direction, we find him advancing in another. Over the Hindus and Muhammadans he throws the chains of Superstition, Idolatry, Self-righteousness,—he makes them choose a murderer instead of the Prince of Life. For the Europeans he has coldness, deadness, infidelity! I noticed at Church that but *one man* stayed to Holy Communion.'

'*Nov. 7.*—I am so much stronger after my visit to Peshawar,—quite a different being. It must be a comfort to Babu Singha, who thought me ageing with wonderful rapidity. But at Peshawar I took a backward spring. I was more than six hours to-day on an expedition to the village of Urduhi, going in my duli; and I was very little tired,—quite ready for Henry viii. and his six wives in the afternoon, and for Agamemnon and Achilles in the evening. It is amusing to go back to the old stories one read in one's childhood.'

TO MISS 'LEILA' HAMILTON.

'Nov. 22, 1881.

'The visit of the two Bishops,[96] Mr. Clark, and the Chaplain, Mr. Deedes, went off beautifully. Everybody seemed pleased with Batala; and the Bishop of Calcutta wrote such handsome things in the school-book, that I am sure dear Babu Singha was gratified. The Bishop of Calcutta is a striking-looking man; tall, with a simple, unaffected dignity.... He gives one the impression of both physical and intellectual strength, combined with true piety. As the vigorous, energetic practical man, he forms an interesting contrast to the fragile-looking, saintly Bishop of Lahore. Then Mr. Clark has a calm charm of his own,—described by a lad as "looking like an angel, with his beautiful white beard." ...

'Of course we had a feast. Then followed brief recitations from Shakespeare, and choruses. To-day the school was examined in Scripture, and pleased the Bishop. We had Divine Service, and an interesting, forcible sermon, well translated, sentence by sentence, by Mr. Clark. The Bishop of Calcutta afterwards went over the place, examining the boys' beds, etc., struck at Native lads having such clean sheets, and at hearing that they were changed weekly. He kindly visited our poor sick M., who is much better, thank God, though still—after six weeks—confined to bed. I gave my guests plenty to eat; and my bottle of wine held out bravely, two of the gentlemen preferring tea, while the wine-drinkers were very moderate. I had to manage a little to make my furniture suffice for four guests. There was a little borrowing, but not much. I put two of your sweet mother's lovely tidies, quite fresh, over chair and sofa, to look elegant. I wore the pretty cap, trimmed with blue, and my graceful grey dress, both gifts from No. 31.[97]

'The Bishop of Calcutta, before leaving, kindly put into my hand a note for 100 rupees. I asked him to what purpose I should apply it; he replied to whatever purpose I liked; so I at once decided on our City Mission School, our Batala *Plough*, which has almost come to the end of its means, and must on no account be suffered to drop through. I was very glad of the seasonable supply.

'Now all the boys' thoughts are turned to the reception of the dear Barings. The Natives take the whole affair into their own hands, I merely helping by paying for the refreshments. I see a wooden arch in course of erection, and hundreds—perhaps a thousand—little earthen lamps cumbering our hall. Perhaps the Bishops wondered what all those funny little concerns could be for. There are to be fireworks too; but I have nothing to do with either illumination or fireworks.'

Before the end of November Mr. and Mrs. Baring arrived, to be received lovingly by Charlotte Tucker, and enthusiastically, not by the boys alone, or even by the Christians alone, but by many of the people of Batala. On the 9th of December a letter went from Mrs. Baring home:—

'My dear Mrs. Hamilton,—I have but few uninterrupted minutes, but long to send you at least a few lines, to assure you that your beloved sister is well. She gave us a most delightful welcome; and a very great joy it is to be with her.

I thought her looking extremely white and thin, although not lacking in her wonted energy, when we first came. Now I think she is looking a little better; and we shall tenderly watch over her, and cherish her, so far as she will allow us; but I assure you it is very hard work to persuade her to reduce her work, or to increase her nourishment. I see that my best plan is quietly to put things in her way that may be strengthening, but not to trouble her by *pressing*; and to ensure soups, puddings, etc., being all thoroughly nutritious, so that the amount she does take may all do her real good. And as to the work, I hope she will gradually let me have part of it, leaving herself more time for writing.

'You will be pleased to see how the people love and honour her. The tahsildar[98] came one day to see us; and reverently bowing his head before her, he asked her to lay her hand upon it, and pray for him,—which she did, most earnestly asking that Heavenly light might be poured into his soul. I think she is very wise in her dealings with the Christians, but is apt to over-estimate some of the heathen,—and to cast precious "pearls before swine," at too great an expense of her own time and strength. However, I am perhaps mistaken about this. We must pray that *all* her loving efforts may be abundantly blessed, and that she may be allowed the joy of seeing some fruit of her city labours. Among the boys she has been *much* blessed. I hope to write often, if you will kindly excuse my notes being hurried. Much love to dear Leila. Kindest remembrances to Mr. Hamilton.— Ever yours lovingly,

Margaret.'

One little touch of depression had appeared a few weeks earlier, in a letter written before the visit of the Bishops, wherein Miss Tucker alluded to a slight sketch or account of herself which had been inserted in a Missionary periodical. The tone of sadness was probably due to those long city labours, spoken of by Mrs. Baring, so few results of which could then be detected.

'*Nov. 16, 1881.*— ... Last Sunday was my sixth *Indian* birthday; it fell on a Sunday, like my natural one. In 1880 I felt joyous on my Indian birthday. Somehow or other I had quite a different sensation this year. I felt so dissatisfied with myself,—my work seemed all sowing, and never reaping! Oh, what a false impression the — — gives of me! And Miss

—— never published my refutation.... Do you remember the noble lines in "Camoens"—

'"Praise misapplied
Is to the generous mind not callous grown
A burning cautery."

'I do not mean that I am burnt; but I feel like one breathing an unwholesome, sickly odour. Here is the Bishop of Calcutta wanting to see me; he has probably been reading some painted description, and imagines me a highly capable and successful Missionary. O dear! O dear! If Miss —— had only published my honest, blunt letter!'

For once in this little fit of down-heartedness, she seems to have somewhat lost her usual balanced view of the comparative unimportance of seemingly successful 'results.' But if in all these years of toil Charlotte Tucker had never known depression, she would have been more than human. Even her brave and dauntless spirit had occasionally to pass under a cloud; more often, as years passed on, and strength decayed. This time it had been a very slight one; and the coming of her two dear friends had brought bright sunshine into her life.

Early in the next year another letter went to Mrs. Hamilton from the bride:—

'Jan. 21, 1882.

'Dearest Mrs. Hamilton,—I often want to have a chat with you,—*so* often! But now how impossible it is to go to the bright, home-like drawing-room at Leinster Square to have it! I must therefore just be content with pen and ink.

'Your own beloved one writes so regularly that you hear all Batala news; but you do not, I fancy, hear much about her own dear self. She had certainly overdone before we came, and naturally, after six years of such continuous effort, in a climate such as this, she looks aged; but she is really just as full of brightness as ever, and her spirit is unflagging in its loving efforts for all around her. It is indeed a privilege and joy to have her here. Just at present she has a troublesome cold, caught by going out in the foggy morning of last week; but I trust it will soon yield to remedies. She is cosily resting in an arm-chair by the log-fire beside me, and has allowed me to take a little care of her to-day. The Native doctor comes every day to see the boys; so if anything is wrong with her we have him upstairs, to have a chat and prescribe. He is a very superior man, and she has great confidence in him.

'She will have told you of the possibility of a Mrs. R. coming out to join us as a Medical Bible-woman.... Not only would she be very useful in the Zenanas, and in taking care of the little boys, but also in taking a look-out for our dear one when we are absent.... My husband thinks of adding a room and dressing-room to The Aloes for Mrs. R. if she comes; so she would be quite near us.... Dinner is announced, so I must say farewell. The dear Auntie kindly consents to let a little low table be drawn close to the fire in the drawing-room for her to-day, as the dining-room is very cold in this weather....

C. M. T. TO MRS. HAMILTON.

'*Jan. 23, 1882.*

'It was rather naughty in Margaret to tell you that I had a cold; I did not know that she would be such a blab! However, she is not an easy person to be angry with. I think that dear kind Doctor, B. D., is quite pleased with me. He thinks that I have done more in the way of getting well in twenty-four hours than I should have done in a week had I been a Zenana lady, because I should not have obeyed him. The Natives are so very lazy about anything in illness which involves any trouble.... Dear Margaret and Francis take great care of me,—coddle me!' (Then comes a pleased reference to the thought of the Medical Bible-woman for the next cold weather.) 'It was such an utterly unexpected thing.... It is so nice to meet with a servant of a true Missionary spirit. Of course she will need taking care of herself. I told Francis that he should calculate on her *pankah* costing £5 a year. I do not need as much fanning as some Europeans do; but I count my pankah as that expense; and it would be folly to grudge it. You see, in the Panjab, if you wish to sleep at night, you must have a pankah in the hot weather even at midnight, unless you can sleep in the open air,—which I find impracticable in a boys' school; and I do not see how good Mrs. R. could manage it....

'Aunt L.'s book is very amusing, even to a grown-up person; there is such vigour in the attitudes, and the colouring is just suited for Orientals. I think of taking it with me when I pay my long-promised visit to Clarkabad. I hope to invade the heathen there and not confine myself—please God—to the Christian village. I feel a special interest in Clarkabad, on account of my dear Rowland. The lovely little gem of a church, partly the work of his own hands, gives a charm to the spot. Now the presence of the excellent Beutels will add to it.

'I expect to find some of the flock very troublesome folk; but that is what Missionaries must expect. These big brown families have their prodigals and sloths and backsliders. What is to be expected from those who have had so little light for generation after generation? We should hail every symptom of improvement. The European idea of a Missionary standing under a tree, preaching,—and numbers listening, understanding, and welcoming the Word of Life,—is often a fancy picture, or gives a most imperfect view of the truth. The seeking to *win* souls is but one part of the real work.

'Only think what a regular workshop of thought has been going on in the heads of such men as — — and — —. *A*. is weak; how is he to be shielded from temptation? *B*. is a stupid, lazy fellow; how is he to be made to work? What is to be done about *C*.'s heathen wife? Are not *D*.'s children growing up like weeds? Can we manage to find employment for *E*. or a Christian wife for *F*.? It is this "care of the Churches" which was a burden to St. Paul, and I suppose has been a burden to most of his most earnest successors. It is not a thing to tell in a Report, or to draw out enthusiasm in a Missionary meeting. But we know, darling, that if a farmer went over a huge field, simply scattering grain, perhaps on ground even unploughed, and then went home, quite sure that all would go right, that he had only to go on for ever sowing and a harvest would certainly rise, he would hardly be likely to garner a crop.... *One* such matured, ripened Convert as — — is worth a hundred of those whose conduct shows that they hardly deserve the name of Christians.'

In the course of this January she wrote lovingly to her sister: 'It touched my heart that you should have had "grief" in your dreams about parting again with your Char! The wrench of saying "Farewell" is what one cannot help shrinking from.'

But despite the pain of long separation from those whom she most loved, and despite many cares and anxieties this year in her work, Miss

Tucker still kept her health. Mrs. Baring, writing early in February, could say: 'I am so very glad to be able to assure you that your precious sister is much better, really looking well; though perhaps not quite so strong as in the days when she could easily outstrip me in a walk, or work from 4 a.m. to 10 p.m. without feeling very tired.' Few women at their strongest could emulate such a day's work, and not feel 'very tired' at the end. It is hardly surprising that at the age of sixty she should not continue '*quite* so strong.'

Money for the proposed Church had been flowing in; yet still it was not begun. 'We have been, I think,' Miss Tucker wrote, 'for nearly two and a half years trying to buy a good site, but the Natives will not sell one to us. We cannot build on air. We have the money—and the will to buy—but we must wait God's time.' A little hospital also was planned, but the same difficulties presented themselves as to a suitable site, and delays were unavoidable.

Here comes a melancholy little touch of the sad side of Missionary work—that side which must inevitably exist in everything belonging to this world:—

> 'Perhaps you sometimes wonder at my so often making the special request for prayer for *wisdom*. But oh, love, if you knew the puzzling cases which meet us! I observe that experienced and sensible Natives are taken in; so can we wonder at being so? I will just give you a specimen case where we have *not* been taken in, because warned in time. I have not even seen the woman in question; I suppose that the parties found out that we have had notice.... A woman professes, I hear, to be an inquirer. She wishes baptism. Why? A Muhammadan man is at the bottom of her inclination towards Christianity. The woman is of low caste, so that the man would be degraded by marrying her, as he desires to do. Let her become a Christian,—that will be a kind of white-washing for her,—she will be received amongst us, be able to eat with us, etc. *Then* the Muhammadan is to pervert her to the faith of Islam, and gain credit for converting a Christian, instead of disgrace for marrying a Mitrani.[99] ... We hope for more than twenty baptisms in C——, but Francis is in no hurry to baptize, nor I to write to Miss —— about our hopes. I think that I have gained more experience in this my seventh year than any other; and dear Francis has also greatly added to his. One of the parts of this experience is the finding out our need of wisdom from above. Only God knows the heart! Do not suppose me dismayed, or that I cease to value the dear

Natives; but it is almost sad to me to see that self-confidence which often arises from lack of experience.'

Miss Tucker might well have said 'very' instead of 'almost' sad. Certain words in a letter of Mrs. Baring's to Mrs. Hamilton, soon after, are something of an echo to the above:—

> 'The blessing she (Miss Tucker) is among those Christian boys is incalculable. Perhaps Eternity will show even more fruit from her bright, loving, holy influence over them, than over the people in the city. They are more able to appreciate her character and teaching than the poor degraded heathen, to whom she is much more like an angel afar off and above them, than a sister-woman whom they may seek to follow and grow like.
>
> 'She does love the boys, and is in her element among them; and they have one and all a chivalrous admiration for her. These years in India have taught her some things, I can see. Formerly her purse was open to every one; now she has the same generous spirit, guided by caution and experience. This winter's painful lessons in the fallibility of our best Native Christians have been to her a very sore discipline, and to us too; but it is really safer for us all to know exactly how far we dare trust, than to be thinking those saints who are very far from it.'

A touching little episode about this time is related in letters from both A. L. O. E. and Mrs. Baring. The latter had been much grieved by quarrelling in one of the Muhammadan schools; and she told her Pandit or teacher about it. He was a Sikh, who knew much of Christianity, though not yet a Convert. The kind words which came in answer were certainly not what might have been expected from a heathen. 'But do not be sad in heart,' urged the Pandit. Satan is strong, but God is stronger. He will hear your prayers.' The speaker could surely have been heathen only in name.

In the end of May it became needful for Mr. and Mrs. Baring to go to a cooler spot, leaving Miss Tucker in charge at Batala,—once more to be the only European in that city. It seemed no great matter to her, and she wrote as usual very cheerily about it beforehand. Little dreamt she that this was to be a final parting; that she and her beloved 'Queen Lily'—her 'Angel-friend'—would never meet again in this life!

> '*May 20, 1882.*—The day after to-morrow my dear friends are to leave me for the Hills. You must not be sad about it, for I am quite happy; indeed, it will be rather a comfort to

me for them to go, sweet as is their society, and valuable as is their affection. Francis stands heat so very badly.... Margaret too loses her pretty pink roses, and gets so tired when she goes to the city. On the other hand, *I* am far fitter for work than in winter.... It is a mistake in kind friends to pity me, or think about *sacrifices* on my part, for the lines have fallen to me in a fair ground. Of course, we have things to trouble us; but the blessings far, far outweigh the trials.'

'*May 23.*—Dear Francis and Margaret started last night, the young May moon and the stars shining beautifully. It was a picturesque scene. The carriage had a lamp within it, as well as one or two outside; the light gleamed on our crowd of boys and men, mostly in white garments. Loud was the cheer when our dear ones drove off....

'Well, love, I and our boys returned to Anarkalli. I did not feel lonely. I went to bed under the swinging pankah; and was ere long wrapped in repose. O what a startling waking at about 3 a.m. What an uproar!—what a fierce sound of struggle breaks on the silence of night,—the call for help—the whack of blows,—it reaches Babu Singha's ears at the Banyans, and brings him in haste from his bed,—but not till the conflict is over. I start up, and am at the window in a minute; but the moon has gone down; there is only starlight; nothing can I see, though much can I hear. I recognise the loud, manly voice of G., our Christian bihisti.[100] I think that he is catching a thief, and that the thief has the worst of it. Of course, boys and men come running. I hear a call for rope,—yes, certainly a thief must have been caught.

'Presently a wee light is brought. I can see, almost below my window, an object crouching on the ground, surrounded by our people. They have bound him; they are examining his face. There is a great deal of noise and talking for twenty minutes or more; and then the robber is evidently led away, and I retire again to rest. My heart beat no faster, but it certainly would have beaten faster, had I known the extent of dear, brave G.'s danger. When I came down in the morning, there was the robber, in iron fetters, with his face all marked with blood,—with the police around. He was crouching on the ground, a picture of a ruffian, a miserable ruffian.

'Babu Singha told me that there had been *five* burglars; but only two had ventured near the house. Our chaukidar[101]

... gave the alarm. G. rushed to the rescue, and he and B. between them, with some help from the dhobi,[102] succeeded in catching the robber; but not without G. receiving hurts from his heavy stick. Babu Singha told me that the robber is a very powerful man. But, oh Laura, what gave me the greatest feeling of the danger G. had been in, was being shown the razor which the robber had had about him. It had been dropped. Thank God, *that* had not been used; indeed, I do not think that the ruffian had been given time to use it. If he had, he might have killed G....'

Two months of busy work followed; towards the close of which came another adventure,—a robber again, but this time one on four legs instead of two.

'*July 18, 1882.*—Our palace was invaded by a wild cat. She caught a poor pigeon in the south room, carried it through the dining-room into my room, and left its half-eaten remains on my floor. Another time she had the impertinence to crouch on sleeping C.[103] A wild cat is not a pleasant visitor; her mode of attack, if incensed, being to spring at the throat. So I set a price, a moderate one, on the wild cat's head. She came again,—she was sure to do so to a house where boys keep pets, and where she had already captured a pigeon. At night I heard a battle-royal going on over my head. I did not rise; I guessed that there was a furious conflict between the boys and the wild cat. On the following morning I saw the animal lying dead, and paid the reward.'

A few days more, and the bolt fell. News came that Mrs. Baring was ill; and that her husband, away from her at the time, had hastened back, to find her in a high fever. Then a rather better report arrived; and Charlotte Tucker was so far cheered as to write to Mrs. Hamilton in much her usual strain, hoping that it might prove to be 'only a passing indisposition.' Before this letter was closed, tidings were received that all was over. Erysipelas had set in, the fair face becoming unrecognisable, and with little warning the gentle saint, so ready to go, had passed away. It was a very heavy blow; and though Miss Tucker, as usual, thought far more of what others felt than of what she felt herself, the letters written afterwards show how much she suffered:—

'*Aug. 9.*—I feel as if I did not care to write much save on one theme. The enclosed letters, which you will read, will give you particulars of the sad, sad event, which must have shocked you much.... How little I dreamed, when I saw the two driven off in the dâk-gari, while the moonlight fell on the picturesque scene, that one, and that the stronger one, ... would never return to Batala again! But the dear Lord knew that she was ready. He does not call His children to mount up as on eagles' wings till the wings are fledged.

'This is the saddest year that I have ever passed in India....'

'*Aug. 11, 1882.*—My dearest Leila, I doubt not that both you and your loved Mother have shed tears over sweet, sweet Margaret's loss,—or rather, our loss,—and that you have tenderly sympathised both with my poor Bhatija and with me. This has been a year of successive trials, not only to us but to others in the Mission field,—a time to make us search our hearts and examine our work. It seems almost as if my two Scripture texts at present are, "Faint, yet pursuing,"— and "Lord, we have toiled all night, and caught nothing, yet at *Thy* Word we will let down the net." ...

'It seems such an age before I can get a reply to any letter addressed to Francis. Time goes *so* slowly now! It is only a week to-day since I received the startling news.'

The especial trials referred to, apart from the death of Mrs. Baring, were numerous difficulties and disappointments among and with the members of their little flock of Indian Christians. One trouble had followed upon the heels of another.

CHAPTER XII
A.D. 1882-1883 THE FIRST STONE OF BATALA CHURCH

About the middle of August Miss Tucker went for change to Allahabad; and very soon after her arrival she was able to speak of herself as 'less tired' than before leaving Batala; despite two nights of severe travelling, inclusive of sixteen hours straight off in her duli. 'The change of air already tells on my bodily frame,' she wrote; 'and the change of scene on my mind and spirits.... I was becoming low in every way.' Before the end of September she was back again in Batala; and there she was soon joined by Mr. Baring, after his most sad absence. For a while, but only for a while, Batala was still to be his home.

In October for the first time the idea came definitely up of building a 'Mission Bungalow' in the place, an idea which afterwards developed into A. L. O. E.'s last earthly home.

It was also in the course of 1882 that some one wrote a sketch of her life, and requested her to revise the same before publication. Miss Tucker had not attained to modern composure on such questions, and she wrote with indignation: 'I am afraid ... neither you nor others may like my note to — —.... I need not dwell upon the part about the little book; it is too personal to myself. What would you think of a little book being written about yourself,—and sent to you to *correct*? Oh! Oh!! Oh!!!'

For some time past Charlotte Tucker had been watching with great interest the movements of the Salvation Army in India; at first with a disposition to admire and approve, which tendency gave place gradually to strong disapproval, as she saw more of the methods employed, and found the exceedingly defective nature of the religious teaching given.

Some very curious glimpses of Indian modes of life and thought, and of the manner in which Miss Tucker dealt with them, appear in the letters of 1882 and 1883, as will be seen in succeeding extracts. Among the singular things constantly happening, an old woman in a Zenana, at about this time, composedly offered to *sell* to A. L. O. E. one of her daughters-in-law. 'If you will give me a hundred rupees, you may have her,' the old woman said frankly. Needless to remark, Miss Tucker did not buy the poor girl!

> '*Nov. 17, 1882.*—I had, I thought, finished my Zenana-visiting to-day, when a man, at a loom in a room which I had not entered, called out to me, "I wish a Gospel. I want to compare it with the Koran." He and the bibi wanted me to come into their room; so of course I went and sat down. Says the man, "I think my religion good. I want to compare our books." "Much better," said I. The man brought his Koran, a translation into Urdu, probably made by some Christian, or at least printed in some Christian press. The good man treated me to such a long reading of the Koran, page after page, I did not know when he would stop! I felt it not only common politeness to sit and listen attentively, but good policy also, for how can I expect an earnest Muhammadan to give the Gospel a fair hearing, if I will not even listen to the Koran?
>
> 'The man was anxious that I should understand as well as hear, stopping every now and then to translate a word that he thought might puzzle me. But the Urdu was particularly simple for anything doctrinal. To understand anything doctrinal, even such sermons as I hear, it is absolutely necessary to know *some* Arabic words. I have written out more than two hundred,—chiefly Arabic,—*all* beginning with M, and mostly three-syllabled words, which I feel that I ought to know; yet they are hardly of any use with women; and if I have them all at my fingers' ends, I shall still be very imperfectly furnished. Is it not a puzzling language? Of course, some of these two hundred words are provokingly similar to each other, but the meaning is different.'

In the same letter she mentions a visit from the Indian Christian Faqir, M., who a quarter of a century before had given up a lucrative situation, and ever since had wandered about India, preaching the Gospel. On 20th November the same subject recurs:—

> 'His type of devotion is thoroughly *Hindu*, transfigured into Christianity.... One part of our conversation, however, amused me.... It was when we came on the subject of celibacy. The Hindu evidently thought it better than marriage. He seemed to regard it as an objection to the latter, that when a husband lost his wife he would cry for two or

three days!—the Faqir's[104] religion is a very joyful one, and when his eyes moisten it is with religious emotion. I stood up for marriage. The dear man is no stern ascetic; he smiled and half gave way, and said that he liked people to be happy. It is pretty clear, however, as regards himself that it is better for him to be unwedded. He walks long distances; sometimes forty—fifty—sixty—miles. He says that he is not so strong as he was. But he thinks nothing of age; the spirit never grows old.... M.'s voice is peculiar; one could always tell without seeing him whether he were in chapel or not; for his "Amen" sounds like a note from a bassoon.'

'*Nov. 21, 1882.*—While it is fresh in my mind I had better give you a description of our grand day, the laying of the first stone of our Church by the Lieutenant-Governor....

'Since the old days of the Sikhs I doubt whether Batala ever saw such a tamasha. Numbers and numbers of boys were gathered together by dear Francis, lining the roads, and cheering. Gay looked the many-coloured turbans. Mr. Wade thought there must be about one thousand boys, for we had Government School, City School, our Village Schools, and our own boys. We had a fine triumphal arch at the opening into our grounds, with "Welcome" in gold on scarlet; but it was far surpassed by the lovely one in Persian Urdu, prepared by our boys for the Church site: "Him that cometh to Me, I will in no wise cast out." Dear Emily Wauton came and helped us greatly; she specially took the luncheon-table under her care; and very elegant it looked, with the cold collation, and plenty of flowers from Amritsar. My bedroom overlooks our front door, so in this room our three *pardah-nishin* were hidden.... I dare say that these poor prisoners[105] of pardah specially enjoyed what was to them so novel. The good Lieutenant-Governor was more than punctual; a happy thing, as we had much for him to do, and only about an hour and a half to do it in. He brought with him his daughter, a winsome young maiden, ... whom I called "dear" before we parted. I liked the Lieutenant-Governor very much; a man of fine presence but simple manners....

'The luncheon was preceded by the reading by one of the Batala non-Christian magnates of an address, emblazoned with gold; other Batala folk, some in very grand dresses, standing in line. The Lieutenant-Governor gave a reply in

English, which I doubt whether many understood. Then we went to our collation; fifteen sat down.... You should have seen our servant ——; he was quite magnificent. He had on such a gold-adorned pagri that it might have graced the head of a rajah, and had as much gold on his dress. I did not think that he looked like a Missionary's servant, but we left him to enjoy his splendour. I had thought, darling, whether I should wear *your* silk dress:[106] but no, thought I; in my Batala I will *not* wear silken attire; so I wore my Laura's purple, which was just the thing, sober and handsome. The collation went over nicely; we could not linger at it long, and no one could drink too much, as water was our beverage. After seeing the view from the roof, we started in the borrowed carriages for the Church. The first carriage, which held the Aitchesons, Mera Bhatija, and myself, had highly conservative horses, decidedly opposed to progress. No use coaxing and urging them; the "nat-khats" *would not* go. The only thing was to get out and go into another carriage.

'Of course, there were many people at the site of our church. We had four surpliced clergymen, my three nephews, Francis, Mr. Wade, and Mr. Weitbrecht, and Nobin Chanda.[107] ... The religious Service was very nice; of course, in Urdu. Then Sir Charles[108] spread mortar over the place on which the marble block was to descend, in what was considered a very workmanlike manner. We sang "The Church's One Foundation" in Urdu; Mr. Weitbrecht's and Mr. Wade's fine voices making it sound so well. Sir Charles made such a nice religious speech; it was almost like a little Missionary address. *He* had had, he said, a very private conversation for an hour with a Native of distinction, who was in concern about his soul; and it ended by the Native saying that he had sometimes prayed to the Lord Jesus, but would now pray to Him *every day*. Thank God for a Lieutenant-Governor who thus shows his Christian colours!

'We drove to the station, after again forsaking the carriage drawn by the "nat-khats."[109] Sir Charles made me come into the railway carriage, to see its comfortable arrangements. Thoughtful Francis had caused tea and cake to be taken to the station. All went off so nicely; and my dear Bhatija feels that he has not had his labour and expense for nothing.'

'*Nov. 28.*—In three days I am to go up to Amritsar, ... where I am to sleep on that Friday night.... By some afternoon train I shall probably then go to Lahore.... On Sunday there are to be special services for the Conference, and Holy Communion is to be administered; a meet commencement for a gathering together of sisters from nine different Societies. But Char has a special interest of her own. We have at least a dozen of those who were Batala boys at Lahore.... I have arranged that my boys should meet me on Sunday afternoon. This is to me one of the most interesting parts of my visit to Lahore.... I have been obliged to prepare two little papers, but have made them mercifully short. I think that one takes about five and the other three minutes to read aloud,—I timed the reading,—so no one will have time to be tired.'

Of the above event Miss Wauton says: 'In 1882 she came to a Conference in Lahore, in which all the Zenana Missions of the Panjab were represented, and was with one consent elected President of the Meetings. None who were present could ever forget the tactful, graceful way in which she conducted the proceedings. Many, I believe, felt that the harmonious spirit, which prevailed in that assembly, was largely due to the loving and Catholic spirit of our President.'

'*Dec. 15, 1882.*—I have written to the — —s about the Salvation Meeting at Lahore, at which I was present. I have not told them, however, how sad an impression it left on my mind.... To *me* there was no real joyousness in the sound of the drum and the tambourines.... The puzzle is to me how such music can be the means of converting any, unless it be English roughs. X.[110] was eager to join the "Army," and go with them for a month to Calcutta. But he went to the meetings, and his wish appears to have evaporated; at least here he is.... The prevailing feeling in my heart (at the meeting) was—*pity*. Though I knelt, I really *could* not pray. The big drum and tambourines seemed to silence any whisper of real devotion in my soul.... I think that I have just ascertained one thing which has cooled our really devout X. It appears that he asked — —[111] about Holy Communion, and found that he had not received it since coming to India! Alas! alas! and if he lets Natives consider themselves saved and sure of Heaven without Baptism,—where will all end? The Blessed Saviour's two clear commands neglected! And —— just killing himself to introduce such a mere—one almost fears—shadow of religion! It is just grievous! How inconceivably artful the Enemy is!'

'*Dec. 21.*—I paid a visit to a village to-day. I first went to the school, then paid my respects to the lady of the place.... She showed me into a pretty bare room,—a chair was brought for me afterwards. But I thought little about the room; its strange occupants attracted my attention. I seemed transported into the Middle Ages, and found myself amongst the retainers of some bold baron,—men who looked like the stuff out of which freebooters are, or were, made. There were four powerful men, with four falcons; and the hoods of the falcons were grand. I suspect that they were valuable birds, used for hunting.

'I had an animated conversation with these burly fellows— not the birds, but the men—if that could be called a conversation, where the talking was almost entirely on one side. I had my Parable of the Two Paths with me, and spoke very plainly about Paradise and Hell;—and they listened to the old lady with perfect good-humour. I dare say that the bold falconers were rather surprised to find such an apparition in the village; for they seemed to have nothing to do with Batala, where of course my face is very familiar.

'As I was returning in my little duli, I saw a bullock-cart in front, with a kind of red, dome-shaped vehicle on it, which of course contained some pardah-lady, perhaps a bride. I noticed that the curtain was drawn back. Probably the prisoned inmate of the red cage had caught sight of the duli, and was curious to see its occupant. As my kahars went faster than the bullocks, I passed the red cage, and a bright jewel-bedizened lady—smiling, as if amused at seeing a white woman—exchanged brief glances with me. I thought her a pretty creature. I wonder what she thought of the old lady who smiled at her.'

Taken at Amritsar about 1882

F. Jenkins Heliog Paris

The New Year begins with a line from Mrs. Wade to Mrs. Hamilton, in reference to the recent Conference:—

'Amritsar, *New Year's Day, 1883.*

'I wish you could have seen dear Miss Tucker as President of our Lahore Ladies' Conference. She did all so perfectly; one only feared her being over tired, but I think she is stronger than she was some months ago. We had the pleasure of her staying a night with us on her way; and her walking powers are wonderful! You will no doubt have a report of the Conference, and of her solemn and helpful words on John xiii., as it is to be printed in England.'

Although Mrs. Wade could speak of her 'walking powers' as 'wonderful,' Miss Tucker had at this period hardly the same unvarying good health as in earlier years. A few days later she was laid by with an attack of 'shingles,' with pain in the side. The Native doctor, called in, informed her that nothing was wrong with either lungs or heart,—the pain which troubled her being 'simply from the nerves,' which were 'affected by the eruption.' Miss Tucker assured him that she was not nervous. Upon which, as she relates, 'the Hindu doctor smiled quietly, and gave me to understand that nerves are real things. He had not meant that I was fanciful. So the whole thing was simple enough,' she philosophically adds. 'To make a bull, I had a little toothache in my side.' The attack gave way readily.

> '*Jan. 25, 1883.*—One is so apt to feel for the poor, downtrodden Muhammadan women, that, until I began to read a novelette written by a Native, I had no idea how they sometimes turn the tables on their husbands. I am reading the book with N. N., who quite confirms the truthfulness of the picture. It appears that a woman will sometimes be asked a question ten times by her husband, before she vouchsafes an answer. Some women burn the soles of their shoes, and make a preparation of them to put on the eyes, believing that by this strange superstitious means they will always keep their husbands *under their feet*! With all the talk about Woman's Rights, we have hardly got so far as this!'
>
> '*Feb. 20.*—Mera Bhatija and I took rather a long walk this afternoon, to look at a lovely little mosque. I had said before to Francis, "How is it that the mosques are so beautiful, and our churches here—unless expensively built—so ugly?" Francis gave me a simple but good reason: "We want people to go *into* our churches; the Muhammadans worship outside theirs." You see, love, we have first to think of room and comfort; so beauty gets shoved into a corner.
>
> 'We went to look more closely at the graceful mosque, to see if we could gain hints. I made a rough sketch of the front. Francis says that it would be much too expensive for us to have anything so ornamental. We want room for one hundred people at least; and that dot of a mosque would hold comparatively very few. Mera Bhatija thinks that we might indulge in two minarets, and ornament our church with clay vessels turned upside down, and painted white, with a little Cross on the top of each. We must have a good-sized Cross, gilt, to glitter in the sun, on the top of all.... The Cross is our Banner, the Sign of Faith in the Son of God,

rejected by Muhammadan and Hindu! It should crown—and sparkle on, too—every religious edifice in this land.'

'*March 8, 1883.*—I had an extraordinary conversation with a Muhammadan boy to-day. His name is Y. He lives in what I consider a nest of bigotry. I am more likely to have to dispute there than in any other place in Batala. I had with me, besides my Bible, the "Mirror of the Heart," which contains beautifully coloured pictures of the human heart, with allegorical vices represented by various animals, the serpent, rat, etc. It is a valuable help to a Missionary. The first heart is that of the natural man, before repentance; the second, that of a man repenting. The fourth is a horrid heart, of a dingy colour, with *a black cross* in it, and seven devils, mounted on the bad emblems, wanting to get in. It is the heart of a hypocrite. Well, dear one, I was showing this picture in a Zenana, and a grave-looking boy, to whom before I had given a portion of Scripture, and who I think once studied in our Mission-School, Y., was close beside me. When I had gone over the various pictures, I said to Y., "Which of these hearts,"—showing the first and second,—"is like yours?" I meant, "Are you repenting or unrepenting?" The boy, perhaps fourteen years of age, would not agree that either was like his. To my surprise he made me turn over to the fourth heart, and told me *that* was like his.

'"But it is not a Muhammadan's heart," said I. "You see the Cross is in it,—but it is black."

'"And how do you know," said the boy gravely, "*that the Cross is not in my heart?*" I think that he repeated this touching question afterwards. In short, he kept firmly to his declaration that *that* heart was the one like his. What is passing in that lad's soul? Does he consider himself a hypocrite, with seven devils surrounding him? If so, he must be a hypocrite as regards Muhammadanism?—for he does not pretend to be a Christian. I suspect that this may be the case. He *has* a cross, but it is a black one, because he does not confess the Saviour.

'There is a great change in dear ——'s mother. (You remember perhaps the dear lad in a bigoted home, who so loved the Lord Jesus, bore persecution for Him, and died in peace.) My last visit to that house was so different to the first! On the first occasion I left the place so shocked, that I uttered the exclamation as I went, "God have mercy on you!" I do not think that I ever left any other house with such an exclamation on my lips. The last time I left the house with the exclamation, "God grant!" The mother had told me the story of her eldest brother, a policeman, who, like her son, had become Christian in heart, and incurred the fierce anger of his father by speaking against Muhammad. A Suni[112] had stabbed the policeman in the side with a knife; but the Christian refused to prosecute. He was very gentle, just like the nephew who followed in his steps. The policeman left Lahore,—this was more than twenty years ago,—and has never been heard of since. Probably he is numbered in the noble army of martyrs.

'I said, "I think that both your brother and son are with the Lord Jesus." "*Without doubt!*" cried this once bigoted woman. I urged her to follow them, and asked her if she had no love for the Lord in her heart. "He is the Apple of my eye," she replied. You must not suppose, love, that there is any immediate prospect of Baptism; but I talked to her about it; and, as I have mentioned, left the house with a "God grant!"'

'*March 24, 1883.*—We cannot see one step before us! I was thinking to-day, as I was going to the City, where my work *seems* of so little use, "Abraham had to wait for twenty years before God kept His promise to him." Perhaps it may be twenty years before the promise is fulfilled—fully—to me, "Your labour is not vain in the Lord."

'O the utter carelessness of some of the women, who will interrupt the most solemn, heart-searching conversation with a question about my dress, or a request for a pin. They seem so utterly frivolous! Then those who do think, and have some concern for religion, are such earnest Muhammadans; it is with them a matter of *heart-love*! It is a mystery how it should be so, when Muhammad was not only a murderer and profligate, but has lowered woman altogether; but it seems especially the women who delight in his false religion. They do not care for its having no proofs; they *love* it.'

'*March 28.*—I had rather an interesting visit to-day, which you may like to hear about.

'I went to the house of a Maulvi ... I had books to take to his sweet young daughter; and soon I found that the ladies had gone to a wedding; but as two servants were in the house, I thought it better to stop and give the "good news" to them. Whether they cared about it or not, I know not. After my interview with them, I was about to leave, when who should come in but the master of the house, the Maulvi himself. (He is not the same one who was so proud, that I could not help an unpremeditated rebuke escaping from my lips.) This Maulvi was fresh from a pilgrimage to Mecca; but the merit ascribed to a Haji did not seem to make him proud at all.

'He courteously addressed me, sat down, and prepared for a *tête-à-tête* with the Englishwoman. He told me that he had none of our books; that he wanted a controversial one, that he might compare the two religions. There was no appearance of bigotry at all. He asked me whether we read prayers. I told him that we not only had regular prayer, but that we sang God's praises,—which the Muhammadans never do,—and opening my Bible, I read aloud several passages in which Hasrat David (Saint David) commands us to do so. My gentle Maulvi made no observation on this proof that Christians pay more obedience than Muhammadans do to the commands of one whom *both* acknowledge as a Prophet....

'Accompany me now to another Zenana. A young man showed himself again and again, as if he wanted to take a share in conversation, but did not at first see his way to doing so. At last he told me that there was great excitement. I could not for some time make out what it was about; it seemed to be about some birth; but then it appeared to be about something else. At last the difficulty cleared up. The young Muhammadan made me understand that it was said that the Imam Mahdi had been born; and on account of this there was great excitement in H— — and over the country.

'I said that I had heard about a man, calling himself the Mahdi, near Egypt. The young man did not seem to have an idea *where* the long-expected Imam is, but he said that when the place should be known all would go to see him. My curiosity was a little aroused. I asked what the Mahdi was to do. "To reign over all kingdoms, and make every one Muhammadan." "But if they should not choose to be Muhammadans?" "Oh, all will be Muhammadans." "But if

I did not choose to be a Muhammadan, would he kill me?" "No, his rule will be like that of the English."

'I would not trust the Mahdi, however, nor that animated young man! This was the only Zenana in which I have heard of the Mahdi; and I have visited plenty. I had more talk with the Muhammadan. I said that I thought that the Dajal was expected to come before the Mahdi. No,—the Mahdi is to come first; then the Dajal; and then Jesus Christ! It is curious to hear these ideas!'

'*March 28.*—I almost think that the Muhammadans are stronger in their bigotry, from an expectation of some coming event at the coming Ramazan (great fast) in July. Perhaps, some of them think, there will be great pestilence; perhaps Christ and the Mahdi will come;—and the sun rise in the west instead of in the east. The more intelligent do not seem to expect the last wonder.'

'*April 27.*—The beautiful monument which Francis is going to place over the grave of sweet Margaret was sent here from Delhi. I have sent a sketch of it to her sisters, and another to Mrs. Baring. I did not find it so easy to draw as I expected, on account of the perspective of the three white marble steps, which support the pure white Cross.... How little we know who will be called! I remember my pleading with her not to delay coming out, or she might find a Cross instead of her friend. The white Cross has been for her, not for me; and I see no likelihood at present of my soon being called, though of course one never knows. I have seen so many young pass away since I came to India.'

In the same letter she says with respect to the Baring High School: 'I hope and expect that our School has reached its lowest ebb,—twenty-three boys, mostly little ones. There is some likelihood of six more coming.'

Mrs. Hamilton had begun to ask occasionally to her house in London young Indians who had come to England for a Western education. Some of them she saw repeatedly, and reference is often made to them in letters.

C. M. T. TO THE REV. W. F. T. HAMILTON.

'*June 19, 1883.*

'Shortly after writing to your dear Mother, I had myself a visit from a Muhammadan. I remembered what I had just been writing,[113] so soon plunged straight into the subject of religion. I had seen Sheik A. twice before; and the first time had had a good talk. Yesterday he listened very well, though I ventured to contrast Muhammad a little with the Blessed One. Sheik A. agreed to his wife visiting me here this evening,—I sending a duli for her, as she is "pardah-nishin"; and as he is going to L— —, he *asked* me for a letter of introduction to some lady there, that she might visit his wife. This was encouraging. Sheik A. took a cup of tea with me, and we parted excellent friends. Perhaps a couple of hours afterwards my dear Faqir, M., came to see me. He too had been having an interview with Sheik A. "Much excitement," said the Faqir. I think that the Muhammadan had probably not been as much on his good behaviour with the dark Madrassee as with the white Englishwoman. There seemed to have been a hot discussion below. Dear M. was inclined to reproach himself. "Harsh!—my loud voice!" said he. Depend upon it, he went at his work like a cannon. But all seemed to end well. I think he told me that Sheik A. and he shook hands as they parted.'

TO MRS. HAMILTON.

'*July 21, 1883.*

'How different it is writing a free and easy letter to you, from a studied one like that to — —! I hope that my Laura will not consider Char a conceited old woman, who likes no one to find fault with her writings. But, you see, love, I know *nothing* of Mr. — —'s capacity to act as critic.... I cannot consent to walk in chains because Mr. — — has a liberal hand and a full purse. I am so glad that I refused pecuniary recompense. In writing I must be *free*. I hope that I have not made a mistake in putting in as many proverbs as I have done. It was difficult to select. How inappropriate—clever as it is!—would it have been to put in such as this, "The sieve said to the needle, You have a hole in your tail"!' ...

'*Aug. 4.*—Yes, love, I dare say that I was mistaken about your entering on religious subjects soon with the young Indians. I often doubt my own judgment. You see, it is a disadvantage to me to have no one to correct me. This has been, I think, my most lonely hot weather.

'I am thankful that I do not hold the doctrine of Perfectionism. I should be very miserable if I did; for sometimes it seems to me as if I went backwards instead of forwards. If I thought that a real child of God ought to be perfect, I must come to the conclusion that I at least am not a child of God. But I do not hold this view, and I see that the holy Simeon wrote clearly and distinctly against it.'

'Alexandra School, Amritsar, *Aug. 15, 1883.*

'Here I am in this big palace, a good deal bigger than my Batala one,—the guest of dear, loving Florrie.[114] ...

'I have been taking my morning walk. I saw the old banyan in the garden of what was my first Indian home with sweet Margaret. The downward shoot which I named "Batala" has now the size of the trunk of a tree.'

A visit of two or three weeks to her nephew at Dunga Gully followed, where the children were a great enjoyment to her, letters home being full of the pretty utterances of little Tudor and Beryl. On the 15th of September, however, she once more gaily reported herself as 'back again in dear old Batala!' and again the steady round of work went on as usual.

'*Sept. 19.*—A lady who knows a good deal about Muhammadanism, and has read from the *Hadis* (Muhammadan traditions), told me something very curious that she had come upon....

'There is a supposed prophecy of Muhammad, that in the latter days a marvellous being, called Dajal, will appear. He will perform marvels, bring a band of musicians, and whoever hears the enchanting sound will follow him, leaving friends, parents, etc.... I, after hearing this, inquired about Dajal from — —. He, having been a learned Muhammadan, of course knew all about the prophecy.... Dajal, who will become a king, is to have but one eye, and ride an ass nine coss (about fourteen miles) long!... Dajal is supposed to be an evil being, drawing downwards those whom he influences. After him the Muhammadans expect the Imam Mahdi;— and then, our Blessed Lord.

'What extraordinary ideas these people have of our Saviour! They think that He never died, but was caught up to Heaven, and some one else crucified in His stead. This is a true doctrine of the devil, for of course it strikes against all belief in the Atonement. It would drive us from the very key and central point of our faith. Often have I tried to show how completely such a doctrine is against prophecy. Well, dear, this is not all. The Muhammadans believe that after our Lord comes again, *to convert the world to Muhammadanism,* He will die! I have spoken with one who has actually *seen the place* where *His future tomb* is to be at Medina! It is near Muhammad's grave, and is considered a very holy place. There is a handsome black marble slab, bordered with white, and fine palings around.'

TO MISS LEILA HAMILTON.

'Sept. 24.

'I have started to-day a temporary drawing-class for the five poor little boys who have to stay here all during the holidays. They are so pleased. It was a pleasure to me to see them all seated, busy with pencil and paper, instead of lounging about wearily. I did not succeed in making them do a bit of carpentering for me.

'The drawing lesson was a lesson to me, dear. After my own fashion, it seemed to me a type, and—strange as it may seem to you—a type bearing on the disputed subject of perfection in this life. We are all children,—the sooner we realise this, the better!—and the Lord sets us a copy; not a poor little one, such as I placed before the boys, but a perfect, exquisite one. Now, I imagine three of our boys drawing as nicely as they can, and then coming to me with their copies.

'The first is very happy indeed. "It is quite perfect!" says he. "My dear child, *you* may think so, but *I* do not think so. Take your measuring paper, and go over your copy more carefully; and you will see that not all the lines are straight."

'The second comes to me, crying. "I shall never manage my copy," sighs he. "It is not a quarter as good as the picture, and yet I took such pains!" "Yes, dear boy, I see that you have taken pains; and that is all that I require. You will do better in time. But dry your tears. Did you really think that I should be angry with you, because your drawing is not perfect?"

'The third looks modestly into my face, to see if he has pleased me. He knows that he has *tried* to please me; and though he has not succeeded in making a perfect drawing, he *has* succeeded in pleasing.

'The third child is the one whom I should most wish to resemble. He trusts me!'

TO MRS. HAMILTON.

'Oct. 14, 1883.

'Do you ever note what is the first waking thought when consciousness returns in the morning?... The other day my thought on awakening was so very odd, that it made an impression by its very strangeness. I could not imagine what could have put it into my head, and you will smile when you read it. *"The snuffers were of gold!"* I have not so much as seen snuffers since I came to India.... Why on earth should my waking thought be of them? "Well," considered I, "snuffers are worthy of mention in the Bible; and those in the Temple *were* of gold. What can I make out of this thought?"

'Then it occurred to me that the office of snuffers, humble enough, being to make candles brighter, the office was emblematical perhaps of that which St. Paul adjudged to the aged women. They were to teach the young women to love their husbands, etc. At last I began to think, darling, that perhaps my place in the Church here *is* a little like that of a pair of snuffers; and now, when I feel that I ought to give a little word in season to Native Christians, I fancy that I have to snuff them—not *out!*—O no!—only to remove some little superfluity....

'I think I must have amused my Laura with my idea of the snuffers; but it may be a useful thought to those who are no longer young. A little gentle snuffing may be the work—unostentatious work—given to us.... What a snip dear H. gave to W. long, long ago, and how the fine boy admired her for it!... But then the snuffers were of gold. No one likes to be snuffed by coarse iron ones.

'What a pity that I have no one to snuff me here! Were we together, it would be your office, love. I have to act as my own snuffers, and take hints never intended to be hints, like noble Tudor's—"I must do my duty." He had no idea that he was acting the part of a tiny pair of gold snuffers. I may almost say that I have taken these snuffers up, and have been snipping away with them at our young Natives ever since. No mortal could object to such a miniature pair.

'*Oct. 16.*—Do not think, from what is written above, that, as I grow older, I think it well to grow more censorious. If I have grown in anything this year, I think that it is in knowledge of my *own* errors and mistakes. I sometimes feel quite disheartened. I do not think that I ever more mistrusted my own judgment than I do now, after my various blunders. But we know that, though snuffers are less straight, comely, and upright, perhaps, than the candlestick, they may be useful in brightening the light which it carries.'

CHAPTER XIII
A.D. 1884-1885 SOME OF A. L. O. E.'S POSSESSIONS

Some little time before this Mr. Baring had, for various reasons, decided to leave Batala, though not, it seems, to give up his interest in the High School. His departure was fixed for the last day of the year 1883; and Miss Tucker, after her usual cheerful fashion, congratulated herself upon the fact that, at least, the New Year would not begin with a parting.

Much uncertainty had prevailed as to who should be chosen to carry on Mr. Baring's most important work among the boys; but before the end of December suspense was ended. Another of Miss Tucker's dharm-nephews, the Rev. Herbert U. Weitbrecht, with his wife and children, would come to live in Anarkalli, and Mr. Weitbrecht would be the Principal. By this time a Mission Bungalow in Batala was finished, and two German ladies, Miss Hoernle and Miss Krapf, came in the course of December to reside in it. Miss Tucker, however, does not yet appear to have thought of changing her quarters. Indeed, the little bungalow was built to contain only two ladies.

On December 27th she wrote home as to arrangements:—

> 'The Weitbrechts are to come here on Jan. 15 for about a fortnight. I am to keep house until they come for good about the middle of March; and then my fair niece, Ellie, is to take the reins. She and her two children must go to the Hills in May. All purpose going to England in the following March. As Herbert did not wish to be buying much furniture, when so soon to be on the wing, I felt it the best plan to take some off dear Francis' hands, and let the Weitbrechts have the use of them. Thus, I find myself the possessor of a very large bed, immensely long table, and a variety of other things too numerous to recount.

> 'There is no use in my not wanting possessions,—they will come! I have even a large coffin, which is not the slightest use to me! I did *not* buy *that* from Francis!...'

The fact of Miss Tucker including a coffin amongst her possessions requires a word of explanation. About this time the Rev. Robert Clark went to pay a little visit to Batala; and on his first arrival he was shown straight to the room which he would occupy while there. Miss Tucker came running in, and exclaimed—

'I hope you have not seen it,—have you?'

Mr. Clark naturally inquired what was the thing in question which she wished him not to have seen.

'I had better tell you all about it,' she said. 'A poor woman was dying, and we thought they would take her away and burn her; and we wished to give her Christian burial. So I ordered a coffin to be made. But they were late in making it, and she died before it was ready; and they took her away and burnt her. And then they brought the coffin. It was a very good coffin, and I thought it would be useful; so I told them to put it under the bed in the guest-room! You did not see it, did you?' Mr. Clark no doubt assured her that he had not yet made the discovery; and she went on eagerly: 'You must not think I kept it for myself; for I have directed in my will that I should be buried without a coffin, and that my funeral expenses must not exceed five rupees.'

The latter injunction was with a view to lessening funeral expenses among Indian Christians generally, many of them being apt to spend heavily at such times. But the whole story is eminently characteristic. Many people shrink from the very mention of a coffin, because of its associations. Not so Charlotte Tucker! There was to her absolutely no sadness whatever in the thought of death. She looked forward to the day of her departure from earth as to a day of release from bondage, of an upward spring into a new and radiant life. It was a subject to be spoken of cheerily, and with a smile.

What became of the coffin in the end Mr. Clark does not say; but he too speaks, as do others, of her entire fearlessness with regard to death. Once, when talking of it to him, she quoted impressively the words, used long before by her gentle sister, Fanny: 'Whenever, wherever, however, He will!'

One time, when Mr. Clark was spending a Sunday at Batala with Miss Tucker, she read aloud to him the 31st verse of the 40th chapter of Isaiah, and drew attention to the fact that the verse had in it instruction and comfort for persons of all ages.

'"They shall mount up with wings as eagles,"—that is something for our young people; they are always soaring and flying. "They shall run, and not be weary,"—that is for our middle-aged people; they run and work on, and never seem to tire. And there is something for us old people too,—

"They shall walk and not faint." We old people cannot fly; we cannot run; but we can walk, and do not faint. And so we all of us renew our strength by waiting on the Lord.'

Mr. Clark, from whom these details have come direct, writes also:—

> 'On another occasion, she came walking up to me in her genial, brisk manner, with a book in her hands, as I entered the room, and said, "You will be surprised when I tell you what book I am reading! You know I am a good Churchwoman; and yet I often like to read Spurgeon's sermons. They are full of apt illustrations, and he never repeats himself. I find them so useful in my writings; and I know hardly any other work which so much helps me." In her latter years she often read Shakespeare, and recommended it to educated Natives, who were averse to the study of the Bible. The recitations from Shakespeare, at the Prize-giving in the Baring High School in Batala, originated with her; and she thought them very valuable in the formation of character. The Prologues in these Prize-givings were, I think, till last year all written by her.'

Not only in later days, but all through her life from very childhood, she had delighted in Shakespeare, as we have already seen; and she had a very high opinion of the value of Shakespeare in the general education of the Indian mind.

In confirmation of certain words above, spoken by herself, Mr. Clark observes: 'As regards her religious views, she was sincerely attached to the Church of England, firmly believing that the teaching of the Church of England, as set forth in the Book of Common Prayer and in the Thirty-nine Articles, is in accordance with the Word of God.' Another also, who knew her well, has said: 'A warm Churchwoman, she would always be ready to see the best of those with whom she could not agree on many points.' This undoubtedly was the case,—in practice, if not always in theory. She was, however, greatly opposed to Ritualism, and would be much distressed when she came across aught of the kind in her various visits to different places.

The subject recalls involuntarily certain words uttered by Bishop French of Lahore,—'our saintly Bishop,' as Miss Tucker called him. When he was at home some years ago, and staying at Eastbourne, I happened to put to him a question bearing on this matter; and his reply was one not soon to be forgotten. He said: 'It is no question out there of High Church and Low Church! It is a question simply of Christianity and Heathenism!' To this wide and comprehensive view Charlotte Tucker could not have fully subscribed. In her letters, from time to time, though not often, the subject crops up, and she expresses her fears strongly as to one individual or another. But it is noteworthy that when, soon after, she meets with the individual himself, her fears are usually quieted; and while conscious of differences on certain points, she is yet able fully to recognise—and to recognise with delight—real devotion of heart and life to the Service of the Master Whom she loved. No more unmistakable token can well exist of true large-heartedness. There was in her no innate love of controversy for its own sake; and though, as might be expected with one of her impulsive temperament, she sometimes expressed her views with energy, she did not love fighting, nor was she a violent partisan. As a general rule, her aim was rather to build up than to pull down.

The years 1884 and 1885 passed in the main quietly, marked by no especial events. Work went steadily on as usual; holidays were short as usual; failure and success fluctuated as usual. Miss Tucker's loneliest time in Batala was over. Now she not only lived with the family of Mr. and Mrs. Weitbrecht, but two other lady Missionaries were settled in Batala, helping to carry on the work. Not that Charlotte Tucker's toil was lessened thereby. She had a less heavy weight of responsibility; but so far as actual work was concerned it could never be overtaken,—and it could not have been overtaken by twice or thrice the number of workers. Fresh openings were continually appearing, continually calling for attention.

In the hot weather, indeed, she had a taste of her old manner of life. Then, when other Europeans were compelled one after another to flee to the Hills, Miss Tucker could safely remain on many weeks longer; up to a certain point even enjoying the heat. On the whole, however, things were altered. Not only were other Europeans in Batala most of the year, but a railway had now been completed between Amritsar and Batala, bringing all the Amritsar friends within a very easy distance. It became possible to run over to Batala for a day's visit; and Miss Tucker grew jealously anxious, lest such visitors should in any wise hinder her work. 'I have let it be known,' she wrote, 'that I do not consider myself *off duty* till 2 p.m., so that if friends come in the morning they visit the house and not me. I must try to be firm in this, and make no exceptions.'

A certain little incident of this period may be mentioned. With a new Principal, naturally new plans were adopted in the training of the boys; and Miss Tucker did not always at first take kindly to fresh ideas. She was now of an age to prefer the old to the new, simply because it was the old. Dr. Weitbrecht writes:—

'In 1885, by way of encouraging muscular exercise in the hot weather, I tried the experiment of having the boys taught wrestling by a Native athlete. The Auntie was at first inclined to be a little shocked at the new development, and would not grace the wrestling practice with her presence. One day, as it was going on, Mrs. Weitbrecht went to a window overlooking the arena, and there found Miss Tucker, stretched on the floor, her head out of the low window. In some alarm lest the old lady should have fainted, she offered to raise her, but was only met with the reply, "Hush! I'm looking at the boys." The ladies soon saw they were discovered, as a handsome young Pathan looked up with a smiling "Salaam."'

Extracts from the letters of these two years, 1884 and 1885, must unfortunately, for lack of space, be very limited in number.

'*New Year's Day, 1884.*—I had a very sore parting with Mera Bhatija; but on that I will not dwell....

'The last day of 1883 was a very sad one to me; but I had some of the little boys in the evening, and amusing them shook me out of my melancholy. I awoke early—as usual—on the New Year's Day, and sang New Year's hymns. After that I heard unwonted music below my window. Good Miss Krapf and three of the Singha girls had come to salute the New Year with a holy song. Of course, I went to the city after breakfast.'

TO MISS 'LEILA' HAMILTON.

'*Jan. 21.*

'I am quite *glad* that my furniture is so simple. Had I had plenty of gimcracks, I might have been a fidgety old maid. As it is, there is no harm in having a nursery instead of a drawing-room. But I have a nice little drawing-room of my own; a screened-off bit of my fine large sleeping-room. I used it for my classes when sweet Margaret was here; for I think that a married couple should not be always having interruptions. This arrangement does nicely in the cool weather; and in the hot weather dear Nellie and her babes will be in the Hills. It will be the old arrangement of Auntie and one choice nephew,—for Herbert *is* choice, and kind to my Leila's attached godmother.'

TO MRS. HAMILTON.

'Jan. 28, 1884.

'I feel as if I must have a talk with my Laura to-night; for my spirit feels pensive and my heart tender. The ladies came and took tea with us; and Miss Krapf brought her music. As Herbert wanted to see a photo of St. George and Francie, I took my dear old album into the drawing-room, which it very seldom enters. While the sweet, rich music was going on, I was—yes, sighing over my Album. More than twenty of the faces in it no longer of earth! Sweet Mother, Fanny, Henry, Letitia, Aunt E— —,—oh, so many gone before! Then my Laura looked so like what she did in old days. I must not look often over *that* Album; it is like my youth between two boards. What a changing world!'

'*March 26.*—I met with a perfectly mad woman in a Hindu Zenana. She came and sat down beside me. V. and others made me change my seat to another bedstead—the usual seat. I did not at first know why, but was soon aware of the cause. The poor, afflicted woman put her head right down on my lap. She did not seem to be mischievous. It was insanity, not idiotcy.'

TO MISS 'LEILA' HAMILTON.

'April 22, 1884.

'Among the little matters which vary our regular life at Batala, I may mention almost nightly alarms about robbers. The servants have got into a nervous state.... It is not a comfortable state of affairs.... The Weitbrechts and I have been putting our heads together. I forget which of us suggested the plan which we hope may succeed. I sleep in the front room, opposite to the servants' house; so a great tumult naturally awakens me, especially as my windows are open for air. The Weitbrechts are more out of the way.

'Herbert is to lend me his revolver, loaded, and we are to take care that every one knows that I have the formidable weapon; but no one but ourselves is to know that I would on no account hurt any one with it. On the next alarm of robbers, I am to jump up, and—fire—at the trees or the stars. The report will probably awake Herbert, who has a rifle. Now you see the double use of this arrangement. My Ayah may possibly even sleep out-of-doors, if she knows that a yell from her may bring a pistol-shot from her vigilant Miss

Sahiba; and robbers, if such there be, will doubtless dread my prowess, not knowing how peculiarly peaceable I am, and that I would prefer being shot myself to shooting another! I am to have a very determined look; and we have all tutored each other *not to laugh*! Both Herbert and Nellie have some fun in them, but they are to look as grave as judges, as if Miss Sahiba were a dead shot; especially on a very dark night, when there is no moon! Have I not spectacles?'

TO MRS. HAMILTON.

'*April 23.*

'Well, my loved sister, if you read my little note to Leila first, you will be pleased to hear that the night went over serenely. Even my frightened Ayah seems to have slept peacefully under the wing of the Buzurg Miss Sahiba, armed with a revolver! Would not dear Rowland have laughed to see old Auntie learning from Herbert how to cock and fire a pistol! I wonder how Nellie kept her countenance, when one of the servants expressed a hope that Miss Sahiba would give some notice before firing, for fear of a casualty to one of the household; and then wanted to know what would happen if Miss Sahiba *killed* a thief! Nellie told the inquirer that we English—she was too truthful to say the Miss Sahiba in particular—only aimed at limbs to disable, not at bodies to kill. Nellie knows pretty well that, if *I* aimed at anything, it would be at the stars.

'I took care to lock up my dangerous weapon before sunrise, treating my revolver with great respect. Do you remember that, when I was known to be coming out to India as a Missionary, dear, kind H. Boswell wanted to make me a present of his pistol? I declined it, as a very unnecessary part of a Missionary's outfit; but I could not help remembering H.'s kindness yesterday. Though I never fired Herbert's revolver, yet the *report* of it—to speak in Irish style—had a great effect.'

'*May 3.*—O yes, my Laura, *love* your K.[115] The Native is affectionate. Indians are not usually considered grateful; perhaps they are not grateful for benefits bestowed through general benevolence or a sense of duty; but my impression is that they readily respond to *affection*. This is one of the great secrets of ——'s power.... I was rather amused yesterday, when I was describing Philemon's funeral to the dear Pandit of O— — (K. S.), and had said that we went singing towards the grave. "I will not sing at *your* funeral," said he. And then he told me how he had *tried* to sing at dear Margaret's—but it was quite a failure; he could not sing, his heart was much troubled. The Pandit is a lovable man; and he loves.'

'*May 8, 1884. (Her Birthday.)*

'When I came down in the morning before 6 a.m. I found in letters of gold on a purple ground over the large front door, "God save our beloved Miss Sahiba." I told dear Babu Singha when we met, as I walked on towards the city, that I liked the "our." He observed that "buzurg" seemed to put me farther away from them. I quite agreed. I like "our," which makes me seem like the boys' property....

'I was surprised in a Zenana to-day by a request for some *old* article of my clothes for a baby. "I will give you some new cloth," said I; for I make exceptions to my rule of not giving presents to Natives in Zenanas, in favour of new babies and brides. But the grandfather did not want *new* cloth at all. He insisted on something old. So I humoured him, and looked out on my return home for something that I had worn....

'How much I have to be thankful for, my Laura! I begin my Tenth September with a quiet, peaceful feeling. "Oh, how kindly hast Thou led me, Heavenly Father, day by day." But the best is to come. "Light after darkness—" Not that my present position is darkness; but there is often weariness, of course.'

'*May 15.*—I can so well enter into the "thought and anxiety" caused by — —. His mind is probably in an effervescing state; but we must trust and pray that, after the froth works down, something precious may remain. Young India is at present in a peculiar state; and — — does not stand alone in his dangerous love for oratory. You must expect, love, to see some of the weaknesses of the Native character even in those on whom our Blessed Religion has made an impression. With the English—Truth, Honour, and a sense of Duty are often found even in those *not* very religious, and it shocks and disappoints one to find the want of this kind of moral foundation in some Natives, whose piety one cannot doubt!!

"I must do my duty,"—"Honour bright!"—are expressions that in this land need to be taught.

'The Native character is a study. *We* can hardly disconnect pious feeling from purity and conscientiousness. One must make great allowance for those brought up in a tainted atmosphere. Do not be easily discouraged, love. India does turn out some really fine fellows; but a school like this is greatly needed, to begin *moral* tuition early. We want our flowers to have stalks and leaves, and not to spread out their petals so close to the earth as to be defiled by its dust. Let — — expand his eloquence in trying to draw ryots[116] to Christ. Close contact with really hard evangelistic work, if persevered in, would probably do much to sober his mind. Let him be persuaded that the Baptism of one true Convert, however ignorant and poor, is a far higher honour than the plaudits of an English audience.'

'*July 3, 1884.*—I have had two comical though not very pleasant incidents.

'I sent dear Mrs. Singha as a present what I believed to be a bottle of lemon syrup, delicious in hot weather.... When next I went to the Banyans, Mrs. Singha told me that I had sent her a bottle of *brandy*! I was astonished,—I, who am virtually a teetotaller! I could hardly believe it. She produced the bottle; and, sure enough, it was full of brandy. What a villain of a grocer must have sold it, thought I, smuggling brandy in this way.... "This is sure to be trashy brandy," thought I, "which I should not dare to give in a case of illness." So, in my indignation, I poured it all out on the grass. I also thought that I would write to good Babu — — at Lahore, who had bought the bottle for me, to tell him of the wicked cheat played on him. Most fortunately, I first mentioned the matter to Herbert. "Do you not remember," said he, "that when we wanted a large bottle, you emptied your brandy into a small one?" I had perfectly forgotten the fact. O stupid, most stupid, old Auntie! And I had emptied my bottle on the grass!

'The next incident was also a provoking one. You know that I have had boils. Well, Herbert said ... that the best way to stop a boil was, at the very first threatening, to put caustic to the place. So I bought a bit of caustic, knowing as much about it as I do of Hebrew.... Just before starting for afternoon Wednesday Service in the city, I thought that I had the slightest possible sensation of a boil on my nose. "Not a pretty place to have a boil on," thought I; so I took out my wee grey stone, dipped it in water, and applied it. It did not burn at all, so I applied it again. Then, seeing a black spot, hardly visible except through spectacles, off I went to Service.

'On returning home, to prepare to go out to Miss Hoernle's, how surprised—I may say almost shocked—was I, on looking in my glass! A big black smutch on my nose; another on my chin; and another on my thumb. Washing was of no avail; salts of lemon none; chloride of lime none; soap useless! I could not help laughing, I was such a figure; and my Ayah laughed too. I determined to give it to Herbert roundly for putting me up to make such a fright of myself.... As soon as I could get hold of my naughty nephew, who was playing at lawn tennis as happily as if nothing had happened, I scolded him in Miss Hoernle's presence as hard as I could,—considering that both of us were laughing. At last my wrath blazed into verse:—

'"You told me it would make me smart,—

The fear of pain was slight;

You have not made me smart at all,—

You've made me just a fright!"'

'*July 10.*—You will like to know that I have managed almost entirely to get rid of those spots, which made me think of Lady Macbeth, and gave me rather a dislike to the use of caustic; for one does not like to appear as if one never washed either face or hands.'

In November another sorrow came; the death of Miss Tucker's nephew in Canada, Charles Tucker, whom she had visited before starting for India. He was one of her 'Robins' of earlier days; and she felt the loss much.

It was in the course of 1884 that Miss Tucker related to her sister a certain Christian Pandit's dream. His wife had long been dangerously ill, and the husband had tenderly nursed her. No other Christians lived in the village except these two; and no one but the husband had been near the dying woman for many days.

'I think it was the day before the sufferer's departure,' wrote Miss Tucker, 'that the Pandit fell asleep; but as he said, "In sleep I was praying." He dreamt that he heard a voice say, "I will take her; she suffers so much!" Another Voice, which he thinks was a Divine one, said, "Wait!" On waking, the Pandit went to his wife. She told him that Jesus Christ had stood by her, and laid His Hand on her head. "How did you know Him?" asked the husband. "*His Side was red!*" Whether the appearance was a dream or not, it gave comfort. The sufferer departed at last in peace.'

There is no necessity for any one to believe this, on the part of either husband or wife, to have been more than a natural dream—a reflex of the state of mind and thought previously. At the same time, it is undoubtedly possible that help or comfort, whichever was required, might be sent through the medium of a dream. Several remarkable instances of dreams are mentioned from time to time by Miss Tucker in her letters,—occasionally vivid enough to decide a Muhammadan on the great step of becoming a Christian. There is many a simple and natural means by and through which God speaks to the heart; and dreams *may* sometimes be one of those means,—especially in 'Early Church days.'

One other instance of the kind can be mentioned here, while the subject is to the fore. In Charlotte Tucker's Journal, some few years later, occurs the following singular little entry, when she is describing a visit to a certain village:—

> '*Aug. 16.*—J. R. told me dream of Christ, which he had had three or four years ago. Indignantly repudiated idea that my pictures were like Him Who was so much more beautiful. I read part of description of Christ in Rev. i.; but the old man, with simple truthfulness, said that *that* was for the superior person who had written. He was a poor man; he had only seen the white dress and beautiful shining Face. I asked if he had seen it distinctly. "Do I see you who are before me?" he replied. "So I saw Him." His nephew certified to J. R. having told him of this dream soon after having it.'

It is very probable that the old man might have been dwelling on the thought of Christ, consciously or unconsciously endeavouring to picture the Divine Form to himself; and the dream *may* have been a perfectly natural consequence of his own cogitations. But to say that a thing is or may be natural is *not* to say that it can have been in no sense Divinely sent, or that it might not bring quickened realisation with it.

The New Year's Day of 1885 was not altogether cheerful, despite courageous efforts made, and parties of Indians: children in the afternoon, seniors in the evening. Two unfortunate Hindus were accidentally drowned in one of the large Batala tanks; happily not that tank which lay close to the palace, wherein the schoolboys were wont to disport themselves. This naturally threw a shadow over the proceedings of the day.

Early in the year came a letter from the Bishop of Lahore to Miss Tucker:—

'*Jan. 10.*

'Dear Friend and Sister in Christ,—May I venture to ask if in the little room you may assign me kindly, during my short visit to Batala, a little cot may be placed for a brother of mine from New Zealand (a brother in Christ also), who is always pleased to *chum* with me, as he does at Bishopstow also, our house being full?

'I am sorry to say my visit must be limited to a sojourn with you from Friday, 30th January, to Tuesday, February 3, as the Ajnala work hedges me in behind, and Lahore and Amritsar Confirmations before. May I ask your special prayers, lest this rather overpowering crush of work may not impair strength of mind or tone of spirit, both of which I have a little reason to dread at this season? It is a comfort to know and to be assured that our Faithful Lord will "stablish and keep us from evil." May His peace, and love with faith, be our portion; and then in the storm we may sing our watchword, "All well."—I am, yours, with ever affectionate and grateful regards,

'Thomas V. Lahore.

'Affectionate good wishes to your whole party.

'This will, alas! break up my itinerating plan; not for ever, I trust.'

A fortnight later Miss Tucker wrote to her sister, on January 24:—

'You will have seen in the paper that our good Bishop has lost his daughter. I wrote to him a little note of sympathy which he was not to answer; but he did reply in his own gracious, characteristic style. We expect the Bishop here next week for a Confirmation; and he has asked leave to bring a Christian brother from New Zealand. Whether the brother be an emigrant or one of the aborigines, we know not. We are prepared for either.'

TO MISS 'LEILA' HAMILTON.

'*Feb. 4, 1885.*

'The interesting Confirmation took place on Saturday, ... after which we partook of the Holy Communion. I think Herbert said that there were 41 Communicants. We never had so many before in our chapel. The dear, saintly Bishop left on Tuesday morning.'

TO MRS. HAMILTON.

'*March 28, 1885.*

'You should have seen Ellie and me down on the floor to-day, pinning down the dusters for the chess-board. It so happens that there is an unusual influx of Native Christian visitors at present—R. R., his winsome lady and two daughters, J.'s mother, and S., a fledged bird, and these with the numerous Singhas and the Native Pastor will make quite a gathering. I rather expect to play badly; but the great thing is to be quick and dashing, and to move as many pieces as possible; and not to be disturbed by the bursts of laughter likely to follow any check given or piece taken. Would you not like to be present,—near me?

'Well, as I rather expected, I was beaten, though I had the best of the game at first. I never heard such noisy pieces of chess as the dear brown boys were, when they were first marshalled on the board, and had to don their crowns, regal or mural, their mitres and their horses' heads. Our Afghan hero, C. C., was a knight, and enjoyed himself very much. I think that there was only one piece, or at most two, that was not moved.'

'*April 23, 1885.*—My nephew Herbert ... is absent again on Mission work. He has heard that there is a spirit of earnest inquiry amongst a number of poor low-caste village folk, I think about ten or eleven miles from Batala. He has gone to look personally into the matter; and if he finds that these lowly peasants are really seeking after God, we will try to make some arrangement for their instruction. Herbert will see if it be advisable for an English lady and Native Bible-woman to go for a short time, and to fix some suitable agent (Native) to reside amongst the poor people, and start a school. Of course, this involves expense; but if corn at last be springing up, it must not be neglected. It is such a comfort to have one, wise, good, and active, like dear Herbert, to look after such matters....

'If you happen to meet with dear Mrs. W——, please tell her that her Cross gleams in my room every night. Her pretty straw basket is so *much* admired in the zenanas....

'Our Church-building is growing rapidly under Herbert's auspices. The "Mission Plough" too surprises me by its growth. I hear that there are 105 boys there now. But we have not a sufficiently strong staff of teachers. The Inspector (Government) was pleased with the school, but said that we should have a stronger staff. We know that too.'

'*May 8.*—I saw Miss B. a few days ago. She saw you in London, and thought that we resembled each other. "But I hope that my sister looks much younger than I do," said I. "Does she look twenty years younger?" To my satisfaction, Miss B. agreed that you did. So my Laura keeps her looks, though not feeling so strong as I should wish her to do.'

'*June 22, 1885.* ... I must amuse —— with the following *perfectly authentic* anecdote. There was a nice young couple, as nice as Fred and Maud perhaps, and they had a nice little baby. One day the inexperienced Mamma banged the baby's head. Accidents *will* happen, you know, in the best-regulated families. The young mother was conscientious; she felt that she ought to confess the banging to the father of the child. With tearful eyes she went to her husband, and owned that she had banged her baby's head. Then the husband, gaining courage from the brave woman's truthfulness, confessed that *he had done the very same*! he had banged the baby's head, but had not liked to own it. The baby does not appear to have been the worse for the two bangs; perhaps they were on opposite sides of the little head, and counteracted each other. Still—fathers and mothers had better not try the experiment of how much banging a baby will bear. Don't you think so, darling?'

'*July 13.*—I was interested in hearing what was said to E. by the lad last baptized.... "I have nearly got through my temptations," said he. Of course, I cannot give his exact words, which were in Urdu; but their drift. The lad thought that forty days of temptation succeed a convert's Baptism, and said, "I have only eleven left." ... "But do you think that you will never be tempted afterwards?" asked E. Poor B. did not think that, but he thought that the first forty days were the worst; and perhaps he is right.'

'*Nov. 13, 1885.*—I think that it will amuse you and my dear god-daughter, if I tell you of my first attempt regularly to make a marriage, and what were the consequences thereof.

'I had been told by the experienced Native Christian, whom I will call M., the proper way to carry on a negotiation. He told me long ago that a "Buzurg" (elder) should ask the parents for the maid. There being a union which we Missionaries thought suitable and desirable, ... I, the most buzurg of all our circle, at the desire of the fine young suitor,—whom I will call B.,—went in my duli to M.'s house, to ask his lovely daughter in marriage for my client. I managed to have both parents present, and sent the maiden away. It would have been a great breach of etiquette for her to have heard me.

'I felt that I was doing all in proper Oriental style. The parents listened; we talked over the advantages of the union; and M. and his wife were to give me their reply on the following day.

'But Orientals take their time. I heard nothing on the following day; so on the third I sent my salaam to M. and desired to see him. He came, smiled, was highly agreeable, said that *he* was willing, but must consult his brother, etc.

'*I* thought that some one else should be consulted; namely, the young lady. I was going to Amritsar ... so I resolved to have a private interview with the maiden, whose future was to be decided upon. The lovely—let's call her X.—had returned to — —; so there I sought her, and had a *tête-à-tête*. I wanted to know whether *she* cared for B., whom she had had many opportunities of seeing from her childhood.... We had almost taken it for granted that X. must care for him.

'Hitherto all had gone pretty smoothly. I had even thought what presents I should give, and the Weitbrechts and I had talked over the day for the wedding. But an unexpected obstacle arose. X. could make no objection to B.; I do not think that she has a thought for any other suitor; but she does not want to marry at all! "I want to read," she said. "I wish to remain *like you*!"

'This opened our eyes to a peril in the infant Church, of which you probably never would dream. Ellie and I set to counting up young maidens who are of a suitable age to become brides,—well-educated, nice girls,—and came to the conclusion that a kind of fashion is setting in *not to marry*. The Native delights in imitating the European. The girls see that most female Missionaries, whom they love and honour, are unmarried. They enjoy freedom.... Christian women are at a premium. *Widows* are eagerly sought as Bible-women....

'Of course, I would never wish X. to marry one she does not care for. I have told her father that the matter is at an end. But *he* looks grave enough, and sees the peril to our Infant Church as clearly as we do. If our nice maidens scorn to marry, where are our fine, well-educated men to find Christian wives? How are girls—except in very rare cases—to work in zenanas without the care of a husband? It would be thought improper, hardly safe.

'"The consequences are" that I have written a little book in honour of the holy estate of Matrimony; which—the new book—has had Ellie's approval, and I am sending it to Herbert for his. What we want in India are good wives and mothers. No science or literature can make up for the lack of such.'

It was in the summer of this year that Miss Tucker mentioned in one letter a curious little scene at the railway station. She had gone there to meet a friend, who failed to arrive. Two young Native Christians happening to be present, and also a young English officer of her acquaintance, she brought them together with a kind of half introduction. When she had left the station, the officer began talking to the two, asking lightly why they had left their own religion for another. 'It's all the same,' he said. 'Muhammadans, Hindus, Christians, all know that there is One God.' This far from brilliant remark received an answer which it well deserved. 'If so,' one of the Indians replied, 'what difference is there between you, us, and the Devil?' The train moved on, carrying the speaker away; and no more could be said. But more might have weakened the force of the retort.

A few slight memoranda, contributed by two Native Christians, come next. The first are sent by Dr. I. U. Nasir, formerly one of the boys in the Baring High School, already quoted in an earlier chapter. He speaks of himself as an adopted 'son' of Miss Tucker's, not, like others a 'nephew.' The second set of extracts, which I give last, not because they are of inferior interest, but because I wish to accentuate one suggestion, by letting it end the chapter, are from the Rev. Mian Sadiq, at one time Indian clergyman in Amritsar, and later the same in Batala.

I

'Of all the India's sons, especially those with whom she had to deal at Batala, it was my privilege to be called her "son." She was an "Aunt" to a good many Missionaries, but only did she allow me to call her "Mother"; and she did love me as a true mother....

'The one thing most noticeable about her was that she was so self-denying and humble, considerate for others' feelings, and tender-hearted. She would tend the sick with such motherly care; and if the disease was a dangerous one, or infectious, she would insist on sitting by the bedside, and not allow others to run the risk of contracting the disease. On one occasion a poor, dirty convert was suffering from fever, and had no clothes. Miss Tucker gave him her bedding for the night, and spent the winter night herself sitting before a fire. Above all she hated "I's." I remember only one occasion when she desired us to do something for her. She had regular morning and evening walks in the fields; but getting a little tired sometimes of waiting till the Church bell sounded, she wished a small terrace to be raised, just sufficient to seat her. A small rude platform was raised for her by the side of a babūl tree. She may have selected that particular spot, because it gave a very picturesque view of the "stately palace," with the "tank with lilies blowing" in the foreground,—now turned into an artificial canal.

'Her reticence regarding her own life and work was extreme. This much I remember from her occasional talks, incidentally dropped from her: that she was eight years old when she read Shakespeare; she was eleven when she began to compose; and at twenty-one she sent her first book to press.[117] She wrote to me once how much she exulted over her first printed composition....

'At that advanced age how much she could accomplish in a single day was a wonder to everybody. Her vast correspondence, reading of books and papers, her literary compositions, her school classes, Bible-meetings, various interviews, were so gracefully and naturally managed. Still, all these were held in the background, and jealously guarded against encroaching upon her Missionary work....

'She was reading the sermon (Spurgeon's) on Christ's first miracle at Cana. She read there that our duty was to fill the jars to the brim; and it was Christ's work to turn them into wine. This led to the self-examining question, "Am I filling the jars to the brim? Can I not work a little more for Christ than I have hitherto done?" This gave her strength in her feebleness; and from that day she spent an hour more in the zenanas than she used to do. Considering the various discouragements she met in her Missionary work, it was no small matter to take this step,—and this too at a time when it was an effort to walk, not to speak of ascending perpendicular flights of stairs in the zenanas....

'The one thing which was not liked by some people about her was that she had an extreme disgust of Natives taking to English dress, which she invariably designated "ugly." She regretted on several occasions that her age and habits did not allow of her adopting the "graceful *dopatta*" (head cover) in preference to her hat....

'Her ideas about the burial system were very definite. She would take up the thread of St. Paul's argument, and compare the human body to a seed of grain, which should be simply buried under the earth, and not shut up in a box and placed in the ground. She several times expressed her desire to be simply wrapped up in a clean sheet and carried by her boys to the cemetery when her turn came, and then laid in the grave as one naturally sleeping.'

II

'During Mr. Baring's absence in England in 1881, one cold night Miss Tucker noticed in the Chapel a man shivering with cold. He was one of the non-Christian servants of the school. After Service she called him, and asked him if he had more clothes. The man said "No." He was shivering, as he had fever. She told him to wait, and ran upstairs. She came back in a minute with a beautiful rug. She told the man she could not give it to him, as it was a present from her sister, but she would lend it to him for the night, and would buy a country blanket for him the next day. I asked her what she was going to do herself. She said she would keep a fire in her bedroom, and that would keep her warm.

'I saw her many times picking up pieces of broken glass or bottles. She said poor people who walk barefoot get hurt by these. She has known cases in which men suffered for weeks from wounds received from these.

'She was not kind to men only, but to animals. One summer morning, as she was coming from the city, after doing her work in the Zenanas, she saw a poor donkey with a sore back, troubled by a crow. She came home, took a piece of cloth, went to the place where she saw the donkey, tied the cloth, and came back and took her breakfast....

'Her example has done a great deal in removing caste feelings among Christians. Batala was a place for feasts. In these feasts all Christians were invited. She generally sat with low-caste Converts, and ate with them....

'Once for sending a girl to an orphanage she sent for a prospectus of the school. In it two warm dresses were put down in the list of clothes. 'It is very unreasonable,' she said, 'to require two warm dresses.' She had herself only one, and that she had been using for the last nine years. Her poem, "What a Missionary Miss Sahiba should be," is an embodiment of what she was.'

One more short sentence from the same source is worthy of particular attention: 'When ill, Miss Tucker did not like to inform her friends of it, lest her friends should leave their work and come to nurse her. She often expressed a wish that there were Mission Nurses, who could attend to the sick Missionaries. Without these, when one got ill, others were taken from their work to nurse her.'

In an earlier chapter it was suggested that some ladies, wishing to find a vocation, might offer themselves as Honorary helpers to the more regular Missionaries in certain lines, among which Nursing was included. Here it seems that the same thought had distinctly occurred to the mind of Charlotte Tucker. Why should not a little Band of Honorary Nurses for India be organised,—Nurses, trained and capable, holding themselves ready to go wherever their services may be required by any sick Missionary, so that the steady work of other Missionaries should not be unnecessarily interrupted by the illness of one of their number? The idea is at least worth consideration, since apparently it would have met with the approval of A. L. O. E.

CHAPTER XIV
A.D. 1885-1886 ON THE RIVER'S BRINK

Changes again were impending. Mr. and Mrs. Weitbrecht, after two years' work in Batala, were to quit the place; and in their stead would come Mr. and Mrs. Corfield,—the former as new Principal of the High School. It is singular to note one Missionary after another thus coming and going, while Charlotte Tucker, with resolute perseverance, held to her post.

At last she too began to think of a change. Not of leaving Batala; not of going home, for even the shortest of furloughs! Such an idea perhaps never so much as occurred to her mind. She simply began to think of altering her residence in Batala. At Anarkalli she had lived with Miss Swainson, with Mr. and Mrs. Beutel, with Natives alone, with Mr. Baring, with Mr. Baring and his wife, with Mr. and Mrs. Weitbrecht; and now another 'upheaval' had become imminent.

The notion of a move was apparently at first her own, though others soon looked upon it as desirable. Two German ladies, Miss Hoernle and Miss Krapf, dwelt together in the cosy little Mission Bungalow, which they had named 'Sonnenschein' or 'Sunshine.' No room remained for a third inmate; but Miss Tucker formed a plan of building a small annexe to the west of 'Sunshine,' for her own use; and to this tiny annexe she resolved to give the name of 'Gurub i Aftab,' or 'Sunset.'

Mrs. Hamilton, on first hearing of the scheme, was somewhat distressed at the thought of such a change for her 'Char'; but Miss Tucker wrote to assure her of no move until the new building should be perfectly dry. Also a long letter from Mr. Weitbrecht set before Mrs. Hamilton, with kind clearness, the advantages of the plan. Among other reasons urged was the overcrowded state of the palace, where more room for the School was urgently needed; and also the desirability that Miss Tucker, in advancing years, should not constantly have to climb a steep and awkward staircase, which had of late greatly tried her strength.

It is probable that for some little time past there had been a certain failure of power, evidenced by such facts as this, though made very little of by herself, and perhaps little marked by others, because of her determined cheerfulness and persistence in work.

Still, as always, she rose at six in winter, and at half-past four in summer; had her little breakfast of cocoa and sweet biscuits; then read and studied till eight. At 8 a.m., whether in summer or in winter, she seldom failed to take her rapid 'Devotional walk' out of doors, up and down, till summoned to Prayers by the Chapel gong. Then came breakfast proper; after which she would still, as always, go out in her duli for three or four hours of Zenana-visiting. Next followed correspondence; lunch; classes of English history and English literature for the elder boys; then afternoon tea; then sometimes more reading of a Native language, and visiting of Native Christians. This was the manner of day that she spent, week in, week out, month after month, often for ten or eleven months at a stretch; varied only by itinerating expeditions into neighbouring villages, or an occasional trip to Amritsar,—the latter seldom, except on business of some kind. And she had been living this life now for at least eight or nine years! Small wonder that a breakdown should come at last. The marvel was that it had not come sooner. A chill and a bad smell were the immediate cause,—they usually are in such cases, acting upon exhausted powers.

Up to Thursday, December 10, things were much as usual. That morning she went on her ordinary city round, and then to a Native wedding, where she was very much tried by a bad smell from a drain, though her innate courtesy would not allow her to hurry away. On reaching home she was in a chilled and shivering condition, with the beginning of a sore throat. In the afternoon fever and drowsiness came on.

For a day or two there seemed to be an improvement. Mrs. Weitbrecht, who was to have left Batala before Sunday, on account of health, deferred her journey until Monday.

Nothing could induce Miss Tucker to remain at home on Saturday. She started as usual for the city; and on her return she told Mrs. Weitbrecht 'how glad she was to have gone,' adding, 'I am always especially glad when I go to the city, feeling it a little effort to do so.' One is disposed to imagine that it must have been more than a *little* effort, on that particular day; and the words contain a revelation as to past 'efforts' when unfit for the work which she never would neglect. Dr. H. M. Clark had been asked to come over, but she utterly declined to see him, except as a friend, refusing to consider herself ill. On Sunday she was at both the Church Services, 'kept up,' as Mr. Bateman said, 'by her indomitable spirit'; and in the afternoon she had, as always, her Class of boys. On Monday morning she made her appearance early, to see Mrs. Weitbrecht off,—very bright and cheery, wrapping up sandwiches, and determinedly hiding how ill she really felt, for fear Mrs. Weitbrecht's departure should be again delayed.

Things could not go on thus much longer. Miss Tucker had made a brave fight,—too brave for her own good!—but illness was now fast gaining the upper hand. She did not again attempt city visiting,—a sure sign of her condition; and much time that day was spent in a half-doze. Towards night she became light-headed, and was so weak that they had to carry her to bed. Miss Hoernle decided to sleep at the palace, so as to be within easy call if needed; but in the early morning she found her patient up, writing a letter, and of course avowing herself 'better.' The improvement, if it existed, was very brief. Fever again set in, with weakness and delirium; and Dr. H. M. Clark was sent for. On Tuesday Mr. Clark came too, and that evening he sent for Miss Wauton to go over from Amritsar on Wednesday morning. Mr. Rowland Bateman also was speedily on the spot. Somewhat later in the week a telegram summoned A. L. O. E.'s nephew and niece, Major Louis Tucker and Mrs. Tucker.

For three days the greatest possible anxiety was felt; and on the Thursday another medical man was telegraphed for, that a consultation might take place. The result of the consultation was not favourable. Dr. P. on first seeing Miss Tucker thought she might live a week, but when going away he expressed a fear that half that time would see the end.

Both before and after Dr. P.'s coming there was excessive restlessness, and a great deal of delirium, though the latter was never of a painful kind, and she always knew those who were about her. She was at times extremely anxious to get up, and she showed vexation at not being allowed to do so. Once, when thus controlled, she said to Mr. Weitbrecht with respect to her nurses:

'Couldn't you take them to see the Church?'

'But, Auntie dear, we have seen the Church already,' they assured her.

'Then take them somewhere else,' she said,—'only take them *a long way off!*'

This evidently remained on her mind; for the next day she began to talk about the Salvation Army, and the doctrine of Perfection in this life, as taught by its devotees.

'It is a doctrine of the devil,' she said emphatically. 'Tell —— that I had an outbreak of anger and petulance only yesterday. I wanted to go to my own room, and I was quite cross when they would not let me. I think the Lord let that be, that we might see how weak and sinful we are. I am sixty-four years old,—and they who are so much younger than I am would not let me get up! They treated me just as if I were a child; and I could not bear to be made into a little child; and so the Lord put me down. These doctrines are the snare of the devil. They make presumptuous people more presumptuous; and they are calculated to drive conscientious people *mad*!' The last words were repeated; and Miss Tucker went on to mention two cases, known to herself, where individuals had become actually insane through 'perfectionist' teaching.

She talked in her delirium almost incessantly, showing extreme mental activity, an activity which never failed, even when exhaustion was greatest. She dictated letters; she composed verses and comic parodies; she repeated texts and long sentences in Hindustani; she sang with animation a cricket-song for the boys, and then a hymn in Hindustani or English. Sometimes her drollery was so intense that her nurses, in all their anxiety, shook with laughter to hear the things she said. And all through, from beginning to end, one thing never failed,—her radiant happiness in the thought of going Home.

While recognising those who were really present, she fancied that others were there also, and talked to them. Generally she could reason quietly about these appearances, saying that she knew they were 'shadows.' She does not seem to have felt thus about the evil spirits, which she thought she saw. She pointed to where she believed them to be, asking, 'Do you see them?' Then addressing the spirits, she continued: 'I am not afraid of you! You can do nothing to *me*! I belong to Jesus! Don't sit there, at the foot of my bed. Go away; you cannot touch me!'

The strong doses of quinine made her very deaf, so that she could hear little of what went on around her bed; but she heard what others could not hear,—sounds of music filling the room.

Sometimes she imagined herself to be in Zenanas, talking to the Bibis, and pleading earnestly with them. Or again she wondered why her kahars did not come to take her thither.

'What to me was most remarkable,' wrote Mr. Clark afterwards, 'was her perfect cheerfulness and happiness; thinking of everything and every one around her, and talking of the most common things, and doing it all in the light of Eternity; standing on the very brink of another world, and yet forgetting nothing, but thinking of almost everything in this.... It was at times even amusing, for there was no sadness in her perpetual sunshine.'

On Friday morning, the day after the consultation, Miss Tucker woke very early, and asked to have her desk, that she might write. This of course could not be allowed. Later in the same day Mr. Weitbrecht went in to see her, just after an interview with Dr. Clark, and she inquired, 'What does the doctor say?'

Mr. Weitbrecht endeavoured to avoid giving any direct reply, speaking only of one symptom which the Doctor had named as encouraging. Then came the point-blank question:

'Yes; but does he think I shall die, or recover?'

'He cannot tell.'

Miss Tucker was not to be so put off. An answer she would have. 'I am very deaf with the quinine,' she said. 'I can't hear what you say. If he thinks I shall stay, do this!'—holding up her hand;—'and if sinking, this!'—dropping it.

There was no choice left. Truth compelled Mr. Weitbrecht to lower gently his hand. 'Whereupon,' as Mr. Bateman relates, 'a smile and an almost shout of joy escaped her.'

'I am so glad!' she exclaimed. 'So glad to be dying in harness! And to think that I shall be no trouble to anybody!.... It is too good to be true, that I am going Home.... The bowl is broken at the fountain!' Then she repeated the simple verse beginning,

> '"And when I'm to die,
> Receive me, I'll cry,
> For Jesus has loved me,
> I cannot tell why!"'

What Charlotte Tucker experienced, on seeing that lowered hand, may be to some extent realised by reading her 'Dream' of the Second Advent, given in an earlier chapter. Heaven to her was 'Home'; many of her nearest and dearest were already in Paradise; and 'death,' so called, would mean re-union with those dear ones. Charlotte Tucker could from her very heart re-echo the poet's words,—with a most practical belief in them,—'There is no Death; what seems so is Transition.' During years past she had longed for this Transition; striving only not to be impatient, but to await cheerfully God's own time.

And now, it seemed, she was to go! Not only to leave sin and sorrow behind; not only to be young and strong again; not only to see such beauty and glory as our Earth can never show; not only to 'mount up with wings, as eagles,' into splendid new spheres of knowledge and thought, of employment and work. All these things, though real, were secondary. *The overwhelming delight of going Home, whether by the Coming of Christ, or* through the 'grave and gate of Death,' was that she would meet her Lord and Master face to face! That was the grand expectation which thrilled her whole being, which drew from her an 'almost shout' of joy, even in extreme weakness,—the prospect of seeing Him, 'Whom, not having seen,' she loved.

So intense was the joy that it had a remarkable result. It appeared to take the same effect as a powerful stimulant upon her sinking strength. The very delight which she had in dying brought her back to life; the very rapture with which she desired to go kept her from going.

It is not needful to suppose that this alone saved her life. Skilled physicians and devoted nurses had done and were doing their utmost; and a fresh remedy was being tried, which brought down the very high fever. But the fact remains the same, that, until Charlotte Tucker was told that she would die, hopes of her recovery had been given up, at all events by those best qualified to judge; and that, from the time when she learned the verdict of the doctors, she began to revive. At the least we must allow that the stimulant afforded by this eager rejoicing was a marked assistance to other remedies; and that, without it, in all probability she might have sunk.

Nor need it be imagined that she was immediately out of danger. Improvement was very gradual, and anxiety lasted long. Weeks later she spoke of her own life as having been on Christmas Day still 'trembling in the balance,' and this was nearly a week before Christmas. But hope had revived, and every day it grew stronger.

Having once made up her mind that she was to die, it was, we may be sure, no easy matter for Charlotte Tucker to turn her mind earthward again. 'She dwelt on the thought continually,' wrote one of her nurses afterwards; and another friend said in a letter home, at the time, 'She is deaf to any suggestion of possible recovery.'

Full directions were given as to presents which she wished to have sent to relatives and friends after her departure; and many messages also, expressive of intense delight in the prospect which she believed to lie before her. She was very particular as to her funeral. 'I wish no one to wear black for me,' she said. 'My funeral must not cost more than five rupees. No coffin; only a plank to keep the body straight. You must make a recess in the grave, so that the earth may not fall on my face. No one must carry me but my dear Christian boys.'

Then she would believe herself to be in a Zenana once more, and she was giving a farewell address in Hindustani to all her Bibis. In the midst of such a serious exhortation would come in quotations from Shakespeare, or odd little remarks about her food, making it impossible for others not to smile, as the active mind passed rapidly from one subject to another. But still her radiant expectation and rejoicing never faltered.

'What a happy thing it is to have conquered!' she said once,—'and to know that I have a crown of glory awaiting me above! What happiness! But I know I have no righteousness of my own. No one has that! My trust is in the Blood of Christ *alone*! "The Blood of Jesus Christ cleanseth us from all sin."'

Repeatedly she remarked how 'happy she was, dying in harness,—just as she had wished!' And again: 'I want to go. You *must not* pray for my recovery. The Doctor *says* I'm worse, doesn't he?' And again: 'If the Ladies of the Committee knew what a wreck I am, they would be glad that I am going now. I cannot do any more work; but tell them that I depart in the full, glad hope of Eternal Life, through Jesus Christ *only*! His precious Blood *only*!... "Nothing in my hand I bring; simply to Thy Cross I cling!" ... I am almost surprised at my ever coming out to be a Missionary. I was so very ignorant! A Missionary needs very great humility.'

At another time she asked: 'How long is it likely to last? My sister will be quite happy about me, now that I have completed my tenth year of Missionary service.'

But near as Charlotte Tucker drew to the Gate of Death, which to her was the Gate of Life, she was only allowed one glimpse inside; and then she had to turn back into the wilderness of Earth once more. It makes one think of the Pandit's dream beside his dying wife. A 'voice' might well have said, with angelic pity, of Charlotte Tucker, 'She longs so to come! I will take her!' But if so, it would seem that the Divine Voice softly interposed, 'WAIT!' Her hour of Rest was not yet reached. She was not very much more than half-way through her toilsome Indian campaign. Ten years of work lay behind. Eight years of work stretched ahead. This was but the Rehearsal of the real Home-going.

By Saturday morning there was so far a distinct improvement that Mr. Clark felt himself able to return to Amritsar. Miss Tucker still counted herself dying; and her last words to Mr. Clark were, 'Give to our dear and honoured Bishop my affectionate *adieux*!'

When Christmas Day arrived, though not yet out of danger, she was allowed to see all her Batala friends who could come, including the boys of the School,—no doubt a mere passing glimpse of each. Much warm interest had been shown by the people of the city, as well as by the Christians who so well knew and loved her. Before Christmas Day, however, Miss Tucker seems to have accepted the fact that, so far as could be seen, she had not yet fought out her battle, had not yet to exchange Cross for Crown. So early as the 21st of December Miss Wauton wrote to Mrs. Hamilton:—

> 'I don't think she will ever attempt so much active work again amongst the people; but she said to me this morning, "Though I shall probably not be able to do much amongst them, I can still *love* them!" Darling Auntie! *how* every one does love and honour her! This week has shown more than ever how she lives in the hearts of those for whom she is spending her life; and how dear she is to a very, very wide circle of friends, as well as to her relations. The boys have been as quiet as mice all the time she was ill; and the only sounds that reached her room were their voices practising the Christmas hymns, which she was delighted with, and fancied she heard them nearly all through the night, long after they were all in bed.'

On December 28th Charlotte Tucker was able to dictate a letter to Mrs. Hamilton:—

> 'My precious Laura,—I have been in deep waters, but I rather think I shall swim. I cannot tell you what I owe to the splendid nursing of —— and ——. You couldn't have nursed me more devotedly and tenderly yourself. Neither you nor I will ever forget it....
>
> 'I've a noise going on for ever in my ears; but my mind has been clear all through. The hard thing was not to be able to pray for what I wished. I should so have liked to depart and be with Jesus; but it didn't seem God's Will; and His Will must be best. I tried to ask for patience and resignation. Good-bye, darling....'

Loving messages to many friends are included in this letter; and she also mentions having received on Christmas Day 'Communion for the Dying,'—though apparently she was then not really counted to be dying. However, unless she misunderstood her doctor, he was not even then hopeful to any great extent. Probably her own recollections were a good deal more confused than she was at all aware of.

It is not a little remarkable that, after all this, she should in letters written somewhat later quietly and decidedly assert that she had *not* reckoned herself to be dying, but had fully expected to get well! The explanation is, most likely, that her strong desire to pass away was so dominant a feeling as to entirely push into the background a consciousness that she would recover. At the time she doubtless refused to listen to the voice of this consciousness; but afterwards it would naturally recur to memory,—possibly in a somewhat exaggerated form.

As soon as she was sufficiently improved for the move to be practicable, she was taken to Amritsar,—being lifted into her duli, which travelled by train, so that she was spared any further changes. At Amritsar she was within easy reach of her Doctor; also she could be better nursed and cared for there than in such an out-of-the-way place as Batala, where personal comforts were few. Letters early in 1886 naturally contain a good deal about her illness.

> 'Batala, *Jan.* 2.—My darling Laura, the last time the Doctor came, I said to him, "Doctor, you're winning the game of chess." He said, "You've been as bad as you could be; but, under God, you owe your life to the excellent nursing." ... My sweet ladies watch me day and night, and seem to think it fun.... I think in England we add to the miseries of sickness by looking so anxious and grave. Then, another thing, love, is this; don't shut out friends, for fear they should tire the patient. On Christmas Day, when my life was literally trembling in the balance, I must have seen more than a hundred, and they didn't do me a bit of harm.... Good-bye, darling. Please give all sorts of kind messages to dear Leila and your other dear ones, and every one who loves me....
>
> 'Please pray for patience. That is the lesson I have to learn. "Be still, and know that I am God." "O rest in the Lord, and wait patiently for Him." I mustn't think even much about Heaven! I mustn't be like a soldier pining to get home, when he's told to keep quiet in the trenches.'

It is impossible not to remember Archbishop Trench's couplet:—

> 'Some are resigned to go; might we such grace attain,
> That we should need our resignation to remain!'

> 'Amritsar, *Jan.* 11, 1886.—I hope that my telegram arrived before the news that would trouble you. The doctor pronounced me "out of danger" last Friday, the 8th; so I almost immediately thought of sending a telegram. Now I'm going to make a little confession of exaggeration. I told you that I saw more than one hundred people on Christmas Day. Babu Singha told me that there were only eighty-four at the feast; so, as babies count at the feast and didn't come up to me, I probably didn't see more than seventy. I questioned the doctor a little time ago as to the influx of visitors; and he

only told me, that, as he thought I was sure to die, it didn't matter whom I saw. But *I* didn't think I was going to die; and you see I was right....'

'Amritsar, *Jan. 18.*—Thanks were publicly returned in Amritsar Church yesterday for the recovery of your Char. "Bless the Lord, O my soul; forget not all His benefits." ... I am floating in a sea of delight, and shall certainly look back to this time of terrible illness as one of the happiest periods of my life. I am as happy as a Queen. A great deal happier than the Queen! One of the images that most frequently rises before my mind, in prayerful thought, is that of our own beloved Queen. There is something so grand and pathetic in that image, as our Sovereign Lady sits with her hand on the helm, solitary at her post of duty, with a revolutionary storm howling and shrieking around her. The Lord shield her head; strengthen her hands; give her increasing grace and wisdom; and grant her the victory over all her enemies.

'I think it would gratify Her Majesty were she to know her *personal* influence amongst the Women of India. In zenana or mud-village, "Maliká Muazima Kaiser-i-Hind"—I generally give our Sovereign her full title among the Orientals, though I love "our own dear Queen" much better!—is an object of interest.... Of course, we inculcate loyalty among our Native Christians, in our Boarding School at Batala. One of the first things that would strike the eye of a visitor is "God save the Queen,"—hung up in the schoolroom.... It would please Her Majesty, could she hear our Christian boys singing:

'"Let the world know,
Be it friend or foe,
We'll be true to our Faith and our Queen!"

The Hindus and Muhammadans might fail us should a storm arise; the Atheists would be our bitter foes. I believe that many of our noble Christians would be Faithful unto Death....

'I have had two such extraordinary attacks of malarious fever.... For three days and nights, and more, I never slept for a moment. My mind was sometimes carried, at other times goaded, in unnatural activity. I had a torrent of thought, which I could not stop; the first week is to me almost a blank.... Dr. P. knew nothing of me, nor what a comically allegorical mind I have. I remember nothing of our interview, but it must have been inexpressibly funny....'

Letters thus far were only dictated. On January 20 is one in her own handwriting, very feeble and shaky:—

> ' ... One does learn such lessons, when lying still for weeks and weeks, with nothing to do but think. For instance, I remember grievous sins of omission, which I have never thought of before.... The duty of Intercessory prayer opens out before me. Of course, I have always prayed for you, love, and a great many more; no danger of forgetting. But I *have* forgotten numbers.'

In a circular letter to English friends, dated January 25, she again and more emphatically asserts her own non-expectation of death during the late illness: 'On the worst day I talked Urdu, nothing else, from morning till night, to imaginary bibis. Almost every one thought me dying, *except myself!*... I asked the dear, kind, skilful doctor of my state; he did not know what to say, for he thought me sinking. I asked dear Mr. Weitbrecht, and he pointed his finger straight downwards. I quite understood, but did not believe myself dying for all that!' This certainly was not the impression of those around her at the time, nor is it borne out by the things she said. No doubt she was striving to believe what she longed for,—was hoping that the doctors' opinion, and not her own inner sense, might prove to be right.

Miss Tucker's 'horror of alcohol' is particularly noted by Mr. Clark. When getting better, she one day remarked to him, 'What a dear, good doctor Dr. Clark is! He has brought me through it all, without giving me any spirits.' Then, turning to one of her nurses, 'Isn't it so, dear?' A judicious answer was returned: 'The doctor gave you just the right medicine, and you were very good in taking it.' A little later, when having another dose of medicine, she said again, 'Are you *sure* there is no alcohol in it?' 'It is what the doctor has ordered for you, Auntie dear. You must just take it, and ask no questions.' As letters show, it was not till February that she learned the true state of the case, which was that she had been kept alive by small doses of stimulant every hour. The strongest brandy had tasted to her like water. As soon as Miss Tucker understood how matters had been, she wrote to her sister, to say:—

> 'I made a great mistake in my letters home. If from them you have given to others a wrong impression, please kindly correct it when opportunity occurs. I wrote that I had had no stimulant in my illness. I thought that I had not; but I

find that I was utterly wrong. I was kept from sinking, not only by quantities of quinine, but brandy also. It was strange that I should not have recognised it; but it was always mixed with something else.'

So steady now was the improvement in her health, that before the middle of February she was able to get out for drives; on the 14th she went to Church; and by the 18th she was back again in 'dear Batala,'—not at the old palace, but in the Mission Bungalow, 'Sonnenschein,' with Miss Hoernle. A crowd of boys welcomed her at the Railway Station, on her arrival; and next day a grand Batala feast was given in her honour.

CHAPTER XV
A.D. 1886-1887 IN HARNESS ONCE MORE

So severe an illness could not fail to leave traces; and Charlotte Tucker came out of it more distinctly an old lady than she had ever been before. Ten years of perpetual toil had used up a large amount of even her superabundant vitality; and she could not expect to be again fully what she had been, either as to vigour or powers of endurance.

But although strength did not return quickly, and work had to be very slowly resumed, her interest in all that concerned Batala was as vivid as ever. The letters of 1886 are full of details about various High School boys,—either those who had been or those who still were scholars. Letters to Mrs. Hamilton were as long as ever,—longer indeed than in times of greater work-pressure,—and the shaky hand soon regained its firmness.

Immediately after her return to Batala, she wrote as to work generally:—

'O, there have been such stirring times in our Panjab Mission field lately! On one side, or rather various sides, the poor, low-caste people are joyfully receiving the Gospel. One hears of them listening, with tears running down their brown cheeks. Dear Miss Hoernle, my chum, is off to Futteyghur, with a new Bible-woman specially for the poor peasants. There, after *due examination*, Mr. Weitbrecht has baptized whole families,—fifty-six individuals,—and I shall probably hear of many more when Miss Hoernle returns.... All this is comparatively smooth, for people do not flare up at poor people being saved; but there has been desperate fighting over dear lads of good family; prosecution, persecution, pelting, lying, hand-to-hand struggling; even our chivalrous Missionary, Mr. Bateman, always ready to be foremost in the fight, owns that he has never had such a hard case as the last. The dear Convert, not yet baptized, refused an offer of 10,000 rupees down and 40,000 in reversion, rather than give up Christ....'

Many other particulars, too long to quote, follow.

The 4th of March was to be, as she wrote, 'a very great day here; the greatest Batala has ever known! Our Church is to be consecrated; and Christians will gather from far and near. One of the most interesting features of the occasion will be, I trust, the presence of converts.... I believe that many of them will gladly walk fifteen miles to be present. One said, in regard to their dress, which is, as you may suppose, of a very rough kind, "We will come in clean clothes, if it take us four days to wash them!"' The last few words were in allusion to very poor village converts.

A letter to a little great-nephew, the day after the Consecration, gave some particulars:—

> 'We had a very grand day in Batala yesterday. The Bishop came to open our fine new Church. A great many ladies and gentlemen came also. There were two meat meals for them; we sat down about thirty-four. But one of the most interesting things was that a good many poor men and boys, whom dear Mr. Weitbrecht had baptized in the villages, came too. Now, some people are proud enough to scorn these poor men, because they are of the low Mihtar caste. But, you know, my T——, that there is plenty of room in Heaven for Mihtars; and when they shine in white garments and crowns no one will despise them then. We thought that it would be a good thing to eat a little with the poor men, to show that we do not scorn them.... Mr. Bateman, Mrs. Weitbrecht, and I sat down on the straw, where the poor folk were eating their dinner, and ate some too. I own that I did not eat much,—I had had the two meat meals already!...
>
> 'Our Church looked very nice. We had to lend three mats for it; and other things were lent also.... But three beautiful cushions were not lent. Dear Aunt Mina, her Wilhelmina, and Cousin Laura worked them years ago for our Church. We took great care of them, and they look in fine condition.'

The Church of the Epiphany at Batala, consecrated on March 4, 1886, by the Bishop of Lahore, is described as being 'of brick, plastered with lime. The style chosen is that of the Mogul period, adapted to the requirements of a Christian Church. The Church at present consists of a nave, with clerestory windows, chancel, and porch. Two side-aisles remain to be added. The present accommodation is 200; when completed it will be about 500. The Church is situated near the chief gate of Batala, on the road leading to the railway.'

Then came the parting with the Weitbrechts; a sorrowful matter, after two years together under the same roof. Miss Tucker, though still far from strong, was sufficiently recovered to travel with them as far as to Delhi, where she paid a short visit to a widowed niece. While there, on March 18, she wrote:—

> 'Here am I, in the famous old city of Delhi, long the capital of India; but I go about to see none of its many sights.... The dear Weitbrechts and I lunched with the Cambridge Mission yesterday. A fine set of Missionaries, whom one is glad to have met. I was invited to dine also, I fancy, but I did not care to have my parting at a dinner-party. I returned here; and dear Herbert came at past 9 a.m. just to bid me farewell. It was very kind in him. We were alone in the verandah; and the parting was almost like that between son and mother....
>
> 'There is an interesting young Missionary here, Mr. Maitland of the S.P.G. He has been almost at death's door, and now appears much in the same state as I was in Amritsar six or seven weeks ago, coddled and taken care of. He wanted me to come and take a cup of tea with him, which I did most willingly; and we had a good chat together. Invalids like visitors, I think. I know that I did....
>
> '*22nd.*—O, my Laura, have you actually been sending *more* money, to meet the expenses of my illness? I do not know what to say or how to thank you. You must indeed stop overwhelming your Char!'

A very troublesome horse, who broke his harness and refused to be controlled, was named by her 'Buzdil,' or 'Coward.' '*I* never attempted to drive,' she observed in an April letter, 'but exhorted him, when I was beside Maria; but he never minded what I said.' Then came some 'rough lines,' adapted to an old Scotch air, 'He's a terrible man, John Tod, John Tod!'

> 'He's a terrible horse, Buzdil, Buzdil,
> He's a terrible horse, Buzdil!
> He gives start and skip,
> Fears all—but the whip,
> And cares not a straw for our will!
>
> 'He's broken his harness, Buzdil, Buzdil,
> He's broken his harness, Buzdil!
> He'd plunge in a hedge,

> Or back on a ledge,
> But when urged to go on—he stood still!
>
> 'He puzzles his syce, Buzdil, Buzdil,
> He worries his syce, Buzdil!
> If you take my advice,
> He'll be sold in a trice,
> Ere our poor Mission ladies he kill!'

Miss Tucker planned starting 'a very sober, safe kind of vehicle' to carry to Church those who could not or might not walk so far, even in cold weather. It was to be a cart, with a cover to ward off the heat of the sun, and was to be drawn by bullocks,—a humble conveyance, which fact was no trouble at all to the mind of Charlotte Tucker. The more humble, the better fitted in her estimation for a Mission Miss Sahiba!

In June she went for a complete change to Murree, and was soon able, while there, to speak of herself as being decidedly stronger, 'able without injury to walk twice to Church and back,' despite a tough hill on the way.

One friend, Mrs. Rowland Bateman, meeting her at this time, wrote afterwards:—

> 'It was so very delightful to see her dear face again, and so nice to get her warm and loving welcome. You know what "pretty" things she says; so on this occasion she said, "I came (to the station) for silver, and I found gold!" Very pretty, was it not? And now let me tell how I thought her looking. It is five years since I saw her; so of course I saw a good deal of change. She is looking very much older; but she is as bright as ever, cracking jokes, and making us all laugh. Then of course, since her illness, she is very thin, and that makes her face look older than she would do, were she a little stouter. And she eats more than she used to do. Five years ago she hardly ate enough to keep a sparrow alive.... Another thing I was very glad of, and that was that she does not attempt to do so much. She gives herself time to rest.'

In July Miss Tucker welcomed with eager pleasure a present from her sister of an 'excellent likeness' of the Queen. Charlotte Tucker's love for Her Majesty went far beyond ordinary loyalty. It was more of the nature of a personal romantic passion.

By the middle of August she was at work again. Mr. Weitbrecht was now gone, and Mr. Corfield had been seriously ill; so once more the School was for some time without a Principal on the spot. Many of the boys did not return to their homes for the holidays; indeed, some young converts literally had no homes to go to. A. L. O. E. therefore exercised her powers to find interests and amusements for them. About this time also she started Shakespeare readings in Batala, of which she says:—

> '*Aug. 11.*—Perhaps I told you that I had begun Shakespeare readings. I had five readings of Henry viii., with fair success; so I thought that I would begin *Macbeth*, which I think the most striking of all Shakespeare's dramas. But it was a dead failure here! The Natives could not understand it; and those who came to the first reading were *non inventus* at the—what would have been the second reading. So I have changed my book, and intend to-day to begin to read aloud my Laura's capital present, the particularly amusing *Life of Buckland*. Fish instead of furies!—salmon instead of slaughter!'

From many letters it may be seen that she was soon in a steady swing again, both with Zenana and with Village visiting; but the amount attempted seems to have been more moderate than formerly. Few quotations must suffice:—

> '*Oct. 15, 1886.*—Now I will tell you about a visit which I paid yesterday to a Zenana, where the Bibi used to be very bigoted. Yesterday I came on her husband, a grave, middle-aged man. So he heard what I had to say. Then he asked me to give him *a picture of Christ*. Very strict Muhammadans object to pictures; but he wanted one of the Saviour. I, as a rule, never give pictures, though I show them; but I happened to have three small pictures, cut out from periodicals,—not coloured,—and I felt impelled to grant the grave man's request. I let him choose. He took the copy of the famous picture—is it not Leonardo da Vinci's?—of the Blessed One, crowned with thorns, and put it carefully by in a paper. Will that suffering, pathetic Face speak to the Muhammadan's heart? N. is no unlearned man. He told me that he had been our K. B.'s teacher. "Were you angry with K. B.?" I asked,—meaning for becoming a Christian! The grave man quietly replied in the negative.'

> '*Nov. 6.*—I have lately been paying more attention to children in the Zenanas,—partly perhaps because they seem to pay

more attention to what I say. When they listen in perfect stillness, one cannot but hope that the young hearts are receiving some seed of life. I had very quiet, attentive little listeners in a Zenana yesterday. When I went to another, some of the children followed me, but the bibi forbade them to come in. In vain I pleaded that they did not make the least noise; she bade them go and play. But after I had read to that woman, and proceeded to another house, children came after me, I think two or three of the same ones. That little book, with gaily-coloured pictures, about little Daisy, which you sent me, is invaluable....'

Miss Krapf in her turn had had a serious breakdown; and she did not return to Batala. In her place, towards the end of the year, came Miss Minnie Dixie, who was to be Miss Tucker's constant companion and fellow-inmate of the Mission Bungalow for seven years or more. By the time Miss Dixie arrived, as 'Sonnenschein' was made only to take in two ladies, and Miss Hoernle was still there, Miss Tucker had doubtless moved into her own little annexe,—the new west wing of the Bungalow, which she had prettily named 'Sunset!'

A ground-plan of the Bungalow gives a good idea of this latest earthly home of Charlotte Tucker. One large room was divided by screens into bedroom and sitting-room. In front and behind were verandahs; while one side was joined to 'Sonnenschein,' and on the other lay dressing-room and bathroom. Miss Tucker lived in her own tiny 'Sunset,' but she took her meals with the other ladies in 'Sunshine,' and their evenings were often, if not regularly, spent together. 'We are a happy little band of Europeans at Batala,' she wrote in the November of 1886.

The year closed with a characteristic little episode, by which it might be seen that the old energy and impetuosity were by no means snuffed out of existence. A young lady, not of the Batala party, was going to a certain doctor at − −, of whose skill Miss Tucker was more than dubious. She had, as we have seen, no very flattering opinion of the medical faculty in general; always with charming exceptions, where personal intercourse interfered with theories. On the present occasion it was not a man but 'a dreadful woman doctor' in the case. On learning that all was arranged, Miss Tucker exclaimed, 'You shall not go alone, dear. I will go with you.' And go she did; regardless of age, of weakness, of cold weather, of long journeying.

Nor was this all! On reaching − −, Miss Tucker was so utterly dissatisfied with the apparent state of things, that she flatly refused to give up the patient to the doctor. After what she describes as 'a fight,—will against will!' she fairly carried off her charge to the house of a friend in the place; and next day ran away with her, by train, to a distant town. The patient happily fell thereafter into kind and skilful hands; and Charlotte Tucker congratulated herself upon her own prompt and decisive action. Whether or no her fears were well founded, one cannot but admire her self-sacrificing readiness to endure any amount of worry, fatigue, and responsibility on behalf of another. The last thing Charlotte Tucker ever did was 'to pass by on the other side,' when a human being was in need of help. She never dreamt of sparing herself.

Many letters this year bear reference to the different pretty and useful articles sent out by friends and working-parties for sale or for gifts. With respect to those for sale, she did indeed exclaim in one letter: 'I wish dear kind friends would sell the things themselves, and simply give us the money! They do not think of the added difficulty of insects and climate! I fear that a good many things get spoiled.' This however was not the usual strain in which she acknowledged such parcels. Here are a few specimen sentences, culled from letters of different dates, to Miss Longley:—

> 'I received your kind letter to-day, and do not delay thanking you heartily for the account of what the dear Warwickshire children are doing for the Mission cause.... The dolls are capital gifts to send. Our little Fatimas and Barakats, etc., like them so much.'

> 'Your very nice box of attractive dolls, those that can open and shut their eyes, and a number of prettily-dressed sisters clustering together like birdies in a nest, safely reached me to-day.... They have come in excellent time, for our annual examination has been delayed.... How pleased our little Panjabi maidens will be with their dolls,—even blind girls would be charmed, I think! The clever dolls that can open and shut their eyes ought to be very special prizes.... Dolls are great favourites with Native children, and I do not wonder at this. The Native toys look very coarse beside the elegantly-dressed little ladies from dear old England.'

> 'Dolls are much liked by our dark-eyed little maidens. Not only little girls; but I suspect that many a mother would be pleased to possess one of the quiet, rosy-cheeked babies from England, that never cry nor give any trouble. Your useful work-basket must, I think, be presented to some Native Christian girl who is fond of work.... Native Christians also would, I think, most value the scrap-books so kindly prepared. At Christmas we have a bran-pie, only

for Christians, and we have to get ready about eighty gifts, even in this out-of-the-way Batala. I begin my preparations very early. I assure you that our children are not "black." Some of the Natives are quite pretty, and I think not darker than Spaniards. I every now and then see a child with brown hair, perhaps curly.'

'We have numbers of young people here. It would amuse some of your workers to hear a few of their names translated. We have amongst girls, Flower, Beloved, Lady of Light, An Offering, etc.,—amongst boys, Valiant, Feet of Christ, Diamond-pearl, Welfare, etc. A nice young convert has the pretty name of "Gift of the Merciful." A little boy is "The Mercy of God." His father's name is "The Power of God." Fancy a number of dark-eyed men, women, and children, with these curious names, assembled around our bran-pie (it is really a bath), and some of the pretty presents from Warwick popping out to delight them.'

Dolls are spoken of again and again, as if too many could not possibly be sent; but many other things are mentioned also,—such as antimacassars, pretty handkerchiefs, boxes of sugar-plums, a nice inkstand, and so on. An unlimited amount of presents for Indian Christians at Christmas-time was evidently a pressing need. Articles for sale had to be sent to Amritsar or elsewhere, as there was no demand for them in Batala.

In February 1887 two little ones came to her for a short stay at Batala on their way to England,—the tiny grandchildren of her brother, Mr. St. George Tucker. Children had always a great attraction for her; and immediately letters became full of the small pair, their pretty ways and sayings and doings. Miss Tucker had to make arrangements for their journey home. Writing on March 17 to her niece, Miss Edith Tucker, she exclaims:—

'O these children! they are such darlings! Edie will not be three till the 19th, but she is as sensible as if double the age; and seems to take a sort of care of her brother. She is such an honourable little girl too. Mrs. C., the very nice matron here, has been very much struck by this. "It must be hereditary," she said; "she could not have got it from her ayah."[118] ... My heart feels very tender towards the loving pets, whom I shall never see on earth again. God grant us a joyful meeting before the Throne!...

'I sometimes think how proud dear Sir Frederick Abbott[119] will be of his descendants. Please congratulate him and dear Lady Abbott from me.'

In another letter, about the same date, and also on the subject of the children, written to Miss Alice Tucker, A. L. O. E. speaks of having been kicked by a horse in a small Muhammadan courtyard,—happily not a severe kick. The horse struck out sharply, but she had just stepped back, and the force of the blow was also broken by the umbrella which she held. She escaped therefore with only 'a harmless contusion.' It might have been a very grave accident.

On March 26 comes a short letter to Mrs. Hamilton, jubilant at the thought of a visit from her friend, Mr. Francis Baring:—

> 'To-day my darlings embark on the wide, wide ocean, dear little "travellers by land and by water"! What sweet blossoms of the fourth generation grow on our honoured Father's family tree! I am sure that you think *your* pet no exception....
>
> 'I received a note the other day, which made my heart joyful: it was from Mera Bhatija.
>
> "He's coming again! he's coming again!
>
> Oh, but he's been long awa',
>
> Far frae his ain," etc.
>
> He is coming all the way from M——, for Batala's ninth birthday. I correct the boys' letters to-day, and am pleased at the tone in which they write regarding his coming.
>
> 'R. "Won't it be a grand thing to see our dear old Principal again?" R. C. "The Rev. F. H. Baring will be here, and I hope there will be a grand feast, and racing, jumping, etc. How happy we shall be to see the father of our school!" ... I shall like to look at dear Babu Singha's face, when he grasps the hand of his old patron.'

Another letter, April 6, refers to a slight operation which she had had to undergo, for continued weakness of one eye. 'It needed the prick of the lancet and the entrance of the probe. It was a mere trifle of an operation; Henry[120] is so gentle and kind, she wrote cheerily; then, later in the same letter: 'Now I must be off for church. We have a great deal of church-going in this Holy Week. I have to play the harmonium to-day. This week Minnie and I have been taking the privilege alternately.'

She was greatly interested this year in a young Muhammadan, who seemed much disposed towards Christianity, yet was never able to make up his mind or to act with decision. He appeared, as she said in one letter, to have clearly 'two wills,—one desiring Baptism,' the other drawing him among the enemies of Christianity. 'He swings from good to evil like a very pendulum,' she observed. 'We cannot keep him from the Muhammadans; yet the Muhammadans cannot keep him from Christ.' In another May letter she wrote of him: 'B. P. interested me yesterday by trying to make me get one of the boys here off with the latter part of a punishment. "You are a kind of mother," said he. "When the father is angry, the mother should plead." Natives do not clearly understand about discipline and justice; even Christian Natives are apt to think that offenders should be quickly forgiven, however disastrous the results might be. Abstract justice to the Oriental sometimes looks like revenge. How often have I heard Muhammadans say, "God is the Forgiver!"—with this they put conscience to rest. But a good many, called Christians, fall into the dangerous mistake of imagining the pure holy God to be too loving to be just. It is the echo of Satan's lie, "Ye shall *not* surely die."'

In June came one of the heaviest blows of all her Missionary career,—a very dark shadow indeed upon its brightness. This was the sudden and unexpected apostasy of one who for years had belonged to their little band of Christians,—one of the first Native Christians whom she had learnt to know on her earliest arrival at Amritsar,—one whom she had loved and trusted, and whom she had looked upon as not only a follower of Christ by profession but in very truth. She felt the defection of this man with exceeding acuteness. He has been once or twice already referred to as Z., or Maulvi Z., and he might have been referred to dozens of times. The first letter on this sad subject to Mrs. Hamilton was written while Miss Tucker was away from home, staying with Mr. and Mrs. Francis Baring.

> '*June 23, 1887.*—I am certainly stronger, and should like the visit to the dear excellent Barings much, if I had not such troubles. From Batala Mission has come such a shock! Fancy Maulvi Z. and his family going over to the Muhammadans,— he who for about twelve years had been such a well-known member of the Church,—she who for eighteen months worked as an Honorary Bible-woman! Both, with their nice eldest son, took the Communion with me this very month! It is terrible! The wretched Maulvi is to receive 40s. for teaching in an opposition school, just set up to injure our Mission School.... The Muhammadans have had rejoicings and fireworks,—the enemies of the Lord will triumph and blaspheme. But I believe that Z. has no faith in the false prophet, and that he *has* loved the Saviour. The prodigal may come back, but probably after terrible judgments, for he is sinning against light and love. I have not the heart to write on other subjects.'

'*June 29, 1887.*—I propose starting for Batala early on Monday the 11th. I must be in time for the prize-givings and a feast. Mera Bhatija had a letter to-day from — —, who does not think that Z.'s terrible apostasy has done any harm to the Christian cause in Batala. The more respectable Muhammadans do not trust him, and our preachers are listened to as well as before. But oh, the wretched man himself and his family! I must not dwell on a subject which has made me so unhappy.'

She could not, however, keep from recurring to it once and again, as darker details came out. Indignation at the conduct of the apostate was equalled by her pity for the unhappy man himself. Writing on July 29, still on the same subject, she said: 'He did harm in the school while teaching here. Some of the Muhammadans despise him. A most sarcastic, *withering* article has come out in a Muhammadan newspaper against the apostate.'

On reaching home another trial assailed her. One of her most trusted servants, mentioned repeatedly as V., proved to be utterly dishonest, and had to be dismissed. Miss Tucker felt this too very acutely. 'In all my Missionary life,' she wrote on July 16, 'I never knew such a year as this.'

Miss Dixie was at this time away, and two or three short extracts from letters to her may be given:—

'*July 18, 1887.*—Welcome, dearest Minnie, *home*! We are to have a picnic in celebration of your return. Please travel in a duli, if the roads are very bad, as they are pretty sure to be. Tell us when and where to send for you. We have had many troubles at Batala since you left,—the unhappy Maulvi not only apostatising himself and family, but slandering his former friends right and left. I have dismissed V., and P. has followed him. A sight of your dear kind face will be a cheer to your affectionate Auntie.'

'*July 30.*—What an adventurous journey my dearest Minnie had! Thank God, dear, that you are all safe and right.... I seem always to be asking you to excuse short letters; but the fact is that almost everything is an effort to me. I just manage to get through a little work, but seem not to be able for much correspondence just at present.'

'*Aug. 10.*—I am glad that you are well and happy. You must not think that I forget you, because I write little. It is rather a case of "duties thronging round," and not much strength to perform them.'

'*Aug. 16.*—We have had *such* floods! On Sunday there was no attempt to reach the large Church. There was Service in Anarkalli; but *that* was surrounded with water. Some went on horseback, some in dulis.'

One letter to Mrs. Hamilton contains a brief description of her own work:—

'*Aug. 31.*—I go, you know, to city work in the morning. After our late breakfast I have a succession of people coming. For instance, to-day,—1st, Munshi and four boys. 2nd, A convert came, to read the Bible to me. 3rd, A teacher came, for me to explain difficult English idioms. 4th, Three lads for English lessons. 5th, A fourth lad more advanced. You see, love, that this is not a sleepy life, though in this warm weather I usually get some sleep in the daytime. I like having the dear boys. They have done much to keep the heart green under various Missionary discouragements.'

On the 9th of September, responding to Mrs. Hamilton's letter upon the unhappy subject related above, she said:—

'I fear that I cannot share your hopes.... A man who for nearly twelve years passed as a Christian, took the Sacrament not many days before he became apostate, spoke coarsely of the Holy Communion to Muhammadans, and bitterly of Christians, ... seems to me *almost* past hope. He has, as far as he could, "crucified the Son of God afresh" and "put Him to an open shame." ... Instead of, as you sweetly write, "bitterly lamenting, like St. Peter," poor Z. day by day sits by his mosque, deceiving the people.'

One more quotation on this sad subject may be made from a letter, dated April 12, 1889, when Miss Tucker was perplexed what to do about seeing some relatives of the unhappy apostate, who were staying with him. 'Bishop French excommunicated — — (we do not call him Z. now), and forbade Christians having intercourse with him.... It would clearly be wrong to throw over the — —s, who had *not* left the Fold. I asked counsel from Herbert, and guidance from One Higher.' Eventually she did manage to see the relatives while avoiding the apostate.

Until the year 1886 Miss Tucker apparently kept no regular written record of her daily work. But in the August of that year, doubtless from a sense that her memory was becoming less trustworthy than of old, she started a Journal, which was kept up until within three weeks or so of her death. The Journal consists of 273 closely written foolscap pages; and, as

Miss Wauton says, they 'give us a glimpse of the earnest, unremitting toil of those seven years in the Batala Zenanas.' The volume opens with a list of about 173 names of those whom she was then visiting; and this continued to be about the average number throughout the seven years; some Zenanas being from time to time closed, while new ones were opened. To quote again from Miss Wauton, whose long Indian and Missionary experience renders her judgment especially valuable:—

> 'Besides being a record of Zenana work, the Diary records many little incidents in connection with the daily life; *e.g.* notices of the arrivals and departures of fellow-workers, and of the many friends and visitors who came to see her. There are numerous references to the boys of the Baring High School, any sickness or death amongst them, the subjects taken in her classes with them and with the boys of the Mission Plough.... All speak of the many objects embraced by her wide sympathies. But the Zenana teaching is always first and foremost. Other things come in, as it were, by the way. The whole Diary shows how carefully and methodically she carried on this visiting, and what infinite pains she took to find out and invent things which would help to attract the people, and open the way for the delivery of her message.
>
> 'Her inventive genius enabled her to do this very effectively; and the wonderful pictures and allegorical designs she took with her opened many doors, which would have probably remained fast barred against a less winning visitor. These charms were very varied. She seems generally to have taken one with her to every place she went to; and to have changed it from time to time, as the lesson to be taught from it had been learnt, or the novelty had worn off.
>
> 'These are all entered in the Diary as "Ladder," "Jewel," "Zouave," "Pagoda," "Prism," "Crosses," "Tree," "Purse," etc. The first was a ladder, painted in various colours, showing the different steps by which the sinner mounts up from grace to glory. The second is a jewel, covered over with several pieces of cloth, representing the different veils, such as ignorance, prejudice, self-righteousness, which, covering man's heart, conceal from his view and hinder his attainment of the jewel of Truth. But these contrivances were not the only key with which these bigoted Zenanas were opened. We find in the Journal frequent memoranda of little gifts to be taken to certain houses,—"sandcloth," on the occasion

of a wedding or birth, "medicine," "quinine," "spectacles," "tea," "soap," etc. The Scripture subjects spoken upon each day are also entered....

'Her love of children was remarkable; and in many cases, where the elder members of the household refused to listen, she would get an interested audience from amongst the little ones. She writes in one place, "Such nice children!" in another, "I found myself stroking little cheeks." ... Another striking feature of Miss Tucker was the courage and indomitable perseverance which she showed in the most difficult and trying circumstances. "Nil Desperandum" was her favourite motto, and she carried it out fully. Sometimes she was rudely treated, sometimes even insulted; but nothing daunted her.'

Here are a few specimen extracts from the Journal, including one or two of unusual length. The majority are exceedingly short. I do not give the correct initials for either Zenanas or people:—

'*Aug. 24, 1886.*—A. very nice sick father, twelve quiet children; Mark ii.

B. a little better, Christ blessing children.

C. disappointing; outburst of bigotry; M. however silent.

D. friendly; read three parables. Good listening.

E. very indifferent. Bibis. Mark vii. N. left.

Aug. 25.—F. fair.

G. Had very nice talk with him. Prodigal Son. From John iii. New. H.'s nice wife. Seemed almost Christian. Ditto.

J. nice. Boy, − −, promised book if he comes. From Matt. x.

K. Send cloth to new baby. Read a little of Xt.'s Birth.

Aug. 26.—L. careless.... I do not remember what I read....

M. Only children attended. Children A., D.'

Sept. 1.—L. very cross, ill-tempered, loud voice. Rebuked by elder woman. I showed picture of Christ healing, quoted "Learn of Me." After a while face quite softened, voice subdued.... Last thing promised she would go to church....'

'*Dec. 15, 1886.*—Rudely treated. Man with unpleasant face and blemished eye shook the charpai (bedstead) on which I was seated four times, to make me get off. Went to second place; people noisy. A man asked me to read of Christ, and

I began. Was asked to go to more open place. Went,—found open place was the *outside* of the village. Had to go off.

'B. H. (another village). Rejected here also. Even a tiny clod was thrown. I told people at both villages that I prayed God to forgive them for their conduct to His servant. Ours is a religion of love.'

'*Jan. 28, 1887.*—P. very nice. Q., a youth, hearing of Last Judgment, says that he wants to be a right-side one, and will pray to be so. He is going to marry; says wife and he will both be right side. He means to send her to our school. He learned in Mission Plough.'

'*May 12, 1887.* ... (List of names.) Except ——'s house, none really satisfactory. My heart very sad. There seems hardly any good ground in Batala.'

The names of Zenanas, villages, and people living in either, are generally printed in dark letters on the left side of the page, while the coming and going of Missionaries and friends, as well as items of home news, are printed on the right side. On February 15, 1887, is the terse entry, 'Operation on eye'; and the very next day, almost equally terse, 'I was kicked by a horse.' Towards the end of the same month is a characteristic notice of the death of one of her nieces, printed large: 'Vesa left earth!' Death to her meant simply this,—leaving Earth for a 'better Country.'

CHAPTER XVI
A.D. 1887-1888 A VISIT FROM BISHOP FRENCH

One matter of marked interest in the year 1887 was the retirement of Bishop French from the Bishopric of Lahore, and his return to the humbler post of simple Missionary. This step appealed strongly to Miss Tucker's sense of admiration. On the 8th of October she wrote to Mrs. Hamilton:—

> 'I have already, as you see, written a good deal by this mail, ... but I will not let the post for England go without at least a few loving lines to my own dearest sister. The dear good Bishop is resigning. I hear that he feels it sorely; but he has no intention of leaving work. He resigns the *English* part into what he feels to be stronger hands,—but will, I believe, continue Missionary work amongst Natives. He was *first* a Missionary; and—dear man!—it is not improbable that he will die a Missionary. To lay down a mitre is no degradation!'

A few days later, having heard that the Bishop purposed paying her a little visit at Batala, she wrote to him direct:—

'Batala, *Oct. 20, 1887*.

Revered Bishop,—Though I know not whether this will reach you till after your return from Batala, I cannot forbear thanking you for your affectionate letter, and intention of gratifying me by visiting my simple little Missionary home. I received your letter at Amritsar, having—for a wonder—left Batala to be present at the wedding of dear old Mr. Newton's grandson at Ludhiana. This has occasioned a little delay in my replying. Mr. Corfield also was absent, having gone to bring his wife from Dharmsala; but we expect him to-morrow morning, and then he shall know your wishes. I think that you will find the Ghurub-i-Aftab very quiet. You will see visitors or not, just as you please,—only give a hint of your wishes. When the dear Lord's Servants honour me with a visit, I say that they gild my floors.

'If it be not presumptuous in me to say so, I would express my feeling that there is something beautiful and elevating in the idea of one who was a Missionary before he was a Bishop, becoming a Missionary *after* leaving his Bishopric; laying down the crozier and mitre, to take up the simple Evangelist's staff. Perhaps, my honoured Friend,—if permitted to call you so,—your grandest work is yet to come.—Yours with affectionate respect,

C. M. Tucker.

'*P.S.*—Please offer my affectionate and grateful remembrances to dear Mrs. French.'

The Bishop's visit came about, as hoped for; and it was a great pleasure to Miss Tucker to receive him. Although they might differ on certain points, they were one in absolute love and obedience to the same Lord and Master; and each thoroughly appreciated, thoroughly delighted in, the whole-hearted and single devotion of the other. In some respects the two were much alike. There was in both, as Dr. Weitbrecht has said, 'a fiery impatience of difficulty or delay which sometimes led to mistakes.' In both also there was a remarkable *upliftedness*,—if the word is permissible,—an absorption in things spiritual, which made earthly matters seem altogether unimportant by comparison.

The one drawback to Miss Tucker's enjoyment was that she gave up to the Bishop her own little 'house,'—and such changes had at her time of life grown to be somewhat of a trial. But she would not hear of a gentleman being permitted to sleep in 'Sonnenschein,' with the younger ladies,—not even her beloved and revered Bishop!! She had not perhaps entirely even yet lost sight of her old favourite idea of a home for Mission Miss Sahibas, into which a man's foot might not enter. At all events, she decided to sleep there herself, and to give up her little Sunset home to the Bishop. Which she did.

'It was beautiful to see them together,' Miss Dixie has said, when speaking of this visit, which lasted somewhat under a week. The Bishop and Miss Tucker went about in company, attended church together, and had many a long talk,—both of them white-haired, fragile in look, worn out with heavy toil, aged beyond their years. Both would be so utterly absorbed in the subject under discussion, as to see nothing around, to hear nothing that went on. There was about each of them a remarkable *Other-worldliness*, to use a curious term, sometimes employed in this sense. They were citizens of Heaven, not of Earth; and they realised the fact to an extent not often equalled.

But with all her 'Other-worldliness,' Miss Tucker never lost the sense of fun and humour, as connected with the things of this world. One amusing little incident is told of the Bishop's visit. He had brought with him a Muhammadan manservant. Miss Tucker habitually kept in her cupboard a small bottle of brandy, in case of need,—the brandy being well dosed with quinine, to render it unattractive. When the Bishop was gone, this little bottle was found to have vanished also. Miss Tucker, on making the discovery, went back to her friends, to exclaim, with an indescribable expression, 'That greedy Muhammadan has taken the brandy?'—then bursting into a fit of laughter at the thought of his surprise on tasting the quinine. She often referred to this afterwards with great amusement.

It was remarkable in A. L. O. E. that she still, in old age, remembered and carefully followed in small matters her parents' wishes. Not of course that her life was shaped by them. Probably old Mr. Tucker would have disapproved of few things more highly than of a woman undertaking such work as she undertook; but here she followed the dictates of her own conscience. In slighter questions, where conscience was not involved, she loved to do what they had of old desired. Still, as always, she rose early to work, and went to bed in good time, according to the promise given long, long before. Still, when she drank afternoon tea, she always took something to eat with it, because 'her Mother had liked her to do so.' And often, though old and weak, when she caught herself to be stooping, she still would pull herself sharply upright, and say: 'I remembered,—my dear Father always wanted me to sit straight.'

While habitually much interested in engagements and marriages, she was particular as to modes of speech on such subjects. Once or twice, when some girl-visitor spoke with what she considered an unbecoming lightness, upon some matter of love or love-making, Miss Tucker observed, after the girl's departure,—'My dear, what a vulgar person!!'

The same curious diversity of opinion as to particular points of Miss Tucker's character which was observable in her English life, is also observable in her Indian life. Here again are opposite opinions. One says, 'She was so peculiarly sympathetic!' Another, with equally good opportunities for judging, says, 'Exceedingly kind, but not sympathetic.' One says, 'She was so well able to put herself into the place of another in trouble!' Another says, 'No tact; the kindest intentions, but she did not always know how to manage.'

The explanation lies, no doubt, at least in part, in her own many-sidedness, and in the very different manner in which she was affected by different people. Some appealed to her tenderness; some only called out her kindliness. She could and did love intensely; but only in particular cases: and though to a wide outer circle she gave love, it was of a less ardent nature. Moreover, she *could* dislike people; and when she once took a marked dislike, though this was seldom, it would be not quite easy to make her view with fairness that person's doings.

She was very impulsive still; the same eager, enthusiastic warm-hearted being, who had lived in girlhood at No. 3,—modified, but not intrinsically different. Possibly, in old age, with weakened health, after living practically much alone, the natural tendency to hasty judgments may have somewhat increased. But if so, there was also an increase in the spirit of humility, a far greater readiness than of old to acknowledge herself mistaken or in the wrong. By nature she was not gentle and had not self-control; and physical weakness doubtless often rendered the fight harder,—yet she persevered in the fight with never-failing resolution.

Sometimes she would hear of a thing done by one of the younger Missionaries, and would at once condemn it, not waiting to learn all the circumstances, and speaking with some severity. A few days later something would turn up, explaining more fully the why and the wherefore of the action in question; and then she would say frankly, 'Well, I think I was wrong, after all! I think you were right to do as you did!' A smaller and less noble nature would probably have refused to see the mistake, and would have clung obstinately to its own way of thinking.

Although she would occasionally *speak* hastily, she did not as a rule *write* hastily. If she could not in her letters praise a person, she would cease to bring forward that person's name,—at all events in letters meant for general reading.

It may also be noted here that, as time went on, Charlotte Tucker, in her extreme desire for Missionary simplicity and economy, had become a little apt to push matters in that direction to an excess. Few people are constituted as she was, to toil hard and to live long upon the smallest possible minimum of food. As some of the weakness of old age crept over her, she was perhaps not always *quite* reasonable respecting Missionary requirements and necessities. She would at times seem to expect others, for the sake of economy, to do with what she herself found sufficient, but which to their different constitutions meant something like semi-starvation. This at least is the impression of one who ought to be accounted a good judge, and it appears to have been in some degree a trouble to certain of her companions.

During all those long years of Indian life, amid the variety of people with whom she was thrown, while there were many whom she could love, and some whom she could love most warmly, there were also naturally a few who did not suit her, any more than she suited them. She may have been somewhat of a trial to them; and undoubtedly they were very much of a trial to her; yet despite all her natural impetuosity and impatience of disposition, she bore long and patiently in such cases. As one says, who was with her in some of those later years, 'Although sometimes hasty in judging, she was also capable of much forbearance.'

It is noticeable that one who knew her well speaks of a remarkable softening and increase of gentleness during the last three years of her life. Naturally very 'up and down' in her moods, she became then far more uniformly bright. The fruit was growing very ripe, almost ready to drop from the tree. Miss Wauton, too, tells of the growing loveliness of expression in her face, as the end drew nearer. But we have not yet quite arrived at those last three years.

By this time Miss Tucker was a little apt to fall behind in new methods of work, and to cling to what was old-fashioned. Needful changes in the High School were at first a trouble to her, even though they might be real improvements, tending to render the school more efficient. She liked, for instance, to drop in at odd hours, and to 'take a class,' after the manner of an English squire's daughter dropping into the village school. As numbers and discipline increased it was found to be not always a convenient plan, and objections were made. Miss Tucker one day, in a fit of depression at having to give up this and other things, is recorded to have said, 'My work is done! I don't care how soon I go now!'

This happily was a mere passing fit of sadness. It was soon after arranged that a Class of the older youths should go to her for instruction on Sunday afternoons; and in the class she found very great interest. She would also ask her 'dear boys,' a few at a time, to spend week-day evenings with her, for games of play, which she enjoyed fully as much as they did. She was very much beloved by the boys; and they were no less delighted to come to her than she was to have them. Her influence over these boys, over Indian Christians generally, and over most of the Missionaries with whom she came in contact, will never be forgotten.

The springy step of earlier years was not quite lost, even in old age. Another thing that she kept remarkably long was, as earlier stated, her voice for singing. It had of course grown thin and weak, and was now a good deal cracked; still she did not sing out of tune; and her enjoyment in singing never failed. It was with her the natural expression of her feelings. When she sang in Church, and when she played the harmonium, her whole face would light up in a marvellous manner. Indians—not Christians—would walk long distances, and be present in Church, simply to look upon the face of the Buzurg Miss Sahiba, as she sang or played. Such an illumination on the face of a human being was counted well worth some exertion to see. Another account tells of a Native who would go to Church for the express purpose of watching her look, when she recited the *Gloria*. It was all so *real* to A. L. O. E. Her very smile was a sermon in itself.

All these years Zenana teaching went steadfastly on. She ever had before her mind a keen sense that her own call might come before another morning's dawn, and that the present might be her last opportunity of speaking. Sometimes she would be depressed when reading of others who had had more apparent results to their work; yet through countless discouragements she never slackened.

The same Native Christian from whom I have quoted earlier as to the non-success, in his opinion, of her Missionary labours, says also about Miss Tucker: 'She was far from being a good judge of the Indian character. I remember her pointing to a Native Christian, and saying that the very light of Heaven was being reflected from his countenance, when in fact he had almost apostatised.' But this was simply a repetition of the old tendency to think always the very best of everybody,—the habit being cultivated to such an excess as materially to interfere with her powers of perception in particular cases. It does not touch the question of her general understanding of the Indian character. Penetration, as to individuals, was hardly one of her gifts; and few would hesitate to agree to the assertion that she thought a great deal better of many Natives than, unfortunately, they deserved. Her eyes were opened slowly through bitter and repeated disappointments. But to the last she would probably have preferred to be sometimes deceived, rather than to be always suspecting.

In the continuous pressure of her work and trials, Charlotte Tucker was a woman of prayer. Not that she was given to long and wordy outpourings; but she lived on the border-land of the Unseen, and she held incessant intercourse with her Divine Master. Whatever she felt, whatever she wanted, when she was afraid, when she was depressed, when things went wrong, when she could not see her way, the first impulse of her heart was always—prayer! Then she would wait to see His Will.

Systematic as were the entries in her Journal, those last few years of life, she was apt to be a little forgetful,—which no doubt was the very reason that she started the Journal. She would come in and say to Miss Dixie, 'Such a sweet young Bibi in a Zenana to-day, dear. She wants to see you.' When Miss Dixie asked where the young Bibi lived, her recollections were confused, and she could not say. The name of Bibi, husband, and house had all escaped. Miss Dixie would then have to question the bearers as to where they had taken Miss Tucker, and so find out particulars.

The writing of books and booklets still continued to some extent; indeed, it could not have been long before this that she achieved a good-sized volume for young English readers, called—*Pictures of St. Peter in an English Home*. As its name might imply, it was controversial in character, being written against the errors of the Roman Church. She could not, however, work so hard now with her pen as in earlier years. Dr. Weitbrecht states that 'her books for publication in England, the proceeds of which went to support local work, were mostly written during her brief summer holiday. It was when she felt her powers failing in this line that she set aside part of her patrimony to endow the "Mission Plough."'

The absence of allusions to her own writings in years of correspondence is remarkable. Once in a way she speaks of what she is doing, but this is quite the exception. Her natural reserve showed strongly here. She had also a curious dislike to being questioned—a fact noticed by relatives in her English life years before; and one of her Missionary companions tells of it also. If questions were put direct, she would say, 'I am not your Mother-Superior; don't appeal to me!'—when her questioner was longing to have the benefit of her years of experience. A story is told of one gentleman, who came from a considerable distance, on purpose to consult Miss Tucker about some books that he meant to publish. The call was a failure. Instead of gradually getting into conversation, and luring her on to tell what she knew, he asked point-blank the things that he wanted to hear; and the result was *nil*. On his way back to the station, he inquired whether Miss Tucker had not lost her memory. Not at all, he was told,—but direct questioning always checked information.

In the November of 1887 the small Star-Dispensary was opened by Dr. Weitbrecht, for Miss Dixie. She had undergone some training in England; and though not 'qualified,' she had it in her power to do much more for the women and children of the neighbourhood than their own people could do for them. Many objections have been made to the idea of a Dispensary anywhere, without a properly qualified doctor; and no doubt as soon as possible the latter should in all cases be supplied. But where a doctor cannot be had, then in default of what is better, a trained nurse can do a great deal to help, in ordinary cases of sickness or accident. The reception given to this little Dispensary soon showed how much it was valued.

In a letter of December 9th are some words of depression under difficulties, especially the difficulty of finding a new master for the 'Plough School,' as the former master was going away.

'I send you and dear Leila a few words of St. Paul's which seem to me so sweet and restful,—a pillow for weary heads. "Beloved of God, called to be saints." It is often difficult to realise that we *are* beloved of God, because conscience says we do not deserve to be so. I have often to fight against discouragements.'

On the 21st of January 1888 is a mention of the 'Missionary Ladies' Conference,' to be held in Amritsar late in February, with a hope that all would be 'as friendly and good-tempered' as on the previous occasion, five years earlier. Towards the close of February comes her report of what had occurred:—

> '*Feb. 24, 1888.*—I found your letter awaiting me this evening, when I returned from the four days' Conference of Lady Missionaries at Amritsar.... Conferences are rather tiring. Sittings each day from 10 to 1, and 2 to 4, and always something besides. We had about sixty ladies, of various Denominations and Societies and Nationalities too, English, German, American, Indian. On Thursday, after our Conference work, we went to Church, and had such a solemn spiritual sermon from our new Bishop.[121] It was the first time that I ever had seen him.
>
> 'In the evening there was rather a large meeting of Christians, both white and brown, to meet the Bishop. I was introduced to him; and we had—in the midst of the room—a quiet talk, which I do not think that I shall ever forget. It was almost as if we could at once meet heart to heart.... I think that he takes up his high office more as a burden and a Cross than a dignity. I felt greatly drawn towards him, and thank the Lord for sending us a holy and humble man.'
>
> '*Feb. 28.*—I must tell my loved Laura a little about the Conference, and the characteristic way in which M., the real, took me down a peg this evening. The first day nice Mrs. Perkins, presided; on the second another nice lady; I was particularly requested to sit in the chair on the third and the first half of the fourth days.
>
> 'Now on the second there had been rather a hot discussion. There had been a show of hands; but numbers were so closely divided that we had to go by ballot. Even then there was only a majority of *one*; and some of the members were absent, and some imperfectly informed. In short, when Char

succeeded to office, the question was brought up again by a strong lady on the one side,—and then a paper was read by a strong lady on the other,—and I proposed that votes should be taken *again*, which resulted in a majority of four, I being one of the four. A lady of the minority called out, "It does not matter what is voted; we will all do just the same as before,"—which was more true than polite. Then there was another lady, who got up time after time, to make impracticable propositions; and she got snubbed and sat down and cried.... Oh dear, it does not do to be so thin-skinned! So you see, dear, all did not go on quite smoothly while I sat in the chair, with the bonnet on my head which you wore at dear Fred's wedding!

'This evening ... Herbert asked M. about the Conference. "I thought the first day nice, when Mrs. Perkins presided," said she. I laughed a little again, and, I think, complimented her on her sincerity.... It was clear that M. did not admire my way of presiding. Now, I had been voted thanks at the meeting; but dear M.'s honesty made me feel more than I had done before that I had *not* been very efficient. It is a good thing to know the truth.

'Is not this a funny little glimpse of life?... I doubt myself that there is much use in Conferences, except that it is nice that some dear workers should meet and know each other. We had many very choice ones.'

More than a year later Miss Tucker referred again to this Conference, when writing to Mrs. Hamilton upon the subject of whether or not secular teaching in schools should be undertaken by Missionary ladies:—

'I cannot explain to you all the difficulties that surround the question. We had a kind of wordy battle on the matter at the Ladies' Conference; and it was no good! When a lady proposed another Conference after another five years, I suggested after *ten*, but no one seconded poor Char! I am not calm and phlegmatic enough for these discussions, and, I am afraid, do not always see both sides of a question. I more and more now mistrust my own judgment, and sometimes feel rather disgusted with—myself!'

There are thousands of people who lack the power of looking on both sides of a question; but among them all few are humble enough to acknowledge the fact!—still more, to distrust their own judgment.

When the Conference was over, Miss Tucker remarked to one of her companions, 'I proposed ten years, because I thought that then I should not be here.' She was 'here' five years later, but was within a few months of her call Home.

> '*March 17, 1888.*—I will tell you of a curious surprise I had a few days ago. I was in my duli in one of the streets of Batala, when I met one of my most highly respected Native friends, the dear old Pandit, now the Rev. K. S.... A crowded street is not the place for a talk. The Pandit asked me to go to his village, O— —, and had evidently some particular reason for his request. As the next day was one of my village days, I promised to go then.... If I thought much about the cause of a visit being desired, I guessed that it either concerned some Mission work, or the health of the good Bibi. But I was utterly wide of the mark, and so I think will my Laura and Leila be, if they take to guessing.
>
> 'The dear couple had set their hearts on presenting me with a beautiful, richly embroidered white Cashmere shawl, which the Bibi, I know not how long ago, had bought ... from some one in distress. In vain I expostulated, in vain said that the lovely shawl was fit for the Queen, and that it was not suitable for me to wear anything so handsome; that it might be sold for the Mission. Both the smiling husband and wife were determined to have it round my shoulders; and I *had* to go away wearing it, though I took it off in the duli, and took care of it, as if it had been a child. Now, the Pandit and his wife want nothing from me; this was no case of giving in hopes of receiving. The whole thing took me by surprise.'
>
> '*April 21.*—We are soon to go—all in the heat—to share a 3 p.m. dinner at the Corfields, and meet the Bishop, Mr. Clark, and dear Herbert,—such a galaxy of good men, that we won't mind the heat, especially as my plump wadded umbrella is a real protection.
>
> 'I am reading—slowly—like a child enjoying a cake, that delightful *Life of Bishop Gobat*. I mean to buy a copy for myself; it would be so good for lending or extracting from. It is such a humbling book too. I feel like a barn-door chicken looking up at an eagle, and chirping, "I'm a bird too!" A pretty difference between them! Now to put on *your* sun-hat, and be off.'

'*April 26.*—You are quite right if you think your unnamed convert's idea of his baptism killing his mother a false one. It seems the *regular trick* here to draw back converts from Christ by telling them of a mother's illness. We feel in such cases the force of our Lord's words, "Let the dead bury their dead!" It seems hard at first; but experience shows us how needful is the caution.'

'*May 1.*—Neither has April gone out smiling, nor did "May come laughing o'er the plain." The one has gone out, the other came in,—in such a passion. It was so dark yesterday that I was reminded of a London fog. Minnie required a lamp to read by; a lamp, at 4¼ p.m. on a summer-day, shed its light on our dinner-table. This is my day for villages when I have extra kahars. I had ordered them not to come, should the day be as bad as yesterday; but come they did. Evidently these hardy fellows do not mind a dust-storm. They rather seem to enjoy it, ... and laughed merrily enough as we went along.'

'*June 1, 1888.*—I have to thank my sweet Laura for helping to provide me with a nice tussore dress for my visit to Murree. I cannot wear white there as I do in Batala, where it does not look odd, as almost every man, woman, and child appears in white. There is nothing like it for such hot weather. But in Murree, where there are many European ladies, I must dress more suitably, and also be prepared for any kind of weather, heat, cold, and torrents of rain. For my cold-weather apparel I have the very elegant grey dress, which dear W. and M. gave me a few years ago. When the weather is warmer my new tussore will be just the thing. I do not like writing so much about dress; but I wished to thank you for your kindness....

'Excuse a short letter, love. I have so much writing in the way of thanking for gifts to the Mission. Friends are so very kind. I have asked a kind Station-lady, Mrs. G., whether she will help me to sell at Murree beautiful things sent from England for the Mission. I am a bad saleswoman myself. I sometimes feel inclined to tell people *not* to buy what they do not require.'

'*June 19, 1888.*—I was so much interested to-day by our young Goorkha J.'s account of his own conversion and adventures, that I will try to write out the gist of it for you and dear Leila....

'Born of a Brahmin family in Nepaul, our Goorkha thought of himself as a kind of god. He would motion to beings of lower dignity to sit at a little distance from him; he was not to be polluted by their touch. The child, however, attended a Mission School at D——, and came a good deal under the influence of a Christian Convert, a Pandit (learned man). At the age of about twelve the boy resolved to leave father, mother, all, for Christ. He was too young to be baptized without his parents' permission, and was advised to go a long way off. To be able to do so, the boy sold his valuable gold earrings and bracelets, and, having thus a good stock of rupees, he made his start, not by any direct route, but through wild, uninhabited jungle.

'He was accompanied and helped by an older Hindu, a sad rogue, who had his own object, it appears, in assisting the flight of the wealthy young Brahmin. The country was rocky and infested by wild beasts. For two nights the fugitives slept in the trees, for protection against leopards, bears, and tigers. But this extreme discomfort could not be endured a third night; so they slept on the ground, after lighting fires to prevent any attack from fierce animals roaming about. The boy awoke,—I am not sure whether it was on that or a succeeding morning,—to find that the false Hindu had decamped with his money, clothes, etc. Happily, the boy-convert had secreted on his own person fifteen or twenty rupees; and with these, in the torn dirty clothes left to him still, the Brahmin went on, and found his way to where some Hindus dwelt. These were kind, but tried to dissuade him from changing his religion. The Goorkha was, however, evidently a boy of strong character. He made his way to a train, the first which he had ever entered, and reached Calcutta at last.

'Here he wandered from place to place, to find a school. Providence at last put the boy under the kind, almost paternal, care of the Rev. —— B., who nursed him through illness, and fed him himself. The Brahmin at first chose only to drink milk; evidently he still clung to caste. However, his prejudices wore away. Mr. B. took the lad on an itinerating tour, and afterwards placed him at school, first at C——, afterwards at R——. At R—— our boy, after receiving more religious instruction,—for he says that he knew very little,—was baptized by the name of J. After a while he was sent to Batala.... I hope that after a while he will study at a Theological College, and become a Catechist and Missionary to his own people. J. has written two or three times to his parents, but his letters have been returned....

'I am writing very early this week, as I propose starting for Murree to-morrow.'

'Murree, *July 11.*—On Friday week I propose beginning my homeward flight to Batala. It will be a different sort of life at the Gurub-i-Aftab. Here there are morning callers, and afternoon visitors, and luncheons, and tea-parties, and many a box-wala[122] or kapra-wala brings his wares, to tempt us, spreading out a variety of pretty things.... One of my pleasures is to see the lovely fair blue-eyed children going about with their ayahs. I am so much accustomed to see brown babies, that some of the English ones look to me almost like cherubs. The church-going is a great gratification; it is so nice to have prayers and sermon in English, and I greatly enjoy the hymns.... I enjoy my quiet morning walks in the lovely wooded paths on the hills. This house is very conveniently situated near the church; so one does not require much *mounting*, which is tiring. I do not attempt long walks, but stroll about. My dear Rowland and Helen have had much anxiety about their little Robin.'

'Batala, *Aug. 9, 1888.*—As our Dr. Miss Sahiba, Minnie, is away, I have now and then to try my 'prentice hand a little, but in a very humble, cautious way. I have nothing to do with making pills, but have invested in big bottles of castor-oil and turpentine. I have quinine, of course, and ammonia in case of bites or stings. I don't revel in physic, like Minnie; and dimness of sight and want of steadiness of hand do not serve to make me more fit to add Doctor to my name. What a blessing it is that some people actually *like* doctoring! I remember saying to my ... kind-hearted ——, now a doctor, that operations must be trying. "I *like* them," was his simple, truthful reply. Well—Buckland liked playing with snails and snakes. *De gustibus non disputandum!*'

On September the 10th, speaking of a planned trip to Lahore, to see her nephew and niece, she continues:—

'I propose after parting with the dear ones to sleep at the Mission House at Amritsar, and to-morrow go to the hospital, to see my dear ayah, Hannah, whom we sent there, not knowing that—as we fear—a deadly illness is on her. Dear, gentle, loving Hannah! she has served me faithfully for about seven years; and in all that time I cannot remember her doing *one* wrong thing, or saying *one* wrong word. A humble, gentle Christian, good wife, good mother,—ah! she is a sad loss to her family of seven, ... and also to your loving Char.'

'*Nov. 1. 1888.*—The first of November, darling Laura, and I am preparing for cold weather. I have taken my chhota janwar[123] (little animal, *alias* dear Fred's splendid foot-muff) out of its bag, to keep my feet warm in the morning, before my bath is ready. Eiderdown petticoat, etc., etc. O luxurious Char! It was a pleasure to me to-day to pay F., my new ayah, her first month's wages; there was a pleasant, half-grateful look in her eyes.... I *like* paying wages.

'My last dear ayah is not forgotten. I have given orders for a modest little monument of brick and mortar, to mark where Hannah sleeps. We have no stones here. I went to the cemetery with the mason, ... to give directions, and was struck by finding a tiny but touching memorial already on the spot. A very little wooden Cross, covered with paper, to facilitate the writing of an inscription. There was the date, of course in Urdu, and "Not dead, but sleepeth"; and "The Lord gave; the Lord hath taken away; blessed be the Name of the Lord." This tribute of love had been placed over his dear Mother's grave by J., the eldest son here, a lad of about fourteen. I mean to keep to his inscription, when the humble monument is placed over Hannah's dust. Dear woman! she was of the meek and quiet spirits who are precious to the Lord.'

'*Nov. 23.*—The last mail brought me letters both from my loved Laura and dear Leila; to both many thanks. My sunstroke was nothing to tell you about; for though I was sickening two days, the illness only lasted about six hours, and left, thank God, no dregs behind. I awoke quite serene from the state which had so alarmed my good friends, was able that very day to hold a little Bible-meeting, and to go to my city-work next day.'

About this time Mrs. Herbert Weitbrecht, who was then in England, wrote to Mrs. Hamilton, upon the question of Miss Tucker being advised to go home. As will be seen from the following little extract, her view was strongly adverse to this step.

> 'For one thing, the cold, in which Mrs. — — revels, would try the Auntie very severely. But there is more than this. You know she used to speak very freely to me; and I have a strong impression that she did not let you and her other friends at home know how much she suffered from the parting, how great a wrench it was to her. She used to say that she ... dreaded above everything the thought of having to go through such partings again.'

Probably no persuasions would have induced Miss Tucker to return. She had steadily made up her mind that in India she would live and die. Unless, indeed, she should be called elsewhere! At this very time she was deeply interested in the Andaman Islands, over which her nephew, Major Louis Tucker, had been appointed Chief Commissioner. On learning that a Mission among the Convicts was sorely needed there, she is said to have offered herself for the purpose,—if she could do good by going. Probably she thought of it as merely a temporary thing; as inaugurating, not as carrying on permanently, the work. But at her age, and in her feeble health, the very suggestion shows marvellous courage and energy.

The next letter is about a difficult case in England: a young Indian, with whom Mrs. Hamilton was acquainted:—

> '*Dec. 1.*—I have not answered your letter about poor Q. in haste. I received it the day before yesterday. Perhaps you will not like my thoughts; but you had better know them, sweet sister....
>
> 'It is a characteristic of the Native character to have little sense of sin. A conscience seems a thing to be created. Q. does not seem to see how grievously he has sinned, *is* sinning. He is clearly denying the Lord Who bought him; and that for worldly gain. Darling Laura, have you *quite* realised the greatness of the sin? To my view it was a mistake to ask Q. to dinner. "With such an one, no, not so much as to eat." Until Q. deeply repents, he is not fit to sit at your table....
>
> 'You may cite the Parable of the Prodigal Son. That is exactly what I would cite for *my* view of the subject. Poor Q., if a son, is the Prodigal Son, beginning to be in want, and hiring himself out,—feeding swine. If, when he was longing for

even husks, he had been coaxed and asked out to dinner, would he ever have "come to himself," would he ever have cried, "I will arise, and go to my Father?" Was it *easy* for him to go, in a far country, as he was? Was *he* not ready to sacrifice his pride, and go amongst his Father's servants as a beggar? If Q. would have the Prodigal's reception, he must do what the Prodigal did.

'Perhaps my Laura will remind me of St. Paul's injunction to the Corinthians to take back and "comfort" a gross sinner. But, remember, that man had first had some mysterious terrible punishment, — "delivered over to Satan for the destruction of the flesh," — and he was so deeply penitent, that there was danger of his being "swallowed up with overmuch sorrow." When Q. repents *like that*, let us all receive him and comfort him.'

Some may count this letter stern, viewed in the light of modern lax and easy notions. But Charlotte Tucker knew what she was about. She was living, at Batala, in the First Century of Christianity. Things would often be very differently viewed by us in England, if we could see them from the standpoint of the First instead of the Nineteenth Century.

CHAPTER XVII
A.D. 1888-1890 THE DAILY ROUND

The year 1888 closed with another sharp attack of illness, not so severe or so prolonged as that of 1885, but sufficient to cause anxiety. On the 16th of December, though 'far from well,' Charlotte Tucker went to church as usual; but all her 'wraps upon wraps could not keep her from catching cold.' On the 21st, Mr. Bateman, reaching Amritsar, was much disturbed by the arrival of a telegram from Batala, requesting Dr. H. M. Clark to go over immediately, as Miss Tucker was in high fever. There was some hesitation whether to start at once by ekka, or to wait for the early morning train; and the latter plan was decided upon. When Dr. Clark went, Mr. Bateman accompanied him; and he wrote to Mrs. Hamilton on the 23rd:—

> 'We reached Batala—"Sonnenschein"—together at 10.30 yesterday. The Auntie was reported sleeping without fever. She woke about 11; and Dr. Clark, after seeing her, telegraphed, "No immediate anxiety," to Mr. Clark, who on receipt would decide whether to go to Batala, or to come here (Lahore) for the "Quiet Day." The Auntie was very much pleased at my going over, and would not rest again till I had been into her room. She is in a comfortable, warm room. To my uninitiated eye she seemed to have everything about her which she could desire.... As I passed into the room Dr. Clark passed out, and behind the screen he whispered, "She is all right." She met me with almost a shout of welcome, and said a number of quasi-comic solemnities, squeezing my hands with great energy. She was a little flushed, and owned that she was weak, but as far as appearances went I have often seen her look worse when in full work. I felt very happy about her; but Dr. Clark said that there was a blueness and a twitching about the lips which he did not like, and that she was very weak. His "All right," he said afterwards, meant only, "You may safely go in." The fever kept off all day, and only returned about four in the afternoon.... It was 105 on Friday night.... I noticed that she

is very much more amenable to discipline than before. She admits that she can't walk or write decently, and she takes her medicine, including five grains of quinine, every three hours, very carefully and with great docility....'

One little remark that she made to Mr. Bateman was, 'Thank God, He has made me quite comfortable'; and again, 'I don't find that I can pray to God about myself; for I don't know what to say.'

'You are in a strait betwixt two,' suggested Mr. Bateman.

Miss Tucker did not like this, and she showed that she did not. Her friend adds, 'I attribute the slight twinge it gave her to her habitual dislike to being thought so well of, as that she might appropriate an Apostolic utterance.'

Another observation was as to the 'Quiet Day' in Lahore,—*she* was having a 'Quiet Week' given to her at Batala instead.

Some slight memoranda of things that dropped from her were jotted down at the time by Miss Dixie. 'Nil Desperandum' was often quoted in this and other illnesses; also she would generally try to sing 'Charlie is my Darling,'—no doubt a reminiscence of her old Stuart enthusiasm.

With reference to a Muhammadan school which had been shut some months before: 'The Muhammadans have done us a good turn! They have rubbed hard against our shield, and have caused our motto on it to shine bright.'

'My little musician is playing all day,' she said once. She was asked, 'What kind of tunes?' 'Now—"The Heavens are Telling." The harmony is beautiful. I can hear every note!' She was asked again, 'Does it play on its own account, or do you express a wish for special tunes?' 'It is sometimes wilful,' Miss Tucker said, 'and plays, "Charlie is my Darling," when I would rather it played something else. It plays tunes I have not heard since I was a child,—so correctly,—all in harmony!' One of her favourite hymns in illness was 'Peace, perfect peace';—but she 'did not like the last verse; it contradicted what went before.'

Happening to speak about different kinds of love, she observed,—'There is a passion, not a love, which I have known some women to have for another. That is not wholesome; it is a passion, not love.' Again, on the question of bringing others to Christ,—'We are only the housemaids! We open the door; but they come in, and go themselves up to the King.'

It was either after this illness, or after another of the same type that she said, 'I have felt that a beautiful Wing has been spread over me, which is lined with down and stitched with gold; and I am quite safe. Nothing can harm me so long as I remain under it!' Somebody rather unnecessarily remarked, 'But it is our own fault if we do not remain under it.' 'No,' Miss Tucker replied, 'we can't say that. Satan does give us a pull sometimes.' She was reminded that God's 'favour is always towards us'; but again she asserted the undeniable truth that God does sometimes permit His servants to be thus tried.

A long letter from herself to Mrs. Hamilton is dated December 21st, or two days before that written by Mr. Bateman, and apparently the very day on which Dr. Clark was summoned by telegram to Batala. This must have been a slip. The handwriting is shaky, but she speaks of her illness as past. With reference to the beginning of the latter, she says:—

> 'When in the afternoon (of the 16th) it was evident that I was seriously ill, the effect was magical. Up went my spirits like a balloon,—the curious effect which severe illness seems to have naturally upon me.... To be bright and cheerful in sickness and suffering costs me nothing, for it seems to come naturally; but I dare say that I get credit for a great deal of grace. It is so difficult for others, so difficult for *ourselves*, to distinguish between Nature and Grace.'

One may perhaps add that it is also unnecessary to do so,—unnecessary as regards ourselves, and utterly impossible as regards others. Better to leave such questions in the Hands of Him with Whom alone 'all things are naked and opened.' But evidently the subject had been much in Miss Tucker's mind. The long letter is half full of it.

On January 4 she wrote:—

> 'Now I dare say that you will want to hear how I am. Wonderfully well, though, of course, not strong. I went a short distance in my duli to-day. My late illness has quite convinced me that God has given me a capital constitution. I had, apparently, so much against steady recovery. Yet—there is no doubt of it—I *am* recovering. Except rather more weakness of the eyes and slight loss of flesh, no dregs seem left.'

> 'Batala, *Jan. 24, 1889.*—Many thanks for the printed extract from good Mr. Clifford's letter about the cure for leprosy.... I dare say that it *is* a valuable medicine when properly used; but probably the secret of its great success in the Andamans is that it was tried on convicts, who dared not refuse to rub themselves properly. Mr. Clifford writes that the exercise is part of the remedy; but I think that it would be wellnigh

impossible to persuade *free* lepers to rub themselves for four hours daily. They would greatly prefer leprosy and begging. Do you not know of the Indian mother who, when one of the Mission ladies told her to rub oil over her poor sick child's body, refused to take such trouble? "I have another!" said she. With dear good Father Damien it would be different.'

TO MISS 'LEILA' HAMILTON.

'*Feb. 16.*—The wood-pigeons are cooing, the little peach-trees displaying pink blossoms, the fields are green with young corn. Perhaps you will half envy us when you read this; but you would hardly envy us six weeks hence....

'In Mission life so much depends on one's companions.... One must not expect too much, for all Missionaries are fallible. One should remember one's own infirmities, and make allowance for those of others. In India we seem to live in glass houses; people are so well known; such a one is quick-tempered, such a one—but you can imagine what it is. There is little privacy even in the dwellings. There is no hall; the upper part of the outer door is glass; people see through, tap, and walk in.... India is a good place for preventing one from growing stiff and precise, and determined not to be put out of one's way. At Batala especially there is no starch.'

TO MRS. HAMILTON.

'*May 2.*—I could give you curious anecdotes of the Ramazan, the grand Muhammadan Fast, which has now begun. Minnie tells me of women in an ostentatious way bringing their bottles, as if for medicine, to the Dispensary; and then saying that they cannot take it—it is their fast. Why did they come then? To be admired for piety! Others come, looking rather piteous, though perhaps not really ill, that the Doctor Miss Sahiba may *forbid* them to fast. Minnie asked one woman whether she fasted. "I am poor; what can I do?" was the helpless reply. One not acquainted with the case might interpret this as, "I am helpless—I am only too often *obliged* to fast." It really means, "I am *too poor* to fast." You might imagine fasting to be rather economical. Quite the reverse! For instance, the — — whom Minnie employs is laying out a whole month's salary in *food for the fast*, to have it extra good. She will have two meat meals every night, to make up for not eating in the day. Does it not remind one of the Pharisees?'

Miss Tucker's birthday this year was signalised by the Baptism of one of the servants, and his whole family, including a little brown baby. After describing the event to her sister, with great delight, she added,—'Of course the new Christians were all invited to the simple feast under a moonlit sky, which dear Babu Singha gave in my honour. It certainly was one of the best, if not the very best birthday, kept by your now aged but truly loving Char.'

'*May 30.*—These last two mornings I have gone to help Miss Dixie by reading to her patients in the waiting-room of her Dispensary. There should always be some one to read, talk, sing, and keep order. Dear good Rosie Singha is wanted to make up medicines. I do not know what poor Minnie would do without her.... It is strange what difficulty we have in getting Native helpers for her (Miss Dixie).... You will have seen in the papers that noble devoted Father Damien has sunk to rest; his form sleeps in a leper's grave. What a wonderful life and death was his!'

'Simla, *June 13.*—Here is Char in Simla, the queen city of the mountain; but I do not think that I shall see much of it. I have a nice quiet walk near, commanding a noble view; and I go backwards and forwards along it, not troubling myself at all with climbing or sight-seeing. The air is very pure and fine; so I drink it in, and if anything is to give strength it ought to do so.... There seems to be a great deal of etiquette here,—people placed exactly according to rank at the grand parties.... I do not care much for what are really trifles, and am thankful that I have not to go out and be gay. I make the most of my age, which enables me, as it were, to sit quietly in a corner, and not even take the fatigue of rounds of visits. A lady had paid sixteen in one day, she said. Evidently, it is a matter of congratulation to find friends (?) not at home.... We take our meals at a table d'hôte, happily a quiet one. I sit between Louis and Lettie, so hardly speak to any one else, for I am shy of conversing across the table.'

'*July 18.*—Your "running about," love, has been on a milder scale than mine. On Friday last, knowing that I was to rise at about 3 a.m. (after a dinner-party at the C.'s), I did not entirely undress. Miss Warren and I started on our long journey downhill by the dim light of a clouded moon.

Laziness might have made us miss the evening train, for we had nearly a hundred miles' drive, in a succession of vehicles, to reach it; and we knew not what the state of the road might be.

'Vehicles, did I write? Would you call an elephant a vehicle? We came to a place where there was a good deal of water; the Gogra swollen by the rains. We were requested to quit the heavy gari, and go across on an elephant. The nice docile creature knelt down; and a man actually wished us to clamber up by its tail! He grasped it, so as to form a kind of loop for me to put my foot in! But I objected to this method of mounting, and managed to scramble up by means of a kind of big bag hung across the animal. There was no saddle or howdah; but the beast's back was broad, its pace gentle, and we held on by ropes fastened across the elephant. The good creature well deserved the two biscuits with which it was rewarded.'

The following letter was with respect to two young Indians, in whom Mrs. Hamilton had been much interested. One might hesitate to quote it, in fear of giving pain to the really true-hearted among Indian Christians; but *they* are not referred to! It seems necessary to show that Miss Tucker, despite her readiness always to think the best of people, was by no means always easily taken in; and that she gained wisdom through sad experience:—

'Batala, *July 31.*—I have received the following reply from —— about that Native in whom you have so long taken kindly, I fear little merited, interest. You do not yet, darling, know how little it costs Indians to write or speak in a way to please. They deceive even old experienced Missionaries....

'It seems almost cruel to throw cold water on my Laura's warm generous feelings, but I confess to an impression that Natives try to deceive one so much more pure-minded and honest than themselves. We get so grievously deceived and disappointed here, where we have much better opportunities of judging. But I hope that your —— may prove one of the real jewels which *are*—though not so often as we could wish—to be found amongst Orientals.

'*Aug. 1.*—Yesterday's post brought me a loving letter from my Laura.... A man[124] whom my Laura calls "my friend, ——," ought to turn out a fine fellow at last. Of course I cannot judge if the going to Paris will be good or not. I do not like hiding colours when a man has been baptized. With secret believers some indulgence is sometimes needed; but after Baptism, it seems to me that to pass for a Muhammadan is a sign—of danger at least. But you will talk over the subject with Rowland. Five minutes with him will be better than five long letters from me. O my Laura, I have so learned to mistrust myself, my judgment, my disposition; and I have been particularly tried this year by inconsistency in those of whom I had thought highly.'

TO MISS MINNIE DIXIE.

'*Aug. 17, 1889.*

'J. D., exemplary young man, has put all three harmoniums to rights. He says that the largest has 223 tongues, and that 25 were dumb. Perhaps I have not given the numbers quite correctly, but nearly so. A live scorpion was found in our drawing-room instrument. It cleverly managed to get away, but was happily found and killed. There was a regularly-conducted Batala Feast yesterday, given by M. in honour of Baby Baring's second birthday. As I walked towards the Singhas, I spoke with regret of the nice old-fashioned feasts, which seem to have gone out, when every one sat on the ground. Pleased was I to behold the cloth laid in the verandah, with no tables! We were to have an old-fashioned feast, after all. And a very nice one it was! About forty partook of it. To-day my nephew gives a smaller party in honour of his dear wife's birthday.'

TO THE REV. F. H. BARING.

'*Nov. 14, 1889.*

'I must give you good news. Another sheaf laid, by God's grace, on our Mission Plough. A nice gentlemanly young Brahmin from that school, K. K., openly received Baptism in the large Church last Sunday. As notice had been given to his family, there was such a tamasha as I had never seen in Batala before. Crowds gathered behind the extempore barricade to divide off the heathen in the Church—line above line of turbaned heads; and the doors were thronged. Without exaggeration, there must have been *at least* 200 people, besides us Christians. R. C., K. B., and A. B. (all converts) made very dashing daring extempore policemen to keep the Hindus from swarming in. The font was very near the sort of barricade; so our young candidate had to face the crowd,—amongst them one or two angry members of his family,—at the distance of only about two yards; but he bore himself like a hero, giving all his answers in a clear distinct tone. The most exciting part was getting our lad out of the church and safe off! The Hindus tried to stop and make the horse back; our boys pushed on behind with energy; and at last the tum-tum was off and away. I would not have missed the scene for something.'

Before entering on the correspondence of 1890, the following verses may be given, written in the course of that year for Batala boys; spirited in style as ever, though Charlotte Tucker was now verging on the age of seventy:—

A GENTLEMAN.

'What is it makes a Gentleman? 'Tis not his high estate, His liveried footmen, or the grooms that on his orders wait,— The horses and the carriages that stand before his gate, The tenants who bow low to him, and think him very great.

Chorus—

These do not make the Gentleman, whate'er his station be! 'What is it makes a Gentleman? Not colour of his skin,— The Negro, black as ebony, may yet be fair within; The weak, the lowly, and the poor, a glorious race may win,— There's nothing makes a man so low as cowardice and sin!

Chorus—

He cannot be a Gentleman, whate'er his station be! 'What is it makes a Gentleman? His dress is not the sign,— Though on each finger of each hand a jewelled ring may shine; His necktie may be elegant—his boots be superfine— Howe'er you dress a monkey, Sir, he is no friend of mine.

Chorus—

He cannot be a Gentleman, whate'er his station be! 'The real Gentleman is he whose aims are pure and high; Who scorns a base dishonest act, and tramples on a lie; Who treats the woman and the child with gentle courtesy, Who holds the Christian's faith and hope, so does not fear to die!

Chorus—

He is the real Gentleman, whate'er his station be!'

All these years, off and on, Charlotte Tucker's pen had been at work; and probably nothing that she ever wrote was of greater importance than the many tiny little booklets for translation into the various languages of India. After being composed by her in English they were rendered by competent persons into Urdu, Panjabi, Hindi, Bengali, Tamil, and were published at exceedingly low prices, to be sold by hundreds of thousands among the Natives of the country. Many were brought out by the Christian Literature Society for India, many more by the Punjab Religious Book Society. A small report of the latter Society, so early as about 1877-78, speaks of thirty-seven of A. L. O. E.'s tiny booklets as already published, and of fresh editions being in some cases already called for. A letter to her English Publishers, Messrs. Nelson & Sons, early in 1890, gives interesting information on the subject:—

'Batala, *Jan. 18, 1890.*

'I am much pleased to hear that *Beyond the Black Waters* is out at last, and return you many thanks for the copies for presentation, kindly sent for me.

'The subject of "cheap editions" of works published long ago is of great interest to me. I am living in an immense country, swarming with Muhammadans, Hindus, and Infidels, where Government is educating tens of thousands of lads, without giving them any religious instruction.... An evident breakwater for the waves of impiety and sedition is religious literature. But it must be very cheap, or hardly any Natives will buy it. I saw long ago in a Report of the Christian Vernacular Society, that for *one* book costing, if I remember rightly, about threepence, *forty* are sold costing a pie, less than a farthing.[125] I resolved to write one-pie stories; did so; and thousands and tens of thousands have been sold.

'A lady here has told me that *The Young Pilgrim* is out of print; she has vainly attempted to buy it. A cheap edition of that might, by God's blessing, be useful in India. Good paper is not needed; but clear type and a bright cover,—not pink, as that soon fades in India.

'As I went along in my duli, a kind of square box carried by men, to-day, to visit villages, I thought that the *Giant-Killer*—only the parable part, which would make a very moderate-sized book—might have a large circulation here. Natives like parables; and though the English portion of the volume, describing the Roby family, might not be suited to Oriental readers, Giant Sloth, Selfishness, etc., are quite as troublesome in India as in England. Would you like to make an experiment with this small publication? If so, I should gladly myself purchase for poor India £10 of cheap copies,—not more than sixpence each,—to be sent as from me to the Christian Vernacular Society's House, Madras. As soon as I heard of the parcel being shipped, I would send the cheque.'

When Miss Tucker was first starting for India, her brother, Mr. Henry Carre Tucker, had written to her upon the subject of literature for that land; and a short quotation from his letter may be appropriately given here. 'The great thing at present,' he wrote, 'is to disseminate widely Christian Vernacular Literature in all the languages, and suitable to the requirements of all classes, men, women, and children; rich and poor; educated and ignorant. Government is rapidly teaching most of the boys to read. We Christians must provide them with a wholesome literature. Few women and girls can be reached personally, but books penetrate everywhere, and may do an untold amount of secret silent good. The preparation and distribution of such Literature ought to be your great object. You might organise Female Colporteurs for the Zenanas and womenkind.' This last suggestion Miss Tucker does not seem ever to have taken up, or attempted to carry out.

Books for English readers still went on appearing from time to time. In 1885 she published *Pictures of St. Paul*; and in 1886 *Pictures of St. Peter* followed. In 1887 came *The Fairy in a Web*, and *Driven into Exile*. The year 1888 also saw two—*The Hartley Brothers*, and *Harold's Bride*, both being continuations of the two Picture volumes, named above. In 1889 *Beyond the Black Waters* was brought out; in 1890 *The Blacksmith of Boniface Lane*; in 1891 *The Iron Chain and the Golden*; and in 1892 *The Forlorn Hope*. When one considers her age, her failing health, and her ceaseless Zenana toil, one cannot but be astonished at the mental energy shown in getting through such an amount of writing as this.

On the 17th of February Miss Maria Hoernle left Batala, with the purpose of soon proceeding to England; and Miss Tucker wrote next day:—

> 'So closes a leaf of my life; for I doubt whether I shall again see on Earth one who nursed me too devotedly in 1885. Maria prefers Bengal to the Panjab; so, if she return, we have hardly a chance of meeting, unless perhaps at some Hill-Station.... I wonder if my dear Bhatija Francis Baring will ever return to India. He was for long my sole European companion.... Think of sixty-five Communicants last Sunday in Batala! We never had so many before.... The Bishop was pleased,—though tired by his village tour, seeing the seven little congregations of the Batala district.'

> '*March 7.*—You must not think of converts, love, as the fruits of my labour, but that, by God's blessing, of others. I have so many Zenanas and villages, with limited strength, that hardly one place gets more than *one* visit from me in a month, some not even that! My employment is trying to pull up weeds that cumber, and to *sow* good seed; but I have no time to *water*,—or very little, so far as Zenanas are concerned.'

The 8th of May, Miss Tucker's sixty-ninth birthday, passed quietly, without the usual feasting, on account of the death, three days before, of Babu Singha's wife, who, as Miss Tucker wrote,—'fell asleep in Jesus,' after some twenty-eight years of happy married life. The letter of May 8 is very full of sympathy with the bereaved husband and the nine children. In the latter half of the same letter, finished next day, comes the mention of 'another book' just written. 'I am making out the fair copy in my seventieth year. I have regarded *Beyond the Black Waters* as my chrysanthemum, a winter plant, lingering on even till December. But my *Blacksmith of Boniface Lane* must be a little sprig of holly. It has its prickles and its red berries. It has a historical—I suppose that I should say—root, not basis.'

TO MISS 'LEILA' HAMILTON.

'*June 4, 1890.*

> 'We had a very uncommon visitor, who came at about 4 a.m. on the 1st of June. I do not think that he ever came before. What say you to a Bagh-i-bilae, or Tiger-cat? He wanted to steal Miss Dixie's chickens, but lost his own life,—six men succeeding in the difficult task of killing the fierce beast. We have kept his skin, which measures three feet five inches from the tip of the nose to the end of his rather shabby tail;

so you see that he was a remarkable cat. The colour pale grey, with a darker stripe down the back. There must have been another curious visitor, and one who also left his skin, but without giving any one the trouble of killing him. The day after the death of the Bagh-i-bilae, Minnie found in her bath-room the overcoat of a snake about four feet long. He has made us a present of it; for there is no use in advertising for the owner of the skin. He gives it us gratis!'

TO MRS. HAMILTON.

'Murree, *June 27, 1890.*

'This day fortnight I expect to start on my long journey to Batala.... Life in a large Hill-Station is hardly congenial to an old Missionary. It is curious how *poverty* is pleaded here by the gay and fashionable, who live in goodly houses, entertain elegantly, ride nice horses, dress well, etc. "Every one is poor at Murree,"—that is to say, when money is required for religious or charitable purposes. L. is collecting for Lady Dufferin's Fund; a rich man's response was that the journey to Murree had cost him so much! The poor Chaplain complained from the pulpit of the shabby collections for the Lahore Cathedral.'

In her letter of July 2 she wrote,—having been told of shaking her head in Church at something that she disapproved,—'I am trying to cure myself of that trick.' It had grown to be so frequent a habit, that one of her younger companions had already mentioned the tendency. If anything was said which she did not quite like, or even if in thought she recurred to something which she regretted, she would say nothing, but would sit silent, gently shaking her head. On being remonstrated with, she showed no annoyance, but at once said cheerfully,—'When I shake my head, you must *rap the table*!' The genuine humility of this answer is even more remarkable than the fact that, at her age, she should soon have entirely overcome the peculiarity.

On July 16 she described herself as 'in a frisky mood, on account of getting back to Batala, and finding things so nice here, weather included;'— and a little later, 'It is so nice to be amongst my brown Christian boys again!'

'*Aug. 22, 1890.*—I must amuse you and dear Leila by a little Oriental episode. A nice simple young widow, called W., is being prepared for Baptism. Female converts, who have not husbands, are specially welcome, as there is a great difficulty to poorer Christians about getting wives. Even before W.'s baptism, therefore, —— wished to secure her for a favourite convert. I spoke for him to W., and she consented just to see M. N., being assured that, if either she or he were not satisfied, there should be no marriage. As we are very proper here, the important interview took place in my presence; but I went a little aside, so as to be no *gêne*. The man seemed very sensible and nice. He began religious conversation at once, questioning the girl to whom he was paying his addresses, as a Pastor might have done with a candidate for baptism.

'So long as the wooer kept to this, all appeared going on well. M. N. questioned, and W. answered in her simple innocent fashion. But when something more personal was said,—I did not hear what, but I suppose that its gist was, "Will you marry me?"—I felt that there was some sticking, and came to the rescue. I asked W. if she were willing; and a little in the spirit, though not in the words of the old song—

'"Amazed was the laird, when the lady said—'Na!'"

'I was surprised, and so I think was the visitor. I asked again, to make sure; and again came a quiet decided negative. So of course I let "Mistress Jean" "turn awa'." ... W. has a perfect right to say "Na," if she prefer a life of sewing, grinding corn, etc., to trying matrimony a second time. I like her the better for her independent spirit.'

'*Aug. 28.*—I think that this August has been the pleasantest month that I have spent this year. The temperature, quite unusually mild for August, suits me admirably; for my idea of a perfect temperature is from 80° to 85° in the house. It is getting into the 90°s that is trying. There is a good deal of sickness about from damp, but damp does not appear to hurt me, and it makes the air so soft.'

'*Sept. 12.*—I have written through dear Leila my triple thanks for the very elegant tasteful dress and pretty jacket. The cloud I am keeping for Minnie, whom I hope to see back on Tuesday. The women in Batala will be so glad to have the "Star" open again. Dear sweet Daisy Key and I will be glad too to have the doctoring in the compound taken off our hands. Some one or other seems to be perpetually ill. Castor-oil and quinine have to be freely used. Happily both are easily procured, especially the first....

'As I was walking in the city early one morning,[126] a party of Government schoolboys passed me, marching in order, in evident imitation of our Christian boys. A minute or two afterwards a very respectable-looking middle-aged Native, probably their master, ran after me. I halted, to know what he wanted; and something like this curious conversation passed between us, in English,—

'Master. "I beg your pardon. Do you pronounce opíate or ópiate?"

'I. "Ópiate."

'M. "Who were the Jacobins?"

'I. "Bad men, who cut off other people's heads."

'M. "Were they Roman Catholics or Protestants?"

'I. "Neither. They had no religion."

'M. "Were Jacobins connected with Jacobites?"

'I. "No; those were followers of King James."

'M. "One more—what is 'Black eye,'—'give a black eye?' I cannot find it in the dictionary."

'To this funny question also I gave a brief answer, and then my volunteer pupil left me,—I hope satisfied with his lesson.'

'*Oct. 14, 1890.*—The shadow of consumption which *may* end fatally is on two dear Native Christians here. One is R. U., a well-educated Convert from Narowal, who has suffered much for the Faith. The other is dear Babu Singha's youngest daughter, Bini. The death of her loved mother in May was a terrible shock to Bini. Babu Singha, a most tender father, has gently intimated to his darling child that perhaps she may be the first to see that dear mother again. Bini is quite pleased at the thought....

'But oh, Laura, we have had in our Mission lately something worse, oh, so much worse! It has been as startling as a sudden thunder-clap. K. K., the young Brahmin, over whose baptism we so rejoiced, who seemed so brave, so true, who sat at our table ... and actually has been employed to *teach the Bible*, ... *he* has apostatised; *he* has become a fearful illustration of our Lord's most terrible parable,—"then taketh he (Satan) others more wicked than himself," etc. I am beginning to believe that this wilful apostasy, after clear light given, is what is spoken of in Heb. vi. I can remember no example, either in the Bible or Mission-life, of any apostate deliberately choosing to forsake Christ, after being received and welcomed, being "renewed unto repentance." We have had so many dreadful backsliders,—who have never returned. Alas! alas!... In no case *fear* the motive, but worldliness or covetousness. When to my surprise I heard that K. K. had fallen, my spirit could not readily recover.... Poor dear N. C. began his sermon on Sunday something like this,—"My spirit is heavy; I am very sorrowful." It was a brave sermon, nevertheless, about "holding the fort." But now he is the only Christian teacher in his school; and we have to face the mockery of the exulting foe! The matter is of course known all over the city. But the Lord reigns, and all enemies shall—*must*—be put under His Feet. Amongst those who *will* rejoice will be those who are saddened now, like your loving Char.'

'*Oct. 25.*—I want to tell you and dear Leila about the trial in the Singha family, but wish to wait till I have had to-day's report of the state of Bini, the dear girl about fifteen, who appears to be dying of consumption. Bini has perhaps never recovered from the effects of the shock caused to her loving heart by her mother, Mrs. Singha's, unexpected death. The poor child, arriving at the Batala station, heard suddenly that her mother was dead.'

'*Later.*—I have just come from the Singhas. Bini lingers still on this side of the river. She is more to be envied than pitied. On Thursday, two days ago, her pain ceased.... She was "quite happy," "quite ready," "why delay?" ... Last night must have been a glorious night for Bini. She spoke to this effect,—"I have been in Heaven, and saw Jesus Christ and my Mother. I did not see the others; they were there, but *somewhere upstairs.*" When some one spoke to Bini of her "dream," she did not like the word. "It was not a dream," she said.... If this be death, it is a blessed thing indeed!'

'*Oct. 31.*—You will see from my note to dear Mr. Baring that sweet Bini's long trial is over. With what joy she departed! I am telling the story in villages and Zenanas. She who had so little opportunity of working for God in her brief life, bears powerful testimony now by her death to Muhammadan and Hindu. To go joyously, in the morning of her life, to death, as to a bridal,—this is a proof of the truth and power of Christianity, which who can gainsay? I went on the day of Bini's departure to three Zenanas, which bigotry has closed. I asked no leave but went in,—I was pretty sure of a hearing, when I went to describe the death of Babu Singha's daughter.

'What a contrast between Christianity and Muhammadanism, Hinduism, *any* other religion! As Bini lay near her pure white coffin, with flowery Crosses above her, a party of the rather upper, educated men of Batala came to pay customary respect to the bereaved father. They were taken right up to where the white-clad form lay peacefully on a charpai.... At Bini's funeral the contrast was most striking; for as the white flowery coffin was carried to its resting-place, we all singing hymns of praise, the Hindus were—about fifty yards to the left of us—burning a corpse. To the right, flowers and music; to the left, fire. The miserable wail of the heathen over their dead was not then heard; only our hymns, and then beautiful words uttered over a peaceful grave.'

'SUNSET,' A. L. O. E.'S THREE-ROOMED HOUSE

CHAPTER XVIII
A.D. 1890-1891 IN OLD AGE

Letters at this late period of Miss Tucker's life become so abundant, from numerous quarters, that the main difficulty is in selection, the main cause of regret is that so few can be used. The history of 1891 and 1892 may be told chiefly by Miss Tucker's details of what went on. Miss Dixie remained her constant companion in the little Mission bungalow all these years,— except when absent for her summer holiday, or on furlough. Others came and went, remaining a longer or a shorter time in Batala. Dr. Weitbrecht had settled down as C.M.S. Missionary in the place; and Mr. Bateman, stationed at Narowal, came and went on itinerating expeditions.

Charlotte Tucker still lived her life of rigid simplicity; though perhaps certain indulgences, immaterial when she was younger and in more vigorous health, had now become a positive necessity. Long Indian toil, as well as sharp illnesses, had told upon her; and at seventy she had every appearance of being ninety. Yet, through weakness, weariness, and languor, she struggled on, and kept up her steady round of work.

The little 'Sunset' house, in which she lived, consisted mainly of the following: bath-room, size 8 feet by 8; dressing-room, size 13 feet by 8; the one large principal room, size 24 feet by 13, divided by a screen into bedroom and sitting-room; and the verandahs. Miss Tucker's chief room has been described to me by one who spent months at Batala, as, at this date,—'Rather bare and shabby, and used to have rather an untidy look.... As you went in from the verandah in front, the fireplace was on your left, and a sofa, with a screen behind it, screening off the bed, on your right. In front of you was the little table, where she used to write. I cannot remember all of the furniture; there was not very much,—I think some shelves on each side of the fireplace.'

This does not sound too luxurious. No doubt Miss Tucker might, without expense, have made her rooms much prettier, but for her passion for giving away. She seldom kept for herself more than was imperatively needed. While on this subject, it may be worth remarking, as regards the food of the Missionary ladies in Batala, that the cost of it has been found to amount, on an average, to about eight annas a day,—an anna being worth rather less than a penny. The said estimate applies to an ordinary time, including a certain amount of entertaining of visitors. Probably the cost would be much the same in other parts of the Panjab, unless it were slightly more in large Stations.

A few scattered sentences from the Journal may precede the letters of 1891:—

> '*April 30, 1889.*—Villages.... Sikh bibi very nice. I said, "I am very weak. If you heard that I died, what would you say?" Reply: "Gone to Jesus! Gone to Heaven!" After a while I asked, "Were I to hear of your death, what should I say?" A little delay; then a bibi observed on the *kirpa*, mercy, of Jesus, and thought that He might take them too.'
>
> '*Aug. 31.*—"Faint, yet pursuing," must be my motto. The two boys from — —, who came to Anarkalli, as if resolved to embrace Christianity, but, being without root, left us again, seem to have done much harm. The Muhammadans more bitter than before. Twice this week I—an aged servant of Christ—have been turned away from the Zenanas, to which I went in gentleness and kindness. To-day I was rejected at a fourth.... It is a strain upon the threefold cord of Faith, Hope, and Love, this deliberate choosing of darkness instead of light, Barabbas instead of Christ. We need the prayers of God's people, and to remember the promise, "In due season ye shall reap if ye faint not."'
>
> '*Sept. 4.*— ... Two places very nice. B. is determined to be a Christian, and teach his wife. Wants Urdu Gospel....
>
> '*Sept. 5.*— ... Felt ill; half-blind; yet generally well-heard....
>
> '*Sept. 6.*— ... Ophthalmia, but managed to go to Q. five places....
>
> '*Dec. 12, 1889.*—D.G. Hindus cross. As I mounted dark stair, heard "Buha band."[127] However, I ventured up, smiling, and said,—"When you come to the Dispensary, the door is not shut." There were four women; the two elder cross, not the younger. At first no seat was offered me; then some one said, "Buddhi,"[128] on which a small mat was brought, and the old woman meekly sat down. I tried to make my visit pleasant, showed my Golden Tree, and sang. It was a kind of breaking of ice. I took care not to stay very long. When I had risen, the two younger salaamed. I turned, smiling,

to one cross old lady, and coaxed her to return my salaam. After a little while she did so; but I wanted to conquer the toughest also. The younger women listened, much amused, to my polite expostulations on her rudeness. At last the old hand went up to the brow, and I departed, contented. The ice was broken. One can go again.'

'*Dec. 25, Christmas, 1889.*—Nice. D., B., and children, made catechumens.'

'*Dec. 27.*—The best day, I think, that I have ever had in Zenanas.... N. B., A very nice visit. Two fine young men, and at least seven women of various ages, appeared pleased, interested, and without any bigotry. So much inclined towards Christianity did one man in particular seem, that I spoke of the advantage of a united family accepting the Truth, and expressed a hope that all would come out. "Sat!"[129] echoed the Hindu heartily, throwing up one of his hands, as though to give force to the word.'

'*June 29, 1890.*—I have, three times in as many weeks, been able freely to show a Bible picture in Islami schools, and speak of Christ. To-day, as I walked in the streets, twice tradesmen in their little shops wished to see my picture. I stopped, and others gathered round, whilst I explained.'

'*Sept. 2, 1890....* K., she sad. Seems to regret death of her poor young S., whom she kept such a prisoner, and of whom I thought, "If any one in that quarter be a secret believer, it is she!" I could seldom get into the house. The sweet S. was quite a prisoner. I have even stood before the window, and sung in the open lane, hoping that S. would hear the sound of my voice, like imprisoned Richard. I hear that S. gave birth to a girl, "a very beautiful tiny child," who only lived for a month, and the young mother soon followed. I have strong hopes that both are with the Lord Jesus.'

'*Feb. 9, 1891.*— ... I have suffered greatly from chilliness this cold weather. Perhaps in no winter during my whole life more. Old age. Ague.'

'*March 25, 1891.*—Song. W. B. Buckle; but my best hearer was R. L., very interesting schoolboy. He met me at my first Zenana, and followed me to all the others. He was so nice,— even singing bhajans—that I thought at first that he must have learned at the Plough. With interest, amid interruptions from women, listened to story of the three Jews in the furnace, and told it afterwards in another Zenana. He was a help to me, explaining the Buckle, etc., very nicely. When the subject was Christ's Ascension, the boy said that He had gone up to God Almighty. I intend to write out the song for the dear fellow.... His heart seemed so impressionable, and his face brightened at the thought of the Crown to be given to "those who believe in Jesus." "I want to be a Christian," he said in English. Lord, bless him. Give him the Crown.'

'*April 13, 1891*.... R. E. took me into her arms; felt so slim encircled by them. I noticed a quantity of jewels on her arms. She popped her bare feet on my knee,—I was seated on the ground,—to show me the jewels on them. Her amount of clothing was by no means proportionate. Presently down went her forehead on my lap. I silently hoped that there was not much oil on her hair.'

'*May 14.*—Hindus very nice. My A. B., cheerful-looking C. D., another whom I do not know so well, E. F. These three all hope to meet me in Heaven. When I said to C. D., "But how can we go? We are sinners!"—her simple reply was, "Jesus Christ, Guide." I have hopes of these three.'

'*May 15.*—F. G., nice intelligent man. I was surprised at a *little* boy, H. I., being able to read. Gave him hymn-book. Was much followed about by boys....'

'*May 25, 1891*.... Felt the weight of years much. Work a struggle! Lord, help me!...'

'*June 4*.... L. very nice. When I said that she was patient, poor dying hand pointed upwards. Peace on face. Many listened....'

'*June 22*.... I am to start to-day for Dalhousie. Feel old and rather worn out. If I live to 1892 must not stay down[130] so long....'

'*Aug 14, 1891*.... I sat outside with Bibis, in front of ——'s house. The door half open, behind it pretty smiling young Bibi, who again and again silently made signs to me to come in. Did so, and sat beside her. She did not utter one word, but by her looks tried to show me that she received the Word, and believed. She only said "Salaam," when I left. I read to her of Christ being the Good Shepherd, His own words.'

'*Dec. 24.*—J. ill; sweet. Told me that, sitting up in bed, she saw beings come in, clothed in white shining raiment. Felt frightened. Asked why they did not speak. Afterwards fell asleep, and dreamed of being taken to a beautiful place. She is, we think, a true believer, confesses herself sinful, and looks to Christ for salvation. Asked her if she would like baptism. "Yes." "Would your husband allow it?" "No."'

These are specimens of the longer entries. The majority are exceedingly brief, consisting for the most part of names, initials, and single words. Letters to Mrs. Hamilton in the early part of 1891 are unusually few: not that the usual number were not written, but few have been kept. In the spring of that year there was some discussion as to the name of 'The Plough School,'—her own favourite name for the School, which meant much to her. One cannot but regret that any stir should have been made about the matter, when she had been the 'mother' of the school. The criticism having been put forward, however needlessly, she wrote to Mr. Baring:—

'By-the-by, the name "Plough" is objected to, as sounding like a public-house.... How could we choose a name that would signify entire dependence on God?... The Plough appears to be flourishing. Boys come to it even from what we call the large Government School. Numbers have arisen to about 113. To-day I had no fewer than seven rather superior boys from the Plough. They come for religious conversation and Bible pictures.'

On the 17th of June 1891 she wrote to Mrs. Gardiner about the recent death of that remarkable man, Bishop French,—no longer holding the position of a Bishop, but working as a simple Missionary.

'My dear Mrs. Gardiner,—Though June in the plains is not the most favourable month for letter-writing, especially to a Septuagenarian, I will not let your kind note remain longer unanswered.

'Yes, indeed, our late loved Bishop French was a saint, one whose memory is sweet, whose example is lofty. You will have seen the article in the *Panjab Mission News*. I think that it was written by Rowland Bateman, who, so like himself, feels not having rushed off in all the heat, to have been at the side of his venerated Friend, left alone in a land of strangers. But the dear Saint was not alone! What a glorious ending to his beautiful course! He reminds one, when dying in the grapple with Muhammadanism in the very home of its birth, of the Swiss hero, who broke the phalanx of the enemy by clasping the spears of the foremost in his arms, and so receiving them into his breast.

"'Make way for liberty,' he cried;

'Make way for liberty!'—and died."

'Of course there will be a Memoir of Bishop French,—but where is the Boswell competent to write it? Who could give all the delicate touches, needed for a perfect portrait of one with so many idiosyncrasies?

'How well I remember the dear Bishop coming all the way from Lahore,—when there was no railway,—to visit me, when I was supposed to be dying.[131] He sat by my bedside, gently talking. I do not remember that I said anything to him. I was looking up at his face, and thinking what a lovely medallion might be made of it in wax! It was an earthly thought; but when you recall the delicate features, pure complexion, and saintly look, of that countenance, you will hardly wonder at the sick woman's reflection.

'My letters, or rather letter, from England came in when I was engaged in writing, and you will not wonder at the blot on the last page.... I feel now disinclined to write at all. My beloved sister, Mrs. Hamilton, has been seriously ill; but, thank God, to-day's account of her is good.—Yours affectionately,

C. M. Tucker.

TO MISS MINNIE DIXIE.

'*(From the Hills) July 4, 1891.*

'I am not timid about snakes; but H. has seen four lately, and it is only common-sense to look under one's bed, as the heat compels open windows and doors. I have only fish-insects and tarantulas at present, but am promised plenty of scorpions, centipedes, and leeches, in the rains. You know I have not your talent for squashing reptiles; and if I called out for help in the unpleasant business, I doubt whether any one would hear me. I rather think that this will be my last visit to the Hills, and that Amritsar will be my Sanatarium in future.'

The two next letters to Miss Dixie are about the outbreak of smallpox in Batala. She was 'quite ready to nurse a smallpox patient, should the malady spread.' And again,—' Why should I delay my return? As a Missionary, I am liable any day to meet children with smallpox full out. I hope to be with you in about a fortnight.'

TO MISS LANGLEY.

'Batala, *July 29, 1891.*

'It is very kind of you to ask what kind of things would be most useful here. For *sale*, pretty little articles of dress for English children, from one day old to five years, are most readily disposed of. We are afraid of woollen articles, as they are so difficult to keep. White ants are a real puzzle at Batala.... Happily cotton or silk they attack much less. Gentlemen's neckties, of a fashionable shape, would be likely to sell well. Station-people in India think *at least* as much about fashion as Londoners do. A few pretty cosies and toilet or tea-table covers would be nice, and some elegant dolls. These would suit for sales. For presents in schools—cheap dolls, gay and rather gaudy; bags, with cotton and tape; kurtas, common gay print, that will wash. I dare say that Miss Cockle could supply a pattern. The kurtas need to be made of Oriental shape, or they would not be worn by the school-children.'

An attack of ophthalmia in her eyes, which must have caused much suffering, is made light of in her letters; and in the same passing manner she alludes to a fall, whereby her face was turned black and blue. The main point in connection with this accident seemed to her to be the kindness and sympathy shown by Batala people, when she went to visit them, and the fact that nobody smiled at her discoloured and swollen features.

TO MISS LEILA HAMILTON.

'*Sept. 12, 1891.*

'You will see a half-sheet; it belonged to a whole one, but the first half, alas! I have had to tear up; for it gave such a bright account of one, who, *only to-day*, I have found out has been deceiving us for many months!... Let us drop the painful subject.

'I had a visit early this morning from a *real* servant of God, dear old K. S.! One thinks of him rather as the learned and pious Pandit, than as the ordained Pastor; he leads such a wandering life. His faithful heart was heavy to-day, from the inconsistencies of professed Native Christians. He thought them better out of the Fold than in it;—so do I, for many are not *sheep* at all!

'I have not yet heard whether dear Mr. Bateman has recovered. I have written to him to-day. My letter will not cheer him, but he must know facts. Blindness is no benefit. We want *light* and *air*. Do you know, dear, that we felt our church dreadfully close,—yes, for years and years. The cause was obvious to us ladies. The doors and *lower* windows were often opened; the *upper* windows *never*! It was troublesome to get at such high ones; so year after year the bad air, which came from breath, ascended, and had no vent. Last Sunday, after my earnest protest, the windows were opened, and we breathed pure air!

'We are very quiet now; but in two or three weeks will begin the rush *from* the Hills; the season for work beginning, and the season for visiting too.... It is possible that in the beginning of October I may go for a week or so to Futteyghur with sweet Daisy Key, to teach the Christian peasants in that out-of-the-way spot. I think that the quietness, with one choice companion, would suit me better than the bustle of many arrivals at Batala. About the 1st of November I am engaged to go for a short visit to dear Louis and Lettie at Rawal Pindi.... The journey is not a very fatiguing one, as I can go all the way by train. Rawal Pindi is a city at the foot of the Himalayas; there is no mounting up.'

'*Sept. 16, 1891.*—My own sweet Sister, I do confess with regret that I wrote too hastily about — —, as dear M. C. does not think him bad, and hopes that he may be useful in time. I was vexed and impatient at my Laura being so worried, year after year.... But I was wrong, dear, I frankly own it! I wonder when I shall be given grace to be really loving, gentle, and patient!

'Poor dear Daisy and I have been sadly tried lately by the wickedness of those in our own compound. We both feel that it will be a relief to get away for a while to Futteyghur, which we shall probably do in the beginning of October.... But oh, let me not be so ungrateful to the Lord, or so unjust to dear excellent Native Christian friends, as to say in my haste, "All men are liars!" Poor Daisy thinks Batala the most wicked place that she has ever been in; and so do I? But precious jewels come *to* Batala, though very few *out* of it....

'But I must not write only of trials, love. If you could have dropped in upon us yesterday evening, you would have thought us a very happy party. See Char, in one part of the room, playing at chess with our good Pastor, Nobin Chanda;[132] ... dear Babu Singha, the excellent and wise, a special comfort to me, looking on in his quiet benevolent way. At the other side see sweet Daisy, animated and bright, playing at our famous Batala game with a choice set of Natives; ... and last, not least, dear Rosie Singha, our honorary and very steady worker in the Dispensary. I feel giving these kinds of parties a real duty; and they give, at little cost, so much innocent enjoyment. It is well for the Missionaries too to have pauses, in a struggle with so much that is repulsive and saddening.... I think that Rowland is not now actually ill, as he writes about being in the midst of a sermon. I hope that he will be able to pay Batala a flying visit before long.... He has so many Missionary troubles, and we cannot help adding to them. But—

'"Soon and for ever, we'll see as we're seen,
And learn the deep meaning of things that have been!"'

'*Sept. 27, 1891.*—I will steal a bit from the morning to write a little to you. We are living rather in a bustle at present; the tide of Missionaries running down from the Hills, rather sweeping over Batala. Dear Rowland is here.... Miss Boyd is here. She is to be married, please God, next week.... Her visit has been a real help to me, at a time of much Missionary difficulty.... Her Betrothed has been to Muscat, to gather information about the last days of dear Bishop French.... Miss —— returned here on Saturday; Miss Dixie and the Corfields start for Batala to-day. One lady comes here from Amritsar to-day; we are to start her from hence at 4 a.m. to-morrow, Tuesday.... I shall be very glad to be quietly off, ... out of a kind of whirlpool. We will have eight at dinner to-day; quite as much as our table will hold.'

'Futteyghur, *Oct. 11.*—I watch with much interest the Christian father, R. M., when at our long Services his little four-years old Z. is beside him. It is lovely to see the peaceful confiding loving clinging trust of the little child, as she cuddles to her strong father, and his gentle tenderness to the wee girl.... It makes me think of our Heavenly Father and us, His weak little ones. But an elder girl of R. M. was bitten by a snake; and then the tender father showed "the hardness of love." He resolutely cut out the poisoned part with a penknife. The poor child screamed terribly, but still the parent cut on. I dare say that his own heart felt gashed. The child was saved. O when our Heavenly Father thus wounds to save, may we have grace to lie still!'

One would much like to know the rest of this story, and how the poor father managed to keep his little girl from bleeding to death. His courage must indeed have been great.

Later in the same letter, when again on the never-failing topic of troubles and disappointments in the work, Miss Tucker says,—'O what need we Missionaries have of wisdom! We are so liable to make mistakes.'

TO — — — —

'*Oct. 24, 1891.*

'I was in Sikh villages this morning. The Sikhs are more friendly than the Muhammadans. I have often told them that if their respectable Guru Nanak were here on Earth now, he would probably become a Christian. I said that I had heard that there was something about our Lord in the Granth. The Sikh with whom I was conversing at once gave me the "Slok," and translated its difficult antique Panjabi. This is the Slok in English; "That Cutter of demons' heads, the world's revered Jesus!" The Sikh said that "Isa" (Jesus) was thought by them to be "Ishur,—God Almighty." I replied that we too called Jesus, God!'

TO MRS. HAMILTON.

'*Oct. 30.*—Many many thanks, mine own sweet Sister, for yours of the 8th, and all your loving thought for Char.'s comfort. You would keep the bird in a golden cage, lined with soft fur! But Char. is a bit of a wild bird, and likes to fly about freely. The fur will be delicious on cold mornings and evenings; but to wear it all day, even in December, would feel exhaustingly warm. One needs to adapt oneself perpetually to the changes of temperature in December and January; this needs a little Indian experience and common-sense. The want of these two things is one cause of Indian break-downs. Inexperienced Missionaries think it safe to do in India what they have done in old England! If you consider, love, that I have kept my health, with some few interruptions, for almost sixteen years in India, you may allow that I am a fair manager of it. I am thought rather a wonder.

'As for having "a really nice capable maid to wait upon" me;—O dear!—*dear*—dear!! I might fill a whole line with such exclamations, to express my almost *horror* at such a proposal! Europeans, except good working Missionaries, who can *help*, are dreadful anxieties and troubles. An Englishwoman in service is always a *possible* invalid, and a *probable* grumbler. I never in my life could stand a person running after me and watching me. I have an ayah to attend to my room,—and could have plenty of darzies to mend my clothes, but I prefer doing a little stitching myself. I am not always tumbling down like a ninepin,—but I would *prefer* tumbling once or twice a month to having any one always watching me. Dear Minnie insists on handing me to my room at night. You must remember that I am the adopted Aunt of a Doctor Miss Sahiba.

'This is rather a frisky note, darling. When I am a *real* invalid, I am said to be a good one; but I am strongly averse to becoming one when I am in fair health.... I know how dear Laura and Leila would constantly be putting soft fetters of love round me; but they would find me an obstreperous bird. I should break the fetters by sudden astonishing efforts,—as I fled from the Doctor lady who came from Amritsar. I knew that the Weitbrechts wanted her to see me. After breakfast she went with Dr. W. into his study, to look at something. I saw my opportunity, hurried down the long stair, and into my duli;—

'"They're gone! she's gone,—over, etc."

I knew that I was safe, as Batala has twelve entrances; and no one could tell which I had taken. It was rare fun, and seemed to do me more good than physic could have done. So take no anxious thought about me, love.'

The being 'handed to her room at night' was found to be a necessity in her old age. After spending the evening in Sonnenschein with the younger ladies,—generally either reading aloud, or playing games,—she had to go out into the front verandah, and to pass along it till she reached the door of her own little 'Sunset' dwelling. If alone, she was apt to stumble, or to run against something, and the regular plan was adopted of either Miss Dixie or one other of her nieces always accompanying the older lady, on this small nightly pilgrimage.

TO MISS LAURA VERONICA TUCKER.

'*Nov. 18, 1891.*

'Oh, dearest Laura Veronica, what a warm capital web you have spread for her whom you call Fairy Frisket. Certainly I look very unlike a *fairy*; and a very comfy rug is far more suitable for me than gossamer wings or glittering wand! A bibi expressed surprise to-day that a weak old woman could sing; but I told her that I sing every day in my life. If I stopped for a week, perhaps my throat might find out my age! I must not give it a chance of so doing. The same with my feet; the dear kind E——s were always offering me a drive, and I often took one with L.; but—oh, my friends, Misses Feet, you had to do your work too. No laziness tolerated; or you might presume to fancy yourselves antiquated. Now I am back in harness again, have been to the city to-day, and intend to visit a village-school to-morrow, unless Daisy Key go instead. She is far better at teaching than I am. But I am afraid that I have not yet thanked my sweet niece for the capital rug. I do so now with a kind kiss....

'Yesterday, in the railway carriage, I offered a wee book by Spurgeon to a tall big man, connected with the railway department. He asked me immediately if I were related to ——, and gave his opinion that —— was a real good man. My frank companion expressed, however, a general dislike to Missionaries. "Why do you not like us?" I asked mildly. He had evidently not been fortunate in some that he had known,—their names were not familiar to me. He disliked their preferring working on Natives instead of their own countrymen, and evidently thought them too comfortable! But what *can* I do, when my dear relatives send such charming gifts to your attached old Auntie Char?'

TO MR. AND MRS. ST. GEORGE TUCKER.

'*Dec. 12, 1891.*

'Your very handsome and very kind—only *too* handsome—gift reached me safely this morning; just the right time for the arrival, as the air in the morning is very keen, and then fur is a real comfort. Much has your fine jacket been admired,—so "beautiful," so "grand." But it does not look unsuitable even for Missionary use. Very many affectionate thanks for this token of your affection. It quite strikes as well as gratifies me, to see how little difference *sixteen* years of absence seems to make as regards the loving-kindness of my dear relatives. They do not seem to forget the aged Missionary, or weary of showing her tokens of love.

'We are to have an interesting Ordination Service next Sunday. F. M. and I. U., Converts from Muhammadanism, tried and true, are to be appointed Deacons. We expect the Bishop on Thursday. He will, we hope, lay the first stone of our Mission School Building, so called,[133] on Saturday.... I have begged that the building may be very plain,—dear Mr. Baring gave the money for it.... It is a great matter for some religious instruction to be given to more than 130 boys from Heathen and Muhammadan homes.'

TO MRS. HAMILTON.

'Dec. 21.

'We have been having a busy time.... On Sunday there was the interesting Ordination. To-day the dear Bishop kindly laid the first stone of Mr. Baring's generous gift to Batala, a building for the City School. A number of Muhammadans and Hindus were present; but the service was most distinctly Christian. The *Gloria Patri* was repeated again and again; the precious Name of Christ was not only on the stone, but in the prayers and portion of the Bible read.... At the gathering I saw many interesting persons, both English and Native.... The Bishop is such a lovable man; gentle, bright, affectionate; showing not a particle of pride. We do not call him "My lord," but "Bishop."'

'(*Undated.*)—Beloved Sister, this is the last Sunday of 1891; may 1892 be rich in blessings to you and your loved ones of two generations. "He leadeth me,—oh, blessed thought!"

'It is good for me to be a while in this quiet place.[134] Batala at Christmas time is too bustling. Merry festivities are more delightful to the young than the old. I expected dear Herbert and Mr. Channing to dine with us; and to my surprise we sat down twelve. It was all right; we should use hospitality without grudging, especially at Christmas time; but you know that Char. has a sorrow at her heart. I retired from the merry games, to prepare for the next day's long journey. O my Laura, ask for me a gentle sympathising spirit,—

'"To meet the glad with cheerful smiles,

And to wipe the weeping eyes."'

Was the 'sorrow' here spoken of, the delicate health of 'her Laura?' If the sister in India was ageing fast, the sister in England was failing fast. Parted as they had been during sixteen long years, the loving sympathy between them was as fresh and ardent as ever. A dread had long oppressed Mrs. Hamilton that 'her Char.' would soon be called away. But though the summons to the elder sister was indeed not far distant, that to the younger sister was to arrive first.

CHAPTER XIX
A.D. 1892 LIGHT AT EVENTIDE

The Evening of Miss Tucker's life was passing fast away. Sixteen years of her long Indian campaign were over. Only two years remained. But the end of her Evening was to be Day, not Night. For nearly forty years she had looked forward with joy to the great change; for more than twenty she had longed with an impassioned craving for a sight, Face to face, of that dear Lord and Master whom she loved. And though she did not know it, the time was drawing very near. Could she have known it, the passing troubles of these months would have seemed easy to bear, in the light of coming glory. Barely two more years of toil and weariness,—and then—the Home-going!

One more heavy sorrow had to come first; one more sharp blow upon the golden staff of her Will. Many a blow had fallen since she wrote her little book, *The Giant-Killer*; many dear ones had been called away by death. And now the summons was going forth for the dearest of all; the sister-friend, who from very infancy had been one with herself. No shadow had ever fallen on their love one for another. Before the close of 1892 the shadow of death was to fall across it, leaving Charlotte Tucker more lonely in heart than she had ever been before. But the shadow was to fall for a very little while. Only a few months of separation; and then the sisters would be together again.

'"Stay thy hand!"' Fides exclaimed, in the story by A. L. O. E., as blow after blow fell on the golden staff. '"It can bear no more!"'

'"Yet a little patience," cried Experience, and struck it again. Then the Will was restored to Fides,—straight, pure, beautiful,—oh, how unlike that staff which had been so deadly in the grasp of Pride!

'As Fides stood gazing on the fair gift before him, once more, and for the last time, the shining robe and star-wreath of Conscience flashed on his sight. Never before had her smile been so glad, so beaming with the radiance of Heaven.

'"The work is done,—the fight is over!" she exclaimed. "Thou art summoned to the Presence of thy King! A messenger is even now waiting to conduct thee to the Home which thou so long hast desired! Go, bearing with thee the offering of a conquered Will, the acknowledgment that not even that should be thine own, and the remembrance of foes bravely met and overcome, through the might of Him Who armed thee for the fight.... Go where all is gladness and rejoicing and peace,—where war and danger shall be known no more!"'[135]

The work was nearly done; the fight was nearly over. But Charlotte Tucker could not yet see the starry form, could not yet hear the gentle accents, which soon would bid her to 'rise and come away.' Before many days of 1892 had passed, she was back again in Batala; deep in her usual round of work and interests.

'Batala, *Jan. 10.*—Here am I at home again. I did so enjoy and benefit by my visit to Narowal. It was not leaving work but leaving cares. I worked every day, but the work was more encouraging, and the feeling of repose so refreshing. If I live to see another Christmas, I think that I shall run away to some quiet spot, like Narowal, where the railway whistle is never heard....

'When I was at peaceful Narowal, I happened to read in a printed paper a kind of fable, which has been such a comfort to myself, that I have put the idea into verse, and my Laura shall have a copy.... As we Missionaries have a great many more *little* annoyances than great afflictions, I am inclined—for myself—to change the last line but one into

'"Change petty worries to plumage on wings."

'You know there are on a bird's pinion, not only the long feathers, but the little tiny ones; but how that fluffy downy sort add to beauty and comfort!...

"WEIGHTS AND WINGS.

'"Sweet is a parable which I have read;
Birds at the first could not soar into air,
Bound to the earth; till their Maker, 'tis said,
Gave to each two little burdens to bear.
Proud ones refused the least burden to lift;
Others, submissive, obediently cried,—
'All that He sends we will take as a gift;

Feeble are we, yet will strength be supplied.'

"Raising her burdens, each bird with surprise
Finds to her weak frame most closely it clings;
Soft, light and beautiful, radiant with dyes,
Lo! every *weight* has expanded to *wings*!
Woe to the creatures that clung to the ground!
They could not flutter bright wings in the sky;
Ne'er could they rise above Earth's narrow bound,—
Whilst their companions were soaring on high.

"Take we up burdens of sorrow or care,
Looking to Him Who the trial has given,
Grace will give courage and patience to bear,
Make burdens wings to uplift us to Heaven.
When disappointment its heavy cross brings,
Lord, in each trial Thy love let us see;
Change e'en our heaviest woes into wings,
Onward and upward to bear us to Thee!"'

'*Feb. 12, 1892.*

'Mine own precious Sister,—Again have you been called to the trial of sickness and suffering.... These trials may seem strange and unaccountable to the children of earth, but how differently they are regarded by the children of light! They make us keep closer to the Father's side,—cling more to His supporting Hand,—the weights *do* turn into wings! O how often have I during late days thought of that little parable! And when we reach the Blessed Shore, and "know as we are known," we shall fully realise *why* it is good that we should be afflicted....

'I was reading the Commandments aloud in a village yesterday, when a bright young Hindu Pandit—rather well read—objected to the Second. The poor fellow was probably conscious that he himself was constantly breaking the Second Commandment. It interested me to hear a middle-aged sensible-looking Sikh take the other side, quietly, and with perfect good-temper. Each of the men afterwards accepted a Gospel, one in Gurmukhi, one in Urdu.'

'*Feb. 18.*—I am thankful for improved accounts of you.... We have had rather an eventful week for Batala.... On Monday the dear Bishop came in. Herbert asked me to take luncheon with him on Tuesday. It was very nice; just the Bishop, Herbert, and four nice Native Christians. I was the only lady.... At half-past three we had a very interesting Confirmation Service in the Church, to which the Bishop drove me. He gave a very nice address, which Herbert translated beautifully into Panjabi, for the benefit of the simple peasants. On the following morning the Bishop gave in English such a practical *heart-searching* address to us workers! He looked so earnestly at us ladies, and was evidently anxious to do us real good. His was no idle display of eloquence; rather did his address resemble the admonition of a kind wise father. We did not see him after we left the chapel....

'We have had a singularly mild and bright cold weather.... How curious it would be to an English farmer to see fields green with corn in February,—the Spring crop,—and, at the same time, other bits of ground being ploughed up for the sowing of another crop! There seems something always growing. There are lovely roses and fruit blossoms, but the weather is now comparatively dark and dull.'

'*April 8, 1892.*—The Muhammadans in Batala seem to be in a much better humour than they may be expected to be during the Ramazan—their grand fast. I have visited a good many Muhammadan Zenanas this week; and in not one, so far as I remember, have I heard a word about the fast, which was apt to make them so bigoted and self-righteous. No one objects when I repeat in Urdu the precious text, "By grace ye are saved, through faith," etc. Indeed, I believe that a good many Batala folk think that after all our religion is better than their own. I repeat "God so loved — —" more often, I think, than any other text; and I have not lately heard the shocked exclamation, "Tauba! tauba!"[136] Perhaps it will be different to-morrow, when I propose visiting two villages, which were so bigoted and disagreeable, that I at one time struck both out of my visiting-list. Minnie induced me to give them—at least one of them—another trial, as she had given medical aid to the wife of the Maulvi (Muhammadan religious teacher of the place), and had found him very polite. No doubt the Dispensary opens doors. I found the Maulvi bigoted but civil, and ... willing to receive a New Testament.... I enjoy the quiet walk, and then ride in my duli, in the cool fresh morning, when I visit villages. The harvest has commenced. Here I see fields of ripening corn, there the scattered sheaves. But the harvest is not so plentiful as it was last year. We had too dry a cold weather; not nearly so chilly as the former one. I am taking out illuminated texts just now. I have beautiful ones, both in Persian, Urdu, and Gurmukhi. It is interesting to see peasants, somewhat more intelligent than their fellows, spelling out the precious verses from Scripture.'

'*April 12.*—Precious darling Laura,—The Mail has to-day brought me in your letter of March 24th; the first *clear* intimation of the nature of your illness. I will not say that my eyes are dry. I own that the selfish thought arose,—"Would that *I* had had it instead!" And yet I prefer knowing the plain truth. I have comfort in the thought, "I am old; whichever of us is taken *first*, the meeting—O what a joyful meeting!—may not be far off!" ...

'I am thankful that you do not suffer greatly. I fondly hope that this trial may be spared. I do not feel inclined to add more. I need not,—you know so much of your own loving Char.'

TO MISS 'LEILA' HAMILTON.

'*April 13, 1892.*

'Though I wrote to your beloved Mother yesterday, and shall only be just in time to catch the post, my heart impels me to send a letter to you, my dear afflicted God-daughter. I know that you try bravely to bear up under your sore trial, so as not to add to that of your precious invalid.... I am glad that I have been told the worst. It has been good for my soul! Only the day before the mail came in, I had been foolishly, sinfully, brooding over trifles, till I even showed outward irritation, instead of reflecting that small annoyances as well as great troubles are God's loving discipline for us. Alas! that I should have shown temper! The next day the Lord sent a *quiet, holy* sorrow, and it did me good,—tears were wholesome,—I felt that I had been petty and irritable, and deserved a different kind of trial. I have been more under discipline since I attained the age of seventy than I have perhaps ever been before in India. But should *trifles* disturb the serenity of a Servant of a Crucified Saviour?... Thinking of your real grief, I hope to be more patient with petty annoyances....

'Write freely to me, dear Leila. To help you in your trouble will not do me harm but good.'

'*April 17, 1892.*—Beloved Laura, "The Lord is Risen indeed!" This is the Easter greeting, and this is Easter morn. I shall soon start for church; but first I would remind my darling sister and myself of words like the clarion of a silver trumpet, followed by the sound of an angel's harp:—

'"The Lord hath triumphed gloriously;
The Lord shall reign victoriously!
Seals assuring,
Guards securing,
Watch His earthly prison!
Seals are shattered,
Guards are scattered,—
Christ hath Risen!"

'"No longer then let mourners weep,
Or call departed Christians 'dead!'
For death is hallowed into sleep.
Each grave becomes a bed."

'"It is *not* exile—peace on high;
It is not sorrow,—rest from strife;
To fall asleep is *not* to die;
To be with Christ is better life!"

'How beautiful are these lines,—how true!...

'Oh, what Heavenly wisdom Missionaries need!... It seems to me that dear people at home have a very imperfect idea of Missionaries, and, in their prayers, probably ask for comfort in trial for God's servants, rather than for the wisdom which is from Above,—the gentle influence of the Holy Spirit. Ask this for me, my Laura. I do get impatient sometimes, and I make mistakes.'

'*May 2, 1892.*—Books are a great enjoyment when I am alone, or sitting, as I am at present, by the bedside of one who has been ill, though now, thank God, recovering. We have had such a sick house, your Char keeping well, when it seemed as if nobody else would; delicate Miss —— coming next on the roll of health. She has been able to take the housekeeping, and to help in the nursing, so we are getting on, and hope that all will come right soon. Miss Dixie took four children to Clarkabad, and returned April 23rd, quite ill.... Miss Wright is nursing her. Then ... Daisy and Miss Copes came almost suddenly in from Futteyghur; Daisy's fever had alarmed Miss Copes.... Miss Copes had her turn next, and has suffered severely.... Char has felt some comfort from being of some use here.'

FROM THE REV. R. CLARK.

'Cheshire, May 3, 1892.

'My dear Mrs. Hamilton,— ... I saw dear Miss Tucker shortly before I left Amritsar. She is, as you know, not strong; 2 Cor. iii. 13, R.V., always occurs to me when I see her. God is daily using her to be a blessing to us all.'

C. M. T. TO MRS. HAMILTON.

'May 8 (Seventy-first Birthday).

'I am sure that my precious Laura has been thinking of me to-day, as I have been thinking of her....

'I think that it was some time before 5 a.m. that Mr. Corfield and his boys came to greet me with a hymn. I was in my dressing-gown, but hastily popped on my bonnet and went out to shake hands with everybody. As it is well known that I do not wish gifts, and prefer simple trifles that are useful, my presents were judiciously chosen, and are, to my mind, curiously symbolical.

'The Corfields gave me a box of soap,—fragrant, and typical of cleansing. Miss Wright, a pretty little box of vaseline. This pleased me particularly. I have said, and I think written, that every Missionary should have a box of ointment, symbol of peace-keeping and peace-making! Now *I* have one myself. Minnie gave *pens.* May I make a good use of them!... Dear Babu Singha has given me a hand-pankah (fan), which I waved gratefully in church this morning. This is an emblem of refreshment in oppressive heat....

'Dear Mr. Baring's admirable building for the Mission Plough is to be opened to-morrow by the Deputy Commissioner; and I suppose that Muhammadan and Hindu big or little wigs will be present. I am glad that my birthday falls on Sunday; so that the tamasha is postponed till the next day. There is something solemn about the Anniversary, when one has travelled so far on the Homeward road. You will feel this, darling, on the 20th.[137] ... Dear Herbert's sermon to-day was on "Seekest thou great things for thyself? Seek them not!" We should never have known Baruch's failing but for that warning word. I have been very much tamed down, dearest.'

TO THE REV. F. H. BARING.

'*May 9, 1892.*

'I must tell you of the grand opening of your beautiful School building to-day, while the scene is fresh in my mind, and before the coming in of the home mail.... The thermometer has been nearly 92° in my room this morning.

'The fine building was well filled; the part nearest the table with Europeans and Baring boys; the Plough boys, very numerous, had the larger space; and in front, on chairs, in stiff dignity, sat the city magnates.... We sang a hymn; Mr. Wright ... read a Psalm; and, we Christians standing, Herbert led the prayer. Then my Nephew[138] made a short speech, followed by a nice one from dear Babu Singha, and a kind of brief, satisfactory report from Nobin Chanda.

'And then up rose the Deputy Commissioner, and, to my great surprise and great amusement, gave, in rough Urdu, such a *whipping* to Batala and her magnates, as I never heard in a speech in my life. First,—Batala, poor Batala, was not like any other city; it was so quarrelsome! Clearly, the Deputy Commissioner (like Mr. — —, who told me nearly sixteen years ago that Batala was the most troublesome and litigious city in the district) has no fancy for the place. Then the whip came down on the shoulders of the poor rais;[139] and it was mercilessly plied. The magnates had to bear the indignation of the Englishman for doing their best— or worst—to prevent our getting ground for the school or the proposed Mission Hospital. For whose benefit was the latter? asked the irate Deputy Commissioner. Not for our own, but that of the women and children of Batala! In short, the Englishman whipped the poor magnates, till he made them bleed—in their purses. He told them that money was wanted for school-benches, etc., and let them know that their aid would be desirable. Paper was on the table.... Some put down rupees; some wrote down promises. About 701 were thus collected.... The whole thing was so funny that I could not help being greatly amused. I wonder what the scolded Muhammadans said, when they went back to their Zenanas....

'Herbert said in his speech that your fine building will also be used as Library, Reading-room, and Lecture-room. I think there will be a Sunday-school also.'

TO MRS. HAMILTON.

'*May 15, 1892.*—My precious Laura, you wish me to ask for you more faith and love. I ask *more*, even for floods of joy. Why not, darling? "Ask, and ye shall receive!" ... My trial, as regards this matter, is different from yours. I have to learn patience to restrain yearning to depart and be with Christ. I have twice, as it were, in dangerous illness,—what men call "dangerous,"—caught a glimpse of the River; and it seems glittering with sunbeams! I *long* to cross it; but I feel that it would be wrong to pray to go. The Master only knows when we are ready to go Home; but how my spirits rise, if I see any likelihood of the time being near! I do not feel this at present, for I have such a good constitution. Three out of four of my Mission ladies here have been seriously ill; with the fourth I can see that it is a weary struggle to get on; and I, an aged woman, am not ill at all! I do not suppose that any of the four really wish to quit the field—or the school. The one who does *may* be kept long at her post. None can tell! I fall back on "The Lord knows best."'

'*May 20.*—This is my own beloved Laura's Birthday,—a day which Char is not likely to forget. Sweet peace and joy be yours, darling. You have added to the happiness of many. You have, as it were, washed the disciples' feet, and you are sitting at the Lord's Feet. That is what dear, saintly Fanny described as "the position of a Christian." Is it not a wondrous thought that you and I may be welcomed by such as Fanny? She was not beautiful on earth; but how fair she will be, raised "in His likeness"! The Saviour will be "admired in His saints,"—a very remarkable expression, and a sweet subject for thought. There is so much in us now *not* to be admired; but when He comes to make up His jewels, *all* will be bright and fair....

'This has been a particularly hot season.... You would think 91° warm in a bedroom at night. Miss —— and Daisy sleep out on the roof: but I think myself too old for the chance of a midnight scramble in my night-clothes, carrying my bedding down an outside stair, should a dust-storm or thunder-storm come on. I keep on the prudent side, which is *in*side.... A Sunday-school has been opened in Mr. Baring's beautiful new School-house. Attendance is of course voluntary; and Mr. and Miss Wright, who have started the Sunday-school, and who only expected to find about twenty boys, were pleased to find about *sixty* pupils; not only the "Plough" boys, but their teachers. Was not this grand?... I hope that dear Francis' new building will be one of the best means of bringing hard-hearted Batala to the knowledge of the Saviour. The laddies are often not hard at all, but pleased and eager to hear about the Christian Faith. The next generation may be very different from the present one.'

'*May 29.*—Do not regret having told me about your state of health. I like to know the truth, and at my advanced age may well face it. Whether my darling Laura or myself be taken *first*, the remaining one will have comfort. It is but a "little while"—

> '"Till He come! O let the words
> Linger on the trembling chords,
> Let the little space between
> In their golden light be seen!"'

Early in June Miss Tucker took the long journey to Simla, accompanied part of the way by Dr. Weitbrecht, and afterwards by Dr. Lankester. Through the thoughtful kindness of various friends, the journey was made as little fatiguing to her as possible. On her arrival she was so worn out as to sleep thirteen hours, with only one break, but was afterwards none the worse. Writing of the kind Cousins with whom she had gone to stay, she says: 'The boys are charming, so clever, bright, and loving. They make of me as much as if I were a pet Grandmother. I bought a little toy for them; and they were so much delighted with it, that I must have had between the three boys nearly a dozen kisses for it. I wonder that they are so fond of kissing a wrinkled old face.'

On June 17 she wrote from Simla:—

> 'I am treated here with great kindness and consideration. I am not pressed to exert myself; but of course I take my part when friends come to dinner. To-day we are to have four Calcutta Missionary ladies for dinner and games. To-morrow an old friend of mine, Carry H., and her husband, and Lord Radstock. One of the most lovable guests that we have had is our own Bishop of Lahore. I am to go to his lecture on Isaiah this evening....
>
> 'There is an excellent piano here, and dear Mackworth Young plays exquisitely.... How you would have enjoyed Beethoven's Hallelujah Chorus, which he has played to me twice from memory! "Worlds unborn shall sing His glory— the exalted Son of God!" Do not those words recall the dear old Ancient Concerts? Yesterday I was tempted, when alone, to open the piano myself; and what do you think was one of the things which I sang and played? My Laura's "The Lord He is my Strength and Stay!" *That* too reminds of old times. O what will Heaven's music be!'

The following letter, written from Simla to Miss Raikes, was on the subject of a translation into Bengali of her little book, *The Story of Dr. Duff*:—

> '*June 20, 1892.*—If I have neglected thanking you for a copy of your translation, pray forgive an aged and half worn-out Missionary;—I am seventy-one, and in weak health. In our Panjab I have no intercourse with Bengalis, except such as know English more or less; and I am not acquainted with a word of the Bengali language, Urdu and Panjabi being what is spoken, so that I could not myself judge of your translation. At Simla, however, where I am on a visit, I hear that there are Bengalis, and I might find some to whom I could present the book, which has been your labour of love. I cannot but hope that you have not published 2000 copies at your own expense. I never do; but a Society prints, and takes the risk. If the Bengalis be like the Panjabis, it will be difficult to sell so many copies at 8 annas each. If I remember rightly, my little *Life of Duff* only costs 2 annas; and *our* people think that a good deal! But Bengal may be more liberal.'

The next letter—like one or two on the same topic, already quoted—is of peculiar interest, because, some three years earlier, Miss Tucker had been a good deal exercised in spirit about the fact of Bishop French's successor being a decided High Churchman, and had more than once written in strong and melancholy terms to her sister on the subject. The tone in which she now wrote, in 1892, is remarkable, as being by no means in accord with her former prejudices. But Charlotte Tucker, as I have had occasion to remark before, was not one of those small-natured people, who always stick fast to what they have said, because they have said it. She was ever ready for fresh light upon any matter. It appears to me that we see here in her some measure of that widening of spiritual outlook, which ought to become visible with advancing years and with a closer knowledge of the Spirit of Christ. Probably she was not herself definitely conscious of any difference.

'Simla, *July 3, 1892.*—My beloved Laura, I have just come from church, from partaking of Holy Communion. Our Bishop preached. It was a sermon whose gist I do not think that I shall ever forget; for it presented a most familiar text in—to me—quite a new and very striking light: "Blessed are the poor in spirit." The Bishop said that many persons—I was amongst them—"took the Blessing as meant for the *humble*"; but he, referring to the parallel passage in St. Luke's Gospel, showed that this is a limitation of the meaning. The poor in spirit are those who count themselves as actually *possessors* of nothing; the goods which are called theirs are merely *lent* of God, to be taken up or laid down simply at His pleasure. In the face of a large congregation, in gay, fashionable, money-seeking Simla, our Bishop with fervent energy preached a sermon on *Unworldliness*! May God write it in the hearts of the hearers!

'I thank God for our Bishop. His influence is of untold value; he is so gentle, courteous, considerate, that he does not, I should think, usually give offence. I had the enjoyment yesterday of, I think, more than an hour's *tête-à-tête* with him. It interested me much, for Bishop Matthews never puts himself on a pedestal. If his Episcopal position resembles one, he comes down at once, with humility and frankness, and seems like a brother. The Bishop never appears to mind in the least my not calling him "lord," either in correspondence or in speaking. One has the impression that he does not care a straw about it. I am struck by the pains which he is taking about the case of a young Native Christian.... The Bishop is investigating the matter with father-like interest.... It is a cause of deep thankfulness that European or Native can appeal to a good, wise Bishop.'

Miss Tucker does not, here or elsewhere, state why she objected to calling a Bishop "my lord."

TO MISS 'LEILA' HAMILTON.

'*July 3, 1892.*

'We had a Missionary Meeting last week, at which the most striking speech was that of Mr. Lefroy[140] of Delhi. I could not help thinking this, though the Bishop, Mr. Young, and my dear nephew, Dr. Weitbrecht, spoke before him. In simple, manly fashion, as one not thinking of human praise, Mr. Lefroy described what seemed to me like a grand single combat between himself and a Muhammadan Hafiz,—one who knows the whole Koran by heart—of great influence. The Hafiz, a great opposer of Christianity, asked Mr. Lefroy to have a *long* discussion with him, not saying that he must go, or was tired, etc. Our champion accepted the challenge at once. The Hafiz appointed a mosque as the place of meeting.

'Mr. Lefroy went at the appointed hour, and, to his surprise, found about 500 Muhammadans waiting for him. They were very attentive listeners; but great, very great, must have been the strain upon the noble and gifted Missionary. Till midnight, for about five hours and a half, in hot Delhi, in the fiery month of June, Mr. Lefroy held up the Christian Banner against the Hafiz and others. At midnight, after one Muhammadan had been arguing against our Faith, the Hafiz said to him: "If you can bring forward no better arguments, *I will take the Missionary's hand, and go out with him!*" He did not do so then; he had not sufficient courage to face the storm of opposition; and again he failed on another occasion, to Mr. Lefroy's great disappointment. But after months, that Hafiz is a Baptized Christian now. God gave His champion the victory at last!'

TO MISS HOERNLE.

'*July 18, 1892.*

'I am still, as you see, at Simla, but expect to start on my long journey downhill on the 21st. We have had a great quantity of rain. I hear that Batala is flooded, so the heat will be much lessened....

'Yesterday was Sunday, and the dear Bishop and a few others dined with us, and we had nice hymn-singing afterwards. How you would have liked to have occupied my seat at the dinner-table! I was next the Bishop, and Dr. Weitbrecht sat just opposite....

'I need not tell you that the mountains are very beautiful; especially, to my mind, when a white cloud, which has been, as it were, quite blotting them out, is lifted, and one beholds the glorious peaks and wooded valleys, lovely in the bright sunshine. It reminds one of the American Poet's striking lines on a yet loftier theme,—

> '"Soon shall the whole
> Like a parchéd scroll
> Before my amazéd eyes uproll,
> And without a screen,
> At a burst be seen,
> The Presence in which I have ever been!"

'Ah, dear Maria, well may we exclaim—

> '"O to be ready, ready, for that Day—
> Who would not cast Earth's dearest joys away!"'

TO MRS. HAMILTON.

'Batala, *Aug. 8, 1892.*—Daisy and I are living in a remarkably damp world, as beautifully green as green can be. The rain is pouring furiously. My kahars had to wade through water to take me to the city. I had a good fire in my Gurub-i-Aftab to-day, not for warmth, but to keep away mustiness.... Damp is by no means as trying to me as cold, and it is a comfort to be in no danger of sand-storms. No dust now; only "water, water, everywhere." Happily I cannot add, "not a drop to drink"!... We have quite a bevy of our Mission ladies up at the Hills. I am very glad that they are there. Hard-working Minnie seems to be enjoying herself so thoroughly. Did I tell you of a Hindu presenting, for her projected Hospital, a piece of ground, worth 700 rupees? Herbert had a meeting of principal Batala folk; and such interest was shown in Minnie's work, that—including a hundred rupees from the kind Deputy Commissioner—551 rupees have been given or promised for the proposed Hospital.'

TO MISS EDITH TUCKER.

'*Aug. 18, 1892.*

'I will tell you between ourselves, for I would not trouble sweet Aunt Hamilton about anything, that, in my old age, since I have attained seventy, I have had more experience of difficulties and worries than perhaps at any other period of my long Indian career. I need not describe the worries; they are things that rub one, chafe one, make life's burden heavier. And why are they permitted, darling? I think that they keep us in a more humble, *clinging* position. We cannot ask sympathy for such little things; we are pitied for some troubles; others we must keep to ourselves,—the latter perhaps try us most. But the dear Saviour knows! He experienced daily trials of patience as well as great afflictions. It is good to remember this. Christ, in addition to cruel persecution from open enemies, had to bear the dulness of perception, the weakness of faith, the ambition, the tendency to quarrel, of His daily companions. If great troubles are like the burdens which expand into wings, it seems to me as if petty worries may turn into the soft, downy little feathers which line the wings. They make our wings softer for those whom we have to shelter beneath them. For as the Lord spreads His great Wing over us, He means us to spread our small ones over others.'

TO MISS L. V. TUCKER.

'*Sept. 21, 1892.*

'You call me "Fairy Frisket," dear. If I be like a Fairy, it is not pretty little Frisket, but rather the old woman of Nursery stories, with wrinkled face and high cap. Yet here I have frisked to Futteyghur. We have a little Christian congregation of peasant converts here, who assemble twice a day in a large, neat room, which serves for a church. It is well matted, and has a red curtain down the middle, to divide the men from the women. All sit on the ground; only Auntie, on account of her age, is allowed a low seat. It is quite easy to me to sit on the ground; but to get up again,— "there's the rub."

'"What o'clock is Service?" I asked of our excellent Native Pastor. "Half-past five in the morning; afternoon half-past five. Before sunrise, and before sunset." I thought half-past five a.m. rather early; but of course we accommodate our convenience to that of the peasants, who have to go to their work. Says I to Daisy, "You may trust me to awaken you at five!" This is no hard matter to Auntie!... When I sallied forth I could see Orion in the sky.'

A few more scattered extracts from Miss Tucker's Journal may end this chapter.

'*Feb. 21, 1892. Sunday.*—The best I have had since Narowal. Prayer seemed answered.

'*Feb. 22.*—Villages. Little B. H. Gave one Urdu Gospel to a young man. Some listened, but I encountered some rudeness. Almost pushed away. Ladder. Widow of Nain.... Went to house of Maulvi F.... He courteous. Some children rude. Sent him one of Gwynn's Gospels.

'*May 3.*—Blessed rain. Three invalids recovering. Thank God.

'*May 4.*—Plough. Subject Passover. K. very nice. Gave Gurmukhi Primer. Saw P. D.... Remembers Maria. Wants to learn Urdu. Had good conversation with S.... Saw pretty bibi and nice brother. He read first part of Acts ii. I lent him *Daybreak*.

'*May 29.*—Too poorly to go to early church.

'*June 1.*—Too poorly to go out. Wrote to poor, dear R. C.

'*June 3.*—Plough. Short work; very weak. Too weak and poorly for work.

'*June 10.*—Left Batala. Dr. Lankester my escort.

'*June 11.*—Reached Simla, much wearied. Slept about thirteen hours.

'*Aug. 3.*—A. B. Man sent me off at once; but almost immediately recalled me; and I had a very good talk with him.

'C.'s Bibi. Courteous and pleasant.

'D. E. Good visit.

'F. Middling.

'G. H. She nice; but grumbling zemindar came in.

'Old J. indifferent as usual.

'H. did not see her, but sweet J. K.'

CHAPTER XX
A.D. 1892-1893 THE LAST GREAT SORROW

With the coming of autumn, accounts of Mrs. Hamilton's state grew steadily worse. In the middle of October Miss Tucker went for a few days to Rawal Pindi; and the last letter which she received there, before starting on her return journey, prepared her for the coming blow. Arriving at Batala station in the early morning, her first question was—

'Is there a telegram?'

There was a telegram, and it was given to her immediately. Before seeing a word, Miss Tucker knew what the missive had to tell,—knew that her dearly loved sister had passed away. She opened it, and burst into a flood of tears. Reaching home, Miss Dixie led her to her own room, and there left her for a little while alone.

Probably no sorrow in all her lifetime, except the death of her Father and the death of Letitia, had touched her so closely as this sorrow; and even they were not the same, because through them she always had still her Laura. Now the sense of loneliness pressed upon her heavily. Whatever she had thought, whatever she had wished, whatever had aroused her interest or appealed to her sympathies, the immediate impulse had ever been to tell it to Mrs. Hamilton,—perhaps even more during these long years in a far-off land, than in her English life. But indeed from very childhood, from the time when Laura was a little rosy, sweet-tempered, merry maid of four, and Charlotte was a wild-spirited, impulsive, and ambitious child of eight, the tie between them had been of a very unusual nature. They did not love merely as sisters, but as the nearest and dearest of intimate personal friends. What made the one happy made the other happy. What grieved the one grieved the other.

And now for a while the tie was seemingly broken; intercourse was at an end. True, Charlotte Tucker had been for sixteen long years and more separated by land and ocean from her sister. But the communion of mind with mind had been incessant throughout. True, the break was for a very little while. But this she could not possibly know. Old as she was, old in some respects beyond her years, she yet had a strong constitution, and a marvellous amount even now of wiry vigour. Weak she might be, in a sense; nevertheless she could get through a round of work daily which few women of seventy would dream of attempting. It was well within the bounds of possibility that her life might be extended through another ten or twelve years, or even longer.

'She felt her sister's death most dreadfully,' one of her nieces has said. Yet she did not lie crushed beneath the weight of her grief. Work had still to be done; and others had to be thought of and comforted.

On the very day that she received the telegram she wrote to Mrs. Hamilton's daughter a letter full of sympathy for her niece's loss, scarcely mentioning her own.

> 'I would take you as it were into my arms, ... and weep with you, so that I might possibly even remind you of the sympathy of the precious Mother, whom you have *not* lost, but parted with for a little while. O, when you meet in Eternity, what a little while it will appear!... You have the blessing of holy memories; you know that you were a great comfort to the precious Invalid; and you have the joy of hope, the hope of re-union. We are only pilgrims on the same road; and one arrives before the other. Both have the same Home.
>
> '"And who can tell the rapture, when the circle is complete,
>   And all the Family of God around the Father meet?"
>
> ' ... It 6will be a solace to you to look after your beloved Mother's poor. I am sure that many had cause to bless her. All her works of love done so quietly and unostentatiously; but every one marked down in God's "book of remembrance." What a wonderful joy the opening of that book will be! Little kindnesses, acts of love, words of holy counsel, all marked down, not one forgotten.... Try to *realise* your Mother's happiness! Has she not looked on the Lord Jesus, heard His Voice, received His welcome?'

And again on the 27th of October:—

> 'Try, dear one, to comfort others; and then you will find comfort yourself. This is a world of suffering; and the best Memorial to your precious Mother will be something that will be a blessing to others. To think of what *she* would have approved will be a solace to your mind.'

On the same day she wrote to her nephew, the Rev. W. F. T. Hamilton: 'I go on with my daily Mission work; it seems what I have specially to live for. Is it not possible that your sainted Mother takes an interest in it still?'

In the first letter to Mrs. J. Boswell, after receiving the telegram, she spoke more openly of her own feelings:—

> '*Oct. 23.* — ... Your letter to Lettie, which I saw at Pindi, before my own followed me there, quite prepared me for Edith's thoughtful telegram. I received that telegram at the Batala station, after my long dark night's journey back from Pindi. I thank and bless God for my precious sister's bliss; but to me the blank— —! I suppose that the funeral will be to-morrow; in thought I follow my poor bereaved Leila,—but my mind dwells less on the grief of those left, than the joy of her who is with her Saviour. I thanked God for her to-day at Holy Communion.
>
> 'I hope that there will be no unnecessary gloom to-morrow. It seems to me so incongruous to throw a heavy black pall over the dear form, when the spirit is wearing the shining white robe. I hate black,—the colour of sin and spiritual death! My own beloved sister had nothing to do with either. My tears fall as I write; but I dare not, cannot, murmur; though life seems to me a weary pilgrimage. I am very home-sick, my Bella; but the Lord will call me when He knows that I am ready. He gives me some work to do for Him. I must live for that.'

And again, on the 4th of November:—

> 'This has been a year of trials. Since I reached seventy, I feel as if my path had grown steeper, and flowers wither. But when the summit of the Hill is reached—what joy! I can hardly help envying my sweet Laura; and, oh, I am thankful that she was spared acute suffering! Her end—as regards this world—was indeed peace; her happiness will be never-ending. You see that I am again at Futteyghur, for about five days, to keep Miss Key company.... It was no sacrifice to me to come out to the village, for I was glad to be in a very quiet place just now. Batala is too full of friends and too cheerful for my present mood. Work is congenial; not cheerful meetings. Mrs. Corfield gave a sort of Concert on Wednesday, to which every one was invited; but I, of course,

stayed at home. There is no one but Daisy Key and myself here.'

From the Journal entries it is evident that Miss Tucker gave herself only one clear day of rest—and that day a Sunday—for indulgence in any wise of her sorrow. She had the telegram on a Saturday; and on Monday the usual round of visiting went on.

'Oct. 20. [141]— ... My precious Laura departed.'

'Oct. 22.—Returned to Batala. Telegram.'

This is the brief Diary notice of what occurred.

The next few months were marked by no very especial events; only the usual ups and downs, anxieties, disappointments, encouragements, of Missionary work. Missionaries came and went as usual; and partings took place, some of which tried her much. Miss Eva Warren, who had spent several weeks with her in 1889, came in November to be a permanent inmate of 'Sunshine'; no small pleasure to Miss Tucker. But Miss Warren, like so many others, broke down under the Panjab climate; and in the spring of 1893 she had to give up her post and return home.

In April 1893 Miss Tucker wrote to her niece, Miss L. V. Tucker:—

> 'Though I have written playfully to your father, I am not in a playful mood. This is such a year of partings for your poor old Auntie. You know about my Louis and Lettie; then energetic Minnie Dixie left us; to-day I go to the station for the last look of the dear, good Corfields ... and their three fine children, accompanied by Rosa Singha, who has been such a help and comfort here. On Monday week sweet Eva Warren, one of my most lovable companions, leaves me.... I do not expect to see her again on earth. Next month Rowland Bateman, my very tip-top favourite amongst all Missionaries, is to start for England. What a blessing it is that there is One Friend Who says, "I will never leave thee, nor forsake"; "Even to hoar hairs I will carry you"!'

A few slight recollections of Miss Warren's may well come in here. They are of particular interest, being almost entirely of this last year of Miss Tucker's life, after the death of Mrs. Hamilton. The two had been very little together before November 1892, when Miss Warren returned from eighteen months' sick-leave, to be again in three months invalided.

'She was very impulsive,' Miss Warren says. 'We used to say of her sometimes that she needed cool young heads to guide her. Her energy was very remarkable. During the last cold weather I was with her, I could see how much she felt the cold, but she would not give in in the least.... Being an Honorary Missionary, she was very scrupulous about not taking any extra privileges in the way of holidays.... My impression is that she had formerly known the language better than she did latterly. In spite of her efforts not to forget what she had learned, some had slipped away from her. She said to me one day: "I speak Hindustani as the Duke of Wellington used to talk French." "Oh," I said, "how was that?" "Bravely!" she said. She had a very merry way of laughing, when anything amused her.

'She said to me once: "I think what is wanted out here is—Missionaries' graves. Not the graves of young Missionaries, who have died here, but the graves of old Missionaries, who have given their whole lives for these people!" ... She was very humble about her own work, and used sometimes to be quite depressed after reading accounts of other people's successful work, thinking that she had met with no success.'

Miss Warren relates also how she would not unfrequently say: 'So-and-so is one of those people who think me a great deal better than I am.' Her conversation was still very bright and full of interest; the active mind had by no means parted with its vigour. Sometimes she would talk eagerly about old days, and tell stories of the Duke of Wellington, a subject which always aroused her. Or again she would plunge into the topic of Shakespeare's Plays. Or she would read some of her favourite Spurgeon's Sermons. Another pet book of hers was Baxter's *Saints' Rest*; and this she read through with Miss Warren. Occasionally still she would read aloud one of her own stories in the evening. Happily, she retained her old love of games; and they must have been a great relaxation after the hard day's work. Sometimes, when Miss Warren had been reading or studying, she would say: 'Now you must come and frisk a little!'

The old untidiness in dress had never been overcome; and the mixture of colours was often remarkable. But though the clothes might not be artistically chosen, or put on with great neatness, they were always daintily clean,—no matter how many years they might have been in use.

Thin and fragile-looking as Miss Tucker had always been, she was by this time hardly more than mere skin and bone; and her face was singularly covered all over with fine wrinkles. This it was, no doubt, which helped to give her the appearance, spoken of by so many, of being far older than she really was,—rather like ninety than like seventy. The vigour and energy which she still retained were, however, certainly not like ninety,—or even like seventy.

Here are a few more selections from the Journal in the year 1893,—the closing year of Charlotte Tucker's Indian life:—

'*Feb. 21.*—Village. B. Saw fourteen girls; only eleven worthy of being counted. Heard of five more. C. D. Did not see him, but E., F., and another familiar face. Men and women listened to story of Knocking, etc. Some man said, did not understand me. I repeated John iii. 16, and asked E. to repeat it too. He did so, and no one could pretend not to understand. I asked E. to instruct them; he said simply that it was difficult for a Hindu to teach about Christ, and twice said that a Christian preacher should be sent. Hindu Bibis nice. Seeing the picture of Knocking, they seemed to understand; and one or two appeared to *have* opened the door of the heart....'

'*Feb. 22.*—G. H. Gentle, pleasing. I lent her *Stories for Women*. J. nicer than I have ever found her. K., a delightful visit. Her husband, L. M., a fine-looking man, has returned, and the family are *so* happy. I saw first one, then another child, on the father's knee; the sweet wife's face is full of pleasure. L. M. says that he is going to be a Christian.... His brother, N. O., seems a thoughtful, nice man. He is puzzled about God's having a Son, but told me that he did not ask questions for controversy, but wishing to be instructed....'

'*March 27.*—Village. P. Sirdar's house. Pretty bibi, not attentive, and bhatija ill-mannered. Other boys listened, specially nice R. ... Take more Urdu and Gurmukhi, and a little Hindi next time. Gave three Gospels and other books. Weather cold.'

'*May 19.*—S. T. Charming. U. V. sixteen years old. Appears to be the wife of the uncle of some and *grandfather* of others, in the house.... Has Gospel and *Pilgrim's Progress*. Read and translated to me some pages of latter, with great emphasis. Seems a believer. I have sent her Psalms in Hindi....'

'*June 15.*—Adopted Lefroy as Nephew.... Fancy-fair.'

'*June 17.*—With W.'s bibi and Ayahs, Ascension and Pentecost. Evening walk, met two respectable-looking men. Had Urdu and Hindi Gospels in my hand. One man's glance at Urdu encouraged me to offer it. Man much pleased. Talked English; in some way belongs to Viceroy. Wished to give me something for Gospel. I said that I did not sell, but gave it with pleasure. Other man readily received Hindi Gospel. A little farther met with a curious-looking man, with appearance of a devotee. Offered him Gurmukhi Gospel.

Accepted eagerly, and, to my surprise, took my hand, and said earnestly in English, "Thanks—dear—Madam!" Lord, bless Thy Word!'

'*June 27.*—Returned from Simla. Happy journey downhill with dear Lefroy. I have left Batala work for four weeks and four days.'

'*June 28.*—Full of difficulties. Lord, help me! CLOSED DISPENSARY.'

'*Aug. 31.*— ... Here closes August, a month of Blessings....'

'*Oct. 28.*—Village. P. started for V. But all V.'s inhabitants seemed to have turned out for the funeral of a young man. Probably eighty or a hundred present. I turned to the left, where about forty women and girls were standing or seated on the ground. I repeated twice over to them, not singing, a little hymn which I had made; also the precious verse, "God so loved." Had not only good listening, but some of the women repeated after me the burden of the hymn. I had chest-cold, so could not have sung without coughing.'

The last page of Miss Tucker's Diary, which follows immediately after this entry of October 28, is reproduced in facsimile.

Writing to Miss Minnie Dixie on July 21, 1893, she asked: 'Have you heard that I have a new nephew, Mr. Lefroy? He is Irish, of Huguenot descent.... He is a gifted man, and a devoted Missionary.' Mr. Lefroy, belonging to the Cambridge Delhi Mission, which is in connection with the S.P.G., has been mentioned in an earlier letter as arguing for over five successive hours with Muhammadans in a mosque. This was probably the latest of her numerous Indian 'adoptions.'

She was for months in much trouble about the Dispensary, as it seemed impossible to find any one, European or Indian, capable of undertaking it and also free to do so. The attendance had been good; often more than a hundred women in one day coming for help; and Miss Tucker was exceedingly desirous to keep it open. But so many had broken down, or were absent on furlough, that for a while the closing proved unavoidable.

That, from time to time, Miss Tucker suffered from depression and moods of sadness, there can be no question. She never allowed such moods to interfere with her work; but she was not always in a state of high spirits and rejoicing. If nothing else showed this, it would be plain from certain brief passages in her journal, occurring at intervals,—sometimes at long intervals. Such passages as these speak plainly:—

'1888.—I have suffered a good deal from bodily languor and mental depression.' '1888. Depression has overtaken me. Thank God, not doubt or despair.' '1891. Felt the weight of years much; work a struggle.' '1892. I begin my seventy-second year with a sense of weakness almost amounting to exhaustion.'

But these and others of the same description were exceptional. In a general way her steadfast courage and cheerfulness were remarkable.

On the 30th of August 1893 she wrote to Mr. Bateman in a strain as cheery as ever, despite the weight of years and worries:—

'O my dearest Rowland,—So you take to lecturing your ancient Auntie, because she has come down to the Plains, where even an old woman is *needed*, instead of being a weak, languishing, fine lady up at Simla, where she was not needed one bit. Why, I am ever so much more frisky here, more cheerful and well, as well as more useful. Barring a few infirmities of age, I am in as good health, I think, as I ever was in England. I paid a good visit to-day to a village about four miles off, and am none the worse. Why, Rowland, I am actually the *only* Missionary, man or woman, now in Batala; and I have not dear Babu Singha, for he is at Chamba. Who would there be to escort our little train of bibis and bachelors to Chapel every afternoon, if an old dame were not here? I feel like a hen with chickens; and Herbert said that we look like a school. We are sometimes the better part of the congregation; for we have little girls home from school, and expect more here, and two little boys also from Narowal. Batala without a Miss T. would be like a teapot without a top.

'But you must not fancy that I am alone. Mr. Clark has considerately sent me a lovely young German lady, to keep house for me, which she does very nicely, and I am becoming a little fatter. I often take her to Zenanas with me; but there she is rather a hindrance than a help.... People will stare at her, instead of listening to me. She cannot help being attractive. She is very happy with me; but of course, as she does not do Mission work, this arrangement must not continue after Miss Clarke comes back from the Hills.

'Now I hope that you are satisfied, dear Rowland, that there has been no foolish imprudence, or worshipping of her old broken net, on the part of your ever attached

Auntie.

'Kind love to Helen. Mr. Gray is to come for next Sunday's services!'

On the 13th of October, in a letter to Miss Edith Tucker, she observed: 'I have such a nice Missionary companion, Miss Gertrude Clarke.... Batala is filling again; it was so empty during the holidays, that, had not Miss L. been sent to keep me company, I should have had no European within twenty miles. I was sole Missionary here.'

On the 31st of the same month, October, she wrote to Miss Minnie Dixie:—

'I made a grand expedition last week,—I have still four days of my six weeks' holiday left; but as we enter November to-morrow, I am not likely to take them. I actually went to Bahrwal, and saw the Consecration of Mr. and Mrs. Perkins' choice little church; simple, but in nice taste.... The dear Bishop was of course there, and held a Confirmation Service in the afternoon, at which about twelve or fourteen Peasant converts were received. I saw a good many friends....

'I send you a little hymn, which you may like to sing. It is perhaps the last thing which may be composed by your affectionate aged Auntie,

C. M. Tucker.'

From these words it would seem as if already some dim sense had come that her time on Earth was nearly over. She was indeed drawing very close to the dark River, which to her did not look dark but bright; and perhaps her eyes had already caught the 'glitter' of its waters. A friend, writing soon after, observed: 'She had been growing more and more conscious of weakness, if not actually weaker, and was looking forward eagerly to release.' In the month of November came what she was wont to call 'her Indian Birthday,'—the day on which she had first landed on Indian shores, eighteen years before. And, as she soon after said, when ill, though not yet so ill as to cause anxiety: 'When the Anniversary of my arrival in this country came round this year, I felt that my work was done, and that I should not live to see another.'

To some minds it may appear as if this perpetual longing for death contained something of a morbid and unhealthy nature. No doubt, as a general rule, it is perfectly natural to cling to life, to shrink from death; and where a desire for the latter exists, it often is romantic and unnatural, or else it arises from impatience of life's troubles, and from a wish to escape those troubles. This, however, was not the case with Charlotte Tucker. Her romance was never unhealthy romance; she was not cowardly, nor was she in the least morbid. On the contrary, she was thoroughly healthy, high-spirited, vigorous in body and mind,—exceptionally vigorous for her years, through the greater part of middle life and old age, till within a short time before her death. And although she had certainly numerous trials in the course of her seventy-two years,—as who has not?—hers was in many respects a very happy life. She had freedom from money cares; she had plenty of interests; she had success in her pursuits; she had abundance of loving and steadfast friends; she had, above all, one most satisfying intimacy; and, in addition to these things, she had a natural buoyancy, a keen sense of fun, a ready appreciation of the ridiculous, which in themselves would brighten life, and which are *not* characteristics usually found in morbid and self-centred people.

What was unusual in her was the strong and intense realisation of the Other World. Spiritual things to her were absolutely real. That which is unseen was to her as if seen. The love of Christ was more to her than the love of all earthly friends. Paradise was more to her than Earth. It was not that she did not love Earth, but that her love for Heaven was greater. It was not that she could not enter into the bright things of this world, but that she found the things of the Other World brighter still. She could never be satisfied with the present life; because she was always craving for the higher existence, always longing to rise 'nearer—nearer' to God. She was like a caged lark, impatient for freedom. And at last, after all these years of waiting, the time was come.

CHAPTER XXI
A.D. 1893 THE HOME-GOING

Up to the end of October Miss Tucker had seemed to be on the whole much the same as usual; though more than one watcher had noted a gradual failure of strength. The expedition to Bahrwal, for the Dedication, proved to be too much for her powers; especially as she insisted on returning to Batala the same evening, so as not to break into another day's work.

At the time she appeared, as Mrs. Wade afterwards wrote, 'though frail, wonderfully bright, ... full of conversation while talking to the Bishop and others.' When the 'feast' took place she sat upon the ground among the Indian Christians, after her old style, utterly refusing a chair. Some who were present left in the middle of the day, so soon as the Dedication was over; but Miss Tucker remained till the evening, so as to be present at the second Service. Notwithstanding her brightness, Mr. Clark was much impressed with the alteration in her look; and he has since said that 'she evidently believed it to be her leave-taking.'

The day ended, Miss Tucker seemed very much exhausted; and when returning by rail, with Mr. and Mrs. Wade, she lay down on the seat to rest. The result of this expedition was a severe cold, with much hoarseness; and though her daily work went on as usual, she must have felt very poorly. Mr. Clark speaks of her as, a few days later, passing through Amritsar, and calling to see himself and his wife. So ill did he think her looking, that the expression he makes use of is: 'Death was even then written on her face.'

Others do not appear to have been so soon alarmed. On November 13, writing to Miss Dixie, Miss Tucker mentioned casually, 'I have a cold,' as an excuse for her shaking hand; and said no more. But it was 'the beginning of the end.'

About this time she kindly took in a friend, Mrs. C——, who seemed poorly and in need of change; and who, after coming to 'Sonnenschein,' proved to be seriously ill. Miss Tucker sat much with her, in a hot room;

going out from thence, late each evening, into the night air, to reach her own little dwelling. On the 11th, two days before her letter to Miss Dixie, she confessed to pain in the side, telegraphed for a nurse, and went to bed. Next day, Sunday, she was up again, and at Church. Then the Nurse appeared, to be sent off on Monday, in charge of Mrs. C——, to Amritsar; after which again Miss Tucker went down.

Dr. Clark came to see her; and though the fever was not very high, and no especial anxiety was felt, it was decided that she ought to go to Amritsar to be nursed—a Doctor there being on the spot. Miss Tucker was much grieved at the decision. She longed to remain, and to die in her dear Batala; and even then, evidently, she was making up her mind to the likelihood of death. But, however unwillingly, she submitted to the wishes of others, and went.

THE LAST PAGE OF A. L. O. E.'S DIARY

The journey did no harm; and on arrival at Amritsar Miss Tucker was most tenderly nursed by her friend, Miss Wauton, and others, with the help soon of a regular nurse. But though the fever yielded to remedies, and the bronchitis improved, both the cough and pain becoming for some days better, she was worn out, and had no rallying power. The weakness was extreme, and the dislike to food could not be overcome. Steadily and slowly she sank, lasting just three weeks from the date of the latest tremulous entry in her Journal.

Dr. Arthur Lankester[142] had written on the 27th of October: 'Sorry to say Auntie has taken a severe chill at Bahrwal; she looks very frail and weak; only, she is so wonderful that we all hope she will soon be about once more, to cheer us all with her bright, sweet smile.' He wrote again on Nov. 22: 'Dear Miss Tucker has been moved to the Mission-house here,[143] and I am thankful to be allowed to be with her. She is very, very ill, but so bright, and longing to go "Home." I fear she is fast sinking. It is a great privilege to be allowed to help look after her.' And again, on Nov. 30: 'Auntie sinking fast; the end can't be far off. O what joy and glory are waiting for her!—for us a terrible blank that nothing can fill. No one could be quite like her.'

The last dictated letter of Charlotte Tucker was to her niece, Mrs. J. Boswell, on the 21st of November:—

> 'My dearest Bella Francis,—You will all like to know how I am getting on. I have come again to House Beautiful in Amritsar, where the four sweet damsels, Faith, etc., glide about to see to my comfort. Yesterday dear Gertrude joined us, and also Miss B. A., so there is a regular bevy. Dr. Clark said yesterday, with a very broad smile, that we were getting on; but I cannot quite see the pith of this. When a worn-out ekka horse tumbles down on the road, and no one can make him get up, one can scarcely say that he is getting on. Getting up must come first. I ought to be very thankful for so much kindness; but you can imagine, darling, that when I hope to soar on eagle's wings, it is rather a trial to have the doctor tie them down so tightly, that when I hope to fly I cannot even creep.
>
> 'I fancy this has been an attack of bronchitis and influenza. Now this is difficult to me even to dictate. Would you have little bulletins roughly printed on my account, and put them in envelopes, and send them to — —?': after which follows a list of relatives and friends in England, together with one or two short messages, and a request that they would ask for her 'patience and perfect submission.'

The day succeeding Miss Tucker's arrival in Amritsar Mrs. Wade came to see her; and during either that call or the next Miss Tucker put the question, 'Is my face altered?' Mrs. Wade hesitated, unable to deny that she saw a change. Miss Tucker immediately added: 'Don't mind telling me. It is harder to be patient on this pillow than to go inside the Golden Gate.' And to Miss Jackson she said: 'To depart and to be with Christ is so *very* much better!'

Many friends came to ask after her; but on account of her excessive feebleness a very limited number could be admitted; only one or two in the day, and merely for a few minutes each.

One day, on hearing Mr. Clark's voice outside, she said, 'Is that Mr. Clark?' They told her that she must not see any one; she was too weak. 'But I must see him!' she replied; and then, 'I *will* see him!'—with a flash of the old determination. When he was brought in she said to him: 'I am dying! I know it. I am very happy,—in perfect peace,—without a doubt or a care,— but I have none of the rapturous feelings of triumph, which I have rather looked forward to!' Then she added: 'It is best as it is!' The next day and the day after, when Mr. Clark was again admitted, she was both times too ill to say anything.

She was indeed this time far too entirely worn out and exhausted, both bodily and mentally, for any shout of joy. All was quiet trust, perfect confidence; but eagerness and exultation were physically out of the question. She could only wait peacefully to be carried through the waters of the River. Rapture would come when she reached the Other Side.

Still, there was the same longing as ever to go. Several times she said: 'Do not pray that I may stay here.' And another time: 'Christ has abolished death! I am longing to go Home!'

On Sunday, November 26th, Mr. Wade came to her room for Holy Communion; Miss Wauton and Miss Jackson being present. Miss Tucker was perfectly clear in mind, and able to join audibly in the responses; but the after-exhaustion was great.

Sometimes she would speak lovingly of her friends, and would wish that she could see one and another. 'It is a pity Rowland Bateman is not here,' she said. Also she would give directions for presents to be sent to one and another after her death. On the 27th she sent for Babu Singha, and mentioned particulars as to the manner in which she wished her funeral to be conducted. The boys—her dear brown boys, as she had so often called them—were to carry her to the grave, on a native charpai. No coffin was to be used; and the expenditure might not exceed five rupees. She was of course to be buried in Batala. Nobody was to shed tears; nobody was to put on mourning; and her own funeral hymn, one which she had written quite lately in Urdu, was to be sung.

One day Miss Jackson repeated the hymn, 'For ever with the Lord!'—and Miss Tucker said, 'That is my favourite hymn!' So it too was afterwards chosen to be sung at the funeral.

On Wednesday, November 29, her temperature fell to 95°; and great difficulty was experienced in restoring it to normal. Two days later it fell again; and this time there was no rally. The cough and other symptoms were exceedingly trying; and all Friday night she suffered greatly from oppression, restlessness, and weariness. Again and again she could be heard to murmur, 'Quickly! Quickly!' Nothing else that she said could be distinguished.

Early in the morning of Saturday, December the 2nd, she became more placid; and when asked if she felt any pain she made a negative sign. Dr. Weitbrecht came to read and pray with her. She seemed to recognise him, and to understand what he said; but she had no power to articulate. Soon after this unconsciousness set in, and lasted to the end, broken only once by a lifting of the eyelids, and an upward look, as if she saw something which others could not see.

At a quarter-past three in the afternoon, calmly and without a struggle, she passed away.

The change which came over her in death was remarkable. A change is often seen; a return sometimes to greater youth and beauty. Death smooths away wrinkles, refines rugged features, sharpens the outlines. But in this case the transformation was of a rare type. 'I never saw a face so altered,' wrote Dr. Clark, who had attended her. 'It became a face of massive power; more like that of the Duke of Wellington than anything else; the nose particularly so, and the jaw. A strong, massive, determined, powerful face. I suppose the power was always there, but masked by the habitual gentleness and tender consideration for all around, which was so beautiful a feature in her beautiful character.'

This allusion to the Duke of Wellington naturally recalls her ardent admiration for him. She would in life have probably counted no compliment greater than to have been called like him. But the description is singular, because her features had never been of the same type as the Duke's features. She had not a Roman nose; and while many describe hers as a 'bright face,' 'a sparkling face,' 'a long, thin face,' and even in one case 'a small face' no one ever uses such words as 'massive' or 'powerful,' as descriptive of her appearance at any period of her life. The touch of death seems to have torn away a kind of veil, leaving bare the original outlines; perhaps to some extent indicating what the face might have become, if unsoftened by the moulding influences of discipline.

Miss Jackson wrote from Amritsar, on Monday, December 4th: 'Yesterday the Dead March was played in Church, and all the congregation stood. It was announced that all who wished to take a last look at the dear face could do so at our house at a certain hour; and about sixty availed themselves of this permission.' And Miss Wauton adds: 'Miss Jackson will have told you that many friends in Amritsar came on Sunday afternoon, to take their last look at the peaceful sleeper. The hands were clasped as if in prayer. The face was thin and worn; but this only brought out a clearer chiselling of the features; and the calmness of death gave a grandeur and nobility to the expression, beyond anything we had seen in the face while living. She looked, as one friend said, "like a Crusader."'

On December the 4th they bore all that remained on Earth of Charlotte Tucker from Amritsar to Batala. As she had forbidden the use of a coffin, the body was laid upon a small Native bedstead, and, being carefully secured in position, was conveyed thus, not by rail but by road. On reaching Batala, the charpai, with its quiet burden, was placed in the Church of the Epiphany,— known colloquially as 'the large Church,' to distinguish it from the little School 'Chapel,'—there to remain till morning. Some of the Baring High School boys took turns in watching beside the loved form all night through.

Next day, Tuesday, was fixed upon for the funeral. It had been delayed unusually long, to allow friends from a distance to be present. A great many came from Amritsar, Lahore, and other stations; and a message from the Bishop expressed his regret at being unavoidably kept away by a Confirmation. The Archdeacon and the Bishop's Chaplain were both present, as also were Dr. Weitbrecht, Mr. Clark, Mr. Wade, Mr. Mackenzie, Mr. Wright, Mr. Wigram, Mr. Shireff, Mr. Hoare, Mr. Coverdale, and Mr. Grey, all in white surplices. A large congregation filled the whole Church, including Missionaries, friends, Native Christians, Non-Christians of Batala, and boys of both the High School and the 'Plough.' The first part of the Burial Service was read there; and two or three hymns were sung. Mr. Clark preached a short sermon from Acts i. 8.

Then began the Procession from the Church to the little Christian Cemetery; the latter being close to 'Sonnenschein,' and nearly two miles away from the Church. Happily it was a cool day; and the roads had been well watered beforehand. A Police-guard preceded the Procession.

First came the surpliced Clergy; then the bier, which was covered with a white chaddah; while many beautiful white Crosses and wreaths sent by friends were laid upon it. Some of the older schoolboys carried the bier, taking turns. Next came the ladies and other Missionaries; also the general congregation, and the rest of the boys. Crowds of leading Batala men were present. A letter from Miss Wauton, written at the time, describes the scene graphically:—

> 'After the Easter hymn, "Lo, in the grave He lay," the congregation then formed into Procession; the Clergy first, then the Bier.... The long line of followers stretched out, till we could scarcely see the end of it. The distance being about two miles, the walk occupied more than an hour. Hymns were sung the whole way; and the groups of people, Hindus and Muhammadans, who lined the road and crowded the tops of the houses, as we passed the city, seemed much interested in looking on. Many of them, I think, came as far as the Cemetery.
>
> 'As we passed through the gates, copies of a hymn were distributed, which the dear Auntie had composed about three weeks before she was taken ill. On sending it to me at the time, she added in her letter: "Perhaps you will like to see my little funeral hymn. Perhaps it may be sung when I go to sleep."
>
> 'We also had the hymn, "Jesus lives"; and closed with her favourite, "For ever with the Lord." Deep feeling was shown; and many of the boys could scarcely restrain their tears. We all felt we had lost a friend, such as we should never see again. The Mission is bereaved,—not only Batala, but the whole of the Panjab; and we all mourn our loss together....
>
> 'Dr. Weitbrecht had arranged everything for yesterday most beautifully. The whole Service was, I think, in perfect

accordance with her wishes; simple, sweet, and solemn, yet with an element of joy and hope about it, which was suitable to her bright, joyous nature. We could indeed give thanks for the fight she had fought, the course she had finished, the crown she had won; and so we laid her down,—till the Day break and the shadows flee away. "Till He come!"'

Another eye-witness, Mrs. Wade, wrote:—

'We were very thankful that it was possible to delay the meeting at Batala till Tuesday, as it gave opportunity for friends from some distance to be present. We all met in the Church for the first part of the Service and sermon by Mr. Clark,—the dear familiar face no longer among the worshippers, but in the King's Presence.... The walk from the Church to the little Cemetery, quite near her own home, is long, and occupied an hour; during which time many hymns of faith and love were softly sung, and at the grave her own hymn, one she had composed not six weeks ago for her own funeral.... Dr. Weitbrecht then completed the Service.... The silence of the onlookers, as one went towards the grave, was very noticeable. Many of them felt that they had indeed lost a friend. A large number of the Native gentlemen of the City were present in the Church and during the Service, with reverent demeanour; and when we had left, I was told, many of the poor women came to weep at her grave.

'We thank God for all she was during the long life, and especially in the eighteen years in India.... Batala will never be the same. Many of the elder boys, who carried her, were weeping.'

And from the pen of Dr. Weitbrecht we have the following:—

'After the Burial was over, I spoke a few words about her to the many people who had assembled from outside, trying to impress on them the motive power of her life: "The love of Christ constraineth us." After most of the Clergy and visitors had left the Cemetery, a number of women from the city came to take a last look, and to wail at the grave. Times without number, gentlemen of Batala and men of lower standing come to tell me how she went to their houses, and sympathised with their wives and daughters in joy and sorrow. Not a few will miss her open-handed charity; and, far more, her bright, ever-ready sympathy.'

The Urdu hymn, written by Miss Tucker for her own funeral, has been roughly translated as follows:—

'The beloved Jesus sleeps in the grave;

Morn breaks, and He Who came to save

Has risen, glorious King of Kings,

Victorious o'er all evil things.

It is Christ's power, Christ's glorious Crown;

His rule shall spread with much renown;

Christ has risen, ne'er to die;

Hallelujah! Victory!'

One fact may be mentioned, as a slight token of the loving esteem in which she was held. When Miss Wauton took the hymn to be printed, the Manager of the Press,—not himself a Christian, but one who had known Miss Tucker,—said immediately, 'Oh, are those lines Miss Tucker's? Then I will do them for nothing.' He printed off some hundreds at his own expense.

Out of the innumerable letters written to friends, after the passing away of Charlotte Tucker, three short extracts alone must be given.

FROM THE BISHOP OF LAHORE.

'For the simple yet always aspiring spirit the change will be a blessed one indeed! Her endurance unto the end, and her constant rejoicing in the Lord, have been a great example, which many of us need to follow.... It was a beautiful and consistent life; and she will still speak, though out of sight.'

FROM THE REV. ROBERT CLARK.

'Miss Tucker ... will not be easily forgotten there (at Batala), nor indeed in India generally, where her name will long continue to be a household word, both for what she was and for what she did. In giving her to India, the Church of Christ gave of her very best.'

FROM THE REV. ROWLAND BATEMAN.

'There is but one voice from India, whether it comes from Natives or Europeans.... Do you know those lines of

Toplady's, beginning, "Deathless Principle arise"? They are old-fashioned and out of date, *i.e.* out of the range of the rising generation, but they are peculiarly beautiful, and keep recurring, as I mentally pass through the ministry which Miss Wauton and others were privileged to offer to our beloved Aunt in Amritsar. There is one touch in Dr. Weitbrecht's p.c. which may not have reached you. He mentions that many women came from the city, to wail at the grave. This is as it should be; for though we know better than to wail or even weep over the grave, in them it is but the expression of love and appreciation and real kindred. Nobody—I speak of non-Christians—weeps and wails except over relatives. We are sorely wounded, and our spirits suffer a sort of collapse; but we have only to go over the hallowed, holy memory of her converse and example, to feel refreshed and braced again.

'"With joy and gladness has she been brought,
And has entered into the King's Palace."'

So ends the story of Charlotte Maria Tucker; for fifty-four years A Lady of England, and for eighteen years A Lady of India. It is the story of a brave and self-sacrificing life, whether in her quiet English home, or in the vicissitudes of her Indian career. I have done my best to present her simply and truly as that which she was,—a very unusual and noble character, with of course some of those defects which are found in even the best and noblest of men and women. Charlotte Tucker would herself have been the first to deprecate any attempt to make her out a faultless being. Faultless she was not; but she *was* singularly true, unselfish, devoted, single-hearted, earnest-minded, and loving.

The one aim perpetually before her eyes was to carry out the Will of her Father in Heaven, alike in the greatest and in the smallest matters. Whether she were striving to bring the Heathen to a knowledge of the Truth, whether she were discussing difficult questions with a Muhammadan, whether she were writing a book, whether she were entertaining a guest, whether she were trying to cheer a sick friend, whether she were playing a game with little brown boys,—in any case she put the whole of herself into the task which she had in hand, and she did it 'unto God.' To the utmost of her ability, all that she undertook was done thoroughly. There was no half-heartedness, no slurring over of one thing or another. Difficulties, oppositions, failures, discouragements, lack of apparent results, all these, instead of disheartening her, seemed rather to spur her on to renewed efforts.

Beyond the few words above, no eulogistic ending to her Biography is needed. If her Life as it was lived does not speak for itself, mere words of praise would be thrown away. It is possible that her example, in going out to India after the age of fifty, will lead others to do the same; and if so, one object of her going will have been accomplished. That may well be the result in England of her eighteen years' toil. The results in India lie beyond our puny powers of measurement.

FOOTNOTES

[1] It was a custom in the family, through several generations, to give a Christmas present to each child of *new silver*, the amount given being one shilling for each year of age, and sixpence in addition. Thus, a child of ten would receive ten and sixpence, all in new silver.

[2] One of a band of robbers.

[3] Chief police-officer.

[4] At the Official East India Company's dinner, given by the Directors; ladies being admitted to a gallery as spectators.

[5] A pet name for her sister.

[6] *Two Noble Lives*, vol. ii. p. 220.

[7] Mr. Tucker. He was never knighted.

[8] Prince and Princess of Wales.

[9] Of the Marylebone Workhouse.

[10] Daughter of A. L. O. E.'s sister Laura.

[11] Mr. Henry Carre Tucker.

[12] The lady's-maid.

[13] Otho's youngest brother, who died an infant.

[14] A tiny Memorial of Letitia, containing some of her verses.

[15] The two chief interests of Otho Hamilton in his short life were— Natural History, and Missions among the Heathen. This is doubtless in reference to the latter.

[16] Marriage of Miss Bella Frances Tucker to her cousin, the Rev. James Boswell.

[17] Mr. St. George Tucker retired this year (1869) from the Indian Civil Service; and his sister Fanny was at this time paying along visit to him and his wife.

[18] Daughter of A. L. O. E.'s brother, Mr. William Tucker.

[19] Father and Mother of Mrs. St. G. Tucker.

[20] As a curious instance of differing views, another relative, who perhaps had had even better opportunities for judging, says: 'Not sympathizing; most kind, but could not place herself in the position of another.'

[21] One of the Zenana Missionaries at Amritsar.

[22] Doubtless covered with snow.

[23] In a letter of Mrs. H. B. Stowe is the following passage, referring to Niagara:—'I felt as if I could have gone over with the waters: it would be so beautiful a death: there would be no fear in it.'—*Life of H. B. Stowe*, p. 75, pub. 1889.

[24] Missionary Ladies.

[25] Show.

[26] Honorary mode of address.

[27] Pronounced *purdah*.

[28] Pronounced *Punjāb*.

[29] Pronounced *Umritsar*.

[30] Her travelling companion from Bombay.

[31] Considerable allowance here and elsewhere must be made for Miss Tucker's habit of seeing things as far as possible *couleur-de-rose*. Large rooms in the Indian climate are, moreover, not a mere luxury, but a necessity for health.

[32] Teacher.

[33] Pronounced *chuddars*.

[34] The Rev. Robert Clark.

[35] Mrs. Elmslie.

[36] Teacher.

[37] Sometimes she would take a week or ten days additional at some other season in the year.

[38] Many Missionaries live upon less than £155. See next page.

[39] A pet name for Mrs. Elmslie.

[40] Often spelt by English writers *doli*, *dooli*, or *dhooli*. Pronounced, *dooly*.

[41] A learned Hindu. Pronounced, *pundit*.

[42] Adopted nephew, the Rev. Rowland Bateman.

[43] Miss Wauton.

[44] Watchman.

[45] Padri Sadiq, Native Clergyman.

[46] German Missionary at Amritsar.

[47] Native bedstead.

[48] Tailor.

[49] Queen.

[50] Carrying things with a high hand.

[51] Miss Swainson.

[52] Mrs. Elmslie and Miss Wauton were away for a few weeks in the Hills with Miss Swainson.

[53] This was an early stage. *Now* the learned Pandit, K. S., is an Ordained Clergyman.

[54] 'My brother.'

[55] Meaning 'bud of a pomegranate.'

[56] A clockwork toy.

[57] Connected with the Government.

[58] Rough roads, unmade roads.

[59] Duli-carrier.

[60] Idle.

[61] Flat cakes of bread.

[62] Native song, or hymn set to Native tune.

[63] Divinities.

[64] A kind of post-chaise.

[65] Bananas.

[66] This, unhappily, proved later to be a mistaken estimate.

[67] The Catechist.

[68] The Rev. Rowland Bateman, just recovered from severe illness.

[69] Cream-coloured dress worn at a Conference.

[70] Precipice or ravine.

[71] Founder of the Sikh religion.

[72] Miss Tucker in this letter ascribes the said change to the work of others; but there can be no doubt that her own influence had largely contributed to bring it about.

[73] Mrs. Elmslie was going home on furlough.

[74] Mr. Bateman, Mr. Wade, Mr. Weitbrecht, Mr. Baring....

[75] Adopted son of the Rev. Robert Clark; afterwards known as Dr. H. M. Clark....

[76] Lentils.

[77] Bishop French.

[78] 'My Nephew'; term constantly used by A. L. O. E. for Mr. Baring.

[79] President of the Zenana Society.

[80] Grove of mango trees.

[81] Not always perfect security. Instances have occurred, though seldom, of Missionaries themselves being attacked and roughly handled on such occasions.

[82] Pronounced *Grunt*.

[83] Teacher.

[84] Bibi Singha.

[85] Muhammadan teachers.

[86] Not *all* actually Batala converts; some having come from Amritsar, in connection with the school, etc.

[87] Threatened war with Afghanistan.

[88] Though I speak in the past tense, the same terms apply to the present.

[89] Cotton mats.

[90] Early breakfast.

[91] Idle.

[92] Hats.

[93] Marylebone.

[94] Native Bible-woman.

[95] Custom.

[96] The Bishop of Calcutta and the Bishop of Lahore.

[97] Mrs. Hamilton's house.

[98] Native official.

[99] Very low caste.

[100] Water-carrier.

[101] Watchman.

[102] Washerman.

[103] One of the boys.

[104] This particular Faqir, Miss Tucker meant.

[105] Some Native ladies.

[106] Mrs. Hamilton's gift.

[107] A Native clergyman.

[108] Sir Charles Aitcheson, the Lieutenant-Governor.

[109] Naughty ones.

[110] A young Native.

[111] A leading Salvationist.

[112] Sect of Muhammadans.

[113] Advice to her sister to enter habitually, without delay, upon the subject of religion with Indians.

[114] Miss Swainson.

[115] A young Indian Convert in England.

[116] Country people.

[117] This is a mistake. She was thirty-one.

[118] A very untruthful woman.

[119] The father of Mrs. St. George Tucker.

[120] Dr. H. M. Clark.

[121] Bishop Matthews.

[122] Pedlar.

[123] So named by the Natives.

[124] Not the same as spoken of in earlier part of this letter.

[125] More strictly, about one-twelfth of a penny.

[126] Miss Tucker had become by this time less strict in her earlier rule of never walking in the city.

[127] Meaning, 'Door closed against you.'

[128] Old woman.

[129] True.

[130] *i.e.* Down in the Plains.

[131] It is not clear which of her severe illnesses is here referred to.

[132] The Rev. Nobin Chanda Das, for years Native Pastor at Batala, and Head-master of the Mission 'Plough' School.

[133] Formerly 'The Plough.'

[134] Narowal, the Station of the Rev. R. Bateman.

[135] *The Giant-Killer*, by A. L. O. E.

[136] Deprecating; meaning something sad, something to be repented of.

[137] The sentence as to her tenth birthday, quoted page 13, comes in here.

[138] Mr. Bateman.

[139] Chiefs.

[140] Later, an adopted Nephew; see pp. 498-9.

[141] This was a mistake. Mrs. Hamilton passed away on October 14; but the telegram was not sent for several days, to permit certain letters to arrive first. Miss Tucker failed to allow for this fact.

[142] Missionary.

[143] At Amritsar.